The Best of

HANDMADE

CRAFT · DECORATING · FASHION

The Australian Women's Weekly

The Best of

HANDMADE

CRAFT · DECORATING · FASHION

The Australian Women's Weekly

Editor: MARY COLEMAN

Craft Editor: ALISON SNEPP

BayBooks

An imprint of HarperCollinsPublishers

Table of British Equivalents

WOOL

8-ply = DK
10-ply = Aran
12-ply = Sport or Chunky
14-ply = Chunky

KNITTING NEEDLES

UK Size	Metric Size (mm)	UK Size	Metric Size (mm)
000	10	7	4.5
00	9	8	4
0	8	9	3.75
1	7.5	-	3.5
2	7	10	3.25
3	6.5	11	3
4	6	12	2.75
5	5.5	13	2.25
6	5		

How to use the Pattern Pieces

- All pattern pieces are printed at 100% unless otherwise indicated. Most pattern pieces are small enough to fit on a page but those that are too large for one page appear on a sequence of pages that are labelled A, B, C etc.
- The pages on which the patterns appear should then be traced off the book, butting up adjoining pages. See example below.

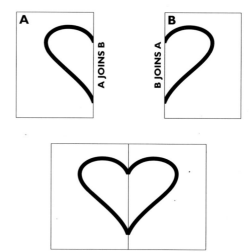

Quite simple!

THE BEST OF HANDMADE HAS BEEN PUBLISHED
BY ARRANGEMENT AND WITH THE CO-OPERATION
OF AUSTRALIAN CONSOLIDATED PRESS

A Bay Books Publication

Bay Books, an imprint of
HarperCollins*Publishers*
25 Ryde Road, Pymble, Sydney, NSW 2073, Australia
31 View Road, Glenfield, Auckland 10, New Zealand

First published in Australia in 1994

National Library of Australia
Cataloguing-in-Publication data:

Coleman, Mary, 1939-
ISBN 1 86378110 2

1. Handicraft. I. Title. II. Title: Handmade.
745.5

Printed in Australia by Griffin Press, Adelaide

9 8 7 6 5 4 3 2 1
97 96 95 94

FOREWORD

Handmade magazine has been entertaining and instructing craftspeople in Australia and New Zealand for over a decade. When first published, the magazine mainly answered the needs of those interested in making wonderfully up-to-date fashion garments and, whether they were sewn or knitted, a hand made *Handmade* garment was distinguished by its avant guard flair. Many of Australia's esteemed fashion designers contributed to its lively pages and many distinguished editors, writers, stylists and artists demonstrated their talents and clever ideas in each edition. As present chatelaine, I pay tribute to them all.

Over the decade the magazine has seen many changes. It has acquired a new publisher, several new frequencies (from quarterly to bi-monthly to bi-annual back to quarterly and now again to bi-monthly), new staff, of course, and new interests. Over the past five years we've responded to the great upsurge of interest in crafts of all kinds and so, without ever losing sight of the genesis of the magazine, have broadened *Handmade's* scope and asked Australia's leading craftspeople to teach us their skills.

We have some very clever people in this country — this book is a testament to that — and it is a privilege to have collaborated with them. What is a double delight to me, and those with me on the magazine, is that all of them are not only wonderful to work with but also extraordinarily generous with their time and talents.

And no mention of talent would be complete without a look at the craftspeople behind the scenes. Sandy Cull, *Handmade's* Art Director is responsible for the look of so many of the beautiful photographs within and Assistant Editor Georgina Bitcon's discriminating taste, gifted writing and meticulous eye have served the book just as marvellously as they shape the magazine.

The pieces in this collection are all from magazines that are now out of print. We're delighted to be invited to help assemble this lovely retrospective, especially as we're often asked for copies of so many of these stories.

MARY COLEMAN

CONTENTS

Crochet and Tatting

Introduction by
Nerée Hartog

Paper Crafts

Introduction by
Nerida Singleton

Folk Art Painting, Stencilling and Marbling

Introduction by
Janet Klepatzki

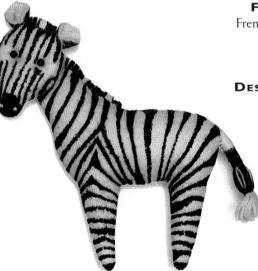

General Crafts

Introduction by
Tonia Todman

Needlework

All forms of needlework are enjoying an exciting revival as stitchers learn to do cross-stitch and become totally addicted to the joy of watching a new design take shape on a plain piece of cloth.

Once cross-stitch has been mastered, it inevitably remains a favourite, but the stitcher is then caught up with the satisfaction which needlework brings and wants to move on to other exciting forms such as wool embroidery and needlepoint.

The exquisite designs in this book will appeal to the beginner as well as the more experienced embroiderer with designs featuring flora and fauna as well as beautiful stylised patterns.

Small projects will be ideal for a quick gift while large projects offer the enjoyment of watching a more detailed design reveal itself in a splendid selection of colours.

Each project will give the stitcher many hours of enjoyment and satisfaction.

ALISON SNEPP

HONEYEATERS AND BANKSIA

Safely preserved in the Australian National Gallery is a large collection of work by a prodigious Australian designer, Eirene Mort, who died in 1977, aged 98. In an artistic career that spanned most of her long life, Eirene Mort produced designs for all manner of craftwork illustration and graphic design, as well as ceramics, leatherwork, metalwork, needlework and woodwork. The magnificent cushion cover, featuring Honeyeaters and Banksias, is a copy of a tapestry originally designed and worked by Eirene Mort in 1906. As part of our 'Stitch in Time' series on historic Australian needlework, we have re-graphed the original, matching Eirene's chosen colours as closely as possible, using the wonderful range of colours from DMC. Re-worked by the Tapestry Guild of NSW, the tapestry brings Eirene's design back to life — a fitting tribute to one woman's extraordinary ability and her importance in the history of Australian decorative arts.

Honeyeaters and Banksia Tapestry

MEASUREMENTS
Finished tapestry measures 40cm square. (The original tapestry measures 41cm square, but was worked on a slightly finer canvas, so where we have allowed a 12-stitch border, Eirene Mort's border was 30 stitches wide.)

MATERIALS
- 50cm square Penelope Antique Canvas (39-count)
- DMC Laine Colbert Tapestry Wool (Art 486-487) in colours and amounts specified on key
- Tapestry frame (optional, but recommended)
- 0.5m material suitable for cushion back
- Cushion insert
- Approximately 12 skeins extra wool for plaited cord and tassels (we used four skeins each of three colours)

METHOD
Using graph on page 14, locate centre stitch. Mark also centre of canvas and start stitching from this point, so that design is centred.

Before stitching design, we suggest that you sew canvas onto a frame, keeping canvas taut at all times.

Each square on graph equals one Continental Stitch. We have used Continental Stitch because it provides padding on back of canvas, as well as front — ideal for items that take a bit of wear and tear.

We have added a 12-stitch border around design. You can, of course, add more or less, depending on finished size that you require.

Cut lengths of tapestry wool, approximately 35cm long. Using longer lengths will wear the wool.

For border, we have used Basket-weave Stitch, see page 15, which looks like Continental Stitch on front of work, but, unlike the latter, does not bias and stretch canvas. It is very useful for large areas of single colour.

Begin each new thread by using a waste knot. To do this, put a knot in end of your thread. Push needle down

through canvas from top side (so knot is sitting on right side of canvas), and bring it up again 10 spaces to the right. Begin stitching back over end of thread, towards knot. When you get back to knot, pull it up and carefully snip knot off. End of knot is then securely fastened. Once you have a section of canvas worked, you can begin new threads by weaving into back of existing stitches.

Finish each thread by weaving into stitches at back of work.

When tapestry is complete, it will probably need blocking, that is, pulling back into shape.

After blocking, stitch canvas to backing to form a cushion cover.

Place insert into cover. To make a plaited cord, cut lengths of wool, approximately twice length of finished side. Using three colours and nine strands per colour, make four 3-ply plaits. Stitch plaits to cushion edges, leaving unplaited ends extending. Gather two adjacent extending ends together and wind with wool, to form a tassel. Trim ends to even.

Reproduced by permission of the Australian National Gallery, the original tapestry is still in remarkably good condition. The design can also be worked on fine canvas, using DMC Stranded Embroidery Cotton, producing a miniature version of the original. We give DMC numbers for both tapestry wool and stranded cotton.

Opposite: A portrait of the artist as a young woman. Taken from the personal collection of Miss Margaret Mort.

With a little ingenuity, a single element can be extracted from the design and featured on its own.

Against a stylised background of intricately intertwined banksia, two honeyeaters are depicted in mid-flight, the subtle tones of the main image gloriously offset by a rich, russet brown.

A JOINS B

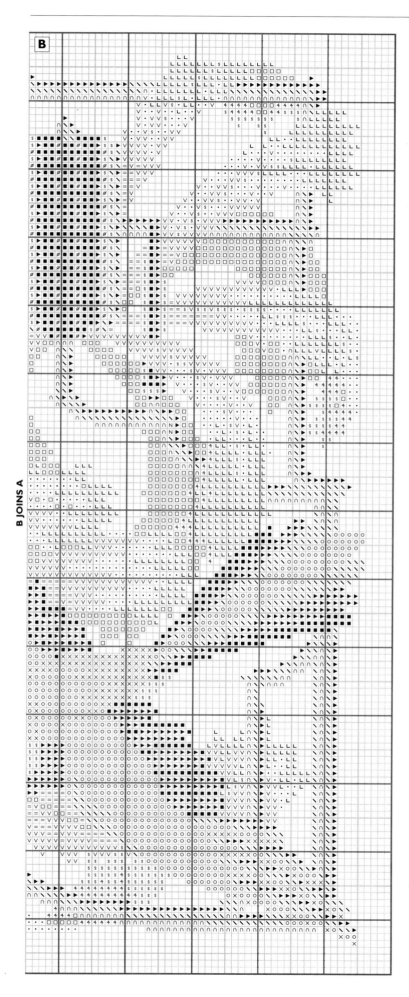

B

B JOINS A

GRAPH FOR HONEYEATERS AND BANKSIA

NOTE: The first number is for DMC Tapestry Wool. The number in brackets indicates the comparable shade in DMC Stranded Embroidery Cotton. The number following the brackets gives the number of skeins of tapestry wool required.

KEY
☐ DMC 7184 (355) x 15
☒ DMC 7535 (3371) x 1
☒ DMC 7739 (739) x 1
■ DMC 7520 (3303) x 2
☒ DMC 7511 (612) x 2
4 DMC 7461 (842) x 1
▶ DMC 7518 (840) x 2
○ DMC 7416 (610) x 2
◣ DMC 7415 (640) x 2
● DMC 7499 (801) x 1
∩ DMC 7432 (839) x 1
= DMC 7925 (939) x 2
∨ DMC 7339 (924) x 2
· DMC 7337 (501) x 3
L DMC 7335 (502) x 3
☐ DMC 7622 (317) x 2
N DMC 7620 (318) x 1

Basketweave stitch

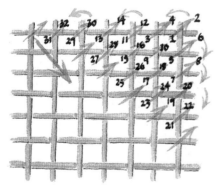

Detail of Basketweave Stitch which has been used for the border as it looks like Continental Stitch but does not bias and stretch canvas in the same way.

Continental stitch – right to left

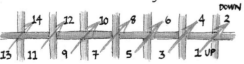

left to right

A close up of the Continental Stitch, used for its padding on back of canvas, helping the work to withstand wear and tear.

A STITCH IN TIME

Wreath of Native Berries

This beautiful wreath of native berries, part of an occasional series on historic Australian embroidery, was first painted in 1860 by Louisa Anne Meredith, and has been translated into exquisite cross-stitch by designer Vivienne Garforth.

Born in 1812 and brought to Australia as a bride in 1839, Louisa Meredith wrote 11 books describing and illustrating the animals, birds and insects she observed around her Tasmanian home. Her skill and enthusiasm led other women of the colonies to record the surroundings of their new country, in embroidery as well as in watercolours and drawings. Following in Louisa's footsteps, Vivienne Garforth is also fascinated with the Australian bush, which is featured in the many books on embroidery she has written.

Louisa's original watercolour, "Wreath of Berries" was included in Some of My Bush Friends in Tasmania, *first published in 1860. The author lists the berries as 'Native Cherry, White Fruited Cherry, Austral Olives, Blue Berry, Largest Black Berry and Clustered Pink Berry'. Collection Tasmanian Museum and Art Gallery.*

The berries from which the wreath
is composed, are from various localities, but
all ripen in late Summer or Autumn. On the
upper side is a spray of the Australian Cherry.
Colonial children pick and eat these mature
cherries with avidity, as children will pick and
eat any wild thing not especially nauseous; but
I sigh, as I see them do so and think, "Ah! they
never knew the glorious blackberry dingles
I can remember!"

LOUISA ANNE MEREDITH

A JOINS B

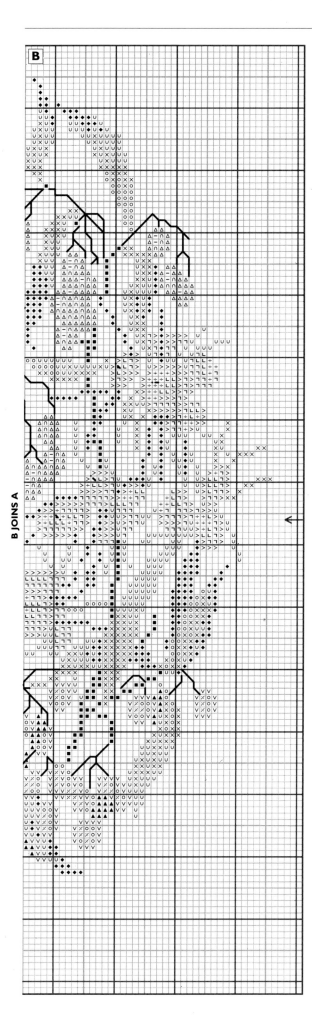

B

B JOINS A

Wreath of Native Berries

MEASUREMENTS
Actual embroidery measures approximately 25cm square.

MATERIALS
- 50cm square cream 14-count Aida cloth
- One skein each DMC Stranded Embroidery Cotton (Art 117) in colours indicated on key

METHOD
Prepare Aida cloth by running a line of tacking thread across centre, both horizontally and vertically, to find centre point.

Divide design into four quarters also and follow cross-stitch graph for one quarter at a time. With a diagram such as this one, that has several small areas to embroider, it is a good idea to colour each section with a highlighter pen as it is completed. This way, it is easier to follow and you are less likely to 'get lost' in the pattern.

Work with two strands of embroidery thread throughout, except for outline around insect on lower leaves, which is worked in one thread.

When embroidery is finished, press gently with a moderately hot iron on wrong side of work and frame as desired.

If Aida cloth has become grubby and you need to wash it, use only warm water and white soap — not detergent — and gently swish fabric up and down through water with your hands. Do not wring.

KEY

- ⊞ DMC 451 grey
- △ DMC 939 navy blue
- ⋂ DMC 792 purple/blue
- ⊟ DMC 932 pale blue
- ⊘ DMC 739 cream
- ▲ DMC 642 stone brown
- ∨ DMC 372 light brown
- ⊙ DMC 734 khaki
- ⊠ DMC 3052 light green
- ⊍ DMC 937 medium green
- ◆ DMC 890 dark green
- ■ DMC 801 stem brown
- ⊞ DMC 327 purple
- ⊠ DMC 3041 mauve
- ⊗ DMC 3042 light mauve
- ⓢ DMC 815 deep red
- ⊞ DMC 776 pink
- ⊡ DMC 3750 dark turquoise blue
- ⊡ DMC 828 pale turquoise
- ⊙ DMC 902 maroon
- ⊠ DMC 902 maroon (also used for French knots and straight stitch stamens)

- Ⓕ DMC 517 turquoise
- ⊳ DMC 223 rose pink
- ⊓ DMC 315 plum pink
- ⌐ DMC 224 pink
- ⊞ DMC 818 pale pink
- ⋈ DMC 730 olive green
- ⊥ DMC 918 rust
- ⊠ DMC 745 lemon
- ⊭ DMC 351 apricot
- ▼ DMC 3021 dark muddy green
- ⊘ DMC 977 orange
- ⊡ DMC 3078 yellow
- ⊤ DMC 976 deep orange
- ⊌ DMC 921 light rust
- ✳ DMC 762 silver grey
- ⊡ DMC 3021 outline – dark muddy green
- ⊠ DMC 730 outline – olive green
- ⊠ DMC 801 outline – stem brown

A CALENDAR OF WILDFLOWERS

Commemorate the Australian year in cross-stitch with this glorious wildflower sampler. Designed especially for *Handmade* by Vivienne Garforth, the sampler features flowers that appear in their appropriate flowering months and includes a sampling from each state and territory.

Bottlebrush — Callistemon

Fringed Lily — Thysanotus

Everlasting Daisies — Helichrysum

Banksia — Banksia

Fan Flower — Scaveola

Giant Water Lily — Nymphaea

Australian Wildflower Calendar

MATERIALS
- 45cm x 60cm cream 14-count Aida cloth
- One skein each DMC Stranded Embroidery Cotton (Art 117) in colours indicated in key

METHOD
Each symbol represents one cross-stitch, embroidered with two strands of cotton in indicated colour, over one Aida square. Work green borders first, then fill in lettering for the months. If you count and work borders inside each square first, it will make it easier to place flowers correctly. Flower name lettering is worked in back-stitch with two strands of No 3021.

Here's a perfect gift for your home or your friends, perhaps especially pleasant for friends overseas who have yet to discover our unique flora.
To make reference easier, we've given the generic name for each of the flowers. As the stitching is decorative rather than botanically specific, you can choose to describe a species that flowers near you.

Gum Blossom — Eucalyptus

Wattle — Acacia

Sun Orchid — Thelymitra

Lechenaultia — Lechenaultia

Waratah — Telopea

Christmas Bells — Blandfordia

KEY

- ☑ DMC 937 medium avocado green
- ⊞ DMC 3328 dark salmon
- ⊡ DMC 3042 light antique violet
- ☒ DMC 640 very dark beige-grey
- ⬆ DMC 815 medium garnet
- ⧄ DMC 321 Christmas red
- ◹ DMC 554 light violet
- ▶ DMC 552 medium violet
- ◺ DMC 742 light tangerine
- ⊤ DMC 3348 light yellow-green
- ⊞ DMC 730 very dark olive green
- ◰ DMC 502 blue-green
- ⓢ DMC 307 lemon
- ◥ DMC 3078 very light golden yellow
- ⊙ DMC 832 golden olive
- △ DMC 899 medium rose
- ⊘ DMC 3354 light dusty rose
- Ⅰ DMC 597 turquoise
- ⊞ DMC 792 dark cornflower blue
- ● DMC 340 medium blue-violet
- ⊻ DMC 434 light brown
- ⊞ DMC 828 ultra very light blue
- ⊥ DMC 826 medium blue
- ⌐ DMC 517 medium wedgewood
- ⫿ DMC 3021 very dark brown-grey

If you've only time to prepare a card for a special birthday, stitch one with blooms that will be in flower in the birthday month. You could add to your offering by writing a little about the flower, using a good reference on native plants as a guide. There's some fascinating information to be unearthed. For example, the Fan Flower, whose five petals are arranged on the flower in a hand-like manner, is named after Scaevola, a Roman soldier who is said to have shown his bravery by burning his hand off in a fire!

Graph for Australian Wild Flower Calendar

Bottlebrush

Fringed Lily

Everlastings

Giant Water Lily

Banksia

Blue Fan Flower

Gum Blossoms

Wattle

Sun Orchid

Lechenaultia

Waratah

Christmas Bells

NATURE NOTES I

Capture a little of the unique beauty of the Australian bush in this magnificent cross-stitch sampler, designed by Marianne Porteners. The extraordinary detail recorded in the embroidery makes this a project to be treasured for years to come. But if you feel a bit daunted about starting on the sampler straight away, we have suggested ways to continue the theme by using motifs on smaller projects. Once you've worked these designs, you'll be inspired to try your own.

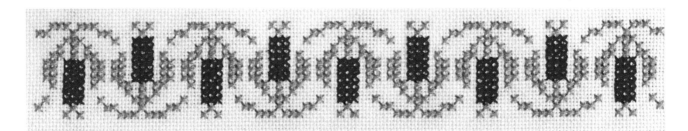

Nature Notes I Sampler

MEASUREMENTS
Finished picture measures approximately 44cm square. Actual embroidery measures approximately 37cm square.

MATERIALS
- 65cm square 11-count linen or hardanger fabric, or 14-count Aida cloth
- One skein each of DMC Stranded Embroidery Cotton (Art 117) in colours indicated on key, plus two skeins No 321 and three skeins No 988
- No 24 tapestry needle

METHOD
NOTE: Each symbol on graph represents one cross-stitch embroidered with two strands of cotton in indicated colour, over two fabric threads or one Aida square.

To begin, overcast fabric edges to prevent unravelling. Commence embroidery with outside border, 14 cm in from edges at righthand lower corner. For first stitch, leave a short end of embroidery thread hanging free at back, to be laced under embroidery when work has progressed.

Work from graph. Personal initials and dates are worked from alphabet and number graph with No 839 thread (see photograph for position).

Work outside border and border above lorikeet design in back-stitch, using two strands of No 988 thread.

Begin and end each thread by lacing ends under embroidery at back. Work top of all cross-stitches in same direction.

Details are worked after all cross-stitches are finished. Embroider with two strands in back- or straight-stitch in following colours: small blue bird tail and outline, No 797; legs, eye and beak, No 321; pine tree top, No 987; small Christmas bell stems, No 840; small spider flowers, No 321; beetle legs, No 839; four stitches of green banksia bouquet, No 987; outline of narrow wattle border, No 988; honey flower styles, No 321.
NOTE: Lorikeet eye is a tiny back-stitch; edges of small Christmas bells are half cross-stitches which pass over one fabric thread (or half an Aida square) in one direction, and two threads (or full Aida square) in other direction.

To finish, frame completed embroidery yourself, or have it professionally framed.

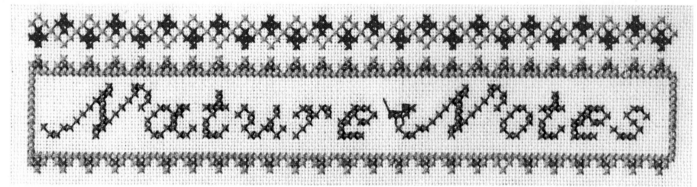

A close-up of the detail in the top left section

GRAPH FOR NATURE NOTES I SAMPLER: TOP LEFT SECTION

A close-up of the detail in the top right section

KEY

☒	DMC 666 bright red	◩	DMC 701 dark parrot green	⑤	DMC 973 wattle yellow
☒	DMC 321 medium red	◣	DMC 3348 light yellow-green	Ⓒ	DMC 972 sunny yellow
⊙	DMC 498 dark red	⠿	DMC 734 light banksia green	Ⓤ	DMC 725 light topaz
⠄	DMC 988 medium forest green	♣	DMC 733 dark banksia green	Ⓛ	DMC 922 light copper
◪	DMC 987 dark forest green	Ⓥ	DMC 840 medium beige-brown	⊙	DMC 920 medium copper
■	DMC 703 bright parrot green	•	DMC 839 dark beige-brown	Ⓘ	DMC 919 red copper
◭	DMC 702 medium parrot green	Ⓣ	DMC 797 royal blue	Ⓥ	DMC 646 brown-beige

GRAPH FOR NATURE NOTES I SAMPLER: TOP RIGHT SECTION

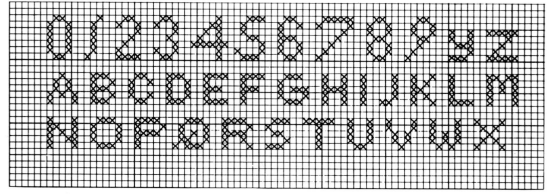

GRAPH FOR NATURE NOTES I SAMPLER: BOTTOM LEFT SECTION

ALPHABET AND NUMBER GRAPH FOR NATURE NOTES I SAMPLER

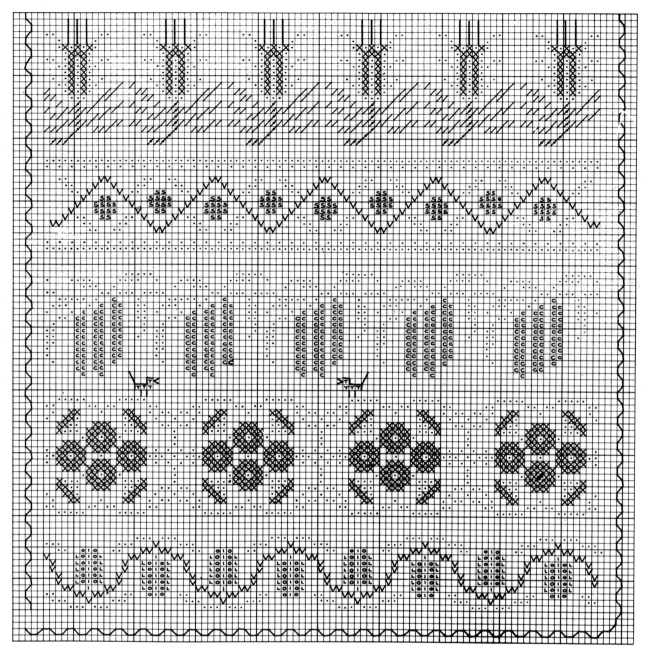

GRAPH FOR NATURE NOTES I SAMPLER: BOTTOM RIGHT SECTION

Using motifs from the larger sampler, these charming bookmarks, embroidered borders, and little buttons are an ideal way to practise your cross-stitch skills. And think what a welcome present a bottlebrush bookmark would be for an overseas friend pining for a little bit of Oz!

NATURE NOTES II

Marianne Portener's second glorious sampler in her Nature Notes series captures the coastal bush of Eastern Australia. In perfect cross-stitched detail, down to the last dangling red spider, Nature Notes II depicts flowering and budding ironbark, crimson rosellas, acacia, pittosporum, coastal banksia and honeyeaters feasting amid grevillea.

Honeyeater Tablecloth

MEASUREMENTS
Finished cloth measures approximately 87cm square, but can be extended to suit your own needs.

MATERIALS
- 110cm square white 11-count Aida cloth
- DMC Stranded Embroidery Cotton (Art 117), in amounts and colours as indicated on key, page 32
- No 22 tapestry needle

METHOD
Each symbol represents one cross-stitch embroidered with three strands of cotton in indicated colour, over one Aida square. For general sewing technique, refer to method for sampler.

To begin, overcast fabric edges to avoid unravelling. Work one horizontal and one vertical line of running stitches across fabric to mark centre. Starting at centre, where marked lines intersect, measure 38cm downwards along one line of running stitches, and mark fabric row here with a pin.

Work first stitch, marked C on graph, page 32, over pinned area,

using three strands of No 937. Continue from graph. Repeat motifs for a border of eight birds and seven flowers along each side, and one flower in each corner. When complete, work green outside border using No 937.

Leave a distance of 13 Aida squares between this border and main border, counting from bird's tail. For corners, refer to small graphs.

To finish, cut cloth 24 Aida squares outside green border. Fold and baste a hem eight squares wide, with a further eight Aida squares turned under. Mitre corners. Sew hem in place against base row of green border.

Don't forget to add your own initials to your finished sampler, for posterity. Included with the main graphs is a full set of letters so you can personalise your work.

For a delightful Australian tablecloth, Marianne has lifted the honeyeaters from the main sampler and given a corner section of grevillea.

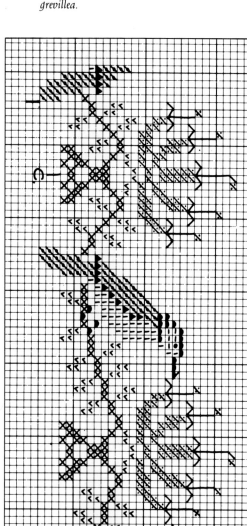

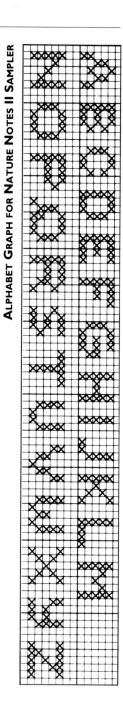

ALPHABET GRAPH FOR NATURE NOTES II SAMPLER

KEY

☒ DMC 937 medium avocado green (4 skeins)
⊟ DMC 798 dark Delft blue (1 skein)
◤ DMC 869 dark hazelnut (1 skein)
◓ DMC 310 black (1 skein)
⊡ DMC 632 dark tan (1 skein)
☒ DMC 321 bright red (3 skeins)
☑ DMC 3347 medium yellow-green (3 skeins)
◩ DMC 732 dark olive green (2 skeins)
◫ DMC 677 very light old gold (2 skeins)

BORDER GRAPH FOR TABLECLOTH

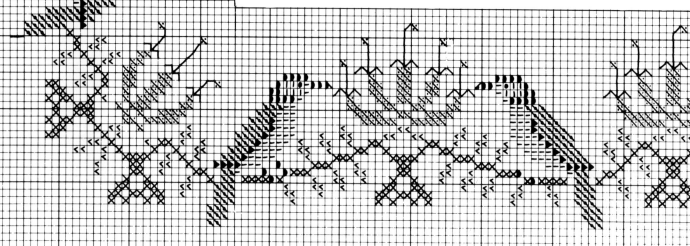

GRAPH FOR HONEYEATERS AND GREVILLEA TABLECLOTH

Nature Notes II Sampler

MEASUREMENTS

Finished picture measures approximately 27cm x 43cm; embroidery itself measures 19cm x 35cm.

MATERIALS

- 50cm x 65cm white 14-count Aida cloth
- One skein each DMC Stranded Embroidery Cotton (Art 117) in colours indicated on key
- One skein DMC No 844, dark grey
- No 24 tapestry needle

METHOD

Each symbol represents one cross-stitch embroidered with two strands of cotton in indicated colour, over one Aida square.

First, overcast fabric edges to prevent unravelling. Commence embroidery with outside border, 15cm in from edges at right lower corner. For first stitch, leave a short end of thread hanging free at back, to be laced under embroidery when work has progressed.

Work from graph. Personal initials are worked from alphabet graph with No 451 thread. Work outside border in back-stitch, using two strands of No 3363 thread. Begin and end each thread by lacing ends under embroidery at back. Work tops of all cross-stitches in same direction.

Details are worked after all cross-stitches are finished. Embroider these in back- or straight-stitch, and make two small French knots for butterflies' antennae. For details, use one or two strands as indicated below, in the following colours: butterflies, two strands No 844; flowering ironbark, one strand No 612; spider, one strand

No 321; spider web, one strand No 451; rosella beak, two strands No 422; pittosporum seedpods, two strands No 680; pittosporum leaves, two strands in same colour green as adjacent cross-stitch; banksia, one strand No 734; grevillea, two strands No 321; ironbark buds, one strand No 3347. Note that Honeyeater beak is ¾ cross-stitch which passes diagonally over half an Aida square in one direction, and full square in other direction.

To finish, frame completed embroidery yourself, or have it professionally framed.

Herb Sachet

Work chosen motif in two strands on 14-count Aida cloth, and sew into bags, about 8cm x 12cm. Hem top edge, finish with crochet, if desired (see below), fill with pot-pourri or dried herbs and tie with ribbon.

CROCHET EDGING

Using fine crochet cotton, sew an even number of blanket-stitches, 2 rows deep and one Aida square apart, around top edge.

1ST RND With a fine hook, work 1dc in each blanket st loop. Join with a sl st.
2ND RND 4ch, *miss 1dc, 1tr in next dc, 1ch. Rep from * to end, join with sl st.
3RD RND *3tr in ch sp, sl st in next ch sp. Rep from * to end, join with sl st.
4TH RND Sl st to centre tr of 3tr group, *3tr in sl st of previous rnd, sl st in centre tr of 3tr group. Rep from * to end, ending with 3tr in last sl st, join with sl st, fasten off.

If samplers and tablecloths seem a little too daunting, why not begin with something smaller? Motifs from the main picture, such as the acacia or the ironbark flowers, can be used to great effect on borders or herbal sachets.

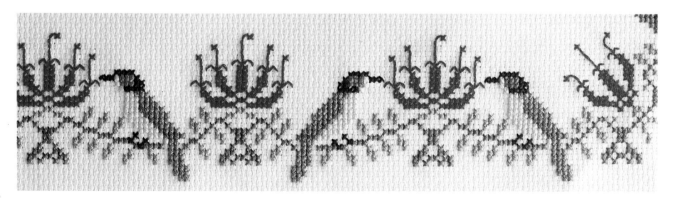

A close-up of the detail on the border of the Honeyeaters and Grevillea Tablecloth.

A

GRAPH FOR NATURE NOTES II SAMPLER: PARTS A AND B

*In order to reproduce the graph at full size, it
has been printed over two pages. To use the
graph, photocopy both pages, join A and B at
the centre edge and tape in place.*

B JOINS A

KEY

- ☒ DMC 451 shell grey
- ⊆ DMC 839 dark beige-brown
- ⌊ DMC 3346 dark yellow-green
- ✔ DMC 3347 medium yellow-green
- ⋒ DMC 471 light avocado green
- ⊠ DMC 937 medium avocado green
- ⊤ DMC 772 light pine green

- ⋀ DMC 3363 medium pine green
- ⊘ DMC 732 dark olive green
- ⋔ DMC 733 medium olive green
- ⊟ DMC 734 light olive green
- ▲ DMC 869 dark hazelnut
- ✚ DMC 422 light hazelnut
- ⑤ DMC 680 old gold
- ① DMC 677 very light old gold

- ● DMC 632 dark tan
- ▣ DMC 612 drab brown
- ⋅ DMC 822 light beige-brown
- ⧄ DMC 321 bright red
- ⋮ DMC 973 bright yellow
- ⊟ DMC 798 dark Delft blue
- ◾ DMC 310 black
- ○ DMC 793 cornflower blue

VICTORIAN SPLENDOUR

When The Strand Arcade in Sydney was opened in 1892, it was the fashionable place to see and be seen. Now restored to its former glory, The Strand boasts delicate wrought-iron lace, cedar balustrades and shopfronts, marble columns and, of course, its famous richly tiled floor. Marianne Porteners has captured the Victorian elegance of The Strand's wrought-iron and floor tiles in her superbly detailed cross-stitch designs for a framed picture and table runners.

Strand Arcade Tapestry Picture

MEASUREMENTS
Finished picture is 45cm square. Actual design is 38.5cm square, with a 2cm border.

MATERIALS
- 65cm square, 10-count, double-thread canvas, allowing four cross-stitches per cm
- Masking tape
- DMC Coton Perle No 5 (Art 115) in amounts and colours indicated on key, page 39
- No 20 tapestry needle

METHOD
Bind edge of canvas with tape to prevent fraying. Following Graph A, page 38, start embroidery 14cm in from edge of lower right corner. Work in cross-stitch with one thread of perle cotton. Repeat graphed design to make a picture of four star motifs. When completed, fill in spaces around all blue squares and pink centre square with cream No 712.

Work a border, eight rows wide, around completed design with very dark beige-grey No 640.

To finish, frame completed embroidery yourself, or have it professionally framed.

Strand Arcade Table Runner

MEASUREMENTS
Finished runner measures 85cm x 41cm.

MATERIALS
- 105cm x 60cm oatmeal or light beige 14-count Aida cloth
- Matching sewing thread
- DMC Stranded Embroidery Cotton (Art 117) in amounts and colours indicated on key, page 39
- No 24 tapestry needle

METHOD
Overcast edges of Aida cloth to prevent fraying. Following Graph B, page 39, start embroidery 9cm in from edges of lower right corner. Work in cross-stitch, using two strands of cotton. For the first stitch, leave a short end of thread hanging free at back. This will be laced under embroidery as work progresses. Avoid

The Strand's wrought-iron lace inspired this motif, which is worked in both cross-stitch and back-stitch, and could be adapted to any number of projects, such as a tablecloth and napkins.

carrying thread across long distances at back. Either weave it under existing embroidery, or end thread and start again. Top threads of all cross-stitches should lie in the same direction.

Repeat graphed design to make a border of fourteen central stars on long sides, and six on short sides. Note that blank squares on graph are left unstitched.

When border is finished, work lines

of cross-stitch on either side of it in dark shell pink No 221, working one stitch in every alternate square. Stay 11 rows beyond border on long sides, and 12 rows at short sides.

To finish, trim fabric edges 5cm beyond outer line of cross-stitch. Make a hem 1.5cm wide, with 1.5cm tucked under, and mitre corners. Press gently with a steam iron on back of fabric, using an ironing cloth.

The gloriously rich colours of The Strand Arcade's tessellated floor tiles make a stunning framed picture.

STRAND ARCADE TAPESTRY GRAPH A

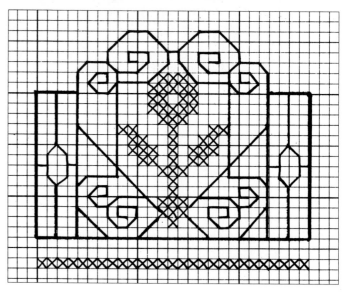

STRAND ARCADE WROUGHT-IRON DESIGN GRAPH C

Strand Arcade Wrought-Iron Design

MATERIALS

- 14-count Aida cloth
- DMC Stranded Embroidery Cotton (Art 117), No 451
- No 24 tapestry needle

METHOD

Using Graph C, work in back- and cross-stitch with two strands of cotton. Use motif to decorate articles as you wish.

KEY

NOTE: Graph A is worked with Coton Perle No 5 and Graph B with stranded cotton. Number of skeins required for Graphs A and B respectively are given in brackets. Where only one figure is given, it is for Graph A only.

- ☒ DMC 221 dark shell pink (6, 9)
- ☑ DMC 640 very dark beige-grey (5, 2)
- ⊤ DMC 334 sky blue (2,2)
- · DMC 729 old gold (2, 2)
- ☐ DMC 712 cream (2)
- ⊡ DMC 3371 rich brown (3)

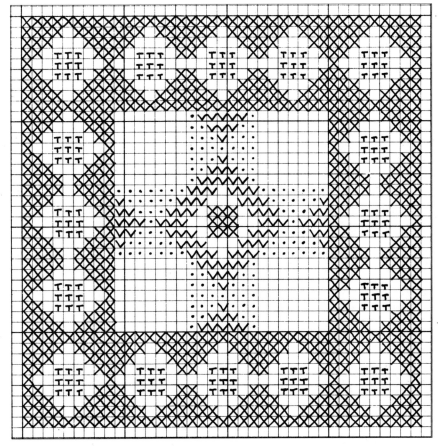

STRAND ARCADE TABLE RUNNER GRAPH B

Right: A detail from the larger tile has been adapted and repeated on this charming table runner. The oatmeal-coloured background enhances its antique effect.

PINS AND NEEDLES

A beginner's guide to cross-stitch

STEP 1

Cross-stitch is habit forming. But, if you haven't yet been bitten by the bug and wonder what all the fuss is about, here's a delightful project to try.

Cross-stitch is an extremely popular and widespread form of embroidery. It is done in cultures all over the world, and has been for many centuries.

Alison Snepp, who designed our pretty pincushion, has been embroidering since she was old enough to thread a needle. These days, she teaches and demonstrates many crafts, foremost among which is her first and best love, embroidery.

STEP 2

Because Alison's design is based on simple repetition, this is an ideal project to sit and stitch while 'watching' the TV. You don't need constant reference to a graph once you've stitched one or two sections of each square.

There are several ways of making the crosses, but the method an embroiderer prefers is not important. The important part is that an entire piece of embroidery is done with the same method, so that the second part of the cross-stitch is always in the same direction. If the stitches are not all crossed the same way, then light will be reflected from the stitches differently, and inconsistently embroidered stitches will stand out.

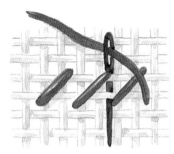

STEP 3

STEP 4

THE BASIC STITCH

The stitch illustrations and instructions show just how simple cross-stitch embroidery is. It is best to use a thread which is about 40cm long. Use a tapestry needle, as it has a blunt point and will not split the threads in the fabric.

Bring needle up through fabric at lower lefthand side of stitch. Count over two threads to the right and two threads up, and put needle into fabric at this point. In the same movement, count two threads directly down and bring needle out through fabric (Step 1). This is a half cross-stitch. Count to the right over two threads

from where top of last stitch went into fabric and put needle in at this point, bringing it out two threads below (Step 2).

Work half cross-stitches along row in this manner until as many stitches have been worked as are indicated in that row on chart.

Without turning embroidery, work back across row, crossing each stitch into same holes as first half of cross-stitches (Steps 3 & 4).

Lefthanded people should follow same instructions, as all rows of cross-stitch are worked from left to right and then back from right to left.

STEP 5

FABRIC PREPARATION

Even-weave fabric will fray very easily. To prevent fraying, zigzag around edge of fabric with a sewing machine. Otherwise, use some machine thread and oversew, or turn in edges of fabric, by hand.

Unless cross-stitch to be worked is a border, it is usual to start embroidery in centre of fabric. It is easy to find the centre by folding fabric in half horizontally, pinching centre on the fold and then stitching a row of tacking across fabric following a thread in the linen. Then fold fabric in half vertically and stitch a row of tacking stitches across fabric following a thread in the linen.

Use machine thread for tacking. Tacking is easier to remove when embroidery is complete if the colour does not appear in embroidery itself. Never use a dark coloured thread for tacking, as it will often shed some of its dye onto fabric, leaving marks behind after stitches are removed.

Leave tacking lines in fabric until work is complete. If tacking threads are cut while work is in progress, they tend to get caught in the cross-stitch. Once tacking is removed, it is difficult to correct mistakes in the embroidery.

Tacking lines on fabric provide a quick and easy reference to the chart. Whenever an area of embroidery crosses a centre line on chart, it should cross centre line on fabric at the same place. This is a most valuable reference, particularly in complicated pieces of embroidery, when tacked lines also help you to keep track of where you are on the graph.

FINDING CENTRE OF CHART

On the pincushion chart, arrows mark centre of the design. Using a pencil and ruler, connect top and bottom arrows and then connect right and lefthand arrows. Centre of chart is now clearly shown.

Centre lines on chart correspond with centre lines which have been tacked onto fabric. Start embroidery with the square which is to the lower right of centre. One square on the graph represents one cross-stitch, that is, a two thread square on fabric.

STARTING WORK

After having established where embroidery is to start, push needle down through fabric about 3cm up from, and to the left of, hole where embroidery is to begin. Leave a tail about 5cm long on right side of fabric. It is easy to control this starting tail on the right side, where it won't get caught in back of embroidery. Later, it can be pulled through to back and threaded under completed stitches.

ENDING OFF

To end off a thread, take needle through to back of embroidery and run it underneath six vertical stitches on the wrong side, as shown in Step 5.

STEP 6

BACK-STITCH

Back-stitch is always worked from right to left. Bring needle out of fabric, and insert it again, two threads to right of where thread is coming out. Bring needle out again two threads to the left of where last stitch finishes. Continue working back-stitch in this manner.

Note from Step 6, that stitch can be worked diagonally, as well as horizontally and vertically. Back-stitch lines on a graph are usually shown by a solid line.

When ending off, finish last stitch by bringing needle through to back of fabric. Whip back over six stitches, pulling thread taut and cut it off close to surface of fabric.

HINTS

- It is difficult to work a new row of cross-stitch which is above the last one completed. Simply turn embroidery and chart upside down and then you will be working down again. It is always far easier to work down in cross-stitch.
- Never turn embroidery and chart on their sides to complete an area of cross-stitch. If work is turned sideways the stitch will be crossed in the opposite direction and will stand out when work is complete.
- When working across a row in which there is more than one colour, do not jump over more than

two stitches, as far as possible. Embroidery will look untidy on the back. Instead, work a panel of stitches in one area and then end off and start again in the separated area.

Cross-stitch Pincushion

MEASUREMENTS
Finished pincushion measures approximately 10cm square.

MATERIALS
- Two 15cm squares of white evenweave linen fabric, 8 threads/cm (18 threads/inch)
- DMC Stranded Embroidery Cotton (Art 117) in following colours and quantities: 2 skeins salmon 760, and one skein each dark salmon 3328, very dark salmon 347 and light salmon 761
- No 22 tapestry needle
- 50cm bias binding (1cm wide when folded) to match one of the embroidery threads
- Small quantity polyester filling
- Machine thread in white and a medium colour
- Embroidery scissors

METHOD
Prepare one of the linen squares as set out under Fabric Preparation. Find the centres of linen square and chart, as described. One square on chart represents a two-thread square on the linen. Start the embroidery at centre. Work cross-stitch first and then back-stitch outlines on the squares. Use six threads of stranded cotton for cross-stitch and three threads for back-stitch.

After embroidery is complete, remove tacked centre lines from fabric and press it on wrong side.

Using medium colour machine thread, tack a line around embroidery, four threads outside back-stitched squares.

Press bias binding open and flat. With right sides together, and using marking on the fold line on the bias as a guide, pin one side of bias binding to tacked outline around embroidery. Snip seam allowance on bias binding to ease binding around corners on pincushion. Join ends of bias binding to fit. Machine-sew binding to embroidery, pivoting at corners.

Prepare second square of linen by outlining a tacked square in centre of it, the same size as outer tacked outline on embroidered square. Backing of pincushion may be embroidered as well, if preferred. Press backing square. Pin backing to other side of bias binding, with right sides together, using corners on each piece of linen to match sides on pincushion. Machine-sew backing to binding, leaving a 7cm gap along centre of one side of pincushion. Trim seam allowances to 6mm.

Turn pincushion right side out. Fill with polyester cushion filling (some lavender, cloves or cinnamon stick may be added, if liked). Slip-stitch opening closed.

KEY

DMC			
▨	347	▨	760
▨	3328	⊡	761
		☐	760 B-S

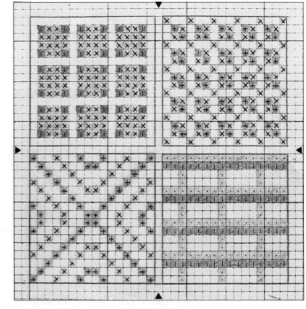

BABES IN THE WOOD

With colourful braid, pretty peasant embroidery and traditional Tyrolean colours, you can transform children's clothes into an Alpine fantasy. Designer Catherine Woram has added sprays of embroidered wildflowers to plain garments and teamed them with a delightful co-ordinating knitted jacket from Karingal, sized to fit three to five year olds.

Edelweiss and field flowers tumble in a pretty cascade down the front of a plain cotton blouse. Worked quickly in satin-stitch, back-stitch and bullion-stitch, the embroidery adds a charming freshness to the Tyrolean green of a simple elastic-waisted braid-trimmed skirt.

Girl's Tyrolean Jacket

MEASUREMENTS
To fit: 3-4 (4-5) years. Fits underarm: 61-66 (66-71) cm. Actual size: 76 (81) cm. Full length: approximately 29 (33) cm. Sleeve length: 28 (30) cm.

MATERIALS
Emu Superwash 4-ply (50g):
- 5 balls (both sizes); we used shade 3620
- Small quantities of blue, white, yellow and red tapestry wools for embroidery
- One pair each 2.75mm (No 12) and 3.25mm (No 10) knitting needles
- One stitch-holder
- Tapestry needle for embroidery
- Eight buttons

TENSION
See Knitting Notes on page 158.
28 sts and 36 rows to 10cm over st st, using 3.25mm needles.

SPECIAL ABBREVIATION
M1 make one st (pick up loop which lies before next st, place it on lefthand needle, knit into back of loop).

BACK
Using 3.25mm needles, cast on 104 (112) sts.
1ST ROW *K1, P1; rep from * to end.
2ND ROW *P1, K1; rep from * to end.
Rep last 2 rows 3 times more (8 rows moss st in all).
Cont in st st until work measures 24 (28)cm from beg, ending with purl row.
SHAPE NECK. NEXT ROW K44 (47), turn.
**Work 8 rows st st on these 44 (47) sts, at the same time, dec one st at neck edge in every row ... 36 (39) sts.
Cont straight in st st until work measures 29 (33)cm from beg, ending with a purl row.
Cast off.**
With right side facing, sl next 16 (18) sts on a stitch-holder and leave. Join yarn to rem 44 (47) sts and knit to end.
Rep from ** to **.

RIGHT FRONT

Using 3.25mm needles, cast on 52 (56) sts.

Work 8 rows moss st as for Back.

NEXT ROW K1, P1, knit to end.

NEXT ROW Purl to last 3 sts, K1, P1, K1.

Rep last 2 rows until work measures 24 (28)cm from beg, ending with a wrong-side row.

SHAPE NECK. NEXT ROW Cast off 8 (9) sts, knit to end.

** Cont in st st, dec one st at neck edge in next 8 rows ... 36 (39) sts.

Cont straight in st st on these 36 (39) sts until work measures 29 (33)cm from beg, ending with a purl row. Cast off.**

LEFT FRONT

Using 3.25mm needles, cast on 52 (56) sts.

1ST ROW *P1, K1; rep from * to end.

2ND ROW *K1, P1; rep from * to end.

Rep last 2 rows 3 times more (8 rows moss st in all).

NEXT ROW Knit to last 2 sts, P1, K1.

NEXT ROW K1, P1, K1, purl to end.

Rep last 2 rows until work measures 24 (28)cm from beg, ending with a right-side row.

SHAPE NECK. NEXT ROW Cast off 8 (9) sts, purl to end.

Work as for Right Front from ** to **.

SLEEVES

Using 2.75mm needles, cast on 45 (49) sts.

1ST ROW *K1, P1; rep from * to last st, K1.

2ND ROW P1, *K1, P1; rep from * to end.

Rep last 2 rows until work measures 3cm, ending with a 1st row.

NEXT ROW Rib 3 (2), M1, *rib 3, M1; rep from * to last 3 (2) sts, rib 3 (2) ... 59 (65) sts.

Change to 3.25mm needles.

Cont in st st, inc one st at each end of 3rd and every foll 6th (5th) row until there are 85 (99) sts.

Cont straight in st st until Sleeve measures 28 (30)cm, or length desired, from beg, ending with a purl row. Cast off.

NECKBAND

Using back-stitch, join shoulder seams. With right side facing, using 2.75mm needles, knit up 8 (9) sts along neck shaping on Right Front, 18 sts evenly along right side of neck, 18 sts evenly along right side of Back neck, 16 (18) sts from stitch-holder, 18 sts along left side of Back neck, 18 sts along Left Front neck, and 8 (9) sts along neck shaping on Left Front ... 104 (108) sts.

1ST ROW *K1, P1; rep from * to end.

2ND ROW *P1, K1; rep from * to end.

Rep last 2 rows 3 times more (8 rows moss st in all).

Cast off.

TO MAKE UP

Sew in Sleeves, placing centre of Sleeves to shoulder seams. Join side and Sleeve seams. Sew pairs of buttons to moss-st edges on Fronts, as photographed. Plait or crochet lengths of yarn to form 15cm ties. Fold ties in half, stitch ends securely behind Right Front, leaving a loop to fasten to buttons on Left Front. Using tapestry wools, and following diagram on page 47, embroider design (as photographed) to Left Front, then reverse design for Right Front. Work white edelweiss flowers in satin-stitch with yellow bullion-stitch centres, red and blue flowers in lazy-daisy stitch with yellow bullion-stitch centres, green leaves in lazy-daisy stitch and green stems in stem-stitch.

Above and left: A bottle-green jacket in Emu 4-ply Superwash, featuring moss-stitch bands and pretty sprays of embroidered field flowers, is worn over a purchased peasant-style skirt, to which we've added matching embroidery on the yoke.

EMBROIDERY DIAGRAM FOR SKIRT YOKE: PART A

yellow

green

blue

blue

white or cream

yellow

blue

blue

A JOINS B

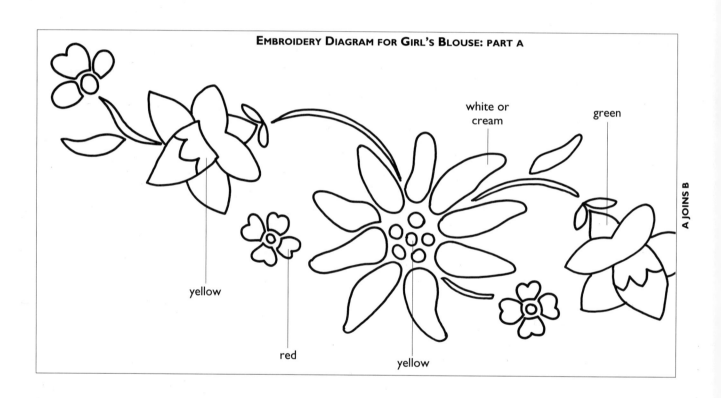

EMBROIDERY DIAGRAM FOR GIRL'S BLOUSE: PART A

white or cream

green

yellow

red

yellow

A JOINS B

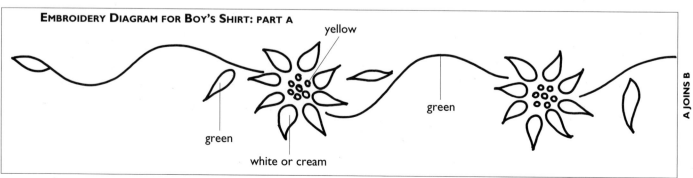

EMBROIDERY DIAGRAM FOR BOY'S SHIRT: PART A

yellow

green

green

white or cream

A JOINS B

EMBROIDERY DIAGRAM FOR SKIRT YOKE: PART B

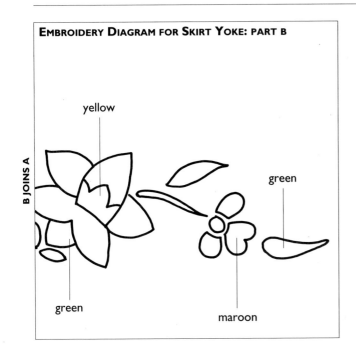

B JOINS A

yellow

green

green

maroon

EMBROIDERY GUIDE FOR TYROLEAN JACKET

EMBROIDERY DIAGRAM FOR GIRL'S BLOUSE: PART B

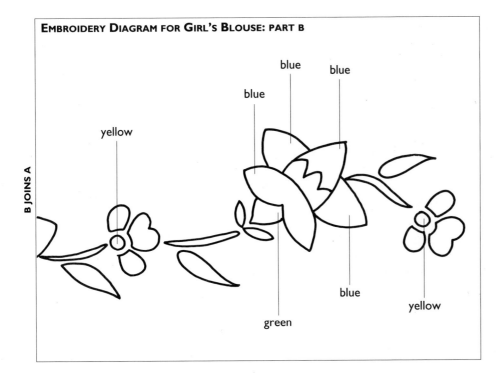

B JOINS A

yellow

blue

blue

blue

blue

green

yellow

green

EMBROIDERY DIAGRAM FOR BOY'S SHIRT: PART B

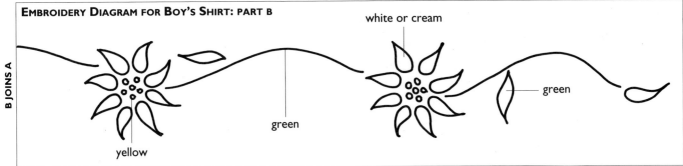

B JOINS A

white or cream

green

green

yellow

Inexpensive, pull-on trousers are teamed with a plain shirt, which we've transformed with a simple trail of embroidered edelweiss twining quietly around small silver buttons. The braces - so practical on small children - are easy to make from purchased braid and elastic.

AND SO TO BED

Traditionally used for decorating babies' bunny rugs and dressing gowns, wool-embroidered blanketing is the natural choice for a snuggly old-fashioned hotwater bottle cover, designed for *Handmade* by Anne's Glory Box. Simple to construct and embroider, the cover is lined with a pretty Liberty print.

Grub roses, forget-me-nots, lily-of-the-valley and tiny sprays of lavender twine in a heart shape on this pretty woollen cover.

Wool-embroidered Hotwater Bottle Cover

MEASUREMENTS

Finished cover measures approximately 24cm x 40.5cm, including frill.

MATERIALS

- 40cm x 54cm cream woollen blanketing
- Tracing paper
- Water-soluble marking pen
- One skein each Appleton's Crewel Wool in White B991, Blue 742, Green 355, Yellow 996, Pale Pink 752, Lavender 885, and DMC Laine Colbert Tapestry Wool (Art 486-487) in Dusty Pink 7951, Pale Dusty Pink 7122 and White
- Large tapestry needle
- 55cm purchased cream satin piping
- 40cm x 54cm fabric for lining (we used a Liberty lawn)
- 10cm x 90cm strip for frill (the same as lining or a contrast)

METHOD

Fold blanketing in half crosswise and cut along fold, giving two rectangles, each 27cm x 40cm. Using a saucer as a guide, carefully round lower corners of each rectangle.

Trace design, below, onto tracing paper. Pin design to centre of one woollen rectangle and, using a thick tapestry needle, prick holes along lines of heart outline and, if you desire, around a few basic features of the flowers. You don't need to transfer all details of design — just enough for a guide. Draw over holes with a water-soluble marker pen, so the result, when tracing paper is removed, is a spotty outline on the wool. Embroidery can be washed gently in cold water, when completed, to remove marker pen.

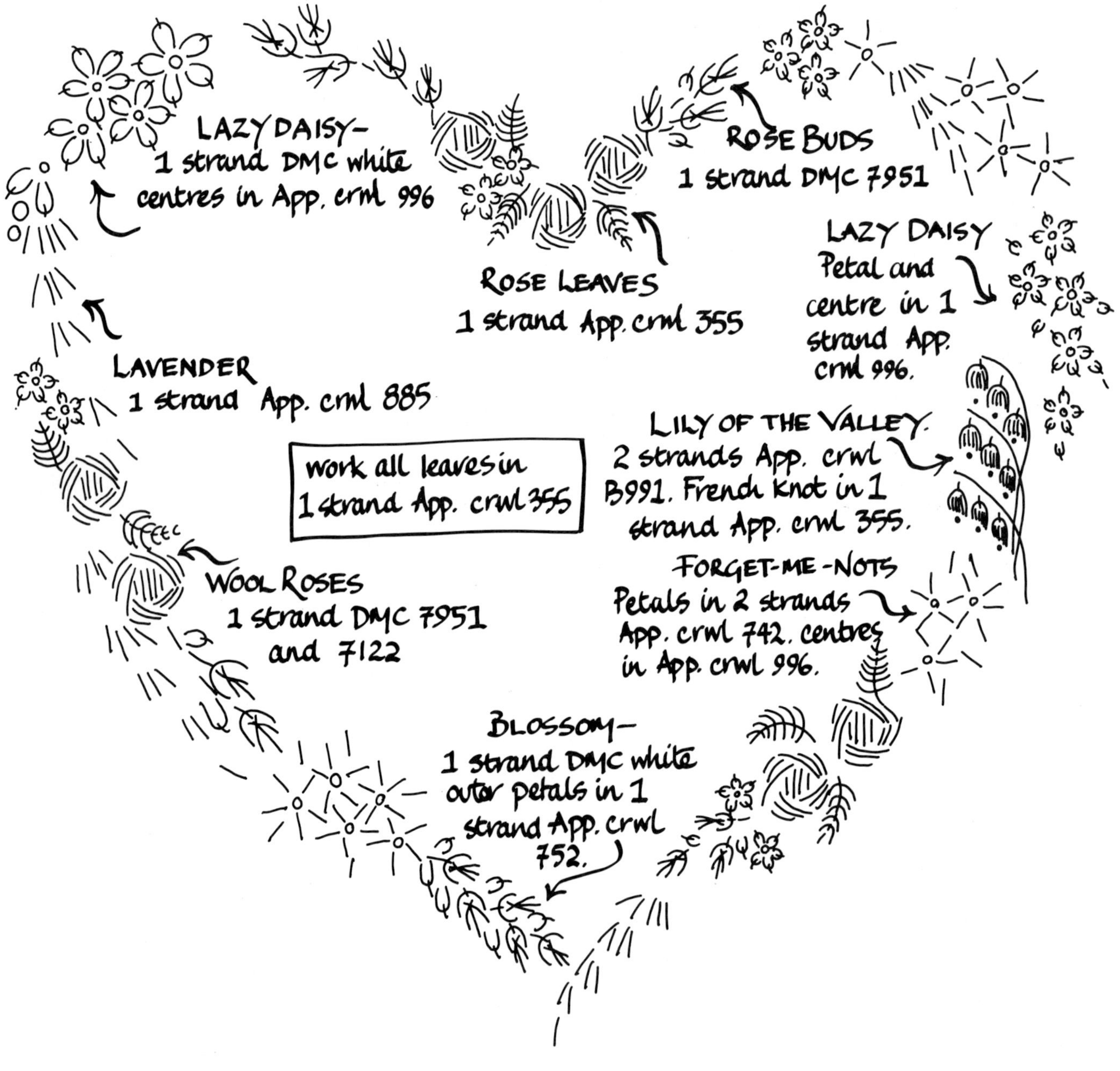

LAZY DAISY—
1 strand DMC white
centres in App. crwl 996

ROSE BUDS
1 strand DMC 7951

LAZY DAISY
Petal and centre in 1 strand App. crwl 996.

ROSE LEAVES
1 strand App. crwl 355

LAVENDER
1 strand App. crwl 885

work all leaves in
1 strand App. crwl 355

LILY OF THE VALLEY.
2 strands App. crwl B991. French Knot in 1 strand App. crwl 355.

WOOL ROSES
1 strand DMC 7951
and 7122

FORGET-ME-NOTS
Petals in 2 strands App. crwl 742. centres in App. crwl 996.

BLOSSOM—
1 strand DMC white
outer petals in 1 strand App. crwl 752.

Following the design diagram (opposite) and stitch guide, embroider design onto blanketing.

With right sides facing, stitch front and back together, allowing 1cm seams. Turn right side out.

With right sides facing and raw edges even, stitch piping to top edge of cover.

With right sides facing, join short ends of frill strip together, allowing a 1cm seam. Press seam open. Fold strip in half lengthwise, wrong sides facing, and run a gathering thread along raw edge. Pull up gathers to fit top edge of cover. With right sides facing, stitch frill to top edge of cover, using piping stitching as a guide.

Fold lining fabric in half crosswise and cut along fold, giving two rectangles, each 27cm x 40cm. With right sides facing, and allowing 1cm seams, stitch lining front and back together, leaving a 7cm opening in one long side.

Place woollen cover into lining, right sides together, and stitch around top edge, once again using piping stitching as a guide.

Pull right side out through opening left in lining and slip-stitch opening closed. Carefully push lining down into woollen cover.

WOOL EMBROIDERY STITCH GUIDE

WOOL ROSE
Using darker of two pinks work 4 straight-stitches beside each other. Work 4 straight-stitches to cover the first 4 stitches. Using lighter of two pinks work 4 diagonal stitches across the corner of the square, starting ¾ of way along side. 4th stitch is very small & almost under 3rd stitch. Continue in this way on all sides. If your roses need to be rounded out a bit, stem-stitch around the outside working clockwise.

ROSE BUDS
Work three straight-stitches in darker pink, 2 and 3 crossing slightly at base.
green open fly-stitch.

LAZY DAISY
When working a 5-petal flower, always follow this order
work a French knot at centre

LILY-OF-THE VALLEY
Using 2 strands of fine white, work 4 stitches over each other. A white open fly-stitch extends beyond centre.
Pale green French knot

FORGET-ME-NOT
Using 2 strands of blue work a 5-petal flower using straight-stitches and working 3 or 4 stitches into the same hole.
work a French knot at centre

BLOSSOM
Using thick wool, work 2 stitches over each other. Using fine wool, work an open-fly-stitch to create outer petals. Work leaves in detached chain-stitch.

LEAVES
Use these with roses. Work one straight-stitch, then as many open fly-stitches as needed to give a nice leaf shape.

LAVENDER
Work in straight-stitch using 1 strand of mauve.

PERFECT POSIES

Flowers have always been a perfect gift, but for flowers that last, try an Embroidered bouquet. These charming brooches, designed by Cassie Donnellan, are very simple to make with scraps of embroidery cotton and curtain rings. You could also vary the finding on the back to make an unusual hairclip, or use to decorate a napkin-ring.

Embroidered Brooch

MEASUREMENTS
Each brooch is 4cm in diameter, but this can be varied according to the size of the curtain ring used.

MATERIALS
- Tapestry needle
- DMC Coton Perle No 5 (Art 115), in two shades of green and one or two colours for flowers
- Curtain ring, approximately 4cm in diameter
- Crewel embroidery needle
- Scrap of green felt
- 20mm brooch finding
- Craft glue
- Small amount of 3mm ribbon

METHOD
Thread tapestry needle with at least 3m of green pearl cotton. Tie end of cotton to curtain ring (Step 1), and work buttonhole-stitch closely all around edge (Step 2). Tie ends together and trim only the unthreaded end. Turn stitches firmly, so that all loops sit on inside of ring (Step 3).

Remove tapestry needle and thread crewel embroidery needle with remaining thread. Lay foundation of bouquet by lacing across ring to create a large fan effect for top of bouquet, and a narrower fan for stems (Step 4). Introduce another shade of green to complete foundation, as well as to draw fans together as shown (Step 5).

Begin bouquet by filling top of foundation with French knots (see Embroidery Stitch Guide on page 55) in both shades of green, and then with flower colours of your choice.

When embroidery is finished, cut a piece of felt, shaped to fit top half of bouquet. Stitch brooch finding onto felt through holes for this purpose, then carefully stick felt onto back of curtain ring with craft glue.

Finally, tie a piece of ribbon around centre of bouquet and arrange in a tiny bow at front (Step 6).

Felt is glued to the back of the embroidery for a neat finish, then a brooch finding is attached to the felt.
A pretty variation can be achieved by using a combination of tapestry wool and silk ribbon embroidery for the bouquet.

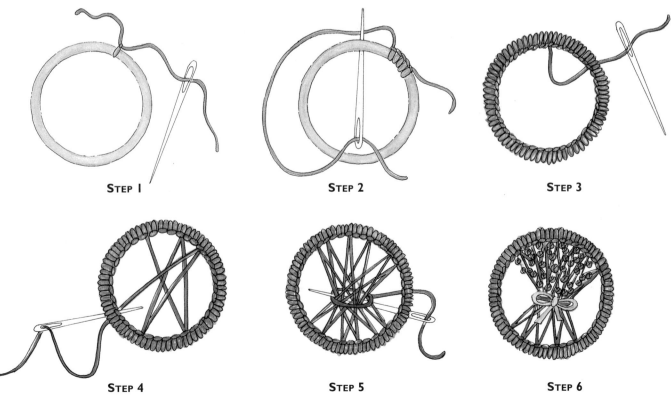

STEP 1

STEP 2

STEP 3

STEP 4

STEP 5

STEP 6

BRIGHT AS A BUTTON

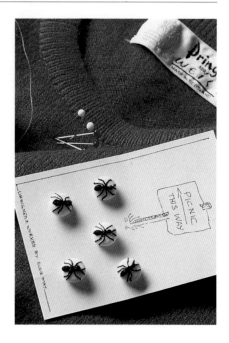

The perfect button to complement a special outfit can often seem very elusive. So, on these pages we show you ideas for making the perfect match. These delightful ribbon rose buttons and an amusing ant design are just two notions to inspire and give a personal touch to any garment. The designs are worked using ribbon embroidery and several basic embroidery stitches.

Ribbon Rose Buttons

MATERIALS
• Small amount fabric
• 30mm-wide self-cover buttons
• 1m pink silk embroidery ribbon
• Small amount green silk ribbon
• Stranded embroidery thread

METHOD
Outline button area with running-stitch (see Embroidery Stitch Guide opposite). Work design in centre of running-stitch circle following diagram.

The large centre flowers are woven over spokes of five straight-stitches. Work five straight-stitches using stranded thread, then weave pink silk ribbon over and under each stitch until straight-stitches are covered. Leaves are worked in open chain by working one chain-stitch either side of flower, using green silk ribbon. Small flowers are French knots; using two strands of embroidery thread work three knots on either side of button. Small leaves are worked in straight-stitch; using two strands of embroidery thread work two stitches, near French knots.

Cover buttons following manufacturer's instructions.

Rose button outline

Ant Buttons

MATERIALS
• Small amount fabric
• 10mm-wide self-cover buttons
• Black stranded embroidery thread

METHOD
Outline button area with running-stitch (see Embroidery Stitch Guide opposite). Work ant design in centre of running-stitch circle.

The head is a French knot made from four turns using two strands of thread. Legs are worked in back-stitch using one strand of thread. Upper body is worked in straight-stitch — three very close stitches using two strands of thread.

Abdomen is worked in chain-stitch encasing two French knots. The top knot has three turns, and the bottom two turns. The abdomen is worked using two strands of thread.

Cover buttons following manufacturer's instructions.

Above: Comical ants will be a hit on children's clothes, or make a humorous addition to more casual garments for adults. Left: Rose motif buttons worked in satin ribbon are an exquisite addition to linen blouses and romantic cardigans. A set of these would also make a gift to be cherished. More wonderful ideas for buttons are included in The Australian Women's Weekly Home Library Fete Favourites Book.

Ant button outline

A Braided Button

Create an opulent button using simple materials. All you need is a rubber washer, your favourite coloured satin braid (narrow braid is easier to work with) and a little beading wire. Just thread braid through centre of washer, securing it with a small knot, or a little glue, when you start. Continue to wind braid through centre and over sides of washer until it is completely covered. An interesting addition to centre of washer is a large knot of braid, which can be glued or sewn in place with tiny stitches. Use beading wire to form a loop at back of button, or work a loop using strong cotton. Choose 2.5cm and larger washers to cover and use the buttons to trim overcoats, boleros and jackets.

Beaded Buttons

Beads look wonderful when they are twisted over the top of a button. It's so simple and the effect is eye-catching. All you need are some small plastic beads (metallic ones look fabulous), cotton thread and glue. Cut a long strand of cotton and make a large knot in one end. Thread a needle with cotton and then thread beads onto strand of cotton, mixing colours if desired. (You may prefer to thread cotton straight through beads, without a needle). When you have threaded on enough beads to cover your chosen button, secure end of cotton with another large knot. Apply some glue to surface of button and secure one end of bead strand in centre. Begin winding it around to form a spiral that covers surface of button. Use extra glue to hold beads in place, if necessary. This technique can be applied to any size or shape buttons. You could also cover button with fabric before applying beads to give a contrasting background, if desired.

Braid-wrapped button

Beaded button

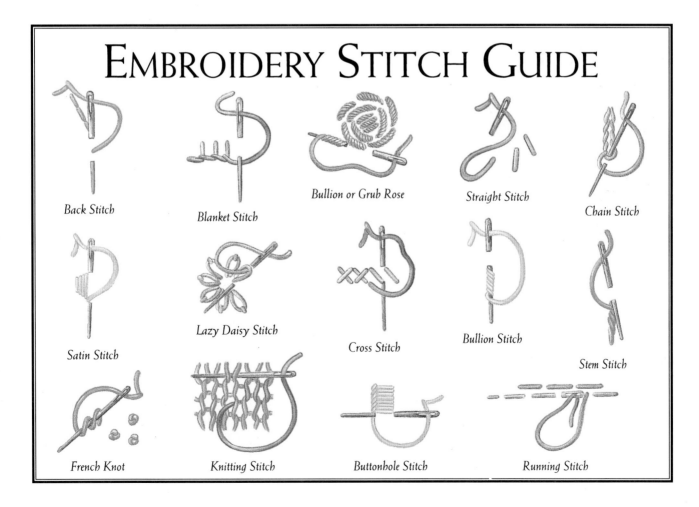

EMBROIDERY STITCH GUIDE

Back Stitch

Blanket Stitch

Bullion or Grub Rose

Straight Stitch

Chain Stitch

Satin Stitch

Lazy Daisy Stitch

Cross Stitch

Bullion Stitch

Stem Stitch

French Knot

Knitting Stitch

Buttonhole Stitch

Running Stitch

Soft Toys

I'm sure that amongst those hazy childhood memories most of us still harbour the image of a favourite toy. Some of us are lucky enough to have the toy still, preserved no doubt by parents who knew how pleased we'd be to find it had lasted the distance! My favourite was a very large rag doll called Pollyanna that my Mother made for me — and despite having lost a shoe (a sensible strapped style made from felt — where did it go?), dishevelled woollen plaits and one almost-detached arm, I still greet her as a very special friend.

Without doubt, all soft toys have the potential to become life long friends, so stitch them carefully and they'll endure all the loving attention they're bound to receive. Assembled on the following pages are many such companions — originals ranging from beautiful bears to marriageable mice — and they are all delightfully easy to make.

So make a start now — all that's needed to bring these captivating friends to life is fabric, notions and thread — plus an all-important dash of love.

TONIA TODMAN

THREE LITTLE MAIDS

Soft and eminently huggable, rag dolls are perennial favourites, and this little trio promises to be no exception — with their sweet expressions, old-fashioned clothes and delightful lacy underwear. Designed by Alison Bushell, they're all made and dressed from the same basic pattern, but as you can see, the possibilities for variety are as endless as your own bag of scraps and remnants.

Basic Rag Doll Body

MEASUREMENTS

Each doll is 36cm tall.

MATERIALS

- 30cm flesh-coloured cotton fabric (see Note)
- Polyester fibrefill
- Strong pink quilting thread, for assembling bodies
- Fabric paints or stranded embroidery thread, in dark brown, white, black, light brown, dark flesh and coral pink
- Toothpick or small paintbrush
- Red and brown coloured pencils
- Fine point brown permanent marker, for freckles
- Clear-drying craft glue (optional)

NOTE: The best fabric for bodies is tightly woven cotton, such as unbleached calico or homespun. It can be dyed a flesh colour with a tiny amount of Dylon Tangerine dye. Do not use a cotton polyester blend, as the fabric will not 'give' and wrinkles will form at curves and stress points.

PATTERN PIECES

All pattern pieces, except rectangles, are printed on pages 64 and 65. Trace Head Back, Head Front, Side Head, Ear, Body Front, Body Back, Leg, Arm and Foot Sole.

CUTTING

NOTE: All pattern pieces include 3mm seam allowance.

From flesh-coloured fabric, cut one Head Back, one Head Front, two side Heads, four Ears (Kathleen only), one Body Front, two Body Backs, four Legs, four Arms and two Foot Soles.

SEWING

When joining pieces, place right sides together, unless otherwise directed.

Join Head Back to Head Front along top edge. Join this central head piece to Head Sides, making sure to sew smoothly around curves. Leave open at neck edge.

Each doll wears lacy pantaloons beneath her petticoat. Underwear can be made from fine lawn or more homely calico.

Previous page: Meet Kathleen, Holly and Collette, all 36cm tall. Red-haired Kathleen has a ponytail and tiny pearl studs in her ears. Dark-haired Holly is dressed for Christmas, with a short fluffy hairstyle created from mohair. Blonde Collette has two thick plaits and legs made from striped fabric to simulate stockings.

Turn right side out through neck opening, taking care as opening is very small.

Sew Body Back pieces together along centre back, leaving open, as indicated on pattern. Sew Body Front to Body Back, leaving open only at neck. Turn right side out.

Sew the Arms together in pairs, leaving top edge open. Turn right side out.

Sew Legs together in pairs along centre front and back seams, leaving open at top and bottom. Make tiny clips along sole edge of feet, then pin and tack Foot Soles in position. Sew, then turn right side out.

Sew the Ears together in pairs around the curved edges, leaving straight edges open. Turn right side out.

Fill head very firmly with polyester fibrefill. To achieve a smooth, firmly packed effect, use a stuffing stick, such as a paintbrush handle, rounded pencil or chopstick. Do not use any implement with a pointed end. Check frequently from all angles that the head is symmetrical and not pushed out of shape. Push small amounts of filling into chin area for a rounded, rather than square appearance. There should be no wrinkles and the head should be firm enough to withstand handling without any dents appearing.

Fill body firmly and smoothly. Use the stuffing stick to ensure that the

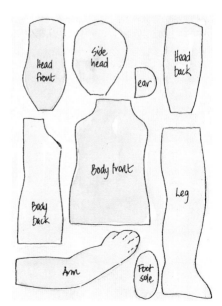

All pattern pieces are printed on pages 64 and 65.

neck is completely filled out. When body is filled, sew closed opening in centre back.

Fill hands softly and top-stitch fingers, as indicated on pattern, by hand or machine. Fill arms firmly up to 2cm from top, leaving remainder empty. Turn in raw edges and sew closed. Sculpt inside of wrist, if desired, with one long stitch, pulled tightly from seam to seam.

Fill legs firmly up to top. If you want the doll to sit easily, leave the top 2cm of legs empty. Turn in raw edges, matching centre front seam to centre back seam, and sew legs closed.

Place head over neck, facing centre front. Brace the body against your chest and press down firmly on head to hold in place. Sew twice around with quilting thread, making tiny stitches and pulling stitches tight. Tuck in raw edges with the point of a needle as you sew. Neck should be shorter at front than back. Place arms at shoulders and sew in position. Legs are sewn to bottom seam of the body.

You might like to read Alison's tips for Making a Doll's Face, on page 62, before starting work on your own project.

Facial features may be sketched freehand, using a brown coloured pencil. Sketch lightly until you are happy with the placement of the features. Mistakes can be removed with a white eraser.

Alternatively, trace the features from Diagram 1 (Kathleen/Holly) or Diagram 2 (Collette) onto a small piece of paper, using a sharp transfer pencil. Position the paper carefully on the face, noting that eyes will be halfway down the face. Pin paper securely to face and check that eyes are level and mouth is on vertical

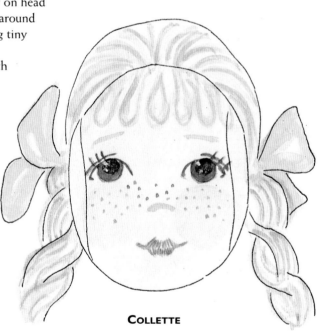

KATHLEEN AND HOLLY

COLLETTE

centre line of face. Iron onto face, then proceed to paint or embroider features as follows.

A combination of fabric paint and embroidery thread is used for the features. Permanent markers (with fine tip) are also ideal substitutes for paint. If you are using fabric paint, a toothpick gives excellent control for fine lines — much easier than a brush. Our dolls' eyes are either blue or brown, with black pupils. The outline of the eye, eyelid and lashes are also brown. The eyebrows are brown lines (either marker or embroidery). Two rows of dark flesh stem-stitch are used for the nose, while the lips are filled in with satin-stitch in coral pink (see Embroidery Stitch Guide on page 55). Use one strand of embroidery thread. Dot freckles across nose area with a sharp brown pencil, permanent marker or a pin dipped in fabric paint. To make rosy cheeks, scribble on a scrap of paper with red pencil, then rub the paper in a circular motion on the cheek area.

To make white highlights in eyes, thread a long needle with white thread (two strands), anchor the thread at side of head behind hairline, then push needle through head into eye, make a tiny straight stitch, then return to starting place. Pull slightly on thread to create eye socket (not so hard that wrinkles appear), then fasten off thread. Repeat for other eye.

Fill ears (for Kathleen) softly with fibrefill, turn in raw edges on straight sides, and stitch closed by hand. Top-stitch by hand or machine, 3mm inside curved edge of ear. Position ear on side of head, noting that the top of the ear should be level with eyebrow and straight edge of ear is about 2cm back from side seam. Stitch ear to head from top to bottom. Tack ear to head with a couple of stitches concealed behind ear, or use craft glue.

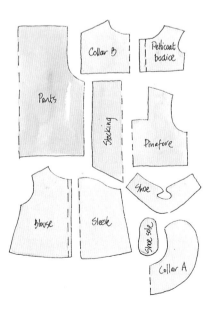

Kathleen

MATERIALS

- One basic doll, with ears
- 0.4m white cotton fabric (such as lawn or batiste) for underwear
- 0.2m light cotton print fabric for blouse
- 0.3m dark cotton print fabric for pinafore
- Scrap of fine voile for collar
- 20cm, or remnant, cream knit fabric for stockings
- Scraps of beige and cream felt for shoes
- 2.25m x 2cm-wide cotton lace edging
- 0.5m x 3mm-wide elastic
- 5-ply apricot yarn for hair (see Note)
- 0.6m x 2cm-wide satin ribbon for hair
- Six small press studs
- 75m x 3mm-wide silk ribbon for collar
- Small amount of narrow ribbon for shoes
- Crochet cotton for shoe ties
- Two tiny pearl beads for ear studs

NOTE: If 5-ply yarn is hard to find, crewel wool is an excellent substitute. You will need five or six skeins for a long hairstyle.

PATTERN PIECES

All pattern pieces, except rectangles, are printed on pages 64 and 65. Trace Petticoat Bodice Front/Back, Pants Front/Back, Blouse Front/Back, Blouse Sleeve, Pinafore Bodice Front/Back, Stocking, Shoe Upper, Shoe Sole and Collar A.

CUTTING

NOTE: All pattern pieces include 3mm seam allowance.

From white cotton fabric, cut two Pants Front/Backs, two Petticoat Fronts on fold, four Petticoat Backs and one 15cm x 50cm rectangle for petticoat skirt.

From light cotton print, cut one Blouse Front on fold, two Blouse Backs and two Blouse Sleeves.

From dark cotton print, cut two Pinafore Bodice Fronts on fold, four Pinafore Bodice Backs and one 15cm x 70cm rectangle for pinafore skirt.

From voile, cut two Collars A.

From cream knit fabric, cut two Stockings.

From cream felt, cut two Shoe Uppers.

From beige felt, cut two Shoe Soles.

SEWING

HAIR

On basic doll with ears, mark hairline lightly on head with brown pencil (see Diagram 1). Cut 45cm strands of apricot wool. Thread a large-eyed needle with one strand of yarn and pull it through on hairline (see Diagram 2). Knot strands together tightly on hairline. Continue this procedure until entire hairline is covered. Pull all strands to top of head and tie tightly with yarn. Trim ends of ponytail, if desired. Knot a few short strands to hairline at forehead and trim as desired, for fringe. Tie 2cm-wide ribbon in bow on ponytail.

CLOTHES

When joining pieces, place right sides together, unless otherwise directed.

Machine-stitch a narrow hem on leg and waist edges of Pants. Stitch centre front seam. Sew flat lace edging to leg edges. Using a long zigzag-stitch, sew flat 3mm elastic to legs and waist, close to hem, stretching elastic as you sew. Stitch centre back and inner leg seams.

Stitch Petticoat Front to Petticoat Backs at shoulders (one set will form petticoat lining). With right sides facing, stitch centre back edge, neck edge and armholes, leaving side seams

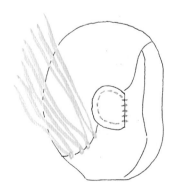

DIAGRAM I

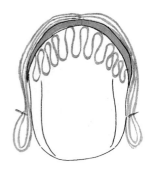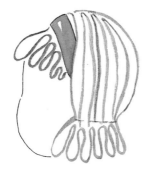

DIAGRAM 2

open. Clip curves, taking care not to cut stitching, then turn right side out and press. Open out sides so that underarm seams and waist edges match on each side and sew through in one long seam. Turn under raw edge on one long edge of skirt rectangle and stitch. Attach flat lace to this edge, just under stitched edge — two rows of lace may be used, if desired. Sew short edges of skirt together, leaving top half open. Machine a narrow hem on open edges, for placket. Run a gathering thread around waist edge of skirt. Pull up gathers to fit bodice and stitch, folding lining out of the way. Hem lining over raw edges on inside of skirt.

Attach two small press studs at back opening, one at neck and one at waist.

Turn under raw edges on cuff end of Sleeves and stitch. Attach flat lace. Stitch Front to Backs at shoulder seams. Gather tops of Sleeves slightly to fit armholes and stitch Sleeves in place. Attach elastic to Sleeves just above lace, as for Pants. Sew underarm and side seams. Machine-stitch a narrow hem on lower edge of blouse. Cut a narrow bias strip of blouse fabric and bind neckline of blouse. Stitch a press stud at neck edge of back opening.

Construct a Pinafore Bodice and Skirt in same manner as Petticoat, omitting reference to lace. Try pinafore on doll and pin skirt up so that lace on petticoat shows beneath dress skirt. Hem skirt by hand. Close centre back at neck and waist with press studs.

With right sides together, stitch Collars together, leaving about 3cm unsewn on outer curved edge for turning. Turn right side out and press.

Turn in raw edges of opening and stitch closed. Slightly gather lace edging to fit the outer curved edge of collar, then neatly sew lace to collar, by machine or hand, with edge of lace just under outer edge. Handsew silk ribbon in place near collar edge. Tie a bow with long ends and stitch to centre front of collar. Close collar at back with a press stud.

Fold Stockings in half lengthwise and stitch seams from toe to heel and up back of leg. Turn right side out and pull onto doll's leg — leg will mould the stocking to shape.

Sew centre back seam of Shoe Uppers by hand, using a small blanket stitch. Gather toe area of Upper to fit Sole, then sew Soles to Uppers, with centre back seam of Upper matching heel. Turn right side out. Stitch a tiny ribbon bow to front of each shoe, and thread a piece of crochet cotton through Upper to tie shoe at ankle.

Stitch pearls to earlobes, for 'earrings'.

Collette's Clothes

Collette is made and dressed in the same way as Kathleen with the following variations:

Make the basic body, but cut Legs from 25cm striped cotton fabric — stockings will not be needed.

Her face is similar to Kathleen's, but her eyes are blue and she does not have ears.

HAIR

To make her hair, you will need 5-ply sandy-coloured yarn. Draw front hairline across head, about 2.5cm above eyebrows. Sew a row of yarn loops across forehead. Cut strands of yarn, 42cm long. Drape across head, so that ends hang down evenly on each side. Using matching thread, stitch securely to head in centre parting, from forehead to nape of neck. Stop about 2cm above neck seam. Cut a few extra 42cm strands, fold each in half and sew looped ends to front hairline. These strands are pulled straight back. Gather yarn into two bundles at ear level. Tie with yarn and stitch securely to head. Plait yarn tightly and tie ends of plaits. Trim to

desired length and tie a bow on each plait at ear level. Leave sufficient ribbon to make a small matching bow for collar. You will need 1m x 10mm-wide ribbon, instead of the silk ribbon used for Kathleen.

CLOTHES

Collette's underwear is made of cream lawn, trimmed with cream lace.

Her clothing is identical to Kathleen's except that Collar B is used and is made of the same fabric as her blouse.

Her pinafore is trimmed with a strip of blouse fabric, 70cm x 2.5cm.

Shoes are made as for Kathleen, except that 3mm-wide ribbon is used for ties, and bow on shoe front is omitted.

Holly's Clothes

Holly has same face as Kathleen, and is made with the following variations:

CLOTHES

Her underwear is white lawn, with broderie anglaise trim. Stockings are made from red ribbed stretch fabric (use an old pair of tights). Collar is Collar A, trimmed with broderie anglaise. Blouse is dark green and pinafore is tartan, trimmed with a ribbon at waist. For sash and hair band, you will need 1m x 12mm-wide satin ribbon. Shoes are black felt, tied with 3mm-wide black ribbon.

HAIR

To make her hair, you will need dark brown fluffy yarn, such as a mohair blend. With matching thread, sew loops of yarn across front hairline (see Diagram 2). Loop yarn across top of head and down sides. Do not cut ends. Keep loops even at bottom. Stitch yarn to head at sides, 2cm up from looped ends. Pull thread tight so that it sinks into fluffy yarn and is not visible. Sew a centre part at top of head. When top of head is covered, tie a ribbon band around head and knot at back of head (hair will cover knot at back). Continue to loop yarn from crown of head to neck and sew loops down, as before.

Making A Doll's Face

No amount of careful sewing or exquisite costuming will make up for a doll whose face is ugly or unappealing — so it's worth taking the time and trouble to get it right.

Facial features can be painted or embroidered. To determine appropriate shape of eyes, nose and mouth, draw a few of each on scraps of fabric, cut out and pin to doll's face. Move and change expression until satisfied.

Having decided on design and placement of features, transfer to face by tracing design onto thin paper with a transfer pencil and then ironing onto face in correct position. You can also draw features freehand with a coloured pencil or a water-erasable pen.

Embroidery is easier to do after head is filled, as cloth will be stretched taut. Use one strand of thread for fine lines or very small dolls. Use two or three strands for filling in areas or for larger dolls.

If you are using ball-point fabric paints, paint face before making up the head, as these paints need to be pressed onto a firm surface.

For permanent fabric paints that do not have this requirement, a toothpick makes a good applicator.

Ordinary coloured pencils can be used for drawing features — just moisten pencil to make colours more intense. A sparing coat of nail varnish will seal colours and prevent them washing out.

Whichever method you choose, practise first on a scrap of body fabric to check if the colours run.

Most dolls look better with rosy cheeks. The best blusher is a red, pink or orange coloured pencil, as this does not run, bleed or smudge, and although it does wash out with repeated laundering, it simply fades out without running onto the face and can be easily replaced when doll is dry. To make round, rosy cheeks, take a scrap of fabric and scribble a solid patch of colour in the centre of it. Place fabric over your index finger and rub colour onto face with a circular motion. Use sparingly at first — you can always repeat the procedure if the

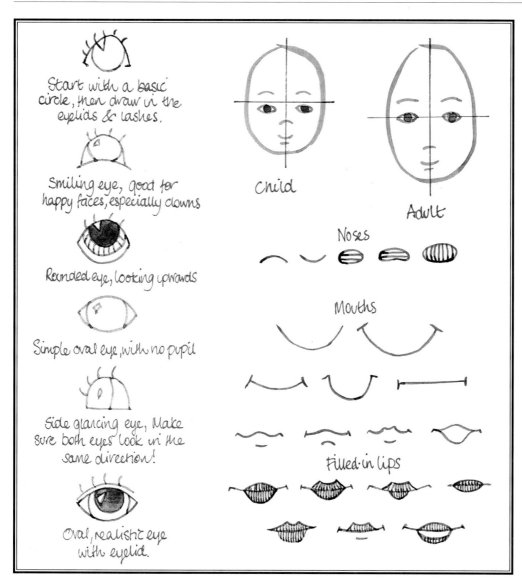

Start with a basic circle, then draw in the eyelids & lashes.

Smiling eye, good for happy faces, especially clowns

Rounded eye, looking upwards

Simple oval eye, with no pupil

Side glancing eye. Make sure both eyes look in the same direction!

Oval, realistic eye with eyelid.

Child

Adult

Noses

Mouths

Filled-in lips

Make sure the spots or circles are level and the same size. Don't rely on glue for attaching felt circles — stitching is much more secure. Add white highlights for an alert, lively expression. Add eyelashes and eyebrows, if desired.

If your doll is large or sophisticated in appearance, you will need more detailed eyes. In small dolls, there is probably no need to draw the pupil — just paint or embroider the iris in a solid colour. For larger dolls, a black pupil can be added.

NOSES

A slightly deeper flesh colour is most suitable for noses. The nose can be represented by an outline only, or the shape can be filled in with satin-stitch. Padded satin-stitch can be used for filled-in types, for extra dimension.

colour is too light. A white tissue will remove excess colour.

All three-dimensional dolls look better if the eyes are slightly sunk into the head, as though they were in sockets. To do this, use a long thin needle with a suitable coloured strong thread. Anchor the thread with a knot or couple of stitches on the side of the head behind the hairline. Insert the needle through the head and into the eye, then take a tiny stitch and return to starting point, pulling the thread slightly. Fasten off securely. Remember to check that both eyes are symmetrical after this procedure. If white thread is used, the sculpture stitch can double as a highlight.

Either white paint or white thread can be used for highlights, but whichever you use, make sure that the highlights are on the same side for both eyes and are the same size.

AGE AND SEX DIFFERENCES

The basic difference between adult and child faces is the length of the face and the position of the features.

Adult: eyes on halfway line, longer nose than child.

Child: rounder face, lower eyes, eyes spaced wider apart, shorter nose.

Male faces: heavier eyebrows, larger or heavier line for nose, squarer chin, narrower lips in brownish pink rather than pink or red, omit eyelashes and eyeshadow.

EYES

The easiest eyes are simple spots or circles. Beware of placing them too close together, or the doll will look mean or cross-eyed. In general, eyes should be the width of one eye apart, with children's eyes being more widely spaced than adults.

MOUTHS

These range from the very simple curved or straight line to shaped lips. For simple faces, a curved line is probably most appropriate. A coin can be used as an outline to obtain an even curve. 'Smile' lines can be added and the expression varied by the depth of the curve.

On soft sculpture dolls, the mouth is generally indicated by a long stitch, pulled tight to indent it.

For child dolls, avoid a dark or bright red, as it looks harsh and unnatural. Any shade of pink or orange is more suitable.

On more detailed dolls, a more elaborate mouth is better.

PATTERN PIECES FOR DOLL AND CLOTHES

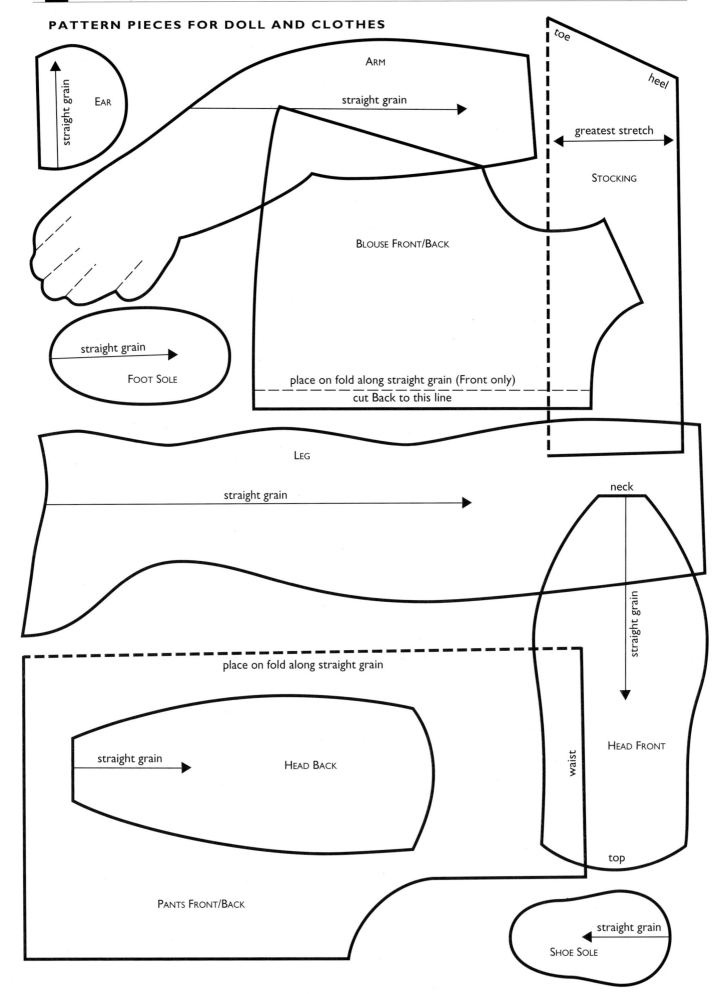

EAR

straight grain

ARM

straight grain

toe

heel

greatest stretch

STOCKING

BLOUSE FRONT/BACK

straight grain

FOOT SOLE

place on fold along straight grain (Front only)

cut Back to this line

LEG

straight grain

neck

straight grain

place on fold along straight grain

HEAD BACK

straight grain

waist

HEAD FRONT

top

PANTS FRONT/BACK

SHOE SOLE

straight grain

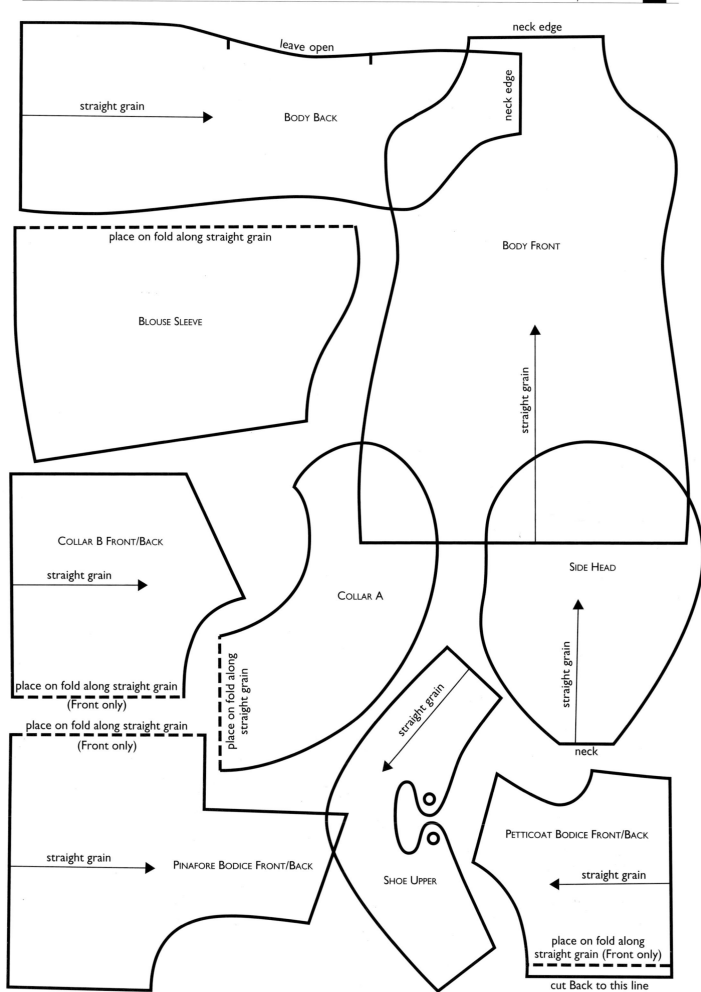

straight grain

BODY BACK

leave open

neck edge

neck edge

BODY FRONT

straight grain

place on fold along straight grain

BLOUSE SLEEVE

COLLAR B FRONT/BACK

straight grain

SIDE HEAD

COLLAR A

straight grain

place on fold along straight grain
(Front only)

place on fold along straight grain

straight grain

neck

place on fold along straight grain
(Front only)

straight grain

PINAFORE BODICE FRONT/BACK

straight grain

PETTICOAT BODICE FRONT/BACK

SHOE UPPER

straight grain

place on fold along
straight grain (Front only)

cut Back to this line

BEAR ESSENTIALS

E veryone deserves at least one teddy bear friend and our lovable fellow is one of the cuddliest, most traditional of teddy bears, to gladden young (and not so young) hearts for years to come. And as no self-respecting ted is without a wardrobe, we've also provided him with his 'bear essentials' — tartan overalls and a jolly red jumper.

Of cheerful countenance and disposed to be friendly, this traditional jointed teddy will be loved by many generations of littlies.

Traditional Jointed Teddy Bear

MEASUREMENTS
Finished teddy is 43cm tall.

MATERIALS
- 0.5m x 150cm fur fabric
- Scrap of black fabric for palms and soles (or soft vinyl, if preferred)
- Two 1.75cm-diameter teddy bear eyes
- Piece of stiff cardboard, or plastic (see Note below)
- Polyester filling
- Four flat buttons with an eyelet on the underside
- Large, strong needle
- Strong sewing thread
- Scrap of black embroidery wool

NOTE: The cardboard is used to reinforce teddy's joints. It may not stand total immersion in water. If you plan to wash your teddy frequently, it might be better to cut the required reinforcing pieces from plastic, such as an ice-cream container.

PATTERN PIECES
All pattern pieces are printed on pages 70 to 73. Trace Centre Front Head, Side Front Head, Back Head, Ear, Front Body, Side Body, Back Body, Inner Arm/Palm, Outer Arm, Inner Leg, Outer Leg, Leg Insert and Sole.

CUTTING
Remember to add 1cm seam allowances to all pieces, except cardboard.

Lay pattern pieces on wrong side of fur fabric, paying attention to straight grain, where marked. Cut pieces from a single layer of fabric, remembering to turn pattern piece to create a mirror image, where two pieces are required.

Palms and soles are made from black fabric. If you wish, you can reverse fur fabric, so that non-fur side faces out, or you can use vinyl instead. For palms, trace pattern piece from Inner Arm, remembering to add seam allowances.

From fur fabric, cut one Centre Front Head, two Side Front Heads, two Back Heads, four Ears, one Front Body, two Side Bodies, one Back Body, two Inner Arms, two Outer Arms, two Inner Legs, two Outer Legs and two Leg Inserts.

From black fabric (or vinyl or fur), cut two Palms and two Soles.

From Leg Insert and Inner Arm pattern pieces, trace markings designated with a broken line and from cardboard or plastic, cut two of each piece. Use point of scissors to make the central hole in each.

SEWING

Before sewing, transfer symbols for joining legs and arms to right sides of Side Body pieces, using tailor's tacks. Do the same on Side Front Head pieces to mark position of eyes.

With right sides together, stitch two Ear pieces to one another, leaving head edge open. Turn Ear right side out and top-stitch, if desired, 1cm from rounded edge. Repeat for the other Ear.

Stitch darts in Side Front Heads and Centre Front Head.

Stitch centre front seam of Side Heads. With right sides together, stitch Centre Front Heads between Side Front Heads, matching tip of nose to centre front seam of Side Heads, and sandwiching part of Ear, from given symbol on Side Front Head. Fold rest of Ear around along side edge and, with raw edges even, sew in place on Side Front Head.

With right sides together, stitch darts in Back Head, then join centre back seam. With right sides together, stitch Back Head to front head section, leaving neck edge open and sandwiching Ears in place at same time. Turn head right side out.

With right sides together, stitch darts in Side Body pieces. Stitch Front Body to Back Body at crotch seam. With right sides together and matching symbols, stitch Side Body pieces to Front and Back Bodies, leaving neck edge open. Turn completed body right side out.

With right sides together, stitch black fabric Palms to Inner Arms. Stitch darts in Outer Arms.

With right sides together, stitch Inner Arm to Outer Arm, leaving a small opening in upper edge for turning. Turn right side out. Repeat for other arm.

Stitch darts in Inner and Outer Legs. With right sides together and matching symbols, stitch Inner and Outer Legs together at centre front and back seams. Insert black fabric Sole at end of each leg.

With right sides facing and matching symbols, stitch a Leg Insert to upper edge of each leg, leaving a small opening on Inner Leg edge. Turn completed legs right side out.

Stuff head firmly and stitch opening closed. (If using safety eyes, attach them to head before stuffing. See Note on page 68.)

Stuff body firmly. Turn in a narrow hem on neck edge of body and run a firm gathering thread around this edge. Tighten neck edge around head and stitch in place with small, firm stitches.

Place a prepared cardboard or plastic disk in upper part of leg, against Leg Insert. Now, place one flat button in leg, against cardboard insert, and push eyelet through hole previously made in cardboard, and then through fur fabric to outside. (If this last bit is difficult, you may need to make a tiny hole in fabric with scissors or a large needle.) Stick a match or a safety pin temporarily through eyelet so that it can't retract.

Stuff leg firmly and sew opening closed. Repeat this procedure for other leg and two arms.

Thread a large needle with a length of strong thread and insert into body at point designated on pattern for fixing leg to body. Push needle across body and out at opposite point. Thread needle through eyelet of leg, then insert it back into same hole,

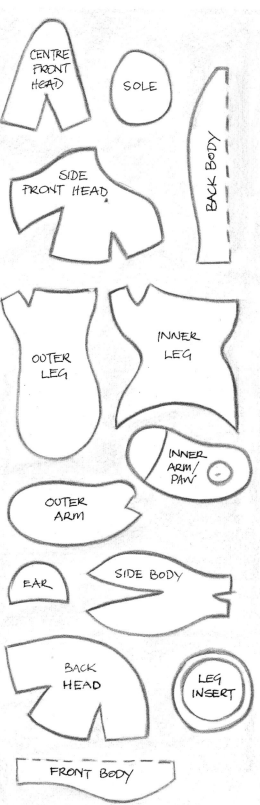

back across body and through remaining eyelet. Knot ends of thread together, pull up tightly so legs are attached firmly, and add another couple of knots. Bury ends back in body of teddy.

Attach arms in same way.

Make tiny holes with a needle in eye positions. Push a large needle, threaded with strong thread, through head from eye point to eye point, through eyelet at back of one eye, back through head and through eyelet of other eye. Knot ends of thread together, pull up very tightly so eyes are pulled into 'sockets', then add more knots to secure. Bury ends in head.

(NOTE: Some teddy eyes are attached without thread, as a safety measure. This sort of eye must be attached before head is stuffed, as it involves the use of a washer that is added to eye shank from behind. After safety eyes are attached and head is stuffed, run a strong thread through

head from eye to eye, to make 'sockets'.)

With embroidery wool, work nose and mouth, using photograph on page 66 as a guide.

Teddy's Overalls

MEASUREMENTS

To fit a 43cm teddy bear. Pattern also fits a Cabbage Patch doll, if straps are shortened and waist is elasticised.

MATERIALS

- 0.35m x 140cm checked fabric
- 0.10m x 3cm-wide braid or ribbon to bind pocket
- Two metal stud fasteners
- Small amount of 6mm elastic (Cabbage Patch doll)

PATTERN PIECE

Pattern piece is printed on page 70 and 71. Trace Front/Back.

CUTTING

NOTE: Remember to add 1.5cm seam allowance on Front/Back, except on lower and upper edges where hem and casing allowances are already included.

From checked fabric, cut four Front/Backs, one 14cm x 33cm rectangle for bib, one 8cm x 9cm rectangle for pocket and two 8cm x 26cm strips for straps (all these measurements include seam allowance).

SEWING

Fold bib in half crosswise, right sides together and stitch sides. Turn right side out, press and top-stitch about 5mm in from top and side edges. Neaten lower raw edges with zigzag-stitch.

Press seam allowances to inside on lower and side edges of pocket, and finish upper raw edge with braid or ribbon. Top-stitch pocket onto centre of bib.

Join Front/Back side seams and inner leg seams. Place one leg inside the other, right sides together, and stitch crotch seam.

Press casing allowance to inside along fold line and turn under raw edge narrowly. Position bib on inside of trousers so that zigzagged edges of bib match folded lower edge of casing. Stitch casing in place, securing lower edge of bib at the same time. Top-stitch along upper edge of trousers, close to fold, making a second line of stitching across bib.

For Cabbage Patch doll, unpick side seams of casing and insert elastic to fit back waist. Secure ends.

Fold straps in half lengthwise, wrong sides together, press in raw edges and top-stitch close to all edges. Insert stud fasteners into top edges of bib and into ends of straps. Try overalls on for fit, adjust length of straps (they need to be much shorter for Cabbage Patch dolls), then hand-stitch straps in indicated position on trousers back, angling ends slightly so that straps can be crossed at back.

Press under raw edge narrowly on trouser legs and stitch. Turn under hem along fold line and slip-stitch in place. Turn finished hem to outside to form cuff.

Teddy's Jumper

MEASUREMENTS

To fit teddy 43cm tall, chest 39cm.
Garment measures: Chest: 40cm,
Length: 15cm, Sleeve: 9cm.

MATERIALS

- Patons 5-ply Machinewash (50g), 2 balls
- One pair 3.25mm (No 10) knitting needles
- One 3mm crochet hook
- One stitch-holder
- Three buttons

TENSION

See Knitting Notes on page 158.
29 sts and 40 rows to 10cm over st st, using 3.25mm needles. To achieve the desired effect, this garment has been designed to be worked on smaller needles at a tighter tension than usually recommended.

BACK

Using 3.25mm needles, cast on 59 sts.
1ST ROW. K2, *P1, K1; rep from * to last st, K1.
2ND ROW. K1, *P1, K1; rep from * to end.
Rep last 2 rows twice more, inc one st in centre of last row...60 sts.
BEG MAIN PATT. 1ST ROW. *P3, K5; rep from * to last 4 sts, P3, K1.
2ND AND ALT ROWS. Knit all knit sts and purl all purl sts as they appear.
3RD ROW. P2, *K5, P3; rep from * to last 2 sts, K2.
5TH ROW. P1, *K5, P3; rep from * to last 3 sts, K3.
7TH ROW. *K5, P3; rep from * to last 4 sts, K4.
9TH ROW. K4, *P3, K5; rep from * to end.
11TH ROW. K3, *P3, K5; rep from * to last st, P1.
13TH ROW. K2, *P3, K5; rep from * to last 2 sts, P2.
15TH ROW. K1, *P3, K5; rep from * to last 3 sts, P3.
16TH ROW. As 2nd row.
Last 16 rows form main patt. Tie a coloured thread at each end of last row to mark beg of armholes, as there is no armhole shaping.**
DIVIDE FOR BACK OPENING. NEXT ROW. Patt 30, turn.

Work a further 37 rows patt on these 30 sts.
Cast off loosely.
With right side facing, join yarn to rem 30 sts and work to correspond with side just completed.

FRONT

Work as for Back to **.
Work 2 rows st st.
BEG 2ND PATT. 1ST ROW. *K6, P6; rep from * to end.
2ND ROW. *P1, K5, P5, K1; rep from * to end.
3RD ROW. *P2, K4, P4, K2; rep from * to end.
4TH ROW. *P3, K3; rep from * to end.
5TH ROW. *P4, K2, P2, K4; rep from * to end.
6TH ROW. *P5, K1, P1, K5; rep from * to end.
7TH ROW. *P6, K6; rep from * to end.
8TH ROW. As 1st row.
9TH ROW. *K5, P1, K1, P5; rep from * to end.
10TH ROW. *K4, P2, K2, P4; rep from * to end.
11TH ROW. *K3, P3; rep from * to end.
12TH ROW. *K2, P4, K4, P2; rep from * to end.
13TH ROW. *K1, P5, K5, P1; rep from * to end.
14TH ROW. As 7th row.
Work 2 rows st st.
Working rem in main patt, work 6 rows.
SHAPE NECK. NEXT ROW. Patt 24, turn and cont on these 24 sts.
Keeping patt correct, dec one st at neck edge in alt rows until 18 sts rem.
Work one row.
Cast off loosely.

With right side facing, sl next 12 sts on a stitch-holder and leave. Join yarn to rem 24 sts and work to correspond with side just completed, reversing shaping.

SLEEVES

Using 3.25mm needles, cast on 43 sts.
Work 6 rows rib as for Back, inc one st in centre of last row...44 sts.
Cont in main patt as for Back, and working extra sts into patt, inc one st at each end of 5th and foll 4th rows until there are 58 sts.
Work 3 rows.
Cast off loosely.

NECKBAND

Using back-stitch, join shoulder seams. With right side facing, knit up 55 sts evenly around neck, dec one st in centre of sts from stitch-holder.
Work 19 rows rib as for Back, beg with a 2nd row.
Cast off loosely in rib.

TO MAKE UP

We do not recommend pressing this garment, owing to textured patt.
Using back-stitch, join Sleeve and side seams to coloured threads. Sew in Sleeves. Fold Neckband in half to wrong side and slip-stitch in position. With right side facing, and using 3mm hook, work one row dc evenly around back opening, working through both thicknesses of Neckband and working three 2ch-buttonloops on right side. Sew on buttons to correspond with loops.

**PATTERN PIECES FOR TEDDY BEAR
AND OVERALLS**

A

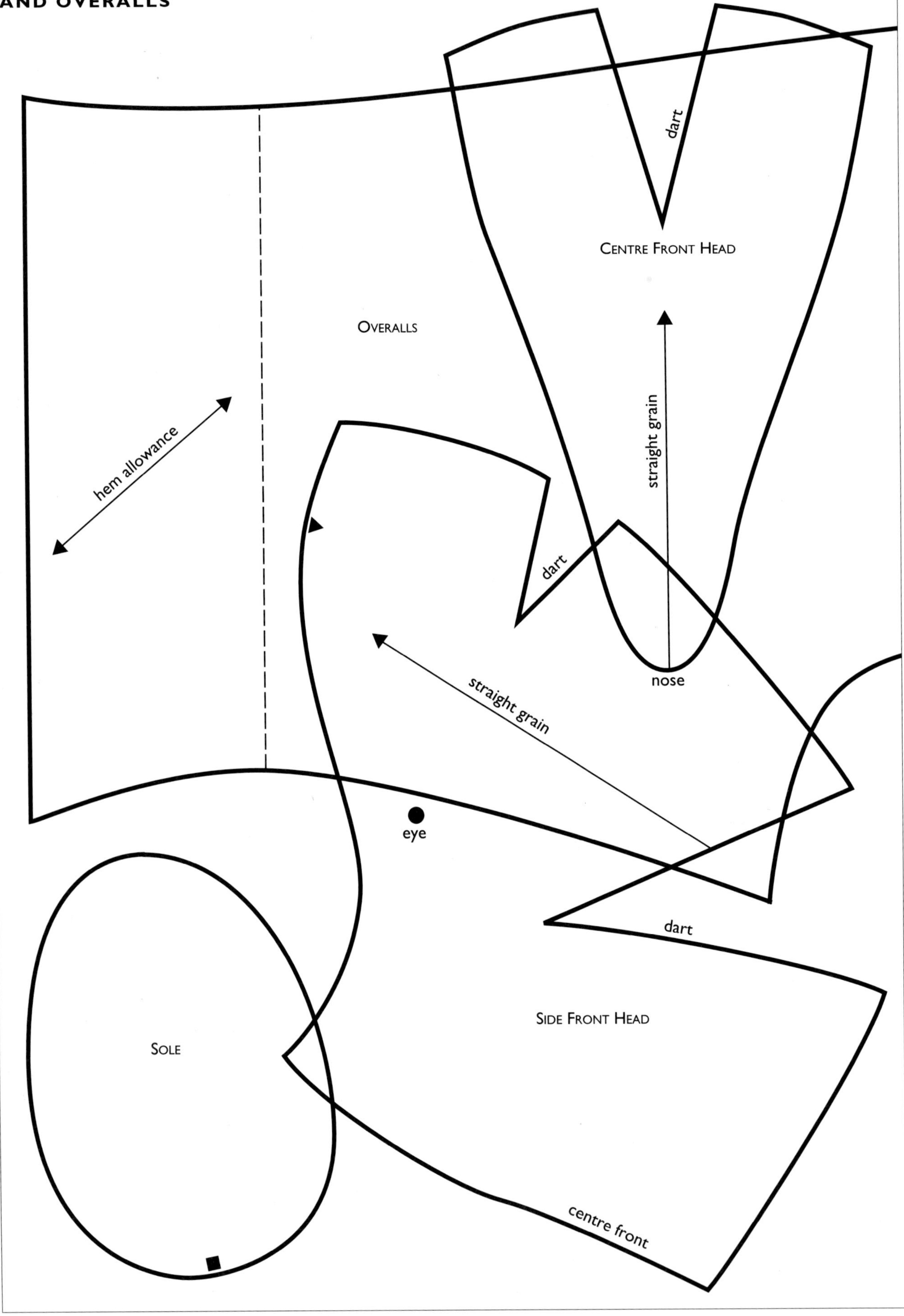

A JOINS B

OVERALLS

hem allowance

CENTRE FRONT HEAD

straight grain

dart

nose

dart

straight grain

eye

dart

SIDE FRONT HEAD

SOLE

centre front

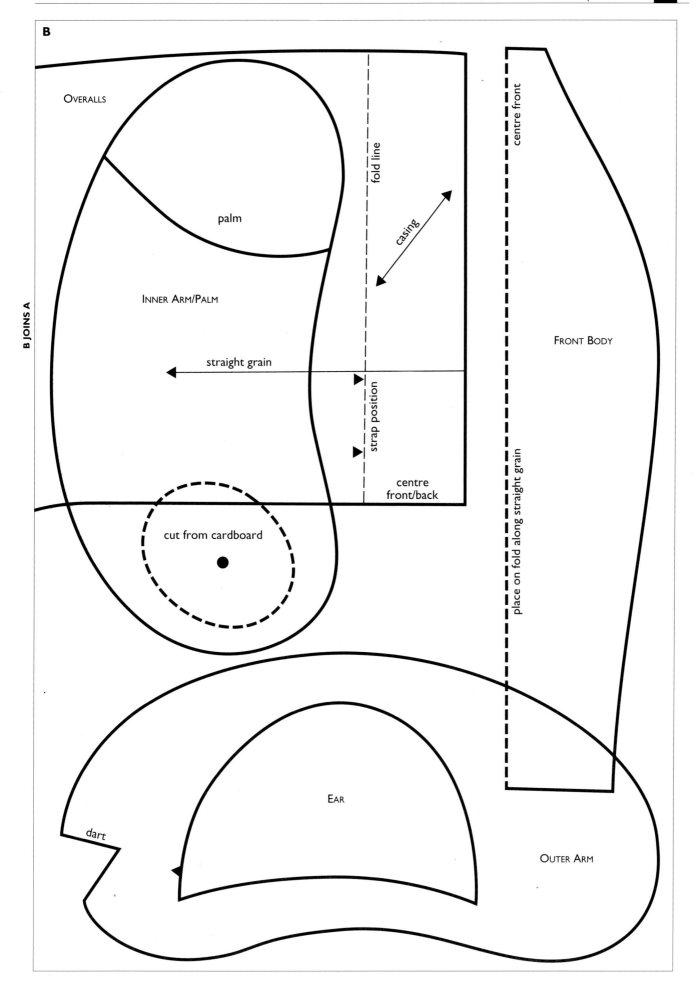

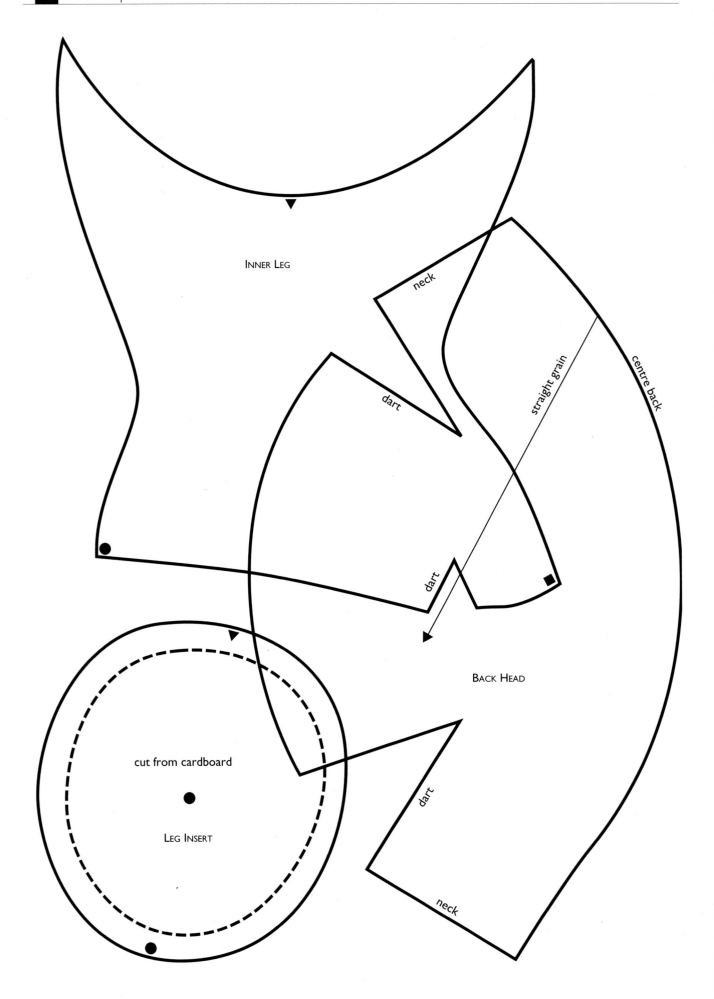

INNER LEG

neck

straight grain

centre back

dart

dart

BACK HEAD

cut from cardboard

LEG INSERT

dart

neck

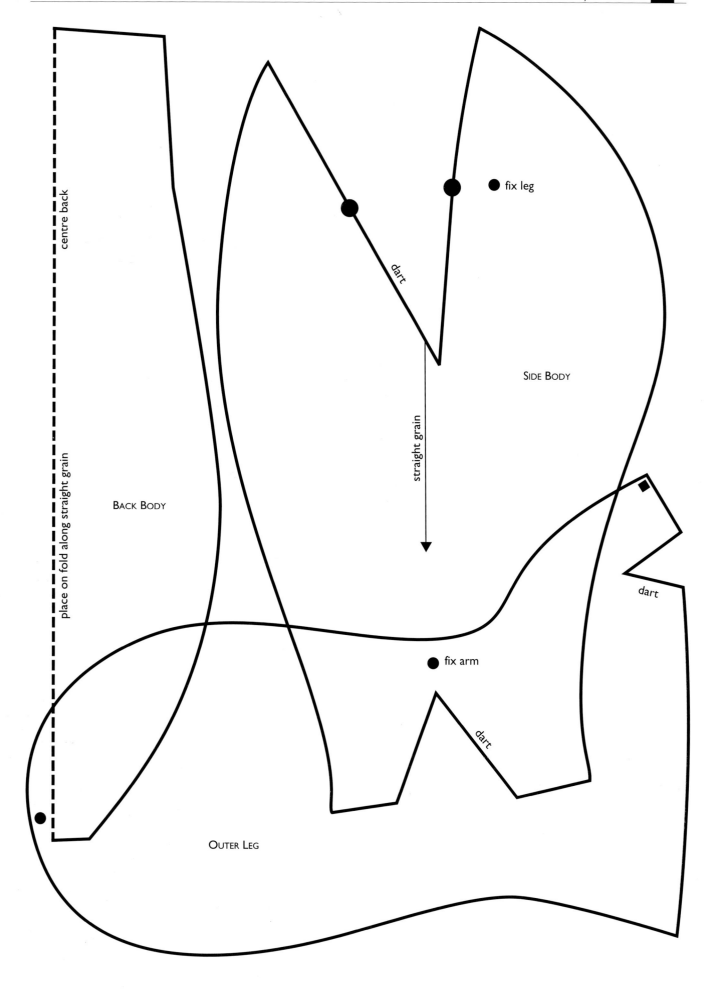

centre back

place on fold along straight grain

BACK BODY

dart

fix leg

SIDE BODY

straight grain

dart

fix arm

dart

OUTER LEG

OF MICE
AND
MARRIAGE

N ow here's a mice idea! Dressed in
wedding finery, from the bride's lacy
satin slippers to the groom's elegantly
embroidered waistcoat, these irresistible
little calico mice, designed by Betty Smith,
would make a charming gift — or a
whimsical decoration for a wedding table,
especially if dressed to match the real
bridal party.

Wedding Mice

MEASUREMENTS
Flowergirl is 16cm tall, bride is 25cm and
groom is 26.5cm.

MATERIALS
For three mice bodies
• 30cm x 107cm calico
• Polyester padding
• Firm cardboard for bases
• Six tiny black beads for eyes
• Iron-on interfacing for ears
• Fine nylon fishing line for whiskers
• Strands of wool for tails
• Scraps of pink jersey for noses
• Pink and bone fabric paints for inside ears
• Craft glue
• Pink chalk or rouge

*Say cheese! Lined up for the family album, our elegant
bridal party — possibly a little overawed by the
solemnity of the occasion — pauses to display all the
glorious detail of their exquisite wedding clothes.*

So excited, she can hardly squeak, the little flowergirl lifts the edge of her pink lace overskirt to reveal her satin slippers and the froth of be-ribboned lace petticoats.

BRIDE'S CLOTHES

- 1.3m x 30cm double-bordered lace
- 30cm x 107cm satin lining (we used palest pink)
- 30cm x 150cm net
- 80cm x 15mm-wide lace
- 30cm x 100cm tulle
- 1m x 17mm-wide satin ribbon
- 1.2m x 3mm-wide satin ribbon
- Two bunches small white ribbon roses
- One bunch white pearl stamens
- One bunch pink pearl stamens

Destined to become a mousewife, the bride — whose blushing cheeks match the inside of her ears — wears a confection of white lace over the softest pink underskirt. Her double tulle veil is held in place with a pretty headdress of ribbon roses and tiny pearl stamens, matching her delicate bouquet.

BRIDEGROOM'S CLOTHES

- 20cm x 90cm striped fabric
- 40cm x 90cm silken fabric for waistcoat
- 20cm x 90cm velvet for coat
- 20cm x 90cm satin lining for coat
- Embroidery threads for waistcoat (optional)
- Five tiny pearl beads for waistcoat buttons
- Scraps of satin for collars, bow and hat trim
- Small amount 16-amp fuse wire for spectacles
- Felt scraps for hat and shoes (an old felt hat is even better!)

FLOWERGIRL'S CLOTHES

- 1.3cm x 7cm-wide pink embroidered nylon banding
- 10cm x 107cm white lining
- 1.1m x 17mm-wide pink frilled lace
- 70cm x 10mm-wide lace beading with 15mm-wide attached frill
- 50cm x 23mm-wide satin ribbon
- 2m x 3mm-wide satin ribbon
- Two bunches small pink ribbon roses
- Pink pearl stamens (from bride's bunch)

PATTERN PIECES

BRIDE

Trace Bride Side Body, Bride Centre Back Body, Bride Centre Front Body, Bride/Groom Ear, Bride/Groom Paw, Bride Base, Bride Bodice, Bride Skirt/Slip, Bride Sleeve and Bride Shoe.

BRIDEGROOM

Trace Groom Side Body/Side Trouser, Groom Centre Back Body/Centre Back Trouser, Groom Centre Front Body/Centre Front Trouser, Bride/Groom Ear, Bride/Groom Paw, Groom Base, Groom Waistcoat, Groom Coat, Groom Collar, Groom Sleeve, Groom Hat Top, Groom Hat Crown, Groom Hat Brim and Groom Shoe.

FLOWERGIRL

Trace Flowergirl Side Body, Flowergirl Centre Back Body, Flowergirl Centre Front Body, Flowergirl Ear, Flowergirl Paw, Flowergirl Base, Flowergirl Bodice, Flowergirl Sleeve and Flowergirl Shoe.

CUTTING

NOTE: 5mm seam allowance is included on all pattern pieces, as well as 1cm hem allowance, where appropriate.

BODIES

For each body, from calico cut (in the appropriate size) two Side Bodies, two Centre Back Bodies, two Centre Front Bodies, four Ears and four Paws. Additionally, cut one base each for Bride and Flowergirl. For tails, cut strips on cross grain of calico, 21cm x 4cm for both Bride and Groom and 15cm x 3cm for Flowergirl.

From Cardboard, cut two Bases for each body.

BRIDE'S CLOTHES

From double-bordered lace, cut one Bride Skirt, one Bride Bodice, two Bride Sleeves, two Bride Shoes, one strip, 20cm x 5cm for waist ruffle, two strips, 15cm x 4cm for bodice ruffles — all strips should include lace border. Scraps of lace border are also used in headdress ruffle and bouquet.

From lining, cut one Bride Slip, one Bride Bodice, two Bride Sleeves and four Bride Shoes.

From net, cut one strip, 75cm x 23cm, and one strip, 75cm x 20cm.

From tulle, cut one half circle, approximately 25cm diameter, and one half circle approximately 18cm diameter.

BRIDEGROOM'S CLOTHES

From striped fabric, cut one Groom Centre Front Trouser, two Groom Side Trousers, one Groom Centre Back Trouser and one Groom Base.

From silken fabric, cut four Groom Waistcoats.

From velvet, cut two Groom Coats and two Groom Sleeves.

From satin, cut two Groom Coats and one Groom Collar. Reserve scraps for bow-tie and hatband.

From felt, cut one Groom Hat Top, one Groom Hat Brim, one Groom Hat Crown and four Groom Shoes.

FLOWERGIRL'S CLOTHES

From nylon banding, cut two strips, 42cm x 7cm, for over-skirts, one Flowergirl Bodice and two Flowergirl Sleeves.

From lining, cut one strip, 42cm x 7.5cm, for underskirt, one Flowergirl Bodice and two Flowergirl Sleeves.

From wide satin ribbon, cut four Flowergirl Shoes and one sash, approximately 40cm long.

SEWING

MICE BODIES

Pin and tack wrong sides of Groom's trouser sections to right side of calico body pieces, following pattern. Waist edge does not have to be turned in, as this will be covered by waistcoat and jacket. Once trousers are basted to body sections, the layers are treated as one.

Pin, tack and sew all sections of each mouse together, matching dot on nose. Sew dart in centre front of Groom.

Turn right side out and fill each body with padding. Insert a cardboard base in each body. Run a gathering thread around lower edge of body and pull up gathers around base.

Cover remaining cardboard bases with fabric Bases (Groom has striped base to match trousers) by gathering around edges, pulling up gathers and gluing to back of cardboard. Pin, glue and sew covered bases onto bodies, leaving shoe and tail positions free.

Press interfacing to wrong side of one section of each Ear. Paint right side of this interfaced Ear with shaded pink and bone fabric paint. Press to set paint. With right sides together, sew Ears leaving opening at base, trim.

Turn right side out and press, turn in raw edges, pleat Ears and hand-sew to head, curving ear towards front.

With right sides facing, stitch around outside edge of Paws, leaving wrist open. Trim, turn right side out and press. Stuff lightly and stitch across opening. Make two lines of stitching (by hand or machine) from tip of paw towards wrist, to define 'fingers'.

Using strong double thread, sew black beads in eye positions, pulling eyes in to give shape to face. Cut small circles of pink jersey, gather up to make noses, pad and sew in position.

Fold tail pieces in half lengthwise and sew in slanted line to create a long tapered wedge shape. Sew across tapered end, trim and turn right side out, using a needle and thread to pull end through. Pad tail with strands of wool, threaded in a darning needle. Insert tail in position and secure with small stitches.

Thread needle with double fishing line and sew through nose twice, dabbing a little craft glue on line before pulling it through. Cut, leaving 1cm long whiskers and carefully remove excess glue. Repeat to give six whiskers on each side.

Colour cheeks lightly with pink chalk or rouge.

Run a gathering thread around waist of Bride and Flowergirl to form smaller waistlines. Finish firmly.

BRIDE'S CLOTHES

Pin and sew a row of 15mm lace around lower edge of Bride.

Join net across the 23cm and 22cm widths to form two tubes and fold each in half lengthwise. Place the narrower width over the wider. With cut edges all even, gather up through all thicknesses to fit 1.5cm below waistline. Sew to body to form a petticoat and sew a row of 15mm lace to cover raw edge.

Sew centre back seam of both Skirt and Slip. Sew small hem around lower edge of Slip. Place Slip inside Skirt, right side of Slip facing wrong side of Skirt and, with raw edges even, run a gathering thread around waist edge, through both layers. Draw up gathers to fit waistline of Bride and hand-sew skirt to waist. Pin and sew Bodice lining and lace to Bride's top, crossing at back.

Pin Sleeve linings to wrong side of lace, turning up 5mm of lining at wrists. Sew Sleeve seams, gather wrists and tops of Sleeves. Pad Sleeves lightly (to form arms) and pin and sew to sides of body. Insert paws into Sleeves, pull up gathers around wrists and sew. Run a gathering thread along raw edge of bodice ruffle strips, draw up gathers and pin and sew from centre front across shoulders to centre back. Hand-sew 3mm ribbon over raw edges of ruffles.

Run a gathering thread along raw edge of waist ruffle, draw up gathers to fit round waist and stitch in place. Pin and sew a sash of 17mm-wide satin ribbon around waist, covering raw edges of ruffle, with a large bow at back and ends trimmed to hem level.

Sew a small 3mm ribbon bow to each wrist. Catch sleeves to body, near waistline. Sew shoes (making top layer of shoe from one lining and one lace layer), pad, insert in position and hand-sew in place. Tie a 3mm ribbon bow to tail.

Make a headpiece of roses, pearl stamens, lace and ribbon to fit over top of head. Gather the two layers of tulle veiling together along straight edge, pull up gathers and sew to head so that short veil is on top. Sew headpiece over raw edges of veil and behind ears.

Make a bouquet of roses, stamens, lace and 3mm ribbon and sew to right hand.

BRIDEGROOM'S CLOTHES

With right sides together, sew Waistcoat and Waistcoat Lining together, leaving sides unsewn. Turn right side out and press. Pin left front over right front and hand-sew together on wrong side. Sew on pearl beads for buttons. Embroider waistcoat fronts, if desired, with tiny grub roses. Pin and hand-sew waistcoat to body, along raw edges.

Press a narrow satin band, finished width 4mm, pressing under raw edges to conceal. Pin band around neck and catch ends at centre front. Make a satin bow-tie approx 35mm x 16mm wide. Stitch to centre front over ends.

With right sides together, sew centre back seams of Coat and centre back seams of Coat Lining. With right

And thereby hangs a tail ... from his splendid topper to his tiny shoelaces, our groom is the acme of sartorial wedding elegance. The dapper morning suit is offset by a pink silk waistcoat, embroidered with miniature grub roses. Clearly a mouse of means!

sides together, pin lining and coat together and sew around edges, leaving hem edge unsewn. Clip corners, turn right side out and top stitch close to edge. Turn up hem and slip-stitch in position.

Turn under hems on Sleeves and top-stitch 5mm from edge. With right sides facing, sew Sleeve seams. Pin Sleeves inside dart area, in marked position. Tack dart and sew, sandwiching Sleeves at the same time.

Pin and sew folded satin Collar to neck edge, turning in Collar front points to inside coat. Catch coat fronts to waistcoat, taking in collar ends but leaving bottom of coat free, to show off embroidery.

Pad Sleeve lightly (to form arm), insert paws into sleeves and sew paws in position against clothing.

Oversew edges of Shoe, pad and sew in position. Sew laces with thick thread.

Oversew ends of Hat Crown. Pin and oversew Hat Top to Crown. Clip Hat Brim where indicated on pattern. Pin Crown over clipped sections and hand-stitch together.

Press in raw edges of a 7cm satin band, join end to end and cover join with smaller satin band. Sew around Crown, so centre join is positioned at the back.

Pin and catch ears so they fit under edge of hat. Sew hat to head.

To make wire spectacles, wind wire around a fine dowel or pencil and twist ends across each other to form nose crossbar. Sew in place.

FLOWERGIRL'S CLOTHES

Pin and sew a strip of lace beading and frill around lower edge of body. Thread 3mm ribbon through beading and tie in a small bow at centre back.

Sew lace beading and frill to lower edge of underskirt.

With right sides together, join 7cm ends of each overskirt, forming two tubes. Press under one raw edge of each overskirt. Sew frilled 15mm lace to one turned in edge of each overskirt. Pin and sew one overskirt to right side of underskirt, so that lower edge of overskirt extends slightly beyond underskirt. Gather unfinished edge of remaining over-skirt and pin and stitch it to waistline. Catch upper layer of overskirt to the lower one with four evenly-spaced 3mm bows.

Thread 3mm ribbon through beading on underskirt, finishing with a bow at centre back.

For remainder of dressing, follow instructions for Bride, omitting bodice and waist ruffles and adding lace frills to sleeve edges.

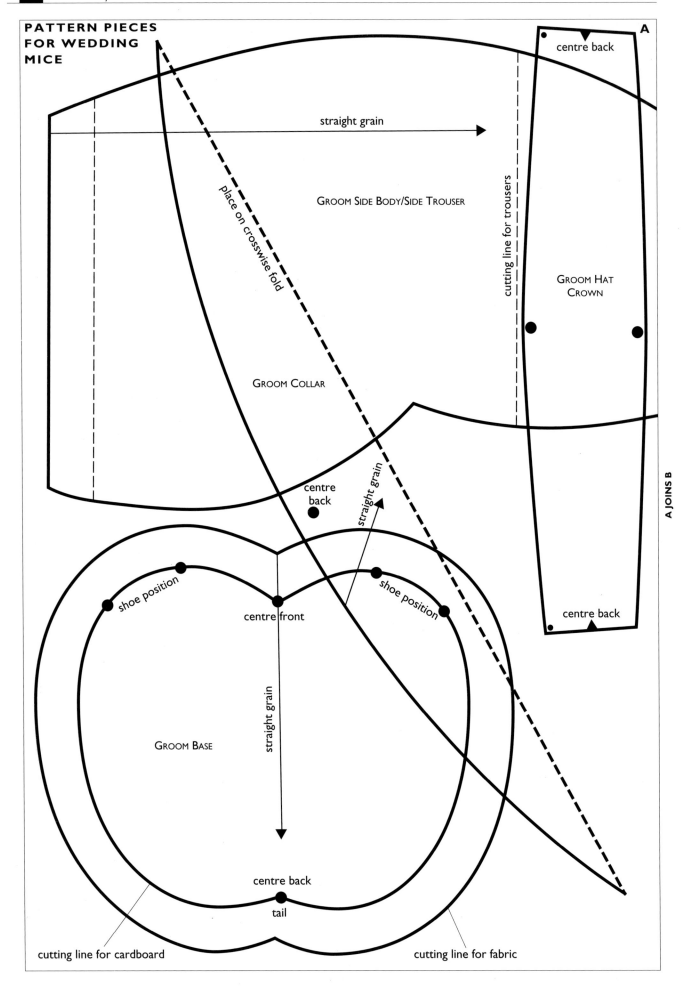

PATTERN PIECES FOR WEDDING MICE

A

centre back

straight grain

GROOM SIDE BODY/SIDE TROUSER

place on crosswise fold

cutting line for trousers

GROOM HAT CROWN

GROOM COLLAR

centre back

straight grain

A JOINS B

centre back

shoe position

centre front

shoe position

straight grain

GROOM BASE

centre back

tail

cutting line for cardboard

cutting line for fabric

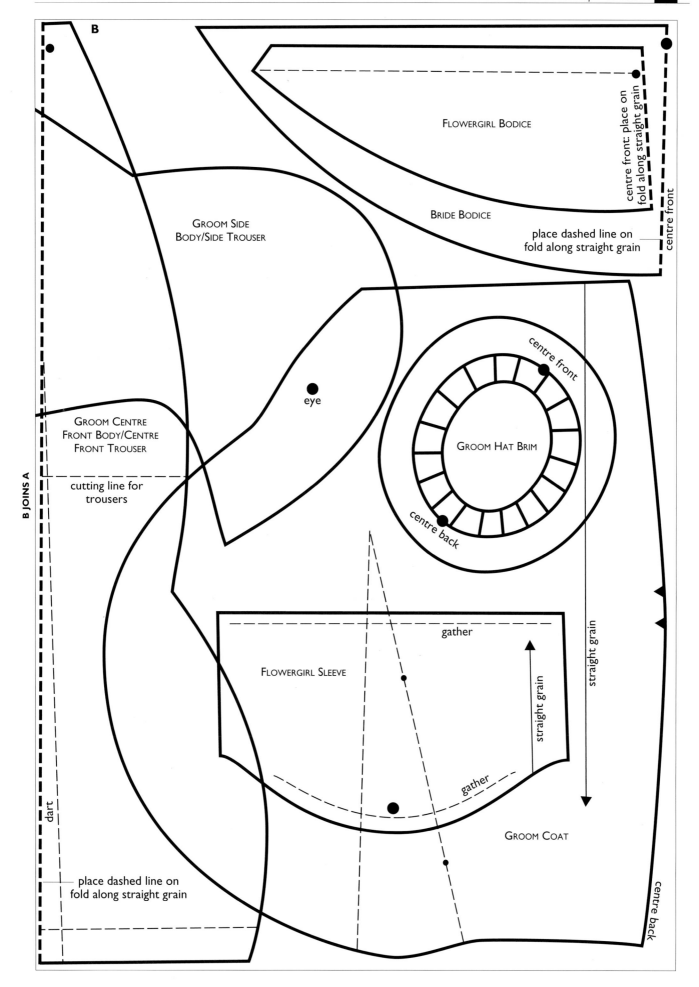

B

FLOWERGIRL BODICE

BRIDE BODICE

centre front: place on
fold along straight grain

centre front

place dashed line on
fold along straight grain

GROOM SIDE
BODY/SIDE TROUSER

eye

centre front

GROOM HAT BRIM

centre back

GROOM CENTRE
FRONT BODY/CENTRE
FRONT TROUSER

cutting line for
trousers

B JOINS A

dart

gather

FLOWERGIRL SLEEVE

straight grain

straight grain

gather

GROOM COAT

place dashed line on
fold along straight grain

centre back

C

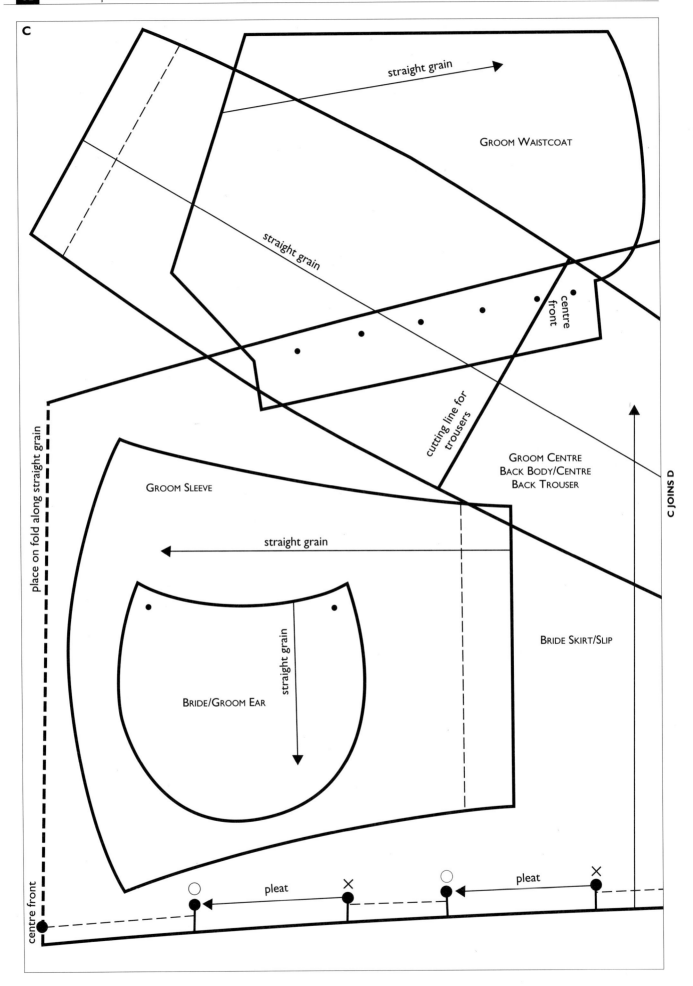

straight grain

GROOM WAISTCOAT

straight grain

centre front

cutting line for trousers

GROOM CENTRE
BACK BODY/CENTRE
BACK TROUSER

C JOINS D

GROOM SLEEVE

straight grain

BRIDE SKIRT/SLIP

straight grain

BRIDE/GROOM EAR

place on fold along straight grain

centre front

pleat

pleat

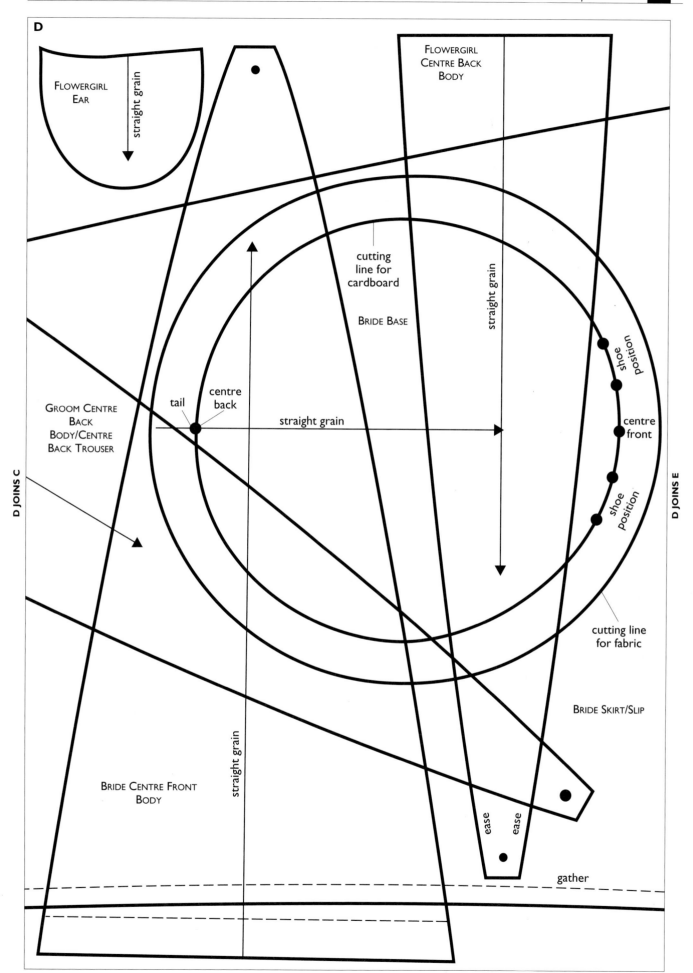

D

FLOWERGIRL EAR

straight grain

FLOWERGIRL CENTRE BACK BODY

cutting line for cardboard

BRIDE BASE

straight grain

shoe position

centre front

tail   centre back

straight grain

shoe position

GROOM CENTRE BACK BODY/CENTRE BACK TROUSER

D JOINS C

cutting line for fabric

BRIDE SKIRT/SLIP

ease   ease

straight grain

BRIDE CENTRE FRONT BODY

D JOINS E

gather

D

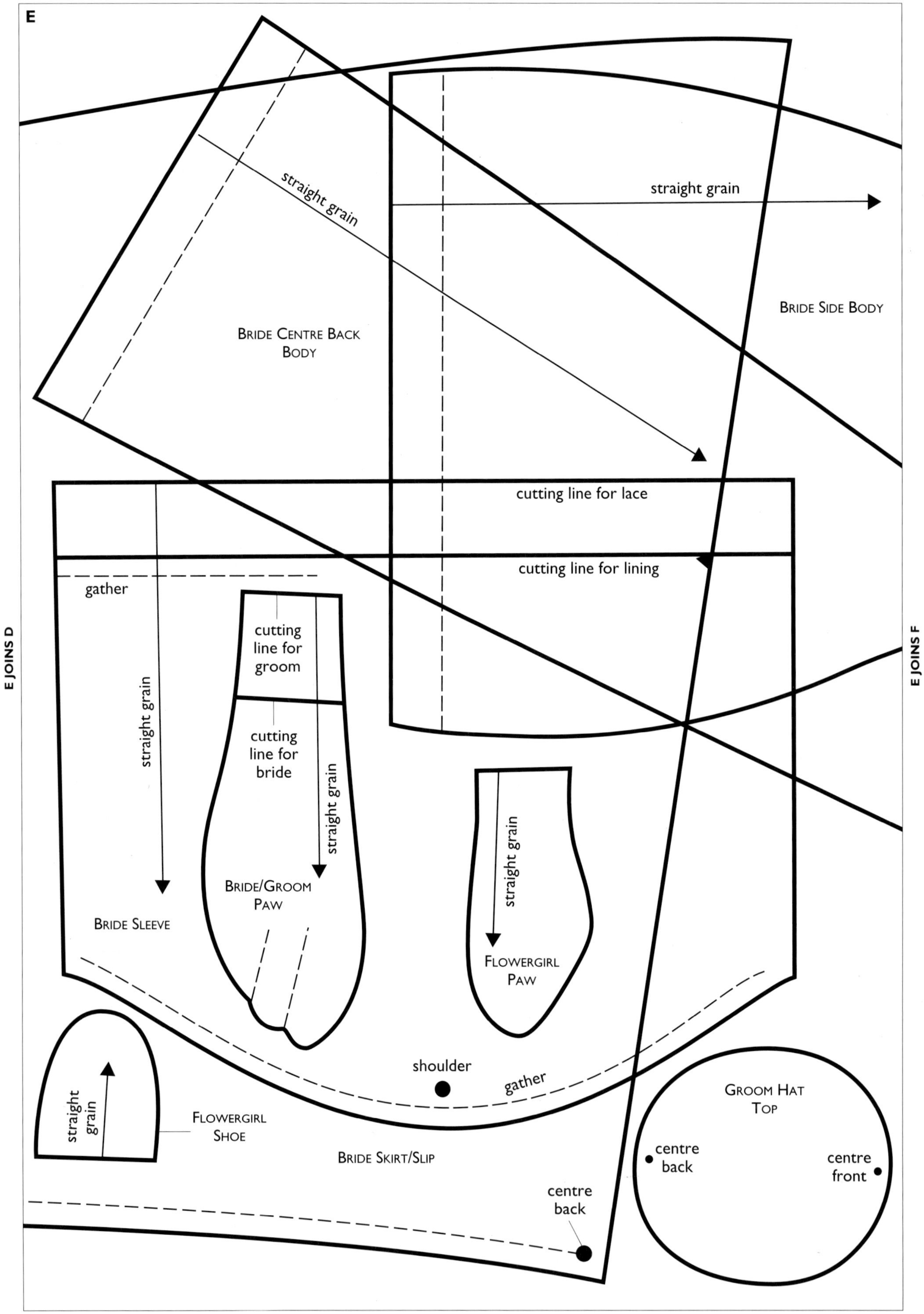

E

straight grain

straight grain

BRIDE SIDE BODY

BRIDE CENTRE BACK BODY

E JOINS D

E JOINS F

cutting line for lace

cutting line for lining

gather

straight grain

cutting line for groom

cutting line for bride

straight grain

BRIDE/GROOM PAW

straight grain

FLOWERGIRL PAW

BRIDE SLEEVE

straight grain

FLOWERGIRL SHOE

shoulder

gather

BRIDE SKIRT/SLIP

GROOM HAT TOP

centre back

centre front

centre back

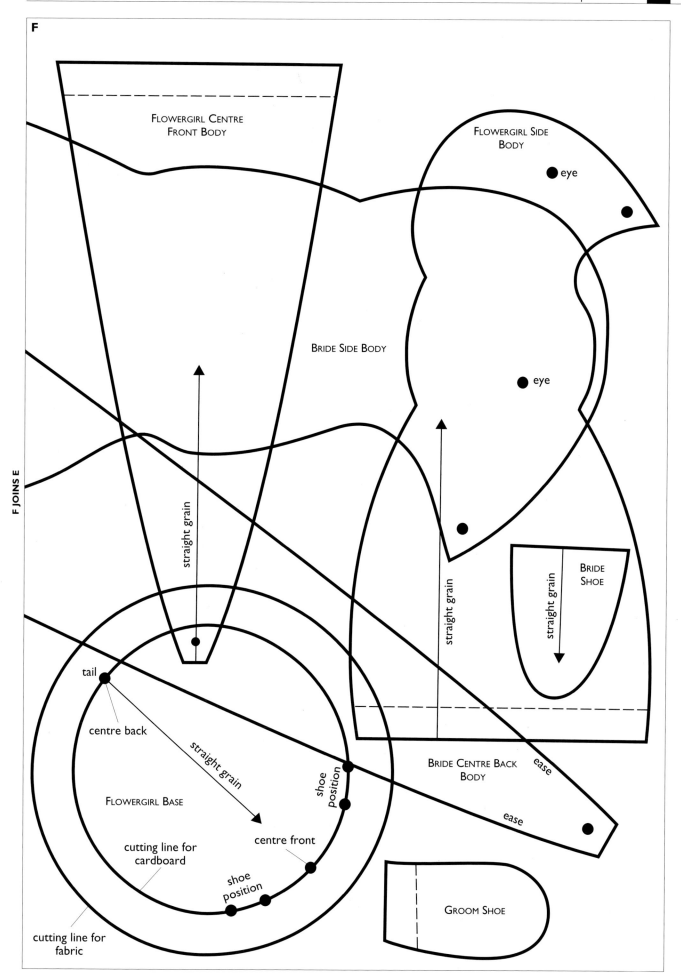

F

F JOINS E

FLOWERGIRL CENTRE
FRONT BODY

FLOWERGIRL SIDE
BODY

● eye

BRIDE SIDE BODY

● eye

straight grain

straight grain

BRIDE
SHOE

straight grain

tail ●

centre back

straight grain

shoe
position

BRIDE CENTRE BACK
BODY

ease

FLOWERGIRL BASE

centre front

ease

cutting line for
cardboard

shoe
position

GROOM SHOE

cutting line for
fabric

IN AND OUT THE WINDOW

Noah's Ark and Animals Wall-hanging

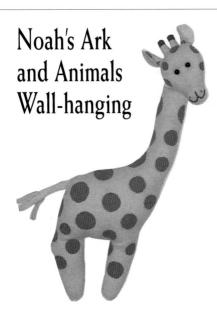

W̶hat small child doesn't just adore sticking things into pockets and taking them out again? This delightful Noah's Ark wall-hanging, designed by Maria Ragan, makes a colourful decoration for the nursery, as well as providing hours of amusement for pre-schoolers. Each figure is backed with re-useable glue, so that it sticks on the outside as well.

Mr and Mrs Noah keep watch over their precious cargo, all of whom like to peep through the portholes of their brightly coloured Ark, and occasionally even take a stroll on the roof!

MEASUREMENTS

Finished wall-hanging is 62cm high and 43cm wide at its widest point.

MATERIALS

- 40cm square light brown fabric
- 40cm square tan fabric
- 60cm x 40cm bright green fabric
- 5cm x 40cm grey fabric
- 10cm x 35cm red fabric
- 1m double-sided, iron-on inter-facing (see Note under Cutting)
- 30cm squares of felt in the following colours and amounts: two sky blue, one light blue, two bright green, two grey, one dark grey, one bright yellow, two white, one orange, one tan, one flesh, one magenta and one light brown
- 50cm x 90cm calico
- Mathematical compass (for drawing circles)
- Craft glue
- Polyester filling
- Knitting needle
- Two keyrings or curtain rings, 1.5-2cm diameter
- Small amounts of embroidery cotton in tan, purple, white and mid-brown
- FolkArt acrylic paints in Rose Garden, Persimmon, Frosted Berry, and Licorice
- Paintbrush
- Red pencil
- 18 small black glass beads
- 12cm square Aida cloth (for Mrs Noah's shawl)
- Small coloured wooden bead, approximately 5mm diameter
- Stikit glue (from Myart)

PATTERN PIECES

For the Ark Hull, Border and Roof, you will need to enlarge the grid, at right, onto squared paper and trace the pattern pieces. All other pattern pieces for the ark and animals, except rectangles and circles, are printed on pages 90, 91, 92 and 93. The facial features can be traced from the faces on these pages as well, but are not listed here. For Mr and Mrs Noah, the details of their dress are superimposed on the pattern pieces, with shaded areas denoting overlaps. You don't need to follow slavishly the colours we suggest.

Trace Ark Window Frame, Giraffe Body, Giraffe Head, Giraffe Ear, Polar Bear Body, Polar Bear Head, Polar Bear Tail, Polar Bear Ear, Leopard Body, Leopard Head, Leopard Tail, Leopard Ear, Elephant Body, Elephant Head, Elephant Ear, Hippo Body, Hippo Head, Hippo Tail, Hippo Ear, Zebra Body, Zebra Head, Zebra Nose, Zebra Ear, Monkey Body, Monkey Head, Monkey Face, Monkey Leg, Monkey Arm, Monkey Ear, Mr Noah and Mrs Noah.

CUTTING

NOTE: Before cutting both fabric and felt, apply double-sided, iron-on interfacing. The paper backing makes it much easier to draw on felt and fabric and to cut out even the smallest pieces. Peel off protective paper after cutting. Remember that the felt pieces do not need seam allowances; the pattern pieces are actual size. For all fabric pieces, add 1cm seam allowance on all sides, unless otherwise specified.

From light brown fabric, cut one 14cm x 32cm rectangle for the ark top and one 18cm x 32cm rectangle for the ark middle (both measurements include seam allowance).

From tan fabric, cut one Ark Hull, three 6cm-diameter circles for portholes (includes seam allowance) and two 7.5cm x 22cm rectangles for window pockets (includes seam allowance).

From bright green fabric, cut one Ark Border.

From grey fabric, cut one 4.5cm x 36cm rectangle for ark strip (includes seam allowance).

From red fabric, cut one Ark Roof.

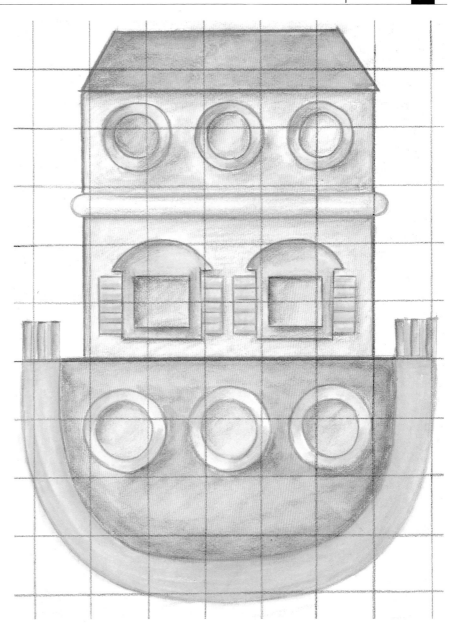

Graph for Ark: 1.5cm = 6cm. Mark 6cm squares on a sheet of graph paper, then transfer outline, working square by square.

From sky blue felt, cut four Ark Window Frames, six 7.5cm-diameter circles (with 5cm-diameter circles removed from the centre) for upper porthole frames and four 0.7cm dots for shutter handles.

From light blue felt, cut three 9cm-diameter circles for lower portholes and two 3.5cm x 8cm rectangles for prow decoration.

From bright green felt, cut eight 3.5cm x 7cm rectangles for shutters, six 9cm-diameter circles (with 6.5cm diameter circles removed from the centre) for lower porthole frames, one 0.5cm x 32cm strip, cut into four equal lengths, for prow decoration, and two Leopard Eyes.

From grey felt, cut two Elephant Bodies, two Elephant Heads, two Hippo Bodies, two Hippo Heads, two Hippo Ears and one Leopard Nose.

From dark grey felt, cut two Elephant ears, one 3cm x 3.5cm rectangle for elephant tail, one Hippo Tail, two 0.7cm-diameter circles for hippo nostrils, one Zebra Nose and one Polar Bear Nose.

From bright yellow felt, cut two Giraffe Bodies, two Giraffe Heads, two Giraffe Ears, two 2cm x 1.3cm rectangles for giraffe horns, one 3cm x 4.5cm rectangle for giraffe tail, and two Giraffe Nostrils.

From white felt, cut two Polar Bear Bodies, two Polar Bear Heads, two

Polar Bear Ears, one Polar Bear Tail, two Zebra Bodies, two Zebra Heads, two Zebra Ears, one 3cm x 5.5cm rectangle for zebra tail, one 0.8cm x 7cm rectangle for zebra mane, six Hippo Toenails, one Hippo Tooth, six Elephant Toenails, and two Elephant Tusks.

From orange felt, cut two Leopard Bodies, two Leopard Heads, two Leopard Tails and two Leopard Ears.

From tan felt, cut two Monkey Bodies, two Monkey Heads, four Monkey Legs, four Monkey Arms, two Monkey Ears, and six Polar Bear Toenails.

From flesh felt, cut one Monkey Face.

From magenta, light brown and various scraps, cut the various pieces for Mr and Mrs Noah, using the photograph as a guide to colour, if desired. Cut the Head backs the same colour as the hair, and remember to cut overlaps where indicated.

METHOD

ARK

With right sides together, join Ark Roof to ark top, lower edge of ark top to ark strip, and lower edge of ark strip to ark middle. Press seams open.

Remove protective paper from back of tan fabric portholes and iron into position on ark top. With wrong sides together, blanket-stitch two sky blue porthole frames together at inner and outer edges. Repeat for other porthole frames. Place over portholes, so frame covers raw edge of fabric, and stitch in place on ark top.

Press in 1cm on a short edge of tan window pocket. Now make another fold 7.5cm from pressed edge, with

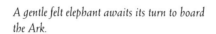

A gentle felt elephant awaits its turn to board the Ark.

right sides together, and blanket-stitch outer edges to form a small pocket. About 5cm from lower edge of ark middle and evenly spaced (use the photograph as a guide), make two 7cm slits. Pull top part of window pocket through slit onto right side of ark middle, so that pressed-under edge of pocket aligns with slit. Pull this edge out and fold over raw edge of slit. Glue in place. Glue top part of window pocket onto ark middle.

With wrong sides facing, blanket-stitch two sky blue Window Frames together at inner and outer edges. Repeat for other Window Frame. Stitch completed frames to ark middle around outside edge and inside frame edge, covering raw edges of window pocket.

For shutters, blanket-stitch two bright green felt rectangles together, leaving a small hole for filling. Fill with polyester filling, using a knitting needle to push filling in. Close opening. Make four evenly-spaced

lines of running-stitch across each shutter, through all thicknesses. Decorate each with a small sky blue felt dot. With small stitches, attach shutters to ark middle at edge of window frames.

With right sides together, stitch Ark Border to Ark Hull. Clip curves and press flat.

Lay completed pieces for ark bottom and ark top on calico, trace outlines, then cut out one ark top and three ark bottoms. With right sides together, join a calico ark bottom to both ark tops, then, with right sides facing, join front to back around all edges, leaving roof edge open for turning. Turn right side out and press. Turn in seam allowance on roof edge and slip-stitch closed.

With right sides facing, stitch remaining calico ark bottom to fabric Hull, around all edges, leaving a small opening for turning. Turn and press. Slip-stitch opening closed. Following position guide on pattern piece, cut three 7cm-diameter circles from Hull. Make tiny clips in curves, turn in allowance on both front and back, and slip-stitch edges together. With wrong sides facing, blanket-stitch two bright green felt porthole frames together at inner and outer edges. Repeat for other two frames. Stitch porthole frames to portholes of Hull, covering turned-in edges.

Glue light blue felt portholes onto calico ark bottom that is already attached to ark top, so that porthole pockets will appear to have a blue background.

Blanket-stitch Ark Hull front to calico Ark Hull back, around curved edges so that Hull front forms a large pocket. Make a couple of stitches at centre front on top edge of Hull so that the pocket does not gape.

Mr Noah and jungle friends — a fabulously spotted leopard, and a rather cheeky-faced monkey.

Mrs Noah with a couple of her colourful felt charges — a one-toothed hippo and a striped zebra.

For prow decoration, fold light blue rectangle in half and blanket-stitch long sides, leaving narrow edge open. Fill with polyester filling, close opening, and stitch to top of Ark Border. Repeat for other side. Glue bright green stripes onto prows as decoration.

To finish, stitch two rings to back for hanging.

ANIMALS

For each animal, decorate front side only. Glue on nostrils and other detail, work features on front side of face (except beads for eyes) and add ears before joining to back piece. All embroidery is done with four strands of embroidery cotton. Insert tail, where applicable, and join fronts to backs with wrong sides together, using a tiny blanket-stitch around outside edge and leaving a small opening for stuffing. Stuff with polyester filling using a knitting needle, and stitch opening closed. Stitch head and body sections together when both are complete. For eyes, attach two black beads to each animal and person, through all thicknesses, pulling tightly to give definition to face.

GIRAFFE

Fold Ears in half lengthwise and attach straight edge to front side of head. For tail, cut a fringe in one end of tail rectangle to a depth of 3cm. Roll tail lengthwise and stitch from top as far as fringe, to secure. Make horns in same manner as tail (without cutting a fringe). Paint tips of horns and centre

of each nostril with Frosted Berry 760. Paint circles on head, body and backs of ears with Persimmon 919.

ELEPHANT

Make tail as for Giraffe, cutting fringe to a depth of 1.5cm. Glue tusks in place on upper trunk. Glue three toenails to each foot. Embroider wrinkles in fold of trunk with purple embroidery thread.

LEOPARD

Paint inside of ears with Licorice 938. Fold each straight side edge of ear towards centre and stitch to front side of head. Paint body spots with Licorice 938. Place green felt eyes behind black beads before sewing.

HIPPO

Glue nostrils and tooth in place on face. Paint inside Ears with Rose Garden 754, fold both edges in and stitch Ear to head. Glue three toenails to each foot.

POLAR BEAR

Paint a small circle inside each ear with Frosted Berry 760. Glue three toenails on each foot.

ZEBRA

Cut fringe in mane to depth of 0.4cm and paint with Licorice 938, leaving some white showing. Cut off a 2cm piece of mane and attach to Head. Attach remainder to neck. Make tail as for Giraffe, cutting fringe to a depth of 1.5cm. Paint backs of Ears and stripes on Body, Head and tail with Licorice 938.

MONKEY

Make Arms and Legs first and stuff them. Embroider fingers and toes with running-stitch. Then attach arms and legs to Body in positions indicated. Stitch Face onto front of Head. Fold edges of Ears in and stitch to front of Head.

MR AND MRS NOAH

Glue overlaps to each other and sew pieces together, stuffing and inserting Arms into sleeves, Legs into trousers and dress, and feet into Shoes as you go. For Mrs Noah's shawl, paint Aida cloth with Frosted Berry 760 and allow to dry. Fold in half diagonally and fray edges a little for a fringe. Wrap around Mrs Noah's body and catch ends together with small wooden bead. Embroider features with mid-brown thread and rub cheeks lightly with a red pencil to give faces some colouring. Define fingers with running-stitch.

Brush Stikit glue on back of all felt figures so that they can be attached and re-attached to Ark.

PATTERN PIECES FOR ARK AND ANIMALS

*Template for Mrs Noah —
the shaded areas show
overlaps.*

LEOPARD BODY

HIPPO
EAR

HIPPO HEAD

HIPPO BODY

LEOPARD HEAD

HIPPO
TAIL

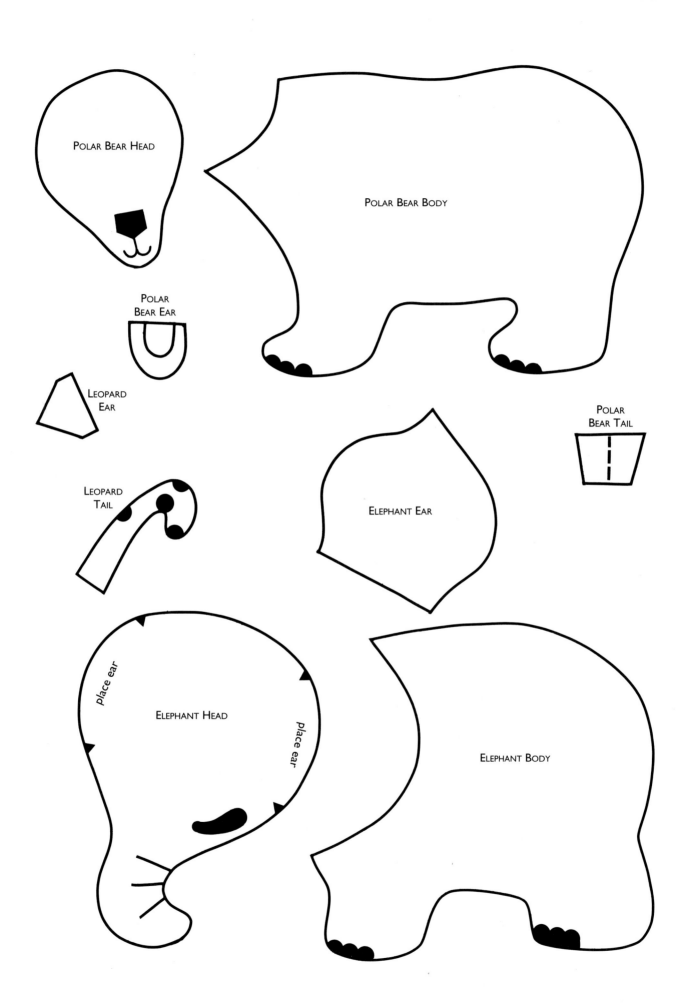

POLAR BEAR HEAD

POLAR BEAR BODY

POLAR
BEAR EAR

LEOPARD
EAR

POLAR
BEAR TAIL

LEOPARD
TAIL

ELEPHANT EAR

place ear

ELEPHANT HEAD

place ear

ELEPHANT BODY

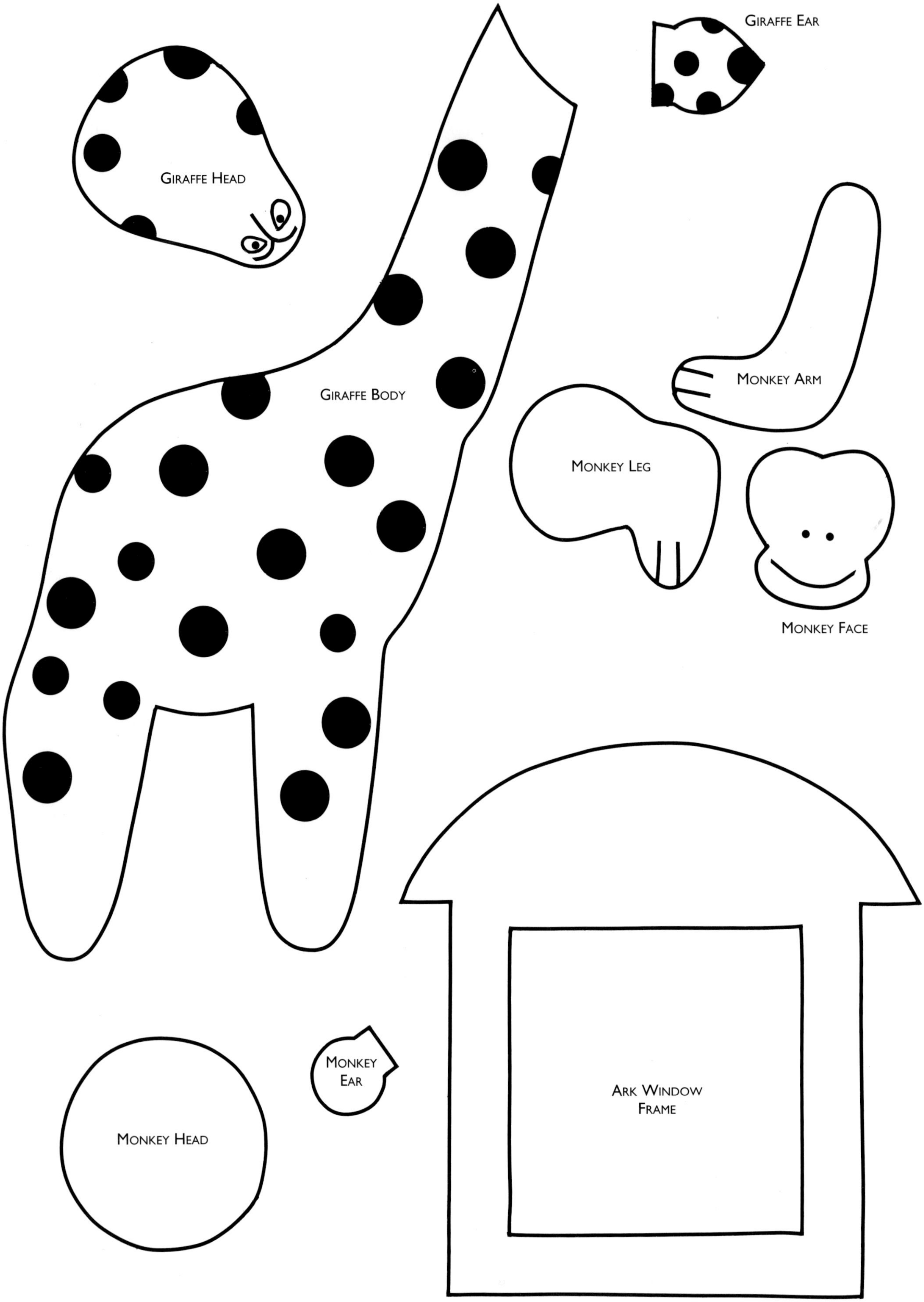

GIRAFFE EAR

GIRAFFE HEAD

GIRAFFE BODY

MONKEY ARM

MONKEY LEG

MONKEY FACE

MONKEY HEAD

MONKEY EAR

ARK WINDOW FRAME

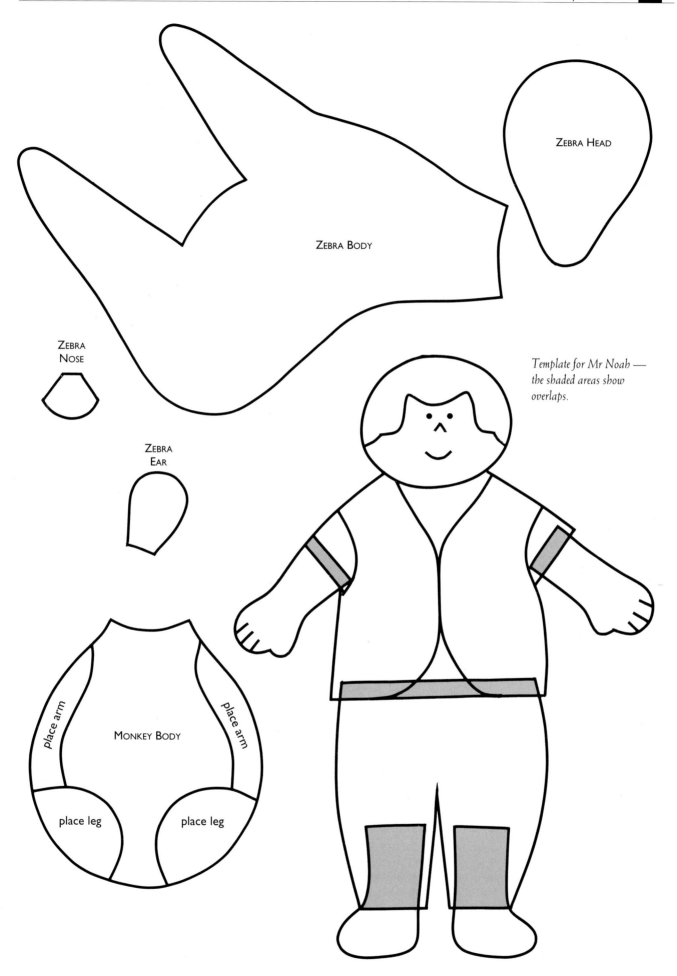

ZEBRA HEAD

ZEBRA BODY

ZEBRA
NOSE

ZEBRA
EAR

*Template for Mr Noah —
the shaded areas show
overlaps.*

place arm

place arm

MONKEY BODY

place leg

place leg

ANIMATED ANIMALS

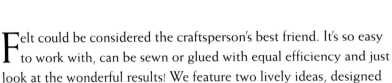

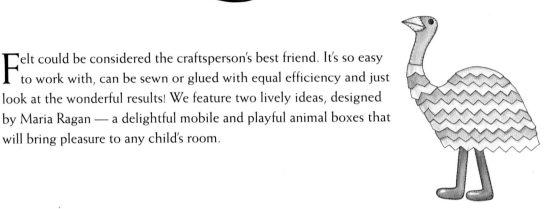

Felt could be considered the craftsperson's best friend. It's so easy to work with, can be sewn or glued with equal efficiency and just look at the wonderful results! We feature two lively ideas, designed by Maria Ragan — a delightful mobile and playful animal boxes that will bring pleasure to any child's room.

Mobile

MATERIALS

- Two 30cm squares tan felt
- One 30cm square each grey, light brown and red felt
- Scraps bright blue, royal blue, flesh, yellow, light green and dark green felt
- 18 small black beads
- Brown stranded embroidery thread
- Polyester filling
- Craft glue
- Knitting needle
- 3m coloured string or fine cord, cut into 2 x 45cm lengths (for koala and kangaroo), 2 x 25cm lengths (for lorikeets), 3 x 20cm lengths (for wombat, possum and emu) and 1 x 1m length for hanging mobile
- Thin dowel, cut into one 45cm, one 25cm and two 12cm lengths
- Nine round and four oval wooden beads
- Electric drill and fine bit

PATTERN PIECES

All pattern pieces are printed on pages 101 to 104. Trace Lorikeet Body, Head, Tail, Beak and Wing; Emu Body, Beak, Leg and Feathers; Wombat Body, Underbody, Head Gusset, Ear and Nose; Possum Body, Underbody, Head Gusset, Ear and Nose; Koala Body, Front Body Gusset, Head Gusset, Ear, Inner Ear, Arm, Leg, Nose and Gumleaf; Baby Koala Body, Front Body Gusset, Head Front, Head Back, Ear, Inner Ear, Arm and Leg; Kangaroo Body, Half Front Body, Head Gusset, Ear, Pouch, Arm, Leg and Nose; Baby Kangaroo Head, Head Gusset, Ear and Nose.

CUTTING

For Lorikeets, cut four Bodies from red felt, four Heads from bright blue felt, four Tails from dark green felt, four Beaks from yellow felt and four Wings from light green felt.

For Emu, cut two Bodies and eight Feather strips from tan felt, two Beaks and ten Feather strips from grey felt and four Legs from royal blue felt.

For Wombat, cut two Bodies, two Underbodies and one Head Gusset from light brown felt, and two Ears and one Nose from tan felt.

For Possum, cut two Bodies, two Underbodies, two Ears and one Head Gusset from tan felt and one Nose from flesh felt.

For Koala, cut two Bodies, one Front Body Gusset, one Head Gusset, four Arms, four Legs and two Ears from grey felt. Cut two Inner Ears from white felt, one Nose from tan felt and five Gumleaves from light green felt.

For Baby Koala, cut two Bodies, one Front Body Gusset, one Front Head, two Back Heads, four Arms, four Legs and two Ears from grey felt. Cut two Inner Ears from white felt and one Nose (a little smaller than Mum's) from tan felt.

For Kangaroo, cut two Bodies, one Head Gusset, four Arms, four Legs and two Ears from tan felt, and two Half Front Bodies, one Pouch and one Nose from light brown felt.

For Baby Kangaroo, cut two Heads, one Head Gusset and two Ears from tan felt, and one Nose from light brown felt.

METHOD

LORIKEET (MAKES TWO)

Place a Head and a Tail onto each Body piece and secure in place with small stitches. Secure Beak to Head and stitch beakline with small running stitches. Attach black beads for eyes. Sew on Wings. Place wrong sides of two Lorikeet pieces together and blanket-stitch around outer edges, catching in hanging cords at top of head, and leaving a small opening. Fill with polyester filling, using knitting needle to push filling into corners. Stitch opening closed.

This irresistible mobile resulted from a fruitless search on behalf of a newborn niece, for a native animals mobile. Handmade asked talented Maria Ragan, who also made the lizard and croc boxes, to design one. The mobile requires very little felt and is easily made.

EMU

With small stitches, stitch Beaks to Head pieces and embroider beakline. Attach black beads for eyes. For legs, place wrong sides of two Leg pieces together, and blanket-stitch around outer edges, gradually filling with polyester filling as you proceed. Stitch opening closed.

Attach feathers to Body using craft glue, starting from bottom with a grey strip, then overlapping with tan, as shown. Trim Feather strips even with outline of Body. Place wrong sides of Body pieces together and blanket-stitch around edges, sandwiching Legs in place at the same time, catching in hanging cord on centre of back, and leaving opening for filling. Fill and stitch opening closed.

WOMBAT

Place right sides of two Underbodies together and blanket-stitch centre seam. With wrong sides together, stitch Underbody to Body pieces, using small, neat blanket-stitch. Fold Ears as shown in diagram. With wrong sides together, blanket-stitch Head Gusset to Head, catching in folded Ears at the same time. Attach Nose with small stitches and sew on black beads for eyes. Embroider mouth in stem-stitch with brown thread. With wrong sides facing, blanket-stitch Body pieces together around outer edges, catching in hanging cord at centre back, and leaving an opening. Fill and stitch opening closed.

POSSUM

Make as for Wombat.

KOALA

With wrong sides together, blanket-stitch Head Gusset to Head, from Point A to back of neck. Stitch Head pieces together from Point A to Point B. With small stitches, attach Nose. Sew on black beads for eyes and embroider mouth in stem-stitch. Glue white Inner Ears to right sides of grey Ear pieces and allow to dry. Gather lower edge of Ears to form folds and attach to Head. Tie a knot in one end of hanging cord and thread the other end through top of head, using a large needle.

Make two Arms and Legs by placing wrong sides of felt together and blanket-stitching around outer edges, leaving a small opening. Fill, using a knitting needle to push filling into corners. Stitch opening closed.

With wrong sides together, blanket-stitch Front Body Gusset to Body, catching in legs on lower edge, as indicated, at the same time. Stitch arms to either side of body. With wrong sides facing, blanket-stitch two Body pieces together, leaving an opening for filling. Fill and stitch opening closed. Take strong thread and tie around koala's head to define neck, burying ends in body. With small stitches, attach Gumleaves to arms.

EMU

bead for eye

embroider beak line

overlap strips of feathers

BABY KOALA

Make Arms, Legs and Ears as for Mother Koala.

With small stitches, attach Nose to right side of Head Front, then embroider mouth in stem-stitch and sew on black beads for eyes.

With right sides facing, blanket-stitch Back Head pieces together along centre seam. With wrong sides facing, sew Front Head and Back Head together with blanket-stitch, catching in Ears at the same time and leaving an opening. Fill, using a knitting needle to push filling into corners. Stitch opening closed.

With wrong sides facing, blanket-stitch Front Body Gusset to Body pieces, catching in legs on lower edge at the same time. Stitch Body pieces together, leaving an opening for filling. Fill and stitch opening closed. Stitch arms in place on either side of body. Stitch completed head to body, positioning it so that baby faces sideways.

To finish, glue or stitch baby onto mother's back.

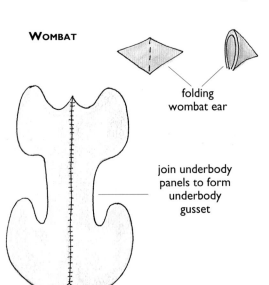

WOMBAT

folding wombat ear

join underbody panels to form underbody gusset

KOALA

ear

head gusset

inner ear

gather ears

body gusset

koala clasping gumleaves

With wrong sides together, blanket-stitch completed Front Body to Body pieces, from Point B to Point C, catching in legs, as indicated, at the same time.

With wrong sides together, blanket-stitch Head Gusset to Head, from Point A to back of neck, catching in folded Ears, as indicated, at the same time. With small stitches, attach Nose. Sew on black beads for eyes and embroider mouth in stem-stitch. Tie a knot in one end of hanging cord and thread the other end through top of head, using a large needle. Stitch arms in position on both sides of Body.

With wrong sides facing, blanket-stitch Body pieces together, leaving an opening for filling. Fill and stitch opening closed. Define top of hind legs by stitching through body and pulling slightly, as shown in diagram.

To make baby's head, follow same instructions as for mother. Secure baby's head to mother's body and glue on Pouch below head.

KANGAROO WITH BABY

Make two arms and legs by placing wrong sides of felt together and blanket-stitching around outer edges, leaving a small opening. Fill, using a knitting needle to push filling into corners. Stitch opening closed. Fold Ears, following diagram.

Place Half Front Bodies together, right sides facing, and blanket-stitch centre seam.

ASSEMBLING MOBILE

With a fine bit, drill holes in both ends and in centre of each piece of dowel. Assemble mobile as shown in photograph, using round beads to keep hanging cords secure and oval beads as spacers between dowels.

Stitch Lorikeets firmly to either end of their perch.

LORIKEET

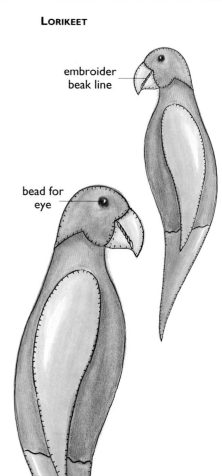

embroider beak line

bead for eye

KANGAROO

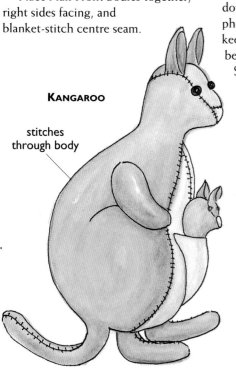

stitches through body

KANGAROO

join half front bodies together to form front gusset

folding ear piece

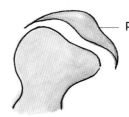

placing head gusset through body

Crocodile Box

MATERIALS

- 30cm square mid-green felt
- 30cm x 15cm red felt
- Scraps blue, white, light green and dark green felt
- Clag clear glue
- Red and blue embroidery cotton
- Two black beads
- Sewing needle and matching threads
- Polyester filling
- Small knitting needle
- Craft glue
- Green Velcro fastener

FELT PREPARATION

Prepare felt before cutting by gently brushing with water, then clear glue. Allow to dry overnight. When dry, it should be paper-like.

PATTERN PIECES

All pattern are pieces printed on page 105. Trace Top Body, Bottom Body, Crocodile Head, Crocodile Tail, Foot, Eye, Patch, Head Scales, Tail Scales, Body Scales and Decorative Spots.

CUTTING

From mid-green felt, cut two Top Bodies, two Bottom Bodies, two Crocodile Heads and two Crocodile Tails.

From red felt, cut two Top Bodies and two Bottom Bodies.

From blue felt, cut eight Foot pieces and as many Decorative Spots to decorate inside of box as desired.

From white felt, cut two Eyes.

From light green felt, cut one Head Scales, one Body Scales and one Tail Scales.

From dark green felt, cut as many Patches as desired, to decorate box.

METHOD

With red cotton, embroider mouth in stem-stitch on right side of both Head pieces. Embroider nostrils with blue cotton. Attach white Eyes and sew a black bead to each.

With wrong sides facing, blanket-stitch Head pieces together, catching in Head Scales, as indicated in photograph, and leaving a small opening. Push filling into corners of

head with a knitting needle and stitch opening closed.

With wrong sides of two Foot pieces together, blanket-stitch around edges, leaving a small opening. Fill and stitch opening closed. Repeat for other three feet.

Use craft glue to attach dark green Patches to right sides of Tail pieces. With wrong sides of Tail pieces together, blanket-stitch around edges, catching in Tail Scales along top edge at the same time, and leaving a small opening. Fill and stitch opening closed.

Stitch darts in all Body sections, as shown in diagram.

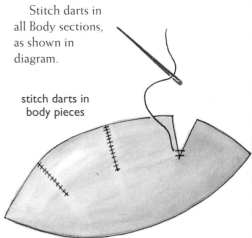

stitch darts in body pieces

With right sides together, stitch green Top Bodies together along darted edge, catching in Body Scales at the same time. With right sides together, stitch green Bottom Bodies together along darted edge, catching completed Tail into seam at the same time. Repeat this process for red Top and Bottom Bodies, omitting reference to Scales and Tail.

Attach Patches to outside of body (green) with craft glue. Attach blue dots to inside of body (red) in the same way. With wrong sides together, place red body sections inside green body sections and secure together around edges with craft glue.

Join top and bottom sections at the back by stitching a hinge at the back, as shown in diagram, then gluing a green Patch over the stitching on the outside to reinforce.

Attach a Patch to front top section with stitching, then glue half of the Velcro fastener to wrong side of Patch. Glue remaining section of Velcro fastener to bottom to correspond.

Attach feet and head to body with glue, as photographed.

Children love little boxes in which to store things or hide favourite treasures. Our croc box and lounge lizard, with their hinged backs and capacious tummies, are a fun alternative. Made from felt stiffened with clear glue, they are hand-stitched together, and you can opt to stitch or glue on the scaly decorations. A Velcro-trimmed flap keeps the box closed for perfect privacy.

Lizard Box

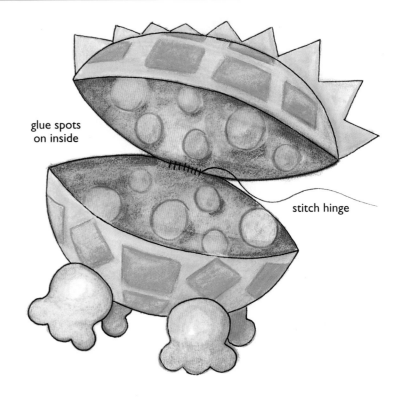

glue spots
on inside

stitch hinge

MATERIALS

- 30cm square yellow felt
- 30cm x 15cm beige felt
- Scraps blue, white, red and orange felt
- Clag clear glue
- Red embroidery cotton
- Two black beads
- Sewing needle and matching threads
- Polyester filling
- Small knitting needle
- 80cm x 8cm yellow nylon net
- Yellow Velcro fastener

FELT PREPARATION

As for Crocodile Box.

PATTERN PIECES

All pattern pieces are printed below and on page 105. Trace Top Body, Bottom Body, Lizard Head, Lizard Tail, Foot, Eye, Patch and Decorative Spots.

CUTTING

From yellow felt, cut two Top Bodies, two Bottom Bodies, two Lizard Heads and two Lizard Tails.

From beige felt, cut two Top Bodies and two Bottom Bodies.

From blue felt, cut as many Decorative Spots to decorate inside of box as desired.

From white felt, cut two Eyes.

From red felt, cut eight Foot pieces.

From orange felt, cut as many Patches as desired, to decorate box.

METHOD

Make as for Crocodile Box, omitting reference to scales. For neck frill, fold net in half across 8cm width and gather along folded edge. Gather and stitch to secure around neck. Finish as for Crocodile Box.

PATTERN PIECES FOR FELT MOBILE AND BOXES

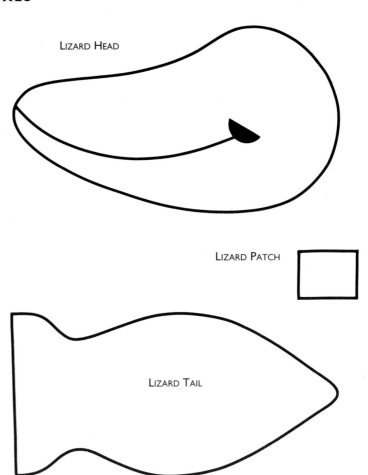

LIZARD HEAD

LIZARD PATCH

LIZARD TAIL

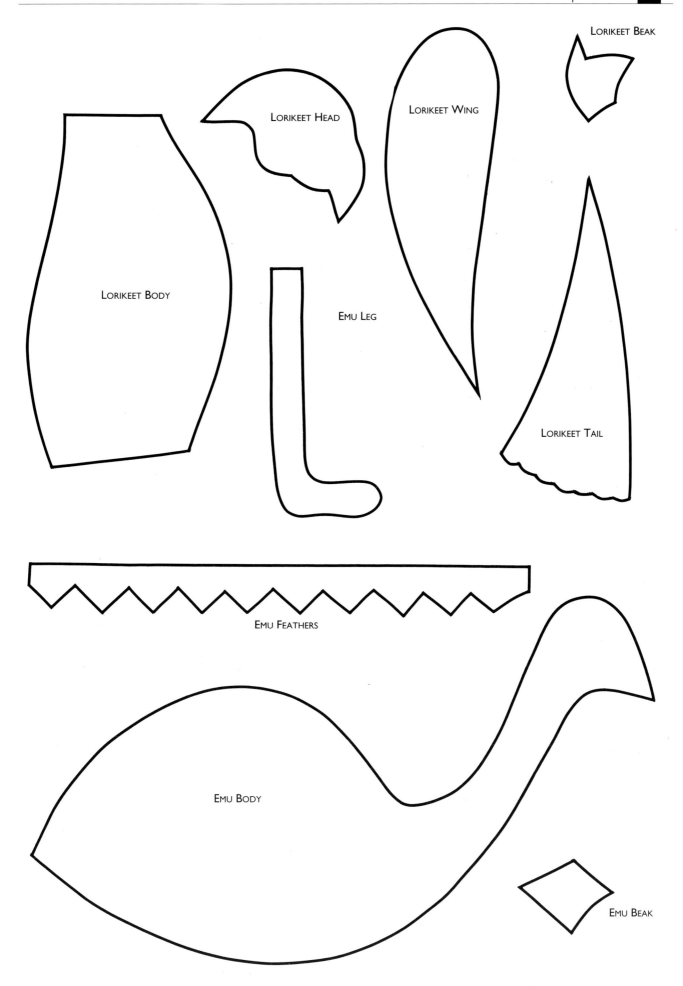

LORIKEET BEAK

LORIKEET HEAD

LORIKEET WING

LORIKEET BODY

EMU LEG

LORIKEET TAIL

EMU FEATHERS

EMU BODY

EMU BEAK

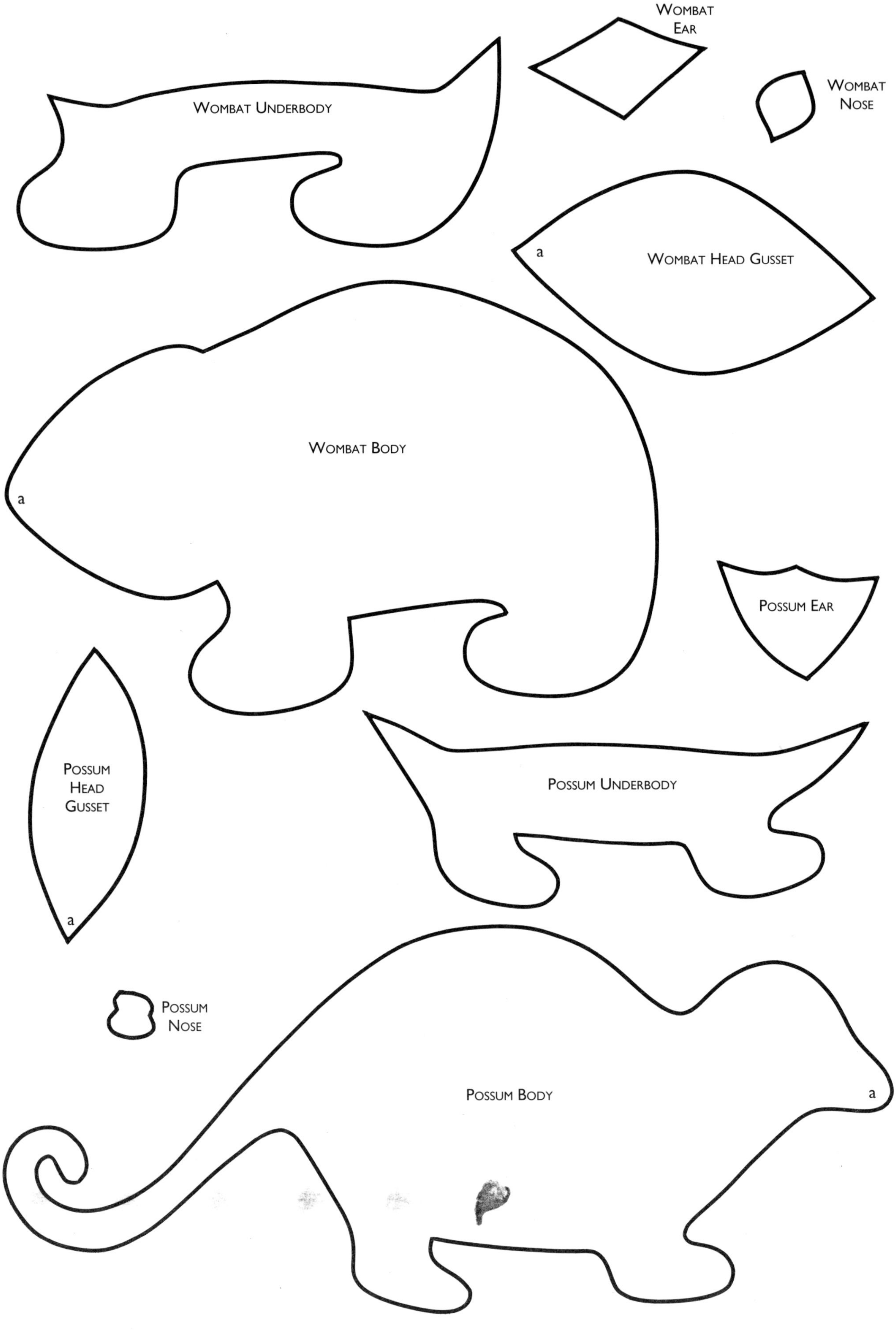

WOMBAT EAR

WOMBAT NOSE

WOMBAT UNDERBODY

a WOMBAT HEAD GUSSET

WOMBAT BODY

a

POSSUM EAR

POSSUM HEAD GUSSET

POSSUM UNDERBODY

a

POSSUM NOSE

POSSUM BODY

a

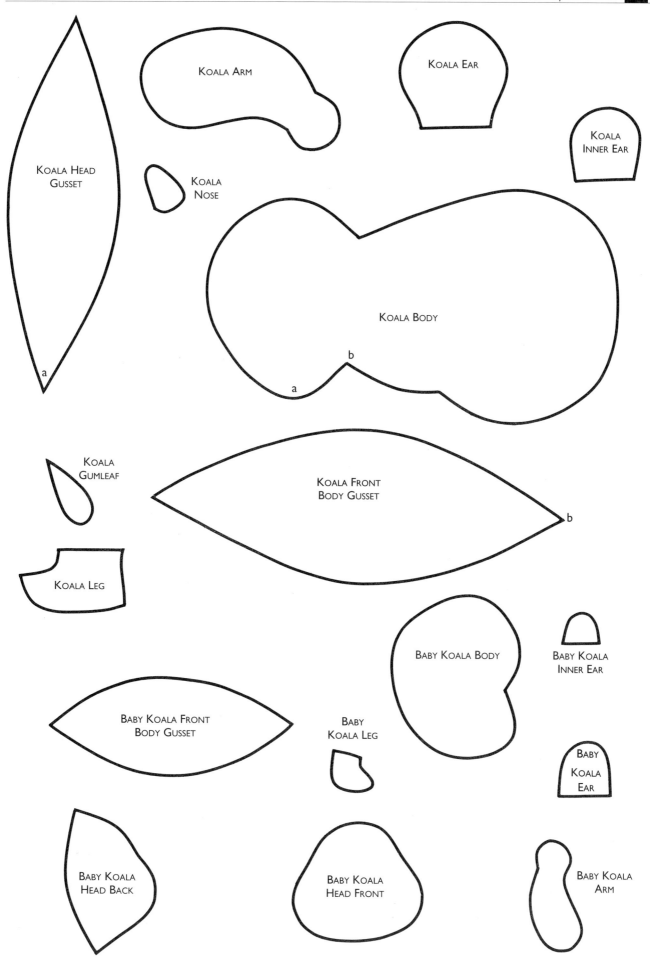

KOALA HEAD GUSSET

KOALA ARM

KOALA EAR

KOALA INNER EAR

KOALA NOSE

KOALA BODY

a

b

a

KOALA GUMLEAF

KOALA FRONT BODY GUSSET

b

KOALA LEG

BABY KOALA BODY

BABY KOALA INNER EAR

BABY KOALA LEG

BABY KOALA EAR

BABY KOALA FRONT BODY GUSSET

BABY KOALA HEAD BACK

BABY KOALA HEAD FRONT

BABY KOALA ARM

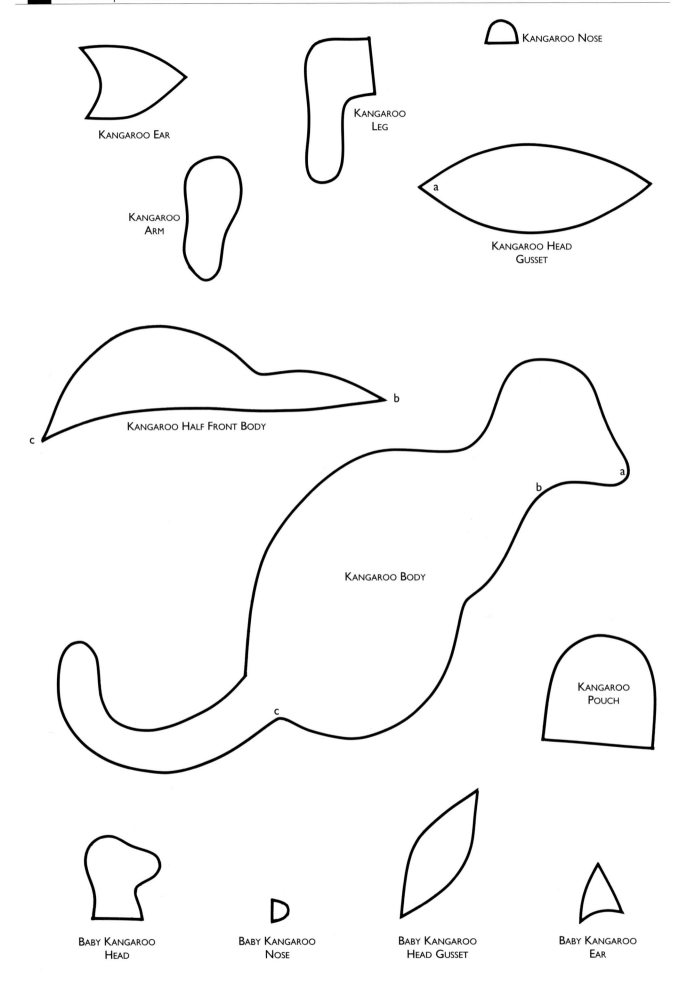

KANGAROO NOSE

KANGAROO EAR

KANGAROO
LEG

KANGAROO
ARM

a

KANGAROO HEAD
GUSSET

c

b

KANGAROO HALF FRONT BODY

a

b

KANGAROO BODY

c

KANGAROO
POUCH

BABY KANGAROO
HEAD

BABY KANGAROO
NOSE

BABY KANGAROO
HEAD GUSSET

BABY KANGAROO
EAR

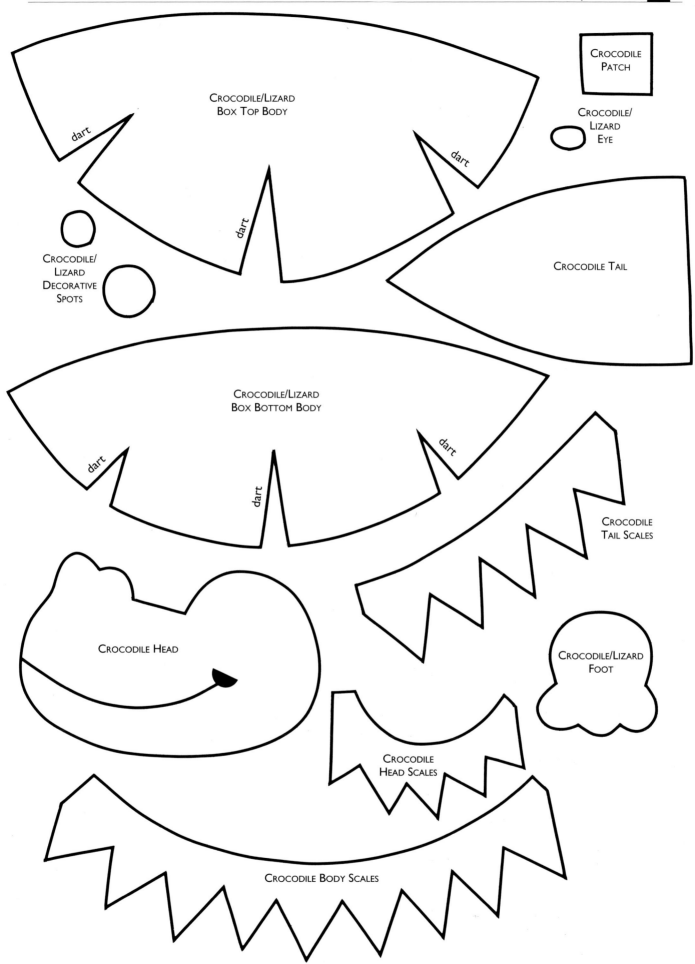

CROCODILE PATCH

CROCODILE/LIZARD BOX TOP BODY

dart

dart

dart

CROCODILE/LIZARD EYE

CROCODILE/LIZARD DECORATIVE SPOTS

CROCODILE TAIL

CROCODILE/LIZARD BOX BOTTOM BODY

dart

dart

dart

CROCODILE TAIL SCALES

CROCODILE HEAD

CROCODILE/LIZARD FOOT

CROCODILE HEAD SCALES

CROCODILE BODY SCALES

SEND IN THE CLOWNS

With their colourful clothes and crazy antics, clowns hold a particular appeal for children of all ages — even grown-up ones! Clever toymaker Maria Ragan has designed a charming collection of clowns for the nursery, not only wonderfully coloured and cheerful, but also engagingly functional. The pyjama case clown has many roles, while the activity book has more things going on than the circus itself!

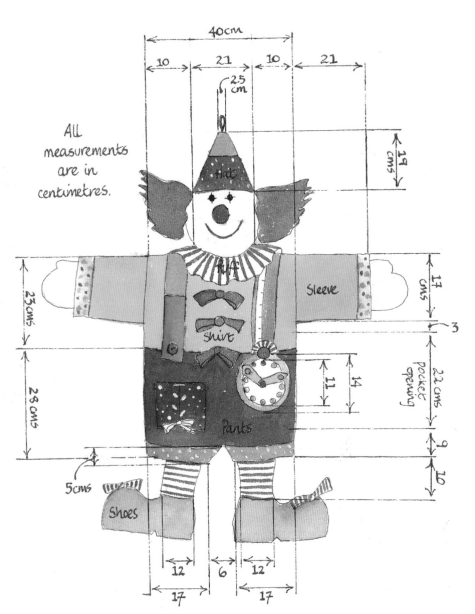

Pyjama Case Clown

MEASUREMENTS
Finished clown is 114cm high.

MATERIALS
- 85cm x 30cm navy blue fabric, for pants
- 85cm x 45cm yellow fabric, for shirt
- 30cm x 60cm brown fabric, for shoes
- 85cm x 45cm light blue fabric, for inner pocket lining
- 52cm x 12cm narrow-striped fabric, for socks
- 30cm x 40cm calico
- 12cm x 110cm wide striped fabric, for ruff
- 20cm x 110cm orange fabric, for ruff and braces lining
- 14cm x 34cm blue fabric, for braces
- 14cm x 24cm green fabric, for braces
- 40cm x 20cm polka dot fabric, for hat and patches
- Scraps of fabric in assorted colours, including red, for nose, bows, trims and watch
- Polyester filling
- Eight eyelets
- One white shoelace
- Craft glue
- Two 20mm black buttons
- Small amount black embroidery thread
- White acrylic paint
- Small amount cardboard
- 25g wool, for hair
- Red pencil
- Four 27mm buttons, for braces
- One purchased tape measure
- Two press studs
- 12 x 15mm flat-faced buttons, for watch
- One 20mm button, for watch (we used a self-cover button)
- A little coloured paper or cardboard
- Paint or marker pen

PATTERN PIECES
Pattern pieces for Head, Hand and Shoe are on pages 112 and 113. Remaining pieces are rectangles, triangles or circles, and can be cut following measurements on the diagram on this page.

CUTTING

NOTE: Add seam allowance to all pieces and measurements before cutting, except where indicated. Pattern pieces can be cut all in one colour or pieces can be sewn together to give a striped effect at cuff and pants edges. If using stripes, sew together and proceed.

From navy blue fabric, cut two Pants.

From yellow fabric, cut two Shirts and four Sleeves.

The oversize pyjama case clown also doubles as a height chart, unravels the mystery of telling the time and teaches little fingers about the intricacies of buttons and laces.

From brown fabric, cut four Shoes.

From light blue fabric, cut two rectangles for Inner Pocket Lining, each 42cm x 47cm (includes 1cm seam allowance).

From narrow striped fabric, cut four Socks.

From calico, cut two Heads and four Hands.

From wide striped fabric, cut a rectangle 12cm x 110cm for Ruff (includes 1cm seam allowance).

From orange fabric, cut a rectangle 12cm x 110cm for Ruff lining, and two strips, each 7cm x 56cm, for Braces lining (measurements include 1cm seam allowance).

From blue and green fabric, cut varying strips, all 7cm wide, which can be joined together randomly to give two Braces, each 7cm x 56cm (includes 1cm seam allowance).

From polka dot fabric, cut two Hats and two 8.5cm x 12cm rectangles for Patch (includes 1cm seam allowance).

From coloured scraps, cut two 8.5cm x 12cm rectangles for Patch

lining, five 5cm x 16cm strips for bows, two 16cm–diameter circles for watch, two 13cm–diameter circles for watch face, four 11cm x 4cm strips for

watch hands and one 3.5cm x 12cm strip for watch handle (includes 1cm seam allowance).

SEWING

With right sides facing, join short edge of a Sock piece to top edge of a Shoe piece. With right sides facing, join completed pieces to each other to form leg and shoe, leaving top edge open. Turn right side out and stuff. Baste raw edges together.

With right sides facing, join Hand pieces together, leaving wrist edges open. Turn right side out, stuff and baste raw edges together.

To make laced patch, join polka dot rectangles to lining rectangles, right sides together, leaving one long edge open. Turn right side out and insert a row of four eyelets down each finished edge. Fold in raw edges, pin patches to trouser front so eyelet edges align, then top-sew in position along folded edges. Thread shoelace through eyelets and tie in a bow.

With right sides together, join Sleeves to Shirts, then join Pants to lower edge of Shirts.

Baste hands and legs to front Sleeve ends and Pants legs respectively (note left and right!), right sides facing and raw edges even. With right sides together, join front to back, securing hands and legs at same time and leaving 20cm open at centre neck edge, and 22cm open down one side for pocket (see diagram).

With right sides facing, join Inner Pocket rectangles together, leaving pocket opening and neck edge opening unstitched. With right sides together, stitch Inner Pocket to clown body at back and front pocket edges. Push Inner Pocket bag inside clown body, wrong sides together, and baste around raw neck edges. Fold seam allowance on neck edges to inside and run a gathering thread around edge, close to fold.

On right side of one Head piece, work clown's face as follows: Glue or sew black buttons into place as eyes. At top and bottom and each side of eye, work a 4mm stitch in black embroidery thread, to give impression of a cross. For nose, cut two 6cm circles from a scrap of red fabric. With right sides together, stitch around circumference, allowing 5mm seam allowance. Carefully make a slit across centre of one circle, turn right side out and stuff. Glue or stitch nose onto

face, slit side down. For mouth, cut a 2.5cm x 12cm strip of red fabric. Fold in 5mm on all raw edges, fold in half lengthwise and hand-sew folded edges together. With white acrylic, paint a large white mouth on the face, then glue or stitch red strip along the centre of it.

With right sides facing, join Heads, leaving neck edge open. Turn right side out and stuff. Carefully stitch opening closed.

Insert head into neck opening, draw up gathering threads and stitch head firmly to body.

With right sides together, join Ruff to lining along one long edge, then join short ends to form circle. Fold ruff in half lengthwise, fold in seam allowance on raw edges and run a gathering thread along this folded edge. Place ruff around neck and draw up gathers to fit, having short seam at centre back. Fasten gathering thread securely, and glue or stitch ruff in place.

To make hair, cut a piece of cardboard, 13cm x 4cm. Wind wool lengthwise around cardboard about 50 times and fasten off by running a piece of wool under all layers and tying securely. Snip ends of wool at one end of cardboard. Repeat for second hank of hair, then secure hanks to head with firm stitching.

Make a loop for the hat by cutting a 7cm x 2.5cm strip of fabric. Fold in raw edges on long sides and stitch together. With right sides facing, stitch loop to top of one Hat piece, raw edges even. With right sides together, stitch Hat pieces, leaving head edge open and securing loop at same time. Turn right side out. Fold in raw edges and hand-sew hat to head.

Shade cheeks with a little red pencil.

With right sides facing, join Braces pieces together, leaving one short end open. Turn right side out, fold in raw edges and stitch opening closed. Work buttonholes in both ends of each brace and sew buttons onto clown's trousers, front and back (about 6cm in from each edge), which braces can be buttoned onto. Cut a piece of purchased tape measure to fit along inside of one brace and glue in place. Cut remaining tape to fit from clown's

brace button to shoulder and glue in place. Do this accurately, so that when brace with tape is buttoned below body tape, the two meet exactly.

Stitch a press stud to each shoulder and brace to stop braces slipping off shoulders.

For bows to decorate shirt and shoes, fold rectangles in half lengthwise, wrong sides together, and stitch, leaving one short end open. Turn right side out, fold in raw edges and stitch opening closed. Tie each strip in a knot in the centre and stitch in place.

Make watch as follows: Fold handle strip in half lengthwise, right sides together, and stitch long side and one short end. Turn right side out and stuff lightly. Turn in raw ends and stitch opening closed.

With rights sides facing, baste ends of handle to top of one large watch circle. With right sides facing, join large circles together, catching in handle at same time. Carefully make two intersecting slits in one side of circle and turn right side out. Insert polyester filling through slit and move it to edge of circle so that edge of clock is slightly puffed. Keep filling in place by running a line of running stitches around circle, about 2cm from edge. Prepare circles for watch face in same way as watch, but do not stuff. Place watch face onto watch back, slit sides together, and glue or hand-sew in place. Sew a button at centre of watch face. Cut tiny circles from cardboard and glue to flat-faced buttons. Number them from one to twelve and glue in place. With right sides together, join strips for watch hands, making one slightly shorter than the other. Turn right sides out, turn in raw ends and close openings. Work a buttonhole in each end of each strip, to correspond to button at centre of watch face and number buttons. Button hands in place.

Clown Activity Book

MEASUREMENTS
Finished book measures 26cm x 23cm.

MATERIALS
- 25cm x 50cm grey fabric
- 25cm x 50cm purple fabric
- 25cm x 30cm calico

The cloth activity book is full of fascinating things to do — buttoning, zipping, tying, counting and learning all about colours. The antics of its collection of crazy clowns will keep a small child absorbed for hours.

- 25cm x 50cm yellow fabric
- 25cm square each green, blue, light brown and striped fabric
- 10cm x 60cm red and white striped fabric, for bow
- Fabric scraps in assorted colours (including red), for appliqué
- 30cm x 90cm Vilene (for appliqué)
- Four 14mm black buttons
- Small amount black embroidery thread
- Polyester filling
- No 1 paintbrush
- White acrylic paint
- Craft glue
- Fabric paints in blue, dark blue, yellow, red, green, purple and brown
- Four 7mm black buttons
- Red pencil
- One 20mm yellow button
- Six 17mm red buttons
- Six Size 2 snap fasteners
- Approximately 1.5m x 0.5cm-wide red-brown ribbon
- 25cm length of fine cord

- Scraps of felt in blue, green, purple, pink and red (or as desired)
- 15cm x 2mm ribbon in each of blue, green, purple, pink and red (or to match chosen felt colours)
- 20cm x 2.5cm-wide Velcro
- 15cm purple zip
- One 20mm yellow button

PATTERN PIECES

Pattern pieces for circles, triangles or rectangles are not given. All other pattern pieces are printed on pages 112 and 113. Trace Hat, Medium Clown Hair, Collar, Box Lid, Box Side, Small Clown A, Small Clown B, Small Clown C, Small Clown Hair, Small Clown Head, Horse Head, Horse Body, Saddle and Horse Legs.

CUTTING

NOTE: Before cutting pieces to be used for appliqué, apply Vilene to wrong side of fabric. Remember to add a small seam allowance to all pieces, unless otherwise specified. Where a measurement is given, instead of a pattern piece, it includes 0.5cm seam allowance, unless otherwise specified.

From grey fabric, cut two 25cm squares (includes 1cm seam allowance).

From purple fabric, cut two 25cm squares (includes 1cm seam allowance).

From calico, cut two 12cm-diameter circles for faces. Cut the following pieces without adding seam allowance: two 6.5cm-diameter circles for faces, four Small Clown Hairs, one Small Clown Head, four Small Clowns A, two Small Clowns B and one Small Clown C.

From yellow fabric, cut one 25cm square and eight 23cm x 4cm rectangles for book binding (measurements include 1cm seam allowances).

From striped fabric, cut sixteen 3cm x 25cm strips for borders.

From fabric scraps, cut four Collars, four Medium Clown Hairs, one Hat, one 8.5cm x 2.5cm strip for hat brim, four 4cm-diameter red circles and four 3cm-diameter red circles for noses, two 10cm x 2cm red strips and two 5cm x 1cm red strips for mouths, two 4.5cm and on 8cm equilateral triangles for hats, one 11cm square for box, one Box Side, three Box Lids, two 8cm x 5cm rectangles for box catch, two 15cm x 4cm rectangles for ruffs, one Horse Body, one Horse Head, two Horse Legs, three 12cm x 2cm strips for horse's tail, one 5cm x 2cm strip for mane, one Saddle and one 6cm-diameter circle for ball.

From felt scraps, cut two 3cm-

diameter circles in each of five colours for balloons, and four 5.5cm-diameter circles for balls.

SEWING

The instructions for sewing will work through the book, page by page.

FRONT COVER

For striped frame around cover, fold each corner of eight striped rectangles in at 45 degrees, then cut off corners along fold lines. With right sides facing, sew four of these pieces together along angled edges, to form a mitred 'frame'. Repeat for other four pieces. Press under 0.5cm on the inside edges (only) of each frame and top-stitch this folded edge in place on the grey and purple 25cm squares. With right sides facing, stitch a yellow binding rectangle to the frame on the lefthand side edge of the grey page and the righthand side edge of the purple page.

Assemble materials for clown face appliqué. You will need one 12cm-diameter circle, four Collars, two Medium Hair pieces, one Hat, one hat brim, two 4cm-diameter red circles and one 10cm x 2cm red strip.

Folding under raw edges, appliqué

pieces in position on grey page, starting with the four Collar pieces, then proceeding to face, hair, hat and hat brim. Sew two 14mm black buttons in place for eyes and, with black embroidery thread, make a straight stitch at top and bottom and each side of each eye, to give the impression of a cross.

To make a nose, stitch red circles together, right sides facing. Carefully make a slit across one circle and turn right side out. Stuff with a little polyester filling and glue or stitch nose onto face, slit side down.

Fold in 0.5cm on all edges of red strip and slip-stitch folded edges together. With white acrylic paint, draw a wide clown mouth on face and glue or stitch red strip along the centre of it.

With right sides facing, place grey and purple pages together and stitch around outer edges, leaving the long edges of the yellow binding strips unstitched. Turn page right side out and press. Press under 0.5cm seam allowance on raw edges of yellow binding and glue folded edges together.

BLUE AND GREEN PAGES

With right sides facing, stitch a yellow binding strip to one edge of both the blue and green 25cm squares.

For appliqué on the blue page, you will need three Box Lids, one Box Side, one 11cm square box front, two box catch rectangles, one ruff, one 6.5cm-diameter calico circle, two Small Hair pieces, one small triangle hat, two 3cm-diameter red circles and one 5cm x 1cm red strip.

With right sides facing, stitch two Lid sections together, leaving lower edge open. Turn right side out and press. Press under seam allowance on remaining box pieces and appliqué in position, starting with lid, then proceeding to inner lid piece (covering raw edges of lid), then side and front of box. With right sides facing, stitch around edges of box catch rectangles, leaving a short edge open. Turn right side out, press and work a buttonhole in finished short edge. Glue raw edges to inside of box lid.

Paint wrong side of calico face with white acrylic paint. This will stabilise the fabric and prevent it fraying. Glue face in position on inner lid, covering raw edges of catch. Paint hair with fabric paint and glue in position when dry. Turn under raw edges of triangle hat and glue in place. Decorate face in the same way as face on Front Cover, using two 7mm buttons for eyes. Shade cheeks with a little red pencil. Press under allowance on all edges of ruff piece and stitch. Gather one long edge and pull up gathers to fit beneath clown face. Secure gathering thread tightly, then glue ruff in place.

Sew yellow button in place on box front to correspond with catch.

For appliqué on green page, you will need one 12cm-diameter circle, two Medium Hair pieces, one 8cm triangle, two 4cm-diameter red circles, one 10cm x 2cm red strip and striped bow fabric.

For green page, assemble appliqué clown face, as for Front Cover. Decorate hat with fabric paint, if desired. To make bow, fold striped rectangle in half lengthwise, right sides together, and stitch edges, leaving one short end open. Turn right side out, press, fold in raw edges and stitch opening closed. Stitch centre of strip in position under clown's chin and tie ends in a bow.

Assemble page, following instructions for Front Cover.

YELLOW AND BROWN PAGES

With right sides facing, stitch a yellow binding strip to one edge of both yellow and brown 25cm squares.

Assemble pieces for yellow page. You will need Small Clown C, Small Clown Head, Horse Head, Horse Body, Saddle, Horse Legs, mane, ten felt circles and three tail strips.

Snip 1cm into main rectangle at 0.5cm intervals and paint with brown fabric paint. Fold under allowance on Horse's Head and baste mane in position along neck.

Fold under raw edges of remaining appliqué pieces and stitch in place, starting with Horse Legs at bottom of page, then proceeding with body, head and saddle. Paint horse's face and reins with fabric paint, using photograph as a guide.

Paint wrong side of Clown Body and Head with white acrylic paint to stabilise. Paint front of Body and Face with fabric paints, as desired, or use photograph as a guide.

Embroider small black crosses on face for eyes.

Stitch felt circles together around outside edges, leaving a small opening for filling. Fill lightly with polyester filling and stitch opening closed, catching in a 15cm length of 2mm ribbon at the same time. On the back of each felt balloon, sew on one part of a snap fastener.

Glue Clown Body and Head in place on page above horse, sandwiching ends of ribbons under clown's hand.

Paint small circles on page, to match balloon colours, and stitch corresponding parts of snap fasteners to circles, so child can match each balloon to a colour.

Fold in raw edges of tail strips and slip-stitch folded edges together. Form a plait from the three finished strips and tie at one end with a scrap of ribbon or a fabric bow. Stitch other ends together, attach a snap fastener and sew corresponding part of fastener to horse's rump, so tail can be snapped on and off.

Assemble materials for brown page. You will need Small Clowns A and B, four 5.5cm-diameter felt circles and one 6cm-diameter circle.

Cut red-brown ribbon into 30cm lengths.

With wrong sides facing, blanket-stitch matching clown sections together around outer edges, catching in a piece of ribbon at top of head and leaving a small opening for filling. Stuff lightly with polyester filling and stitch opening closed. Embroider small black crosses for eyes, then paint clowns with fabric paint, as desired. Paint backs as well, but omit fine detail. Paint will stop edges fraying.

Blanket-stitch felt circles together around outer edges, leaving small opening for filling. Stuff lightly and stitch opening closed, catching in a piece of ribbon at the same time. Decorate balls with fabric paint, if desired.

Glue a small patch of Velcro on back of each clown and ball.

Glue length of cord across page, about 4cm from lower edge. Turn under edges of fabric circle and top-stitch in place above cord. Paint ball as desired.

Trace numbers from pages 112 and 113 and cut out in Velcro. Stitch Velcro numbers to various positions on page. Paint numbers on fronts of clowns and balls (trace them from pages 112 and 113, if desired).

With right sides facing, assemble yellow/brown page as for Front Cover, catching ends of brown-red ribbon into top edge of yellow binding.

BACK COVER

Cut purple 25cm square in half and join with a zip, decorating zip tag with a small bow, if desired.

Make 'frame' for inside and outside back cover, following instructions for Front Cover.

Appliqué outside back cover with a clown's head, following instructions for clown on blue page.

Join purple and grey pages as for Front Cover.

To assemble book, place all pages in order and glue, or sew, yellow binding strips firmly together. Sew red buttons along 'spine' of book at intervals on front and back.

**PATTERN PIECES FOR CLOWN PYJAMA
CASE AND ACTIVITY BOOK**

1

SMALL CLOWN
HAIR

SMALL CLOWN HEAD

SMALL CLOWN C

2

SMALL CLOWN A

CLOWN SHOE

3

HORSE HEAD

SMALL CLOWN B

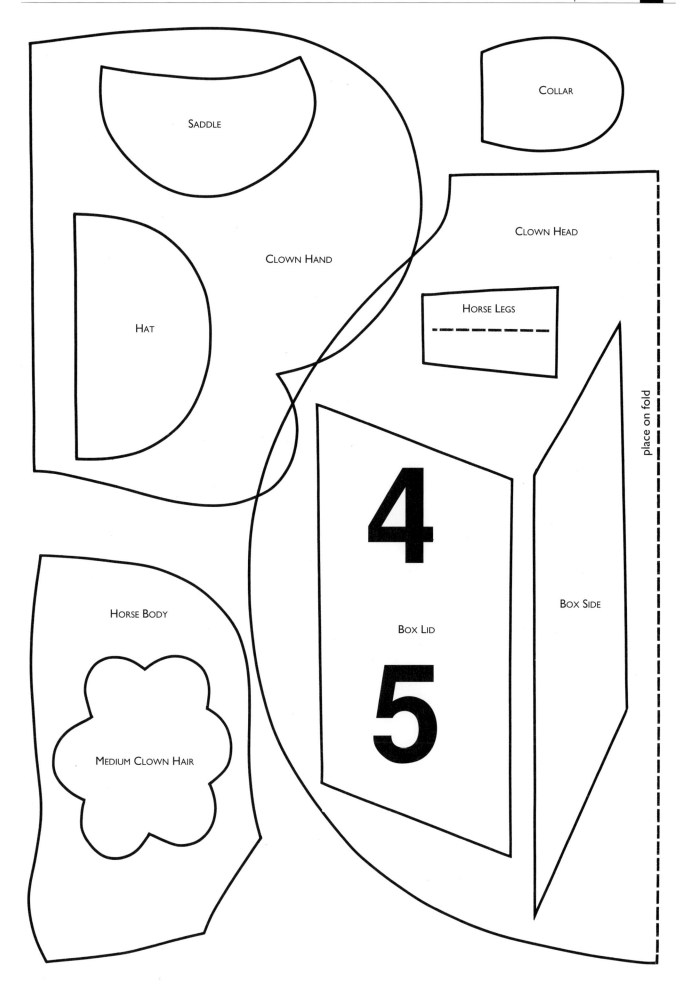

SADDLE

COLLAR

CLOWN HAND

CLOWN HEAD

HAT

HORSE LEGS

place on fold

4

5

HORSE BODY

BOX SIDE

BOX LID

MEDIUM CLOWN HAIR

BUSH BABIES

Australia's most dearly loved marsupial now comes in a variety of cuddly styles — sewn, knitted or crocheted. Designed by Maria Ragan, each koala is accompanied by a winsome youngster, a detail that's sure to delight small human owners.

Fur Fabric Koala and Baby

MEASUREMENTS

Finished mother koala measures about 30cm high, when sitting. Baby is about 12cm high.

MATERIALS

- 40cm x 90cm grey fur fabric
- 30cm square white Sherpa fabric
- 15cm x 10cm grey felt
- Thin plastic, such as icecream container
- One pair 21mm-diameter safety eyes
- One pair 10mm-diameter safety eyes
- One 5cm safety koala nose
- One 2cm safety koala nose
- Polyester filling
- Large needle
- Strong sewing thread
- Four flat buttons with shank and eyelet
- Four safety pins
- 2.5cm Velcro

Choose your favourite method of construction for this very cute trio. Each will provide its owner with a favourite bedtime friend.

PATTERN PIECES

All pattern pieces, except rectangles, are printed on pages 117 to 120. Trace Head, Head Gusset, Ear, Body Front, Body Back, Stomach, Arm/Paw, Leg, Sole, Baby Head, Baby Gusset, Baby Ear, Baby Body Back, Baby Body Front and Baby Stomach.

CUTTING

NOTE: Remember to add seam allowance to all pieces before cutting — 1cm for mother koala and 0.5cm for baby.

From grey fur fabric, cut two Heads, one Head Gusset, two Ears, two Body Fronts, two Body Backs, two whole Arm pieces and two Arm pieces with Paw section removed (remember seam allowance), four Legs, two Baby Heads, one Baby Gusset, two Baby Ears, two Baby Body Backs, two Baby Body Fronts, two 4cm x 2.5cm rectangles for Legs and two 4cm x 3cm rectangles for Arms (measurements include seam allowance).

From white Sherpa fabric, cut two Stomachs, two Ears, two Baby Stomachs and two Baby Ears.

From grey felt, cut two Soles and two Paws.

From plastic, cut two 6cm circles and two 5cm circles, to reinforce limb joints.

SEWING

With right sides together, join Head Gusset to Head pieces, from A to B. Join chin seam, from B to C. Turn head right side out.

Trim pile a little on Stomach pieces. With right sides together, join Stomachs to Body Fronts, then, with

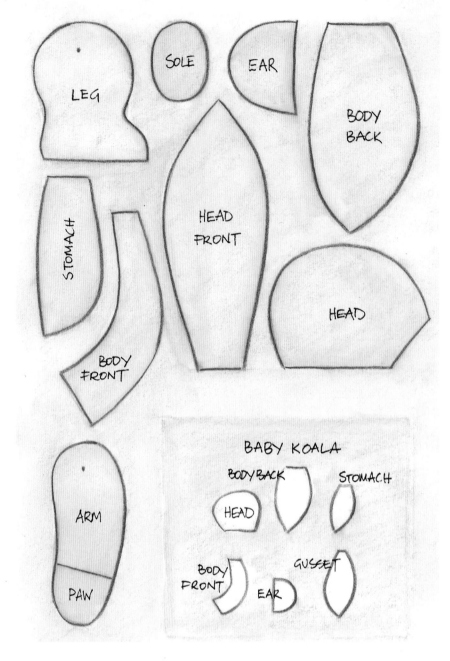

right sides facing, stitch Stomachs together down centre front.

With right sides together, join Body Backs at centre back seam, leaving an opening in the middle for turning.

Place back and front together, right sides facing and stitch side seams, leaving neck edge open.

With right sides together, stitch head to body around neck edge. Turn right side out through back opening.

Using dot on pattern piece as a guide, mark position of eyes. Attach safety eyes in position and stuff head lightly with polyester filling — not too full, just enough to give a sense of the head shape, so that you can attach nose in correct position at point A. When nose is attached, finish filling head.

To further contour face, thread a large needle with strong grey sewing thread and, keeping stitches hidden behind eyes, pull a thread across from eye to eye and from each eye down to the neckline, to create an eye 'socket'. End thread securely and bury threads in head.

To create a contoured mouth, pull

a strong thread from behind nose, through head, down to a point halfway between A and C. Take a stitch across seamline at this point and pull thread back up to behind nose, pulling enough to create a pucker below nose. Tie off threads securely and bury ends in head.

With right sides together, join Ear pieces in pairs (one grey, one white), leaving straight edge open. Turn ears right side out, fold in raw edges and slip-stitch closed. Position ears on head and stitch securely in place.

Stuff koala body firmly and stitch back opening closed.

With right sides facing, stitch Leg section together in pairs, leaving foot end open, as well as a small opening in back seam of each leg.

With right sides together, stitch a felt Sole to each leg, matching centre front and back. Turn leg right side out and put aside.

With right sides together, stitch Paws to shortened Arm sections. Stitch Arms together in pairs, leaving

a small opening in underside seam. Turn arms right side out.

With nail or hot skewer, make a hole in centre of each plastic disc. Push shank and eyelet of flat button through each disc and insert a disc and button into upper section of each arm and leg (larger discs are for legs), pushing shank and eyelet through fabric to outside in spot marked on pattern. Use a safety pin through each eyelet to prevent buttons falling back through the holes.

Stuff arms and legs and close openings. To attach legs, with large needle and strong thread, used double, insert needle into body at leg joint symbol, shown on Body Front pattern piece. Push needle across body and out at opposite point. Take needle through eyelet then back into body at same point, across body and out again, then through second eyelet. Pull thread ends until limbs feel firmly attached, then knot ends several times and bury threads inside body. Attach arms in same way.

Stitch a small square of Velcro to inside of one paw and outside of the other, so that paws can be joined to hold Baby.

BABY

Construct head and body of Baby in the same way as Mother, above.

For Arms and Legs, fold each rectangle in half crosswise, right sides together and stitch with a narrow seam, leaving ends open. Run a gathering thread around one open edge, pull up tightly and secure ends. Turn limbs right side out and fill with polyester filling. Turn in raw edges and slip-stitch limbs to body.

PATTERN PIECES FOR BABY KOALA

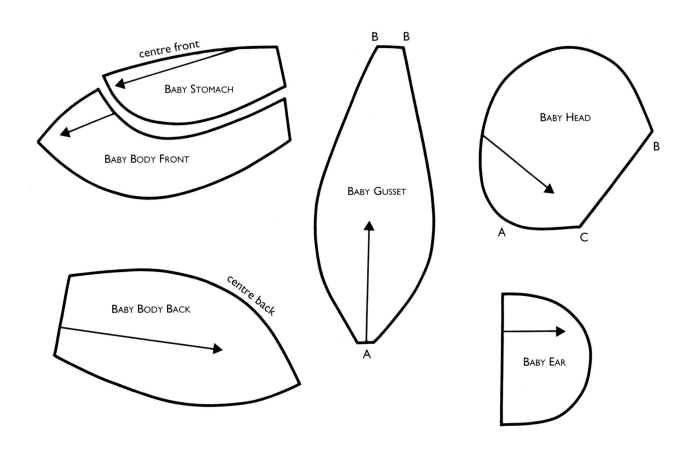

PATTERN PIECES FOR MOTHER KOALA

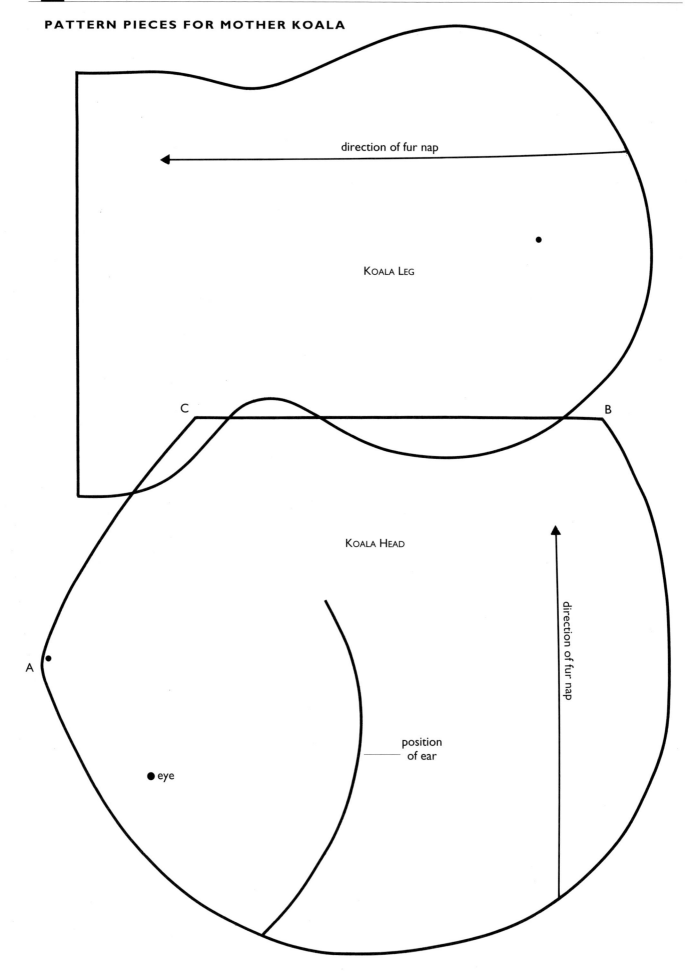

direction of fur nap

KOALA LEG

C

B

KOALA HEAD

A

direction of fur nap

position of ear

● eye

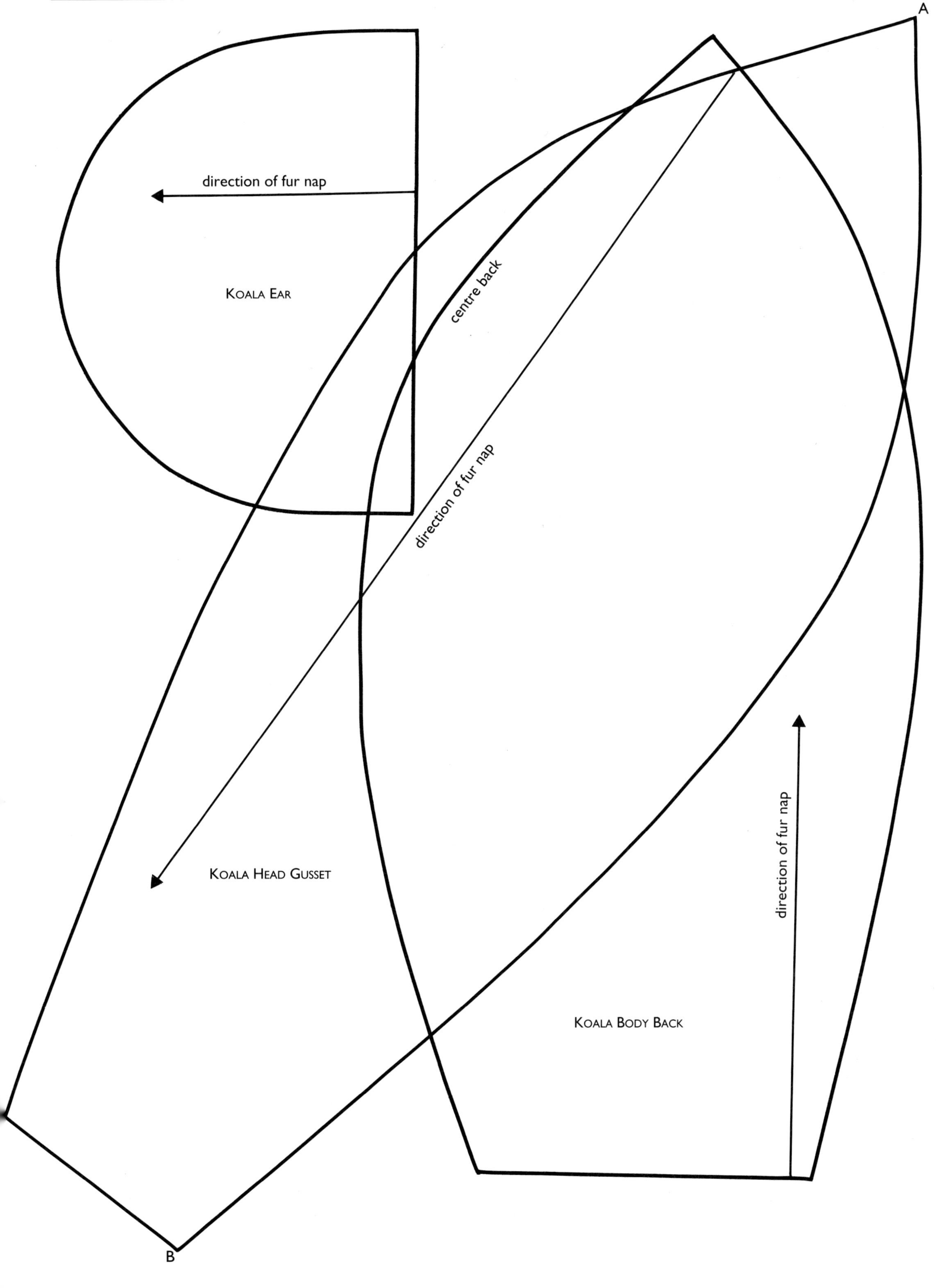

A

direction of fur nap

KOALA EAR

centre back

direction of fur nap

KOALA HEAD GUSSET

direction of fur nap

KOALA BODY BACK

B

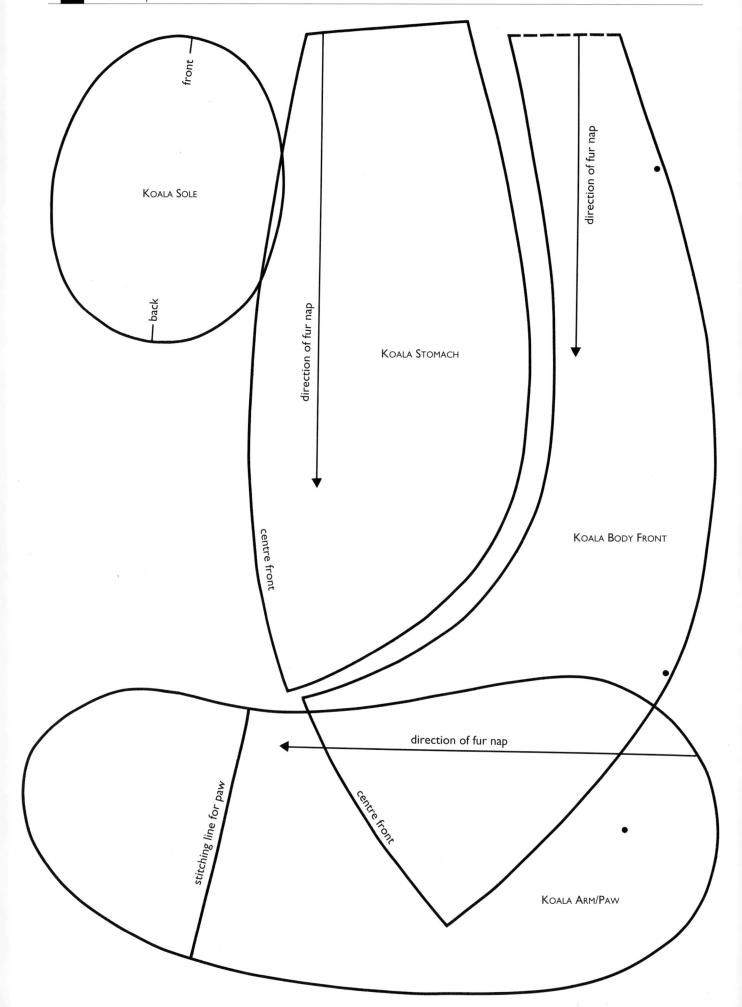

KOALA SOLE

front

back

KOALA STOMACH

direction of fur nap

centre front

direction of fur nap

KOALA BODY FRONT

direction of fur nap

stitching line for paw

centre front

KOALA ARM/PAW

Crocheted Koala and Baby

MEASUREMENTS
Finished mother koala measures about 30cm high, when sitting. Baby is about 12cm high.

MATERIALS
Panda Angoretta 8-ply (50g):
- 6 balls grey (MC)
- 1 ball white (CC)
- One 3mm crochet hook
- 25cm x 10cm white Sherpa fabric
- 15cm x 10cm grey felt
- Thin plastic, such as icecream container
- One pair 21mm-diameter safety eyes
- One pair 10mm-diameter safety eyes
- One 5cm safety koala nose
- One 2cm safety koala nose
- Polyester filling
- Large needle
- Strong sewing thread
- Four flat buttons with shank and eyelet on underside
- Four safety pins
- 2.5cm Velcro

TENSION
See Crochet Notes on page 201. 10 sts and 10 rows to 4.5cm over double crochet.

PATTERN PIECES
The pattern pieces for any parts not crocheted are printed on pages 117, 119 and 120. Trace Ear, Paw, Sole and Baby Ear.

CUTTING
NOTE: Remember to add seam allowance to all pieces before cutting — 1cm for large koala, 0.5cm for baby.

From Sherpa fabric cut two Ears and two Baby Ears.

From grey felt, cut two Paws (without seam allowance) and two Soles.

From thin plastic, cut two 6cm-diameter circles and two 5cm-diameter circles, to reinforce limb joints.

METHOD — MOTHER
All body pieces are worked in double crochet fabric, from graphs on pages 122 and 123, working increase and decrease as indicated. For Mother Koala work Left and Right Back, Left and Right Front, Left and Right Head, one Head Gusset, four Arms, four Legs and two Ears.

To make up, follow instructions for Fur Fabric Koala, on pages 116 to 117. The only difference is that Paw is simply oversewn in position on Arm, rather than being attached to a shortened arm.

METHOD — BABY
Body pieces are worked in double crochet, with the same tension as Large Koala, working increases and decreases from graphs on page 123.

Make up and shape head in similar manner to fur fabric koala. Before making up ears, trim fur fabric to a shorter pile.

LEGS (MAKE 2)
Using 3mm hook and MC, make 3ch and join to form a ring.
RND 1 Work 6dc into ring.
RND 2 Work 2dc in each dc of previous rnd ... 12 dc.
Cont in dc in these 12dc, working 5 rnds.
Fasten off. Break off yarn, leaving end for joining.

ARMS (MAKE 2)
Work as for Legs, but working 7 rnds dc instead of 5 rnds.
Place small amount of filling in each Arm and Leg, close openings and attach to body.

GRAPHS FOR CROCHETED MOTHER KOALA

ARM
Make 9ch, 1dc in 2nd ch, 1dc in each ch to end (8dc). Make four, reversing shaping for two sections.

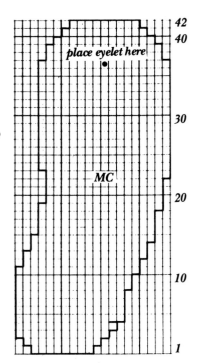

place eyelet here

MC

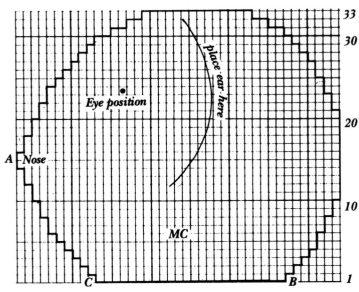

place ear here

Eye position

A — Nose

MC

C   B

LEFT SIDE HEAD
Make 25ch, 1dc in 2nd ch, 1dc in each ch to end (24dc).

RIGHT SIDE HEAD
Work as Left Side Head, reversing shaping.

RIGHT FRONT
Make 4ch, 1dc in 2nd ch, 1dc in each ch to end (3dc).

LEFT FRONT
Work as Right Front, reversing shaping.

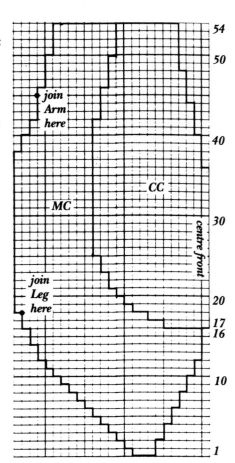

join Arm here

CC

MC

centre front

join Leg here

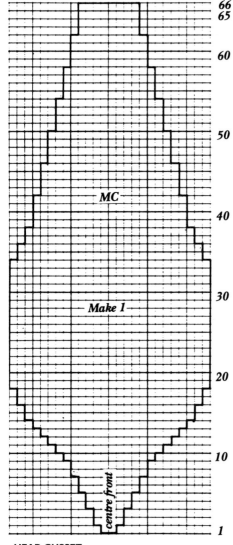

MC

Make 1

centre front

HEAD GUSSET
Make 3 ch, 1dc in 2nd ch, 1dc in next ch (2dc).

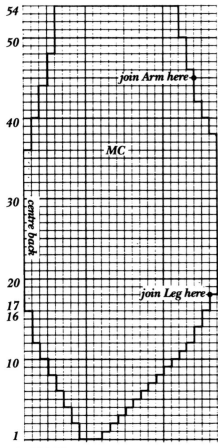

RIGHT BACK

Make 4ch, 1dc in 2nd ch, 1dc in each ch to end (3dc).

LEFT BACK

Work as Right Back, reversing shaping.

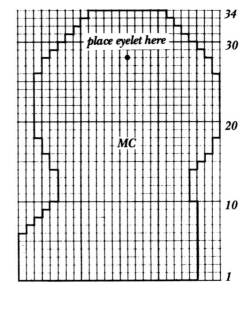

LEG

Make 24 ch, 1dc in 2nd ch, 1dc in each ch to end (23dc). Make four, reversing shaping on two sections.

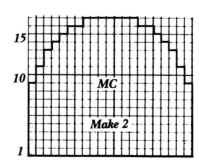

EAR

Make 22ch, 1dc in 2nd ch, 1dc in each ch to end (21dc).

GRAPHS FOR CROCHETED BABY KOALA

EAR

Make 9 ch, 1dc in 2nd ch, 1dc in each ch to end (8dc). Make 2.

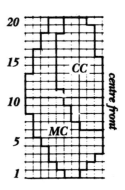

RIGHT BACK

Make 3ch, 1dc in 2nd ch, 1dc in next ch (2dc).

LEFT BACK

Work as Right Back, reversing shaping.

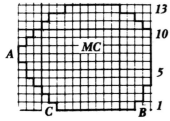

LEFT SIDE HEAD

Make 11ch, 1dc in 2nd ch, 1dc in each ch to end (10dc).

RIGHT SIDE HEAD

Work as Left Side Head, reversing shaping.

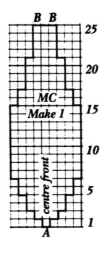

HEAD GUSSET

Make 2ch, 1dc in 2nd ch (1dc).

RIGHT FRONT

Make 3ch, 1dc in 2nd ch, 1dc in next ch (2dc).

LEFT FRONT

Work as Right Front, reversing shaping.

Knitted Koala and Baby

MEASUREMENTS
Finished Mother Koala measures about 30cm high, when sitting. Baby is about 12cm high.

MATERIALS
Panda Angoretta 8-ply (50g):
- 5 balls grey (MC)
- 1 ball white (CC)
- One pair 3mm knitting needles
- 25cm x 10cm white Sherpa fabric
- 15cm x 10cm grey felt
- Thin plastic, such as icecream container
- One pair 21mm-diameter safety eyes
- One pair 10mm-diameter safety eyes
- One 5cm safety koala nose
- One 2cm safety koala nose
- Polyester filling
- Large needle
- Strong sewing thread
- Four flat buttons with shank and eyelet on underside
- Four safety pins
- 2.5cm Velcro

TENSION
See Knitting Notes on page 158.
10 sts to 4.5cm and 10 rows to 3cm over reverse stocking st.

PATTERN PIECES
The pattern pieces for any parts not knitted are printed on pages 117, 119 and 120. Trace Ear, Paw, Sole and Baby Ear.

CUTTING
NOTE: Remember to add seam allowance to all pieces before cutting — 1cm for mother koala, 0.5cm for baby.

From Sherpa fabric cut two Ears and two Baby Ears.

From grey felt, cut two Paws (without seam allowance) and two Soles.

From thin plastic, cut two 6cm-diameter circles and two 5cm-diameter circles, to reinforce limb joints.

METHOD — MOTHER
All body pieces are worked in reverse stocking stitch fabric (ie, right side purl, wrong side knit), from graphs on pages 125 to 127, working the increase and decrease as indicated. For Mother Koala work Left and Right Back, Left and Right Front, Left and Right Head, one Head Gusset, four Arms, four Legs and two Ears.

To make up, follow instructions for Fur Fabric Koala, on page116 to 117. The only difference is that the Paw is simply oversewn in position on the Arm, rather than being attached to a shortened arm.

METHOD — BABY
Body pieces are worked in reverse stocking stitch, with the same tension as Large Koala, working increases and decreases from graphs on this page.

Make up and shape head in similar manner to fur fabric koala. Before making up ears, trim fur fabric to a shorter pile.

LEGS (MAKE 2)
Using 3mm needles and MC, cast on 12 sts.
Beg with a P row, work 10 rows reverse st st. Cast off, leaving end for joining.

ARMS (MAKE 2)
Work as for Legs, but work 12 rows reverse st st instead of 10.
Thread end through cast off sts and draw up firmly to form ring. Join sides, leaving end open. Fill with small amount of filling, close opening and attach to body.

GRAPHS FOR KNITTED BABY KOALA

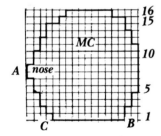

LEFT SIDE HEAD
Cast on 11 sts, purl to end (right side).
Purl all sts on right-side rows, reading graph from right to left, and knit all sts on wrong-side rows, reading graph from left to right.

RIGHT SIDE HEAD
Work as Left Side Head, reversing shaping.

EAR
Cast on 2 sts, purl to end (right side). Purl all sts on right-side rows, reading graph from right to left, and knit all sts on wrong-side rows, reading graph from left to right.

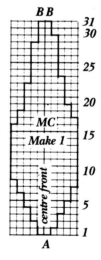

GUSSET
Cast on 10 sts, purl to end (right side). Purl all sts on right-side rows, reading graph from right to left, and knit all sts on wrong-side rows, reading graph from left to right.

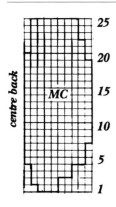

RIGHT BACK

Cast on 3 sts, purl to end (right side). Purl all sts on right-side rows, reading graph from right to left, and knit all sts on wrong-side rows, reading graph from left to right.

LEFT BACK

Work as Right Back, reversing shaping.

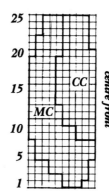

RIGHT FRONT

Cast on 3 sts, purl to end (right side). Purl all sts on right-side rows, reading graph from right to left, and knit all sts on wrong-side rows, reading graph from left to right.

LEFT FRONT

Work as Right Front, reversing shaping.

GRAPHS FOR KNITTED MOTHER KOALA

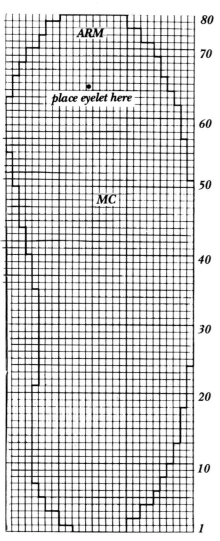

ARM

Cast on 8 sts, purl to end (right side). Purl all sts on right-side rows, reading graph from right to left, and knit all sts on wrong-side rows, reading graph from left to right. Make four, reversing shaping for two sections.

LEFT SIDE HEAD

Cast on 35 sts, purl to end (right side). Purl all sts on right-side rows, reading graph from right to left, and knit all sts on wrong-side rows, reading graph from left to right.

RIGHT SIDE HEAD

Work as Left Side Head, reversing shaping.

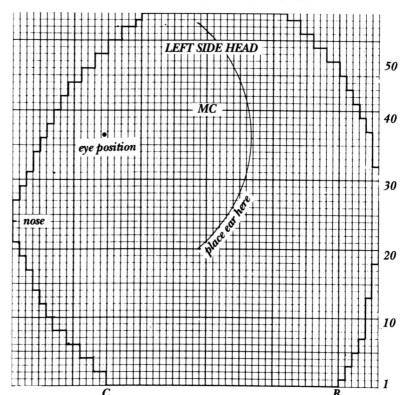

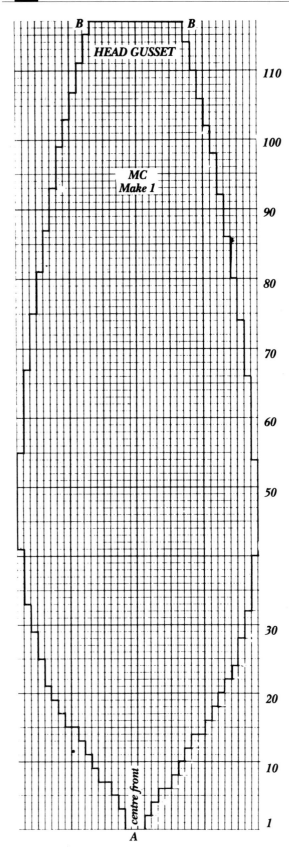

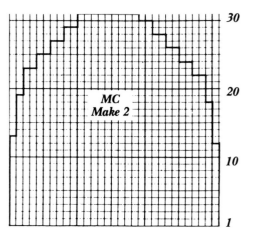

EAR

Cast on 31 sts, purl to end (right side). Purl all sts on right-side rows, reading graph from right to left, and knit all sts on wrong-side rows, reading graph from left to right.

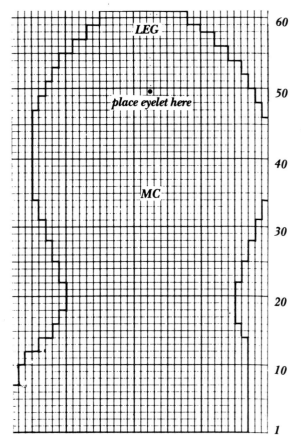

HEAD GUSSET

Cast on 3 sts, purl to end (right side). Purl all sts on right-side rows, reading graph from right to left, and knit all sts on wrong-side rows, reading graph from left to right.

LEG

Cast on 35 sts, purl to end (right side). Purl all sts on right-side rows, reading graph from right to left, and knit all sts on wrong-side rows, reading graph from left to right. Make four, reversing shaping for two sections.

RIGHT FRONT

Cast on 3 sts, purl to end (right side).
Purl all sts on right-side rows, reading
graph from right to left, and knit all
sts on wrong-side rows, reading graph
from right to left.

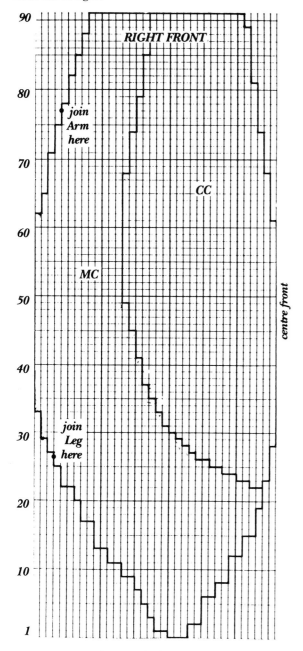

RIGHT BACK

Cast on 3 sts, purl to end (right side).
Purl all sts on right-side rows, reading
graph from right to left, and knit all
sts on wrong-side rows, reading graph
from left to right.

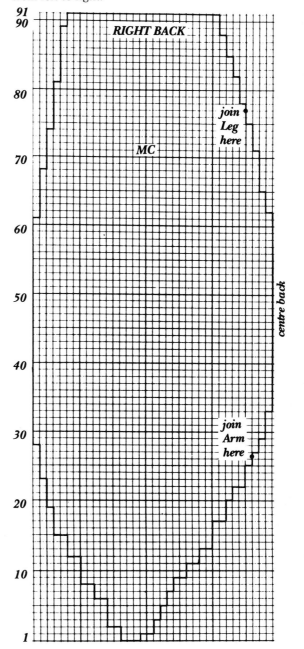

Patchwork

From possum rugs, patched together from skins by aboriginals, to the latest in clothing and decorating, patchwork and quilting has a long and colourful history in Australia. As well as the ever popular quilt, patchwork clothing, cushions, even a favourite teddy, take on new dimensions when they are made from pieced or appliquéd fabrics that are quilted.

Whether leftovers from favourite clothes, gifts from friends or newly-purchased fabrics, the scraps of fabric are a memory bank to be treasured.

The colours can be restricted to the restful harmony of many tones of one colour, or can be a riot of saturated colours, making the quilt sing exultantly. In fact, Australian quilts are renowned worldwide for their exciting use of colour and for unexpected combinations of fabric design.

The piece can be as abstract as a crazy-patch jacket or as organised as a repeat block quilt. The design possibilities are infinite.

DIANNE FINNEGAN

Appliqué and Quilting

QUILT QUICK-STEP

If you love the look of country patchwork, but ache at the thought of all that cutting and piecing, then here's a project for you! This lovely scrap patchwork picnic quilt and cushions can be made up quickly and easily, using a sewing machine, a rotary cutter — and some revolutionary sewing techniques. Designer Julia Curran's clever shortcuts produce spectacular results in next to no time. Beginners beware — painless patchwork ahead!

Above: The studio, every quiltmaker's dream.

Above right: Quiltmaker Julia Curran at work in her beautifully equipped studio.

Opposite page: The triangles in this charming quilt and cushions are not individually cut and painstakingly sewn together in the manner of traditional patchwork. They are, in fact, the result of diagonally sewing one square of fabric to another. Cutting takes place after the stitching is done.

Patchwork Picnic Quilt and Cushions

MEASUREMENTS

Finished quilt measures 118cm x 120cm, but this can be varied according to the size of the border you choose. Each finished block, for quilt or cushion, measures 44cm square.

MATERIALS

- Fabric (see Note)
- Sewing machine
- Size 70 machine needle
- Rotary cutter and cutting mat
- Perspex quilt rule (6″ x 24″) or large square
- Thread
- Pencil
- Pins

NOTE: As this is a co-ordinated scrap quilt, fabric required for each different patchwork block will be given individually. See Joining Blocks and Adding Borders and Finishing Quilt on page 133 for fabric amounts needed to complete your quilt.

BASIC DRAWING, STITCHING AND CUTTING TECHNIQUE

Using Quilt Block One as an example and starting point, count the number of squares. There are, actually, 16 squares, that is, 12 squares made up of 'two triangle' squares, and 4 uncut corner squares.

Understanding this concept will help you design you own block patterns using squares and triangles, as well as enabling you to following these directions.

QUILT BLOCK ONE
(three fabrics)
Cut and pair:
- Two 5½" (140mm) squares dark fabric with two 5½" (140mm) squares light fabric
- Two 5½" (140mm) squares dark fabric with two 5½" (140mm) squares medium fabric
- Two 5½" (140mm) squares medium fabric with two 5½" (140mm) squares light fabric

Cut:
- Four 5" (127mm) squares light fabric.

QUILT BLOCK TWO
(three fabrics)
Cut and pair:
- One 11" (280mm) square dark fabric with one 11" (280mm) square light fabric
- Two 5½" (140mm) squares medium fabric with two 5½" (140mm) squares of light fabric

Cut:
- Four 5" (127mm) squares medium fabric for corners.

QUILT BLOCK FOUR
(five fabrics)
Cut and pair:
- One 11" (280mm) square dark fabric with one 11" (280mm) square medium fabric
- Two 5½" (140mm) squares second medium fabric with two 5½" (140mm) squares light fabric

Cut:
- Four squares second light fabric.

QUILT BLOCK THREE
(three fabrics)
Cut and pair:
- One 11" (280mm) square dark fabric with one 11" (280mm) square light fabric
- One 11" (280mm) square medium fabric to one 11" (280mm) square light fabric.

STEP 1

STEP 2

Carefully draw a pencil line, diagonally, from one corner to the other, on backs of lighter fabric of each pair. Pin securely.

STEP FOUR
Sew two lines of stitching, one on either side of each diagonal, ¼" (6mm) away from diagonal pencil lines on all pairs . For most machines, outer edge of presser foot will skim along pencil line, automatically forming a 6mm seam from where needle penetrates

STEP 3

STEP ONE
Cut all pieces for Quilt Block One (see page 131), using a rotary cutter.

STEP TWO
Pair 11" (280mm) square of light fabric to 11" (280mm) square of dark fabric, carefully matching edges, with right sides together. With a pencil, on back of lighter side of pair, draw four long lines as follows: Two lines are drawn from corner to corner, making an X, and two lines intersect the X horizontally and vertically, forming a cross (note that picture shows a pairing of light and medium fabrics, rather that light and dark).

STEP THREE
The pair of 11" (280mm) squares should now be divided by lines into four 5½" (140mm) squares, and subsequently, eight triangles.

Pin pair securely and away from pencil lines.

Next, pair two 5½" (140mm) squares of medium fabric to two 5½" (140mm) squares of light fabric, right sides together and matching edges.

STEP 4

fabric, to line. Maintain a consistent seam allowance.

STEPS FIVE AND SIX
Rotary cut, carefully, all pencil lines on all three pairs . Open out the 'two triangle' squares and, from the back, press 6mm seam toward darker fabric.

STEP SEVEN
Lay the 16 pieces (including the four 5" (127mm) squares of light fabric) on

the table in the same placement as Quilt Block One.

EASY BLOCK ASSEMBLY
Look at the 16 unassembled pieces as being placed in four rows of four pieces running across, and four columns of four pieces running down.

STEP EIGHT
Sew column one to column two, using a technique called 'string sewing', that is, sewing from first pair to next pair below without snipping threads between them. Connecting threads hold your pieces together as you add them and are never cut except to add next column . After adding columns three and four in the same manner, flip top joined row, right sides together, onto joined row below and sew the horizontal seam. Sew remaining two horizontal seams. Press completed Quilt Block One.

Use the same Basic Drawing, Stitching and Cutting Techniques, as described above, to make 16 pieces for Quilt Block Two and

STEP 5

STEP 6

remaining Quilt and Cushion Blocks.

Following photographs of each block, lay out design, and use Easy Block Assembly method to complete.

JOINING BLOCKS AND ADDING BORDERS

- Block dividing strips: Cut two 3″ (76mm) strips by width of 100cm–115cm fabric. Cut each strip into two.
- Centre square: Cut one 3″ (76mm) square of fabric.
- Borders: Cut five x 5½″ (140mm) strips by width of 100cm–115cm fabric.

FINISHING QUILT

Sew blocks, dividing strips and centre square together. Cut any excess dividing strip back to quilt top. Add border strips (joined if necessary) and measure quilt top. Cut quilt backing and quilt wadding 6″ (153mm) longer and wider than quilt top. Safety-pin, baste or hand-baste (every 4″ or 102mm) three layers together, being sure to smooth as much fullness as

STEP 7

STEP 8

DIAGRAM 1

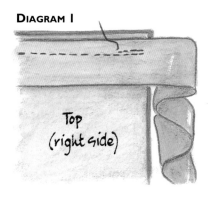

Top (right side)

DIAGRAM 2

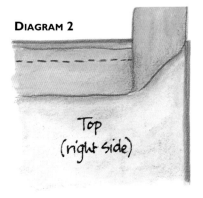

Top (right side)

DIAGRAM 3

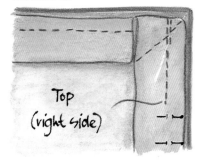

Top (right side)

possible to outer edges. Avoid basting pleats into backing by firstly smoothing and taping backing to your work surface.

Machine- or hand-quilt, as preferred. Hand-baste edges of quilt and neatly cut excess wadding and backing to edge of quilt top.

To bind quilt, cut five x 2½″-wide (64mm) strips on the straight of 110–115cm fabric. Join strips on bias-cut ends and press these seams open. Press long joined strips in half, wrong sides together.

Sew two raw edges of binding to top and through all three layers of quilt, using a generous 8mm seam (see Diagram 1). Stop stitching 8mm from corners and fold a mitre into corner with binding (Diagram 2). Begin

stitching again, from off edge of quilt onto quilt, after pivoting quilt a quarter turn (see Diagram 3). Repeat with remaining three corners.

Join binding on bias cut ends, remembering to add 6mm seam allowance to both ends.

Turn folded edge of binding to back and secure with an invisible hand-stitch. At back of each corner, fold mitre in opposite direction to front of corner, so that it will sit neatly.

POINTS FOR PERFECT PATCHWORK

- Patchworkers and quilters tend to use imperial measurements because most of the available tools are American. We have given the exact metric conversion in brackets after the imperial measurement.
- Select a satisfying mix of print sizes, ranging from large to small, to give your quilt visual texture.
- Good contrast between light, medium and dark fabrics will give your quilt visual depth.
- 100% cottons, manufactured specifically with patchwork in mind, will give best results.
- Pre-wash all fabrics separately in a mild pure soap or eucalyptus wool soap, using cold water. Spin and tumble dry fabrics to shrink them.
- Use cotton or cotton-wrapped sewing thread. Pure synthetic thread will saw at the seams.
- All seams are ¼″ (6mm), and allowance is already included in measurements.
- A propelling pencil with soft lead will give a consistent and easy to see line while sewing.
- All 'two triangle' squares began as 5½″ (140mm) paired squares.
- All one-piece squares are cut at 5″ (127mm).
- Care for your finished quilt by hand washing in cold water with a mild pure soap or eucalyptus wool wash.

CUSHION BLOCK ONE
(four fabrics)
Cut and pair:
- Two 5½″ (140mm) squares medium fabric with two 5½″ (140mm) squares second medium fabric
- Two 5½″ (140mm) squares medium fabric to two 5½″ (140mm) squares light fabric
- Two 5½″ (140mm) squares second medium fabric to two 5½″ (140mm) squares light fabric

Cut:
- Four 5″ (127mm) squares dark fabric.

CUSHION BLOCK TWO
(three fabrics)
Cut and pair:
- One 11″ (280mm) square medium fabric with one 11″(280mm) square light fabric
- One 5½″ (140mm) square medium fabric with one 5½″ (140mm) square light fabric

Cut:
- Two 5″ (127mm) squares dark fabric
- Four 5″ (127mm) squares light fabric.

CUSHION BLOCK FOUR
Cut:
- 16 x 5″ (127mm) squares from leftover light, medium and dark fabrics. Arrange as desired and use Easy Block Assembly method on page 132 to complete block.

CUSHION BLOCK THREE
(five fabrics)
Cut and pair:
- Two 5½″ (140mm) squares dark fabric with two 5½″ (140mm) squares medium fabric
- Two 5½″ (140mm) squares dark fabric with two 5½″ (140mm) squares light fabric
- One 5½″ (140mm) square medium fabric with one 5½″ (140mm) square second light fabric
- One 5½″ (140mm) square medium fabric with one 5½″ (140mm) square second dark fabric

Cut:
- Four 5″ (127mm) squares first dark fabric.

WELCOME HOME

Stitch a welcome gift for a new baby, with Tonia Todman's pretty patchworked and appliquéd cot quilt and matching teddy bear. Soft pinks and blues are the basis of the overall colour scheme and the cotton fabrics are a happy mixture of small checks, stripes and solid colours from the Tajmahal range by Ray Toby.

Patchwork Cot Quilt

MEASUREMENTS
Finished quilt is 90cm square.

MATERIALS
NOTE: Fabrics have been given numbers to help you identify them from the photograph. No 1 is blue and pink check, No 2 is plain pink, No 3 is blue and white check and No 4 is pink and cream stripe.
- 1.6m x 115cm fabric No 1
- 0.3m x 115cm fabric No 2
- 0.3m x 115cm fabric No 3
- 0.6m x 115cm fabric No 4
- 15cm Vlisofix bonding webbing, for appliqué
- Matching sewing thread for appliqué
- 1m medium thickness quilter's batting, either pure wool or polyester
- Hoop for hand-quilting
- Cream quilting thread
- Hand-quilting needles

The piecing methods for this quilt could not be simpler and the assembly is very straightforward. It's an ideal first project for a beginner.

PATTERN PIECES
Three heart templates for appliqué and quilting are printed opposite. Trace Small, Medium and Large Heart.

CUTTING SQUARES, BACKING AND BINDING
NOTE: Measurements given are for finished size of pieces — remember to add seam allowances. The usual depth of patchwork seams is 6mm or ¼". When cutting squares, draw a thread across fabric, to be sure of cutting straight on the grain. Continue to draw threads at required intervals and use these as cutting guides. Providing your cutting is accurate and your seam allowance is always identical, your patchwork pieces should always meet accurately.

From fabric No 1, cut twelve 8cm squares, and four 10cm-wide strips across fabric width for binding. Use remainder of fabric for heart appliqué and quilt backing.

From fabric No 2, cut twelve 8cm squares and five 16cm squares.

From fabric No 3, cut twelve 8cm squares.

From fabric No 4, cut twelve 8cm squares and eight 16cm squares.

CUTTING HEARTS
NOTE: When cutting hearts for appliqué, do not add seam allowance, as edges are oversewn.

Trace five Medium Hearts onto paper side of bonding webbing. Cut these out, allowing 5mm margins. Using a medium hot iron, press these onto fabric No 1, paper-side uppermost, making sure hearts sit straight along grainline of checks. When cool, cut out hearts around traced outlines and reserve.

Trace off Large Heart and cut it in halves down the centre. Trace eight half hearts onto paper side of bonding webbing, adding centre seam allowance. Using same technique described above, bond four half hearts from each of fabrics No 1 and 3, remembering to allow for four left and four right sides. Cut around outlines, peel away paper and stitch two different halves together, then press seam open with your thumb, not the iron.

APPLIQUE, PATCHWORK AND QUILT ASSEMBLY
Peel and discard paper from back of reserved fabric No 1 hearts, then place peeled side of fabric hearts onto five squares of fabric No 2, using a ruler to be sure they are centred. Press them into place with an iron. (Glue residue left on back of fabric from paper melts and bonds fabrics together.)

Centre and press the four joined hearts onto squares of fabric No 4.

Adjust your machine to a medium-width satin-stitch and, starting at top dip in heart, and using machine sewing thread, work satin-stitch around edge of all hearts, enclosing raw edges.

Assemble 8cm squares together as follows: Place all squares of fabrics No 3 and 1 together and stitch down one edge, right sides facing. Repeat for fabrics No 2 and 4. The joining of these squares can be speeded up by continuing to place aligned pieces under machine-foot and not stopping to clip threads. This is called 'chaining' and when all squares are joined, you then clip threads between them and press seams open. Place pairs of joined 8cm squares together, following sequence in photograph, then join them to make 16cm squares.

Following photograph, assemble quilt top by pinning 16cm squares into vertical rows, starting at one top corner. Check that all is in order, then proceed to stitch squares together to make a complete row. When rows are complete, press seams in one direction, not open.

Stitch rows together in sequence until all rows are joined, again pressing seams to one side. Press completed quilt top.

On a large flat surface, place your backing fabric No 1 right side downwards and smooth it out, taping it down at edges to keep it flat. On top of this, place batting, then quilt top, facing upwards. Secure all layers together with pins or safety pins, then baste all layers together, starting at centre and fanning out towards edges in straight lines, similar to a sunburst pattern. Trim batting and backing fabric equal with quilt top and baste around edges.

With right sides facing and raw edges even, stitch one 10cm-wide binding strip to opposite side edges of quilt (they will be too long, but will be trimmed to correct length later). Open out these strips, then stitch remaining strips across top and

bottom quilt edges, taking top and bottom strips over opened-out edges of side strips. Leave unfinished until quilting is complete.

QUILTING

With area to be quilted clamped in an embroidery hoop, using small, even running stitches and quilting thread, and making sure you stitch through all layers, quilt around each small square, just inside seam lines, and around each appliquéd heart, stitching two rows of quilting 3mm apart around hearts on fabric No 2. Using soft lead pencil, trace a Small Heart into each corner of plain squares of fabric No 4 and quilt these as well.

FINISHING

Turn in 1cm on remaining raw edges of binding strips and then fold binding over raw edge of quilt. Slip-stitch this folded edge neatly over seam line on back of quilt.

HEART TEMPLATES

Patchwork Bear

MEASUREMENTS

Finished bear is approximately 36cm tall.

MATERIALS

NOTE: See under Materials for Patchwork Cot Quilt, on page 136, for details of fabrics.

- 0.4m x 115cm fabric No 1 for squares, head, paws and soles
- 0.3m x 115cm fabric No 2 for squares
- 0.4m x 115cm fabric No 3 for squares and neck tie
- 0.3m x 115cm fabric No 4 for squares
- Polyester stuffing
- Two buttons for eyes, or a set of safety eyes
- Four 2cm-wide buttons for joints
- Long doll needle
- Strong sewing thread, such as linen thread or quilter's thread
- Hand-sewing needle
- Embroidery thread for nose and smile
- Spray starch

MAKING PATCHWORK FABRIC

NOTE: Remember to add seam allowance to all edges, as measurements given are for finished size.

Cut 25 x 8cm squares of each of the four fabrics, then cut diagonally through each square. Place them together in un-matched pairs (we put Nos 1 and 3 together, and Nos 2 and 4), right sides facing, and stitch, creating full squares. Press seam

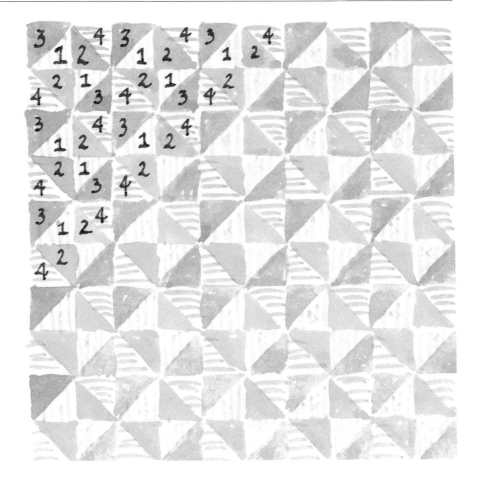

allowance to one side. Place squares onto a flat surface in rows, 10 squares by 10 squares, following diagram on this page. Stitch squares together to make rows, then press seam allowances to one side. Stitch rows together to create finished fabric. Press and lightly spray starch.

PATTERN PIECES

Pattern pieces are printed on pages 140 to 143 (overview below). Trace Centre Head, Side Head, Ear, Front Body, Back Body, Arm/Paw, Leg and Sole.

CUTTING

NOTE: 8mm seam allowance is included on all pattern pieces, unless otherwise specified.

From fabric No 1, cut one Centre Head, two Side Heads, four Ears, two Paws and two Soles. When cutting head, try to match fabric pattern at centre front under nose, by first cutting one Side Head, then using this fabric piece as a pattern, aligning it exactly on fabric before cutting second piece.

From prepared patchwork fabric, cut two Front Bodies, two Back Bodies, four Arms and four Legs, placing pattern pieces at random, either on or across the grain, but not on the bias. Try not to have any bulky patchwork seam allowance points right on the stitching lines.

From fabric No 3, cut an 8cm x 85cm strip for the neck bow (includes seam allowance).

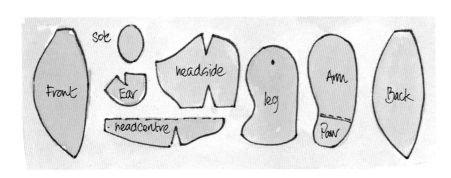

CONSTRUCTING BEAR

Place Body Fronts and Body Backs together in pairs and stitch centre front and centre back seams.

With right sides facing, stitch back and front together around sides, starting and finishing at neck. Turn right side out.

Place Paws over end of Arms, along marked stitching line, right sides together, and stitch in place. Fold Paw down over seam and press flat. Baste raw edges together.

With right sides facing, stitch Arms together in pairs, leaving an opening in back seam for stuffing. Turn right side out.

With right sides facing, stitch Legs together in pairs, stitching from centre front around to heel, leaving an opening in back seam for stuffing. Clip foot edge at intervals, for easing when pinning Sole to foot opening. Stitch only when you are satisfied with fit. Turn right side out.

With right sides facing, stitch Side Heads together, from nose down to neck. Press seam open. Pin Centre Head between Side Heads, then stitch, starting at back neck, matching ear darts and aligning centre front with nose seam. Clip head seams near nose and proposed eye positions for easing when head is turned out.

Above: A gift with heirloom potential – this friendly fellow is fully jointed using buttons as joints.

Top left: An illustration to show how fabric has been numbered.

Stitch darts in Ears and press seam allowance to one side. With right sides facing, stitch Ears together in pairs around curved outer edge. Clip seam, turn right side out and press.

Place Ears in head dart splits, right sides facing. On one side of head, stitch from one end of one dart through to end of other, stitching in

Ear as you sew. Repeat for remaining Ear. Turn head right side out through neck edge.

Insert safety eyes now, if using, following manufacturer's instructions.

Fold neck bow in half lengthwise, right sides facing and cut ends at an angle. Stitch around all edges, leaving an opening in centre for turning. Turn, press edges neatly and stitch opening closed.

Stuff head, body, arms and legs evenly and firmly with polyester filling. Stitch openings in arms and legs to close.

Hand-stitch a row of running stitch around neck edge of body, draw up slightly and secure end.

Turn under 1cm on raw neck edge of head and pin this folded edge to body, aligning centre front seams and centring head over centre back seam. Check alignment, then stitch head securely to body with tiny, invisible hemming stitches.

Thread doll needle with strong double thread and knot end. Stitch from one arm position, through body to other arm position, and out. Hold a button against joint position on outside of one arm (be sure paw is facing body), then take needle through arm and out through button, then back through button into body at arm position. Continue through body and out other side, through second arm and button, pulling thread firmly as you stitch.

Repeat this process, stitching through body and arms several times until arms are very secure. Tie off thread and bury ends in body.

Repeat this process to secure legs.

Stitch on button eyes, if using, taking thread through from one eye to the other, while pulling on it gently, to create slight indentations in the face. Using photograph as a guide, embroider nose in satin-stitch, and a smile in small chain-stitch.

Tweak your bear's ears forward in a shell shape, and tie his bow tie.

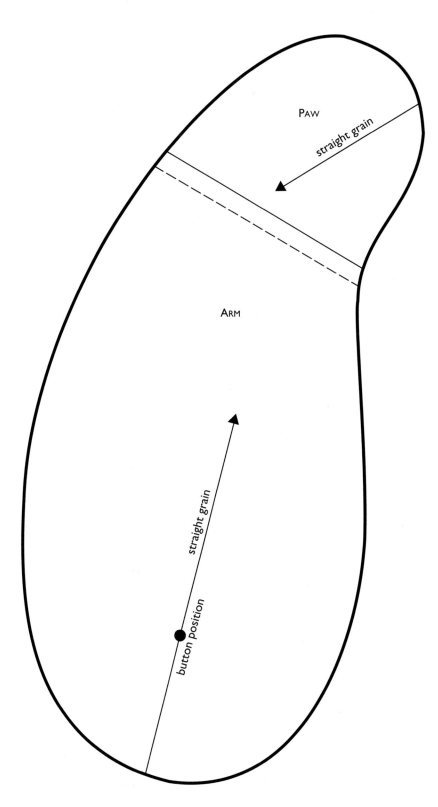

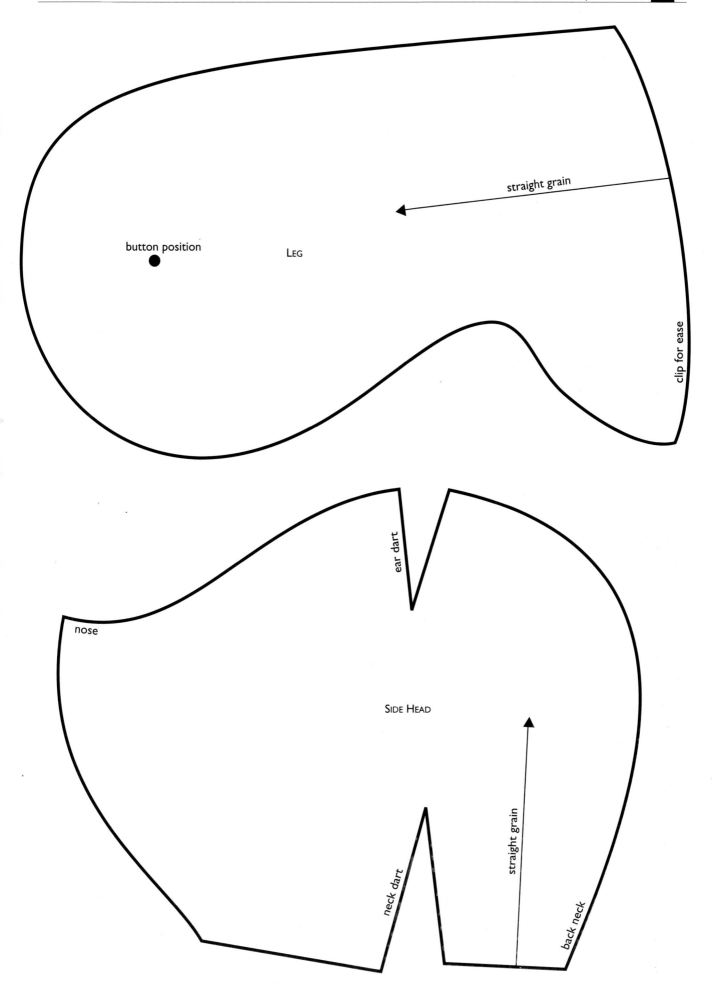

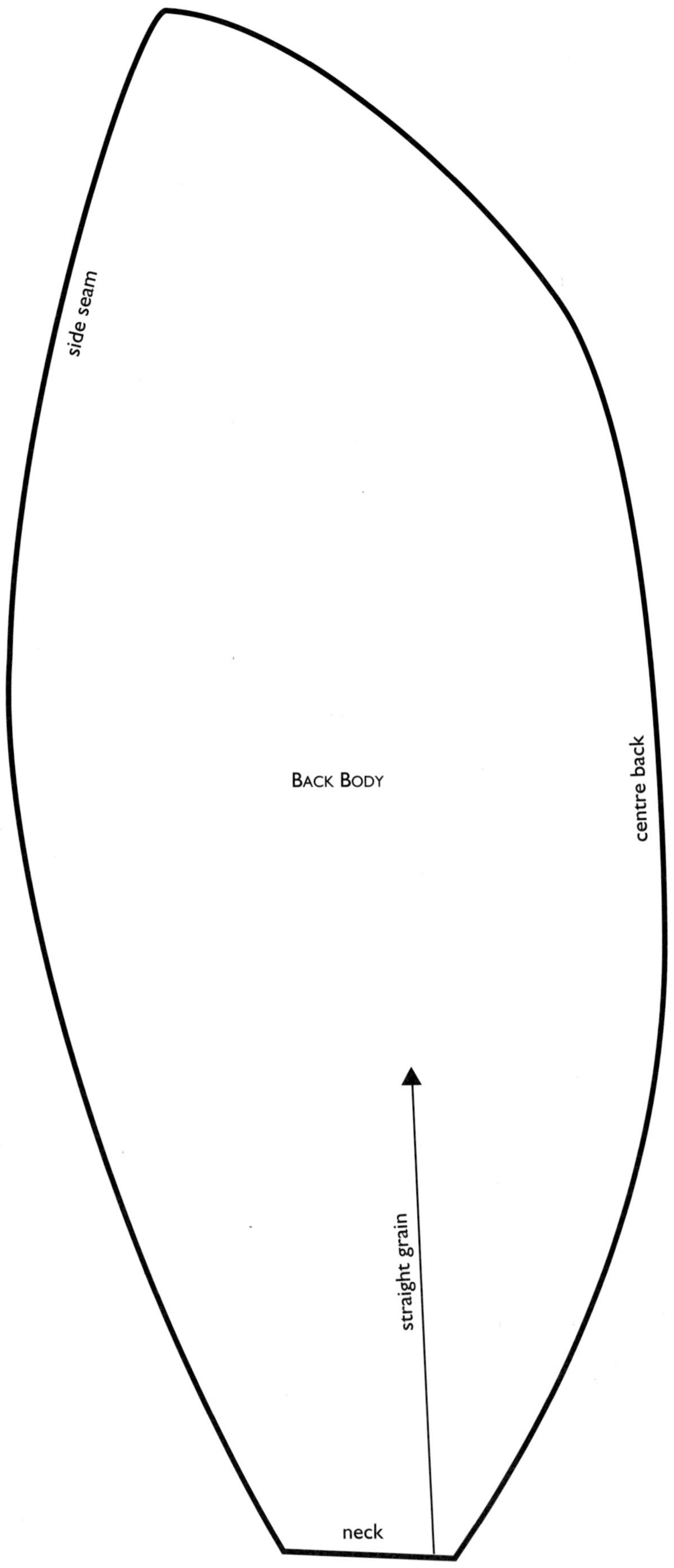

side seam

BACK BODY

centre back

straight grain

neck

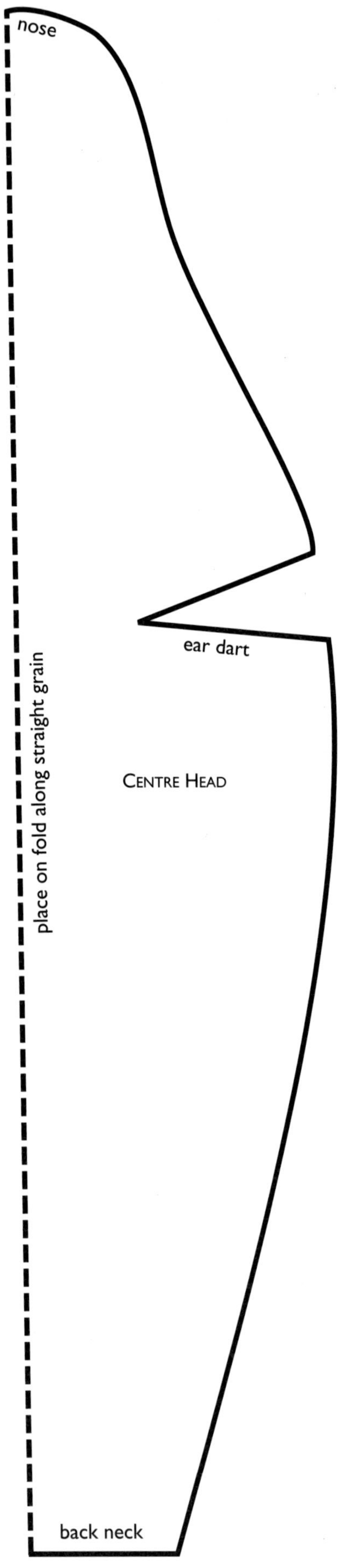

nose

place on fold along straight grain

ear dart

CENTRE HEAD

back neck

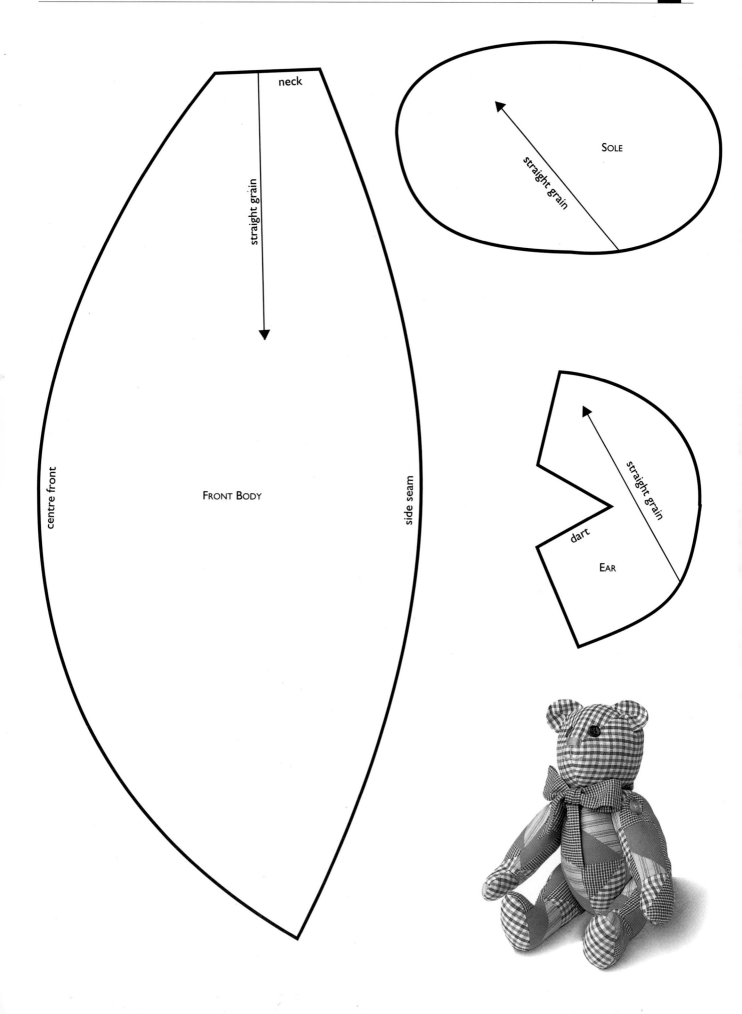

neck

straight grain

SOLE

straight grain

centre front

FRONT BODY

side seam

straight grain

dart

EAR

neck

PERFECTLY PATCHED

Discover the delights of a crazy-patch jacket made from all the old scraps of fabric you can't bear to discard. Dianne Finnegan demonstrates a simple machine patchwork technique that can be applied to any pattern with wonderful effect. Whether worn casually over jeans to keep out the cold or donned for a party, your crazy-patch jacket will be perfect for every occasion.

Step-by-step photographs illustrate the techniques involved in patching the jacket and instructions for sewing it are on page 148.

Once you have mastered the crazy-patch technique, you'll find it can be adapted and used for many other designs – for example, a stunning sash, or patchwork skirt?

HINTS FOR SEWING A PATCHWORK JACKET

If you're starting from scratch and want to buy fabric for the jacket, choose a variety of colours and patterns. For cutting, Dianne finds it easiest to make a separate length of fabric for each pattern piece, rather than making one long length, which leaves more wastage. Measure your pattern pieces, then allow 3cm of extra fabric around all edges of each piece. Altogether, we made five rectangles: one for Back, two for Fronts and two for Sleeves.

STEP 1

Crazy-Patchwork Technique

MATERIALS

- Fabric scraps or purchased meterage (see page 148)
- Pelon batting to line entire garment
- Matching sewing thread
- Safety pins
- Ruler
- Marking pen or chalk
- Scissors
- Black or gold contrasting thread for top-stitching

STEP 1

Begin by making a rectangular piece of fabric for Back of jacket. Lay pieces of scrap fabric on a flat surface and move them into different positions until you are happy with combination of colours and shapes.

Dianne works by incorporating the existing shapes of her fabric scraps into the main piece and finds that darker patterns look better when placed towards the bottom of a garment. Number of patches used in each large rectangle is your choice. Straighten all edges by trimming before proceeding.

STEP 2

STEP 5

STEP 6

STEP 2

Stitch fabric patches together, allowing 0.6cm seams. (Dianne lines up edge of her fabric with presser foot on machine. She recommends working upwards from bottom when joining patches.) If you are unsure of sewing neat, straight seams, pin or tack pieces together before machining them.

STEP 3

After sewing each patch, it is important always to press seam back to one side with an iron and square-off new piece so it is in line with patches that have already been joined. To square-off fabric, draw a line along top of piece using a ruler and marker pen, then cut along this line with scissors. Keep pressing seams back and squaring off fabric as you set patches together.

STEP 4

Seams need not be back-stitched or finished with overlocking or zigzag-stitch, as they are all secured by other lines of stitching and are protected by Pelon batting.

STEP 5

As you join patches, you will find yourself constantly filling gaps with smaller pieces. You might like to vary the shapes by including triangular pieces.

To make a triangular piece, first measure a square and cut it in half on diagonal. It is easiest to stitch triangular piece to a square.

With right sides together, lay triangular piece of fabric over fabric you wish to join it to, then cut a large square, allowing about 2cm around edges of triangle.

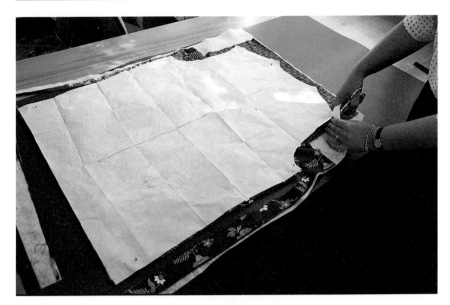

STEP 7

STEP 6
Place triangular and square pieces of fabric, right sides together, so diagonals match, and stitch along this line. After stitching, fold triangular piece back, press seam to one side, then trim edges to form a square.

STEP 7
When you have joined enough pieces to form a rectangle slightly larger than pattern piece, lay Back pattern piece on fabric, pin it in place and cut it out.

Follow steps 1 to 6 to make lengths of fabric for Fronts and Sleeves.

STEP 8
Cut out Pelon batting pieces for Back, Fronts and Sleeves using pattern pieces, allowing 2cm extra around all edges.

STEP 9

STEP 9
When joining batting to fabric pieces, Dianne recommends pinning it in place at intervals with safety pins, then top-stitching along patchwork with a selection of machine-embroidery stitches, using black or gold thread — this gives the crazy-patchwork effect. (Make sure safety pins are placed at a distance from seams you want to top-stitch.)

When machining, it is best to roll up Pelon batting that is not being stitched, as this allows you to manoeuvre the piece you are stitching, and stops batting and fabric from becoming bunched.

When stitching around patches, always consider pieces you want highlighted as blocks. Dianne does not top-stitch around each of the smaller patches, but prefers to create larger blocks of fabric. When each piece is top-stitched as desired, trim batting even with fabric edge.

STEP 10
Once pieces are quilted and trimmed, you can make up jacket following instructions on page 148. Because of the batting, you will need to line the jacket, so don't to forget to calculate fabric for this.

STEP 10

Patchwork Jacket Sewing Instructions

MEASUREMENTS

Pattern is given for sizes 10, 12, 14, 16.

PATTERN OUTLINES

.... Size 10

———————————— Size 12

- - - - - - - - - - - Size 14

-.-.-.-.-.-.-.- Size 16

MATERIALS

- 2.2m x 115cm fabric (or patched rectangles of fabric)
- 2m x 115cm lining fabric
- 2m x 115cm pelon batting
- Matching sewing thread
- Non-woven iron on interfacing

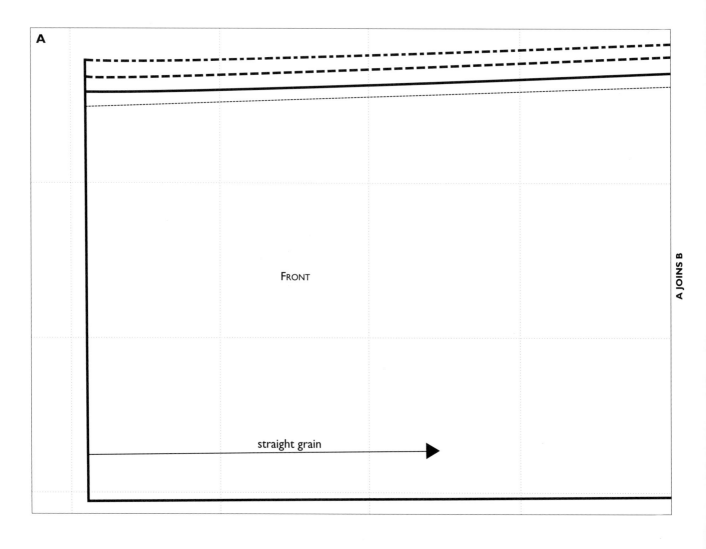

A

FRONT

straight grain

A JOINS B

PATTERN PIECES

All pattern pieces are printed on a scaled grid on pages 148 to 153. Each 4cm square on grid = 10cm. Rule up a 4cm grid and transfer pattern lines, square by square. Draw up Back, Front, Sleeve, Front Band and Back Neck Band.

CUTTING

From patched fabric, cut two Fronts, one Back, two Sleeves, four Front Bands and two Back Neck Bands. From lining, cut two Fronts, one Back and two Sleeves. From interfacing, cut two Front Bands and one Back Neck Band.

SEWING

Apply interfacing to wrong sides of two Front Bands and one Back Neck Band.

With right sides together, stitch Fronts to Back at shoulders and sides. Trim, neaten and press seams. Repeat for lining pieces.

With right sides together, stitch lining to jacket at cuff and lower edges. Turn right side out and baste front and neck edges together.

With right sides together, stitch Front Bands to either end of Back Neck Band. Repeat for remaining band pieces. With right sides facing, stitch Bands together around outside and across lower edges. Trim and neaten seam, turn right side out and press. Press under 1 cm on inside raw edge of Band.

With right sides together and raw edges even, pin unpressed edge of Band to neck and front edges of jacket. Stitch, trim and neaten seam and turn Band to right side. Slip-stitch pressed edge of Band over seamline.

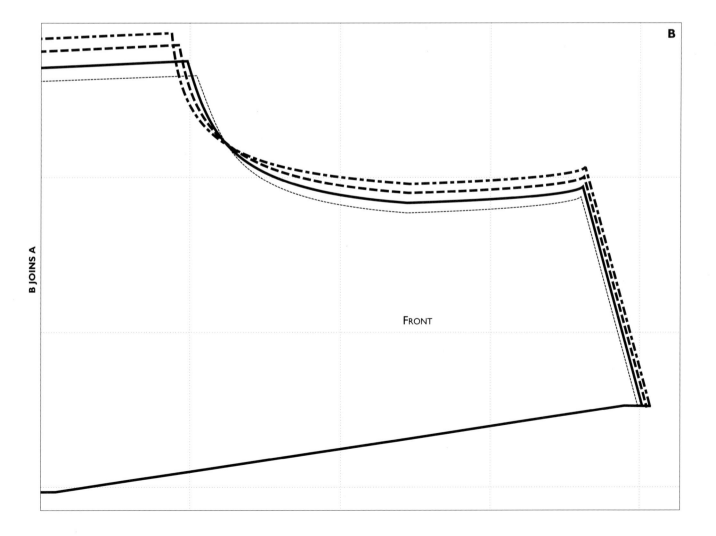

B

B JOINS A

FRONT

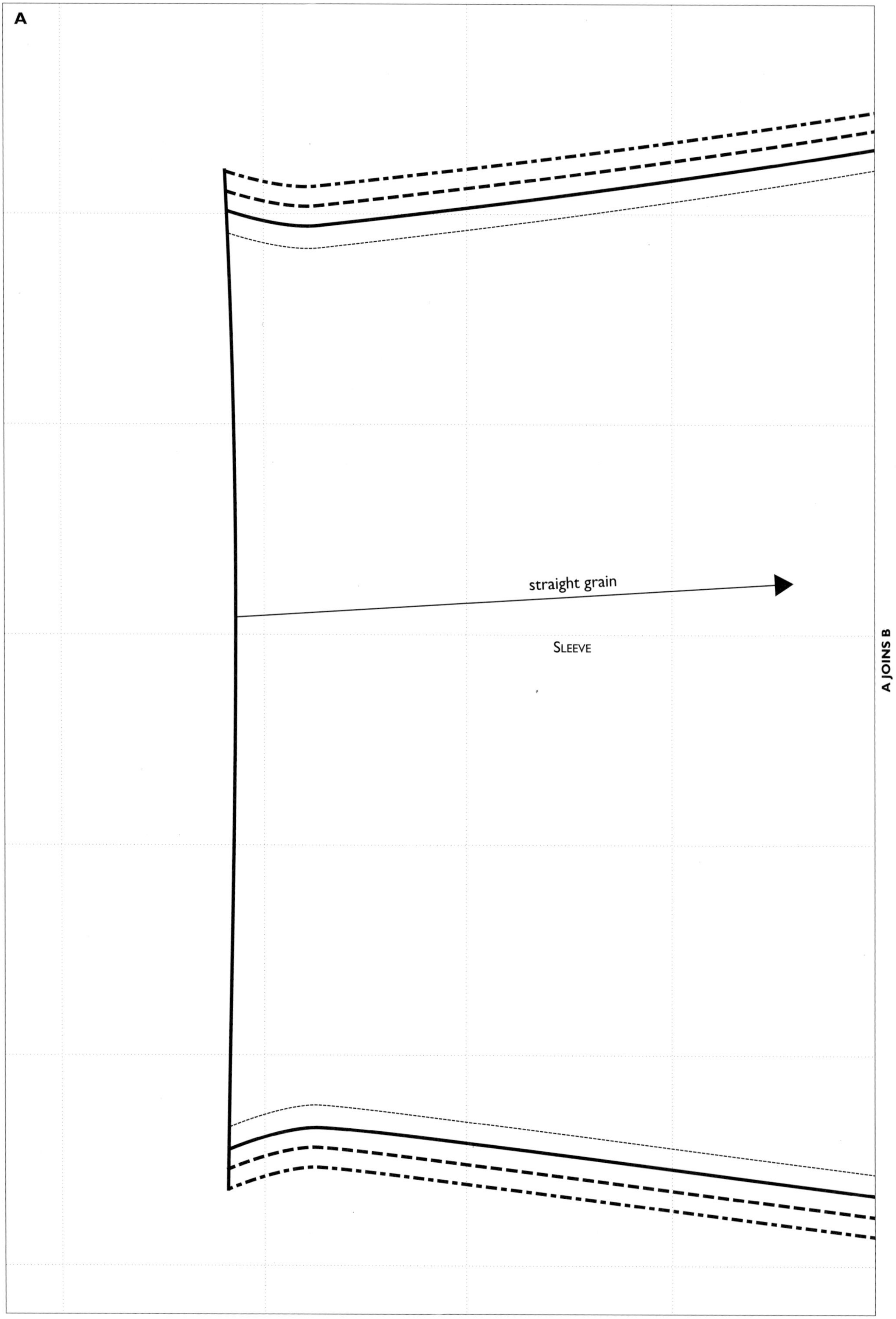

A

straight grain

SLEEVE

A JOINS B

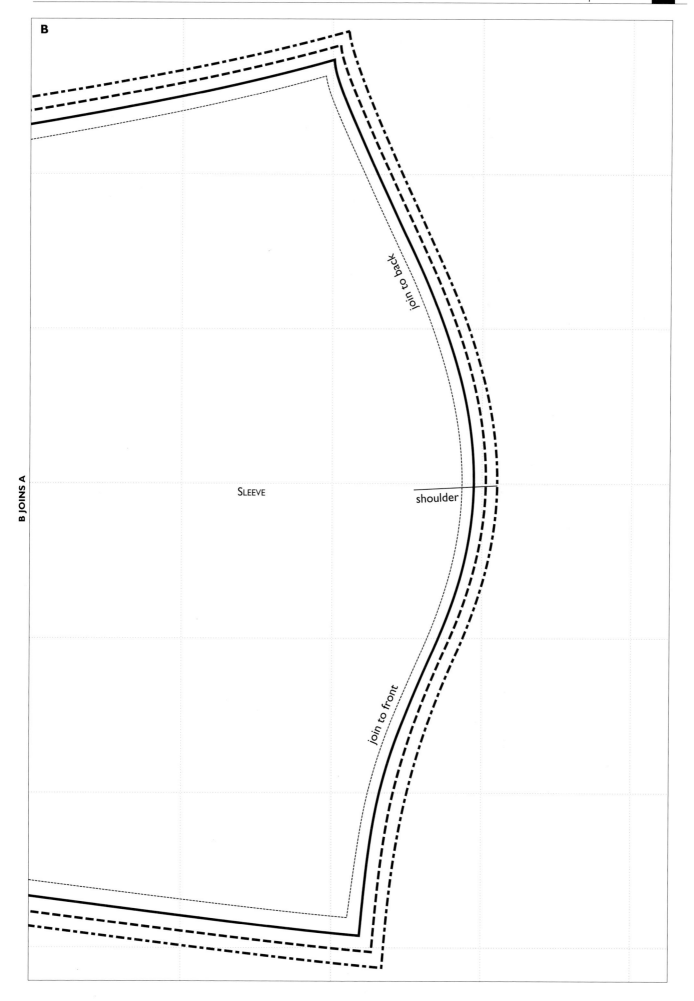

B

B JOINS A

SLEEVE

shoulder

join to back

join to front

A

place against fold along straight grain

foldline for facing

BACK

A JOINS B

A

FRONT BAND

A JOINS B

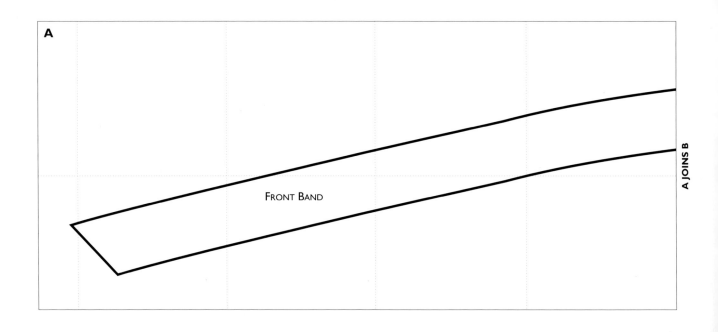

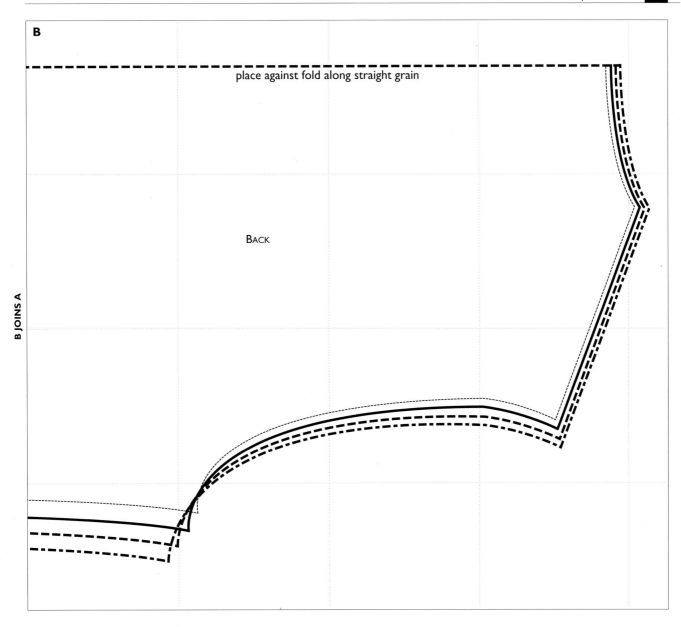

B

B JOINS A

place against fold along straight grain

BACK

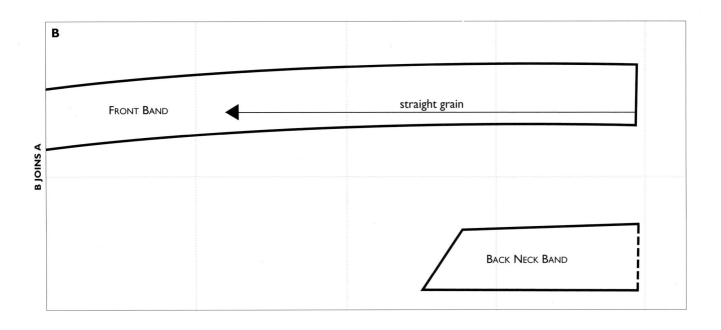

B

B JOINS A

FRONT BAND

straight grain

BACK NECK BAND

STACKING UP THE ODDS ... AND ENDS

Simple solutions for storage problems

If all your possessions rush to greet you every time you open a cupboard, read on! Re-organising your limited storage space doesn't have to mean vast expenditure or a tearful parting from junk you've known and loved for years. Why not allot it a place of its very own, in a series of sturdy and attractive storage boxes? You'll be amazed at what a tidy person you've suddenly become!

Covered Storage Boxes

MATERIALS

- Cardboard boxes and lids (see Note)
- Furnishing or heavy-weight cotton fabric (length depends on size of box — generally, you will need between 0.5m and 1m x 120cm–137cm fabric)
- Craft glue
- Calico or lightweight cotton for inside covering
- Lightweight cardboard for lining box and lid
- Contrast piping (purchased, or make your own), optional
- Iron-on interfacing (for appliqué)
- 37mm-wide grosgrain ribbon for decoration, optional
- Polyester filling (for padded appliqué)
- Brass card-holder, optional (see Note)

NOTE: Large stationery shops or speciality storage shops often have cardboard box kits, in a variety of sizes, from about $5.00. You can also use boxes scrounged from supermarkets, of course, and make them lids to fit, if necessary. Brass card-holders are a lovely finishing touch, and are handy for listing the contents of your boxes. We obtained ours from Mother of Pearl & Sons at 34–36 McLachlan Ave, Rushcutters Bay, NSW 2011, ph (02) 332 4455, who will advise you of your nearest stockist.

METHOD

Box

Carefully measure sides and base of box and cut five fabric pieces to match, allowing 0.5cm seam allowance and 3cm fold-over allowance around top edge. This method will allow you to match large patterns or stripes at the sides.

With right sides facing, stitch sides together to form a circle. With right sides together, carefully stitch base piece to sides to form a cloth 'box'.

If you are using a plain fabric, or small print that does not need matching, it is simpler to place box on wrong side of fabric, trace around its base and cut base and sides from a single cross-shaped piece of fabric, remembering to add seam and fold-over allowances.

If using this method, simply stitch side seams, right sides facing, and turn right side out.

Whichever method you use, fabric should be a snug fit on box, so adjust if necessary.

Slip fabric covering onto box, stretch fabric firmly, fold allowance to inside of box edge and glue in place.

From lightweight cardboard, cut side and base panels in same measurements as box, less 1cm in height.

Cut corresponding pieces of calico or lining material, allowing an extra 2cm all around. Place cardboard rectangles squarely in centre of calico rectangles (on wrong side), fold in edges and glue in place.

Next, glue lining panels to inside of box, wrong sides together, noting that panels are about 1cm shorter than top edge of box.

Lid

The lid is covered in exactly the same way as box, except that lining panel cardboard should be cut to the same size as side of lid, not 1cm shorter, and piping can be added, if desired. If piping is added to top edge of lid, it can be secured in the seam. If it is added to lower edge of lid, it should be glued in place along edge after outer cover has been secured, and raw edge then concealed by fabric-covered lining panel.

Applique

If you wish to decorate box or lid with appliqué, remember that flat shapes can be glued in place after box is finished, but it is easier to stitch padded appliqué to cover before it is glued to box.

Choose simple shapes, such as diamonds, triangles, circles or half circles, and arrange according to your taste, or follow our photograph. If you wish to use the shapes flat, iron interfacing onto wrong side of fabric

before cutting out. This will prevent fraying and the shapes can simply be cut out, then glued in place.

For padded appliqué, cut two pieces for each shape, allowing 0.5cm seam allowance. With right sides facing, stitch right around outer edge, then carefully make a small slit in centre of one side only, and turn right side out. Stuff with polyester filling and over-sew opening closed. Stitch or glue in place on cover, with slit to inside. If desired, grosgrain ribbon can

These stylish storage boxes, designed by Maria Ragan (right), once contained photocopying paper, but any sturdy, lidded box will do. Once transformed, they're almost too nice to keep hidden away.

be added to edge of box or lid first, then appliqué added to ribbon.

FINISHING
As a last touch, add a brass card-holder to side or end of box.

Kids' Knits

For a knitter, one of life's most joyous pastimes is knitting for children and babies.

Small and quick to knit, with cheerful, bright colours or fine, intricate lace patterns, a handknit for a special baby or child has always been a favourite choice for knitters.

To know that the jumper or shawl you so lovingly purled and plained will keep a special tot snug and warm and dressed with individual flair adds a unique charm to such a personal gift.

Perhaps that is why the most popular knits of all are those for the younger set.

In this collection you will find an irresistible selection of knits to choose from.

Bright and breezy designs for boys, pretty pastels and flowers for that special Miss, and cute clowns and teddies for tots. And not forgetting an easy-to-knit layette and shawl for the new arrival.

There's a stunning design in this collection for every child you love. And you'll get as much fun out of knitting them as they will when they wear them.

JO-ANN CITTADINI

Pictured this page: Warm and cosy — and oh, so sweet! The little knitted dress features garter-stitch at the cuffs, lower edge and yoke, combined with a simple lace pattern.

SMALL BEGINNINGS

A fter all the excitement surrounding the birth, it's finally time to take your new little person home. What could be more special for the big day than this beautiful layette, featuring dress, matinée jacket, cap or bonnet, bootees, and circular shawl? The tiny garments and shawl are knitted in Patons Baby Wool or Feathersoft, and the unfussy design would suit either a girl or boy.

Baby's Dress

MEASUREMENTS
To fit size: A (B, C). Approximate age: 0 (3, 6) months. Fits underarm: 35 (40, 45) cm. Length: 42 (47, 53) cm. Sleeve fits: 11 (13, 16) cm.

MATERIALS
Patons 3-ply Baby Wool or 3-ply Feathersoft (25g):
- 6 (7, 8) balls
- One pair each 2.75mm (No 12) and 3.25mm (No 10) knitting needles
- One 3.25mm (No 10) circular needle (60cm long)
- Four stitch-holders
- Three buttons

TENSION
See Knitting Notes below.
31 sts to 10cm in width over st st using 3.25mm needles.

BACK AND FRONT (ALIKE)
Using 2.75mm needles, cast on 157 (181, 205) sts (if this number of sts will not fit comfortably on needle, we suggest using a 2.75mm circular needle).
Knit 5 rows garter st (1st row is wrong side).

Change to 3.25mm needles.
1ST ROW K1, *yfwd, K4, sl 1, K2tog, psso, K4, yfwd, K1; rep from * to end.
2ND ROW K1, purl to last st, K1.
Last 2 rows form patt.
Cont in patt until work measures 32 (36, 41) cm from beg, ending with a purl row. Tie a coloured thread at each end of last row to mark beg of armholes.
Work a further 7 (7, 11) rows patt.
NEXT ROW P2, *P3tog; rep from * to last 2 sts, P2...55 (63, 71) sts.
Leave rem sts on a stitch-holder.

SLEEVES
Using 2.75mm needles, cast on 37 (39, 41) sts.
Knit 5 rows garter st (1st row is wrong side), inc 4 sts evenly across last row...41 (43, 45) sts.
Change to 3.25mm needles.
Cont in st st, inc one st at each end of 5th and foll 4th (4th, 6th) rows until there are 53 (57, 61) sts.
Cont straight in st st until work measures 10 (12, 15) cm from beg, ending with a purl row.
Tie a coloured thread at each end of last row to mark end of Sleeve seam.
Cont in st st, dec one st at each end of next and foll alt rows until 45 (49, 49) sts rem.
Work one row, dec 3 (5, 3) sts evenly across row...42 (44, 46) sts.
Leave rem sts on a stitch-holder.

KNITTING NOTES

TENSION
Correct tension is essential. If your tension is not exactly as specified in the pattern, your garment will be the wrong size. Before starting any pattern, make a tension swatch, at least 10cm square. If you have more stitches to 10cm in width than recommended, use larger needles or hook. If you have fewer stitches to 10cm than recommended, use smaller needles or hook.

KNITTING ABBREVIATIONS
Alt: alternate; beg: begin/ning; cm: centimetre/s; cont: continue; dec: decrease, decreasing; foll: following; garter st: knit every row; inc: increase, increasing; incl: including, inclusive; K: knit; 0: no rows, stitches or times; patt: pattern; P: purl; psso: pass slipped stitch over; p2sso: pass 2 sts over; rem: remain/s, remaining, remainder; rep: repeat; rnd/s: round/s; sl: slip; st/s: stitch/es; st st: stocking st (knit row on right side, purl row on wrong side); tbl: through back of loop; tog: together; ybk: yarn back (take yarn back under needle from purling position); yft: yarn front (bring yarn under needle from knitting position to purling position); yfwd: yarn forward (bring yarn under needle then over into knitting position again, thus making a stitch); yrn: yarn around needle (take yarn around needle into purling position, thus making a stitch).

KNITTING GRAPHS
Knit odd-numbered (right side) rows and purl even-numbered (wrong side) rows unless otherwise stated.

Baby's Jacket

The small dress and matching matinée jacket would make a superb gift for an impending arrival. The layette also includes tiny bootees with practical crocheted bobbles on the ties, and two hats — a traditional bonnet and a very sweet three-cornered pixie cap that looks quite adorable.

MEASUREMENTS

To fit size: A (B, C). Approximate age: 0 (3, 6) months. Fits underarm: 35 (40, 45) cm. Length: 23 (26, 29) cm. Sleeve fits: 11 (13, 16) cm.

MATERIALS

Patons 3-ply Baby Wool or 3-ply Feathersoft (25g):
- 3 (4, 4) balls
- One pair each 2.75mm (No 12) and 3.25mm (No 10) knitting needles
- One 3.25mm (No 10) circular needle (60cm long)
- Five stitch-holders
- Four buttons

TENSION

See Knitting Notes opposite.
31 sts to 10cm in width over st st, using 3.25mm needles.

JACKET

Worked in one piece to armholes.
Using 3.25mm needles, cast on 175 (199, 223) sts (if this number of sts will not fit comfortably on needle, use a 3.25mm circular needle).
Knit 5 rows garter st (1st row is wrong side).
6TH ROW Knit.
7TH ROW K5, purl to last 5 sts, K5.
Rep 6th and 7th rows until work measures 13 (15, 17) cm from beg, ending with a 7th row.
DIVIDE FOR ARMHOLES. NEXT ROW K43 (49, 55), cast off 4 sts, K81 (93, 105), cast off 4 sts, knit to end.
Cont on last 43 (49, 55) sts for Left Front.
Cont in st st and keeping garter st border correct, dec one st at armhole edge in alt rows until 38 (42, 46) sts rem.
Work one row, dec 6 (7, 8) sts evenly across st st section.
Leave rem 32 (35, 38) sts on a stitch-holder.
With wrong side facing, join yarn to next 81 (93, 105) sts for Back.
Cont in st st, dec one st at each end of alt rows until 71 (79, 87) sts rem.
NEXT ROW P7 (6, 5), *P2tog, P3; rep from * to last 4 (3, 2) sts, P4 (3, 2)... 59 (65, 71) sts. Leave rem sts on a stitch-holder.
With wrong side facing, join yarn to

YOKE

Using back-stitch, sew Sleeves to Front and Back above coloured threads. With right side facing and beg at right back seam, sl all sts from stitch-holders onto 3.25mm circular needle, then sl first 30 (34, 38) sts on to other end of needle... 194 (214, 234) sts.
1ST ROW (right side). Cast on 5sts for underlap, knit to end... 199 (219, 239) sts.
Turn and work in rows.
Knit 5 rows garter st.
7TH ROW Knit.
8TH ROW K5, purl to last 5 sts, K5.
Rep 7th and 8th rows once.
11TH ROW K12, *(K2tog, K5) twice, K2tog, K4; rep from * to last 7 sts, K4, yfwd, K2tog (buttonhole), K1... 172 (189, 206) sts.
Rep 8th row once, then 7th and 8th rows twice.
17TH ROW K11, *(K2tog, K4) twice, K2tog, K3; rep from * to last 8 sts, K8...145 (159, 173) sts.
Rep 8th row once, then 7th and 8th rows 1 (2, 2) time/s.

NEXT ROW K11, *(K2tog, K3) twice, K2tog, K2; rep from * to last 8 sts, K5, yfwd, K2tog (buttonhole), K1...118 (129, 140) sts.
Rep 8th row once, then 7th and 8th rows twice.
NEXT ROW K10, *(K2tog, K2) twice, K2tog, K1; rep from * to last 9 sts, K9...91 (99, 107) sts.
Rep 8th row once, then 7th and 8th rows 0 (1,1) time/s.
Knit 2 rows garter st.
NEXT ROW K6 (7, 9), *K2tog, K3 (2, 1), K2tog, K2; rep from * to last 4 (4, 7) sts, K1 (1, 4), yfwd, K2tog (buttonhole), K1...73 (77, 81) sts.
Knit 2 rows garter st.
Cast off.

TO MAKE UP

Do not press Feathersoft. With a slightly damp cloth and warm iron, press Baby Wool lightly, taking care not to flatten patt. Using back-stitch, join side and Sleeve seams. Sew underlap in position. Sew on buttons. Press Baby Wool seams.

rem 43 (49, 55) sts for Right Front and work to correspond with Left Front, reversing shapings and keeping garter st border correct.

SLEEVES

Using 2.75mm needles, cast on 39 (41, 43) sts.
Knit 5 rows garter st (1st row is wrong side), inc 6 sts evenly across last row...45 (47, 49) sts.
Change to 3.25mm needles.
Cont in st st, inc one st at each end of 5th and foll 4th (4th, 6th) rows until there are 57 (61, 65) sts.
Cont straight in st st until work measures 10 (12, 15) cm from beg, ending with a purl row.
Shape raglan. Cont in st st, cast off 3 sts at beg of next 2 rows, then dec one st at each end of next and foll alt rows until 41 sts rem.
Work one row, dec one st in centre.
Leave rem 40 sts on a stitch-holder.

YOKE

Do not press Feathersoft. With a slightly damp cloth and warm iron,
press Baby Wool lightly. Using back-stitch, join Sleeve and raglan seams.
Sl all sts from stitch-holders onto a 3.25mm needle so that right side will be facing (if this number of sts will not fit comfortably on needle, use a 3.25mm circular needle)...
203 (215, 227) sts.
1ST ROW K2, yfwd, K2tog (buttonhole), knit to end.
2ND ROW K5, purl to last 5 sts, K5.
3RD ROW K9, *sl 1, K1, psso, yfwd, K1, yfwd, K2tog, K7; rep from * to last 2 sts, K2.
Rep 2nd and 3rd rows twice more, then 2nd row once.
9TH ROW K8, *sl 2, K1, psso, yfwd, K1, yfwd, K3tog, K5; rep from * to last 3 sts, K3...171 (181, 191) sts.
10TH ROW As 2nd row.
11TH ROW K2, yfwd, K2tog (buttonhole), K4, *sl 1, K1, psso, yfwd, K1, yfwd, K2tog, K5; rep from * to last 3 sts, K3.
Rep 10th and 11th rows twice (omitting buttonhole), then 10th row once.
17TH ROW K7, *sl 2, K1, psso, yfwd,
K1, yfwd, K3tog, K3; rep from * to last 4 sts, K4...139 (147, 155) sts.
18TH ROW As 2nd row.
19TH ROW K7, *sl 1, K1, psso, yfwd, K1, yfwd, K2tog, K3; rep from * to last 4 sts, K4.
Rep 18th and 19th rows once, then 18th row once, working a buttonhole (as before) in 2nd row.
23RD ROW K6, *sl 2, K1, psso, yfwd, K1, yfwd, K3tog, K1; rep from * to last 5 sts, K5...107 (113, 119) sts.
24TH ROW As 2nd row.
25TH ROW K6, *sl 1, K1, psso, yfwd, K1, yfwd, K2tog, K1; rep from * to last 5 sts, K5.
Rep 24th and 25th rows once, then 24th row once.
29TH ROW K6, *sl 1, K1, psso, K1, K2tog, K1; rep from * to last 5 sts, K5...75 (79, 83) sts. Knit 4 rows garter st, working a buttonhole (as before) in 2nd row...4 buttonholes.
Cast off.

TO MAKE UP

Sew on buttons. Press Baby Wool seams.

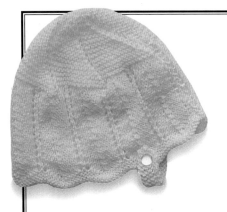

Baby's Cap or Bonnet

MEASUREMENTS

To fit size: A (B, C). Approximate age: 0 (3, 6) months. Fits head: 35 (40, 45) cm.

MATERIALS

Patons 3-ply Baby Wool or 3-ply Feathersoft (25g):
• 1 ball (all sizes)
• One pair each 2.75mm (No 12) and 3.25mm (No 10) knitting needles
• One button

TENSION

See Knitting Notes on page 158. 31 sts to 10cm in width over st st, using 3.25mm needles.

CAP OR BONNET

Using 2.75mm needles, cast on 121 (133, 145) sts.
Knit 5 rows garter st (1st row is wrong side).
Change to 3.25mm needles.
1ST ROW K1, *yfwd, K4, sl 1, K2tog, psso, K4, yfwd, K1; rep from * to end.
2ND ROW K1, purl to last st, K1.
Last 2 rows form patt.
Cont in patt until work measures 8 (9, 10) cm from beg, ending with a purl row.
SHAPE CROWN. 1ST ROW K4 (1, 1), *K2tog, K5 (3, 4), K2tog, K4; rep from * to end...103 (109, 121) sts.
2ND AND ALT ROWS Knit.
3RD ROW K1, *yfwd, K3tog, K14 (15, 17); rep from * to end... 97 (103, 115) sts.
5TH ROW K1, *yfwd, K3tog, K13 (14, 16); rep from * to end...
91 (97, 109) sts.
7TH ROW K1, *yfwd, K3tog, K12 (13, 15); rep from * to end... 85 (91, 103) sts.
Cont dec in this manner (working one st less between dec each time) in alt rows until 19 sts rem.
Break off yarn, run end through rem sts, draw up and fasten off securely.

STRAP

Work as for Pixie Hat.

TO MAKE UP

Do not press Feathersoft. With a slightly damp cloth and warm iron, press Baby Wool lightly, taking care not to flatten patt.
Cap: Using a flat seam, join entire back seam. As your baby's head grows, you can unpick this seam and then turn Cap into a bonnet.
Bonnet: Using a flat seam, join crown seam only.
For Cap or Bonnet: Sew Strap in position; sew button in position.
Press Baby Wool seam.

Baby's Pixie Hat

MEASUREMENTS

To fit size: A (B, C). Approximate age: 0 (3, 6) months. Fits head: 35 (40, 45) cm.

MATERIALS

Patons 3-ply Baby Wool or 3-ply Feathersoft (25g):
- 1 ball (all sizes)
- One pair each 2.75mm (No 12) and 3.25mm (No 10) knitting needles
- One button

TENSION

See Knitting Notes on page 158. 31sts to 10cm in width over st st, using 3.25mm needles.

HAT

Using 3.25mm needles, cast on 103 (115, 127) sts.
Knit 5 rows garter st (1st row is wrong side).
6TH ROW K1, *yfwd, K15 (17, 19), sl 1, K2tog, psso, K15 (17, 19), yfwd, K1; rep from * to end.
7TH ROW K1, purl to last st, K1.
Last 2 rows form patt.
Cont in patt until work measures 11 (12, 13) cm from beg, ending with a purl row.
Knit 5 rows garter st.
Cast off loosely.

STRAP

Using 2.75mm needles, cast on 5 sts.
Knit in garter st (1st row is wrong side) until work measures 5cm from beg, ending with a wrong-side row.
NEXT ROW K2, yfwd, K2tog (buttonhole), K1.
Knit 3 rows garter st.
NEXT ROW Knit, dec one st at each end.
Knit one row.
NEXT ROW Sl 1, K2tog, psso, fasten off.

TO MAKE UP

Do not press Feathersoft. With a slightly damp cloth and warm iron, press Baby Wool lightly. Fold cast-off edge into three peaks so that lines of eyelets meet at centre, and then join with a flat seam. Now join back seam. Sew Strap in position. Sew button in place. Press Baby Wool seam.

Baby's Shawl

MEASUREMENTS

Diameter: approximately 135cm.

MATERIALS

Patons 3-ply Baby Wool or 3-ply Feathersoft (25g):
- 12 balls
- One pair 5mm (No 6) knitting needles
- One 5mm (No 6) circular needle

TENSION

See Knitting Notes on page 158. 20 sts to 10cm in width over garter st, using 5mm needles. To achieve desired effect, this Shawl has been designed to be worked on larger needles at a looser tension than usually recommended.

SHAWL

Begin at centre.
Using 5mm needles, cast on 9 sts.
1ST AND ALT ROWS Knit.
2ND ROW K1, (yfwd, K1) 8 times...17 sts.
4TH ROW K1, (yfwd, K2) 8 times...25 sts.
6TH ROW K1, (yfwd, K3) 8 times...33 sts.
8TH ROW K1, (yfwd, K4) 8 times...41 sts.
10TH ROW K1, (yfwd, K5) 8 times...49 sts.
Cont in this manner (working one st more each time) until the row 'K1, (yfwd, K44) 8 times' has been worked...361 sts (when sts feel uncomfortable on needle, transfer sts to circular needle).
NEXT ROW Knit.
NEXT ROW Inc at each st to last st, K1...721 sts.
WORK BORDER. 1ST ROW K1, *yfwd, K4, sl 1, K2tog, psso, K4, yfwd, K1; rep from * to end.
2ND ROW K1, purl to last st, K1.
Rep last 2 rows until work measures approximately 63cm from beg, ending with a 2nd row, turn, cast on 8 sts for edging.
WORK EDGING. 1ST ROW K7, K2tog, turn.
2ND ROW Sl1, K5, yfwd, K2.
3RD ROW Yfwd, K2tog, K6, K2tog, turn.

A potential family heirloom, this beautiful circular shawl with a pretty lace edge is actually not as difficult to knit as it looks.

4TH ROW Sl 1, K4, yfwd, K2tog, yfwd, K2.
5TH ROW Yfwd, K2tog, K7, K2tog, turn.
6TH ROW Sl 1, K3, (yfwd, K2tog) twice, yfwd, K2.
7TH ROW Yfwd, K2tog, K8, K2tog, turn.
8TH ROW Sl 1, K2, (yfwd, K2tog) 3 times, yfwd, K2.
9TH ROW Yfwd, K2tog, K9, K2tog, turn.
10TH ROW Sl 1, K2, K2tog, (yfwd, K2tog) 3 times, K1.
11TH ROW As 7th row.
12TH ROW Sl 1, K3, K2tog, (yfwd, K2tog) twice, K1.
13TH ROW As 5th row.
14TH ROW Sl 1, K4, K2tog, yfwd, K2tog, K1.

15TH ROW As 3rd row.
16TH ROW Sl 1, K3, K2tog, yfwd, K2tog, K1.
17TH ROW Yfwd, K2tog, K5, K2tog, turn.
Rep rows 2 to 17 incl until all border sts have been worked off.
Cast off loosely.

TO MAKE UP

Using a flat seam, join edges to form a circle, taking care that you do not make the seam too tight. Roll Shawl in a damp towel, leave for several hours, then spread out flat in a circle. Pin each point out separately with rustless pins and leave until Shawl is completely dry.

Baby's Bootees

MEASUREMENTS

To fit size: A (B, C). Approximate age: 0 (3, 6) months. Fit foot 7 (8, 9.5) cm.

MATERIALS

Patons 3-ply Baby Wool or 3-ply Feathersoft (25g):
• 1 ball (all sizes)
• One pair 3.25mm (No 10) knitting needles
• One 3mm (No 10–11) crochet hook

TENSION

See Knitting Notes on page 158 and Crochet Notes on page 201.
31 sts to 10cm in width over st st, using 3.25mm needles.

BOOTEES

Begin at sole.
Using 3.25mm needles, cast on 27 (35, 45) sts.
1ST AND ALT ROWS (wrong side). Knit.
2ND ROW *Inc in next st, K11 (15, 20), inc in next st; rep from * once more, K1...31 (39, 49) sts.
4TH ROW *Inc in next st, K13 (17, 22), inc in next st; rep from * once

more, K1...35 (43, 53) sts.
6TH ROW *Inc in next st, K15 (19, 24), inc in next st; rep from * once more, K1...39 (47, 57) sts.
8TH ROW *Inc in next st, K17 (21, 26), inc in next st; rep from * once more, K1...43 (51, 61) sts.
10TH ROW *Inc in next st, K19 (23, 28), inc in next st; rep from * once more, K1...47 (55, 65) sts.
Knit 3 (5, 7) rows garter st.
NEXT ROW Knit.
NEXT ROW K1, purl to last st, K1.
Rep last 2 rows once more.
Knit 2 rows garter st.
SHAPE INSTEP. 1ST ROW K28 (32, 37), sl 1 knitwise, K1, psso, turn.
2ND ROW P10, p2tog, turn.
3RD ROW K3, sl 1, K1, psso, yfwd, K1, yfwd, K2tog, K2, sl 1, K1 psso, turn.
Rep 2nd and 3rd rows 6 (7, 9) times, then 2nd row once.
NEXT ROW Knit to end...31 (37, 43) sts.
PROCEED AS FOLLS. 1ST ROW K1, purl to last st, K1.
2ND ROW *K1, yfwd, K2tog; rep from * to last st, K1.
3RD ROW As 1st row, dec (inc, dec) once in centre ... 30 (38, 42) sts.
4TH ROW K2, *P2, K2; rep from * to end.
5TH ROW K1 *P1, K2, P1; rep from

* to last st, K1.
Rep 4th and 5th rows once.
Knit 8 rows garter st.
Cast off loosely.

TIES

Using hook, make 4ch. Miss 3ch, 9tr in last ch, join with a sl st in top of 3ch, make a ch a further 35cm long, miss last 3 of these ch, 9tr in next ch, join with a sl st in top of 3ch. Fasten off.

TO MAKE UP

Do not press Feathersoft. With a slightly damp cloth and warm iron, press Baby Wool lightly, taking care not to flatten patt. Using a flat seam, join leg and foot seams. Thread ties through holes at ankles (or use ribbon, if desired). Fold cuffs to right side.

TOTS' TOP 20

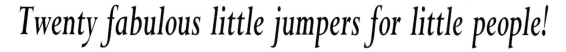

Twenty fabulous little jumpers for little people!

Tumbling teddies, clowns, animals, plains, stripes, pastels and brights — there's every jumper you can imagine, and then some! Designed exclusively for *Handmade* by Patons, to fit sizes 1 to 5, each jumper is knitted in one of two very easy basic patterns, with variations according to your choice. Patterns can be knitted in, or added later in knitting stitch. Happy knitting!

Tots' Top Twenty Jumpers

BASIC INSTRUCTIONS

Here are the Basic Jumper (with ribbed lower bands) and Basic Tunic (with a hem at lower edge) patterns. Follow these instructions in conjunction with directions for the variation you have chosen, working stripes or pictures as described. For picture variations, you can use the winding yarn method to knit them in as you go along, or embroider them afterwards using knitting-stitch embroidery (see page 191). We suggest that best results may be achieved by knitting-in any large areas, then embroidering smaller, more intricate, areas later. Work knitting-stitch embroidery before pressing or sewing up your garment.

MEASUREMENTS

To fit size: 1 (2, 3, 4, 5). Fits underarm: 52.5 (55, 57.5, 60, 62.5) cm. Garment measures: 59.5 (63, 66.5, 70, 73.5) cm. Length: approximately 36 (38, 40, 42, 44) cm. Sleeve fits: 21 (23, 25, 28, 31) cm.

MATERIALS

Patons Totem 8–ply or Patons 8–ply Machinewash (50g):
• See individual patts for colours and amounts
• One pair each 3.25mm (No 10) and 4mm (No 8) knitting needles
• Two stitch-holders
NOTE: In individual requirements, 8–ply Machinewash is written as 8MW.

TENSION

See Knitting Notes on page 158.
22.5 sts and 30 rows to 10cm over st st, using 4mm needles.

Basic Jumper Pattern

BACK

Using 3.25mm needles, cast on 69 (73, 77, 81, 85) sts.
1ST ROW K2, *P1, K1; rep from * to last st, K1.
2ND ROW K1, *P1, K1; rep from * to end.
Rep last 2 rows 4 (4, 5, 6, 6) times...10 (10, 12, 14, 14) rows rib in all.
Change to 4mm needles.
Work 56 (60, 62, 64, 68) rows st st. Tie a coloured thread at each end of last row to mark beg of armholes as there is no armhole shaping.**
***Work a further 40 (42, 44, 46, 48) rows st st.
Shape shoulders. Cont in st st, cast of 5 sts at beg of next 8 rows, then 3 (4, 5, 6, 7) sts at beg of foll 2 rows.
Leave rem 23 (25, 27, 29, 31) sts on a stitch-holder.

FRONT

Work as for Back to **
****Work a further 24 (24, 26, 28, 30) rows st st.
SHAPE NECK. NEXT ROW K29 (31, 32, 33, 34), turn and cont on these sts.
Cont in st st, dec one st at neck edge in alt rows until 23 (24, 25, 26, 27) sts rem.
Work 3 rows st st.
Shape shoulder. Cont in st st, cast off 5 sts at beg of next and foll alt rows 4 times in all.
Work one row.
Cast off.
With right side facing, sl next 11 (11, 13, 15, 17) sts on a stitch-holder and leave. Join yarn to rem 29 (31, 32, 33, 34) sts and work to correspond with side just completed, reversing shapings.

SLEEVES

Using 3.25mm needles, cast on 35 (35, 37, 39, 41) sts.
Work 10 (10, 12, 14, 14) rows rib as for Back, inc 6 (8, 8, 8, 8) sts evenly across last row...41 (43, 45, 47, 49) sts.
Change to 4mm needles.
Cont in st st, inc one st at each end of 5th and foll 6th rows until there are 53 (57, 59, 63, 67) sts. Work 13 (13, 15, 17, 17) rows st st.
Cast off very loosely.

NECKBAND

Using back-stitch, join right shoulder seam. With right side facing, using 3.25mm needles, knit up 83 (89, 93, 97, 101) sts evenly around neck, incl sts from stitch-holders.
Work 9 rows rib as for Back, beg with a 2nd row.
Cast off loosely in rib.

TO MAKE UP

Press with a slightly damp cloth and warm iron. Using back-stitch, join left shoulder and Neckband seam (if desired, an opening may be left and fastened with buttons and loops). Join Sleeve and side seams to coloured threads. Sew in Sleeves. Press seams.

Basic Tunic Pattern

BACK

Using 3.25mm needles, cast on 69 (73, 77, 81, 85) sts.
Work 9 rows st st, then knit one row to form ridge (hemline).
Change to 4mm needles.
Work 66 (70, 74, 78, 82) rows st st. Tie a coloured thread at each end of last row to mark beg of armholes as there is no armhole shaping.**
Complete as for Basic Jumper from *** to end.

FRONT

As for Basic Tunic Back to **.
Complete as for Front of Basic Jumper from **** to end.

SLEEVES

Work as for Basic Jumper.

NECKBAND

Work as for Basic Jumper.

TO MAKE UP

Press with a slightly damp cloth and warm iron. Using back-stitch, join left shoulder and Neckband seam (if desired, an opening may be left and fastened with buttons and loops). Join Sleeve and side seams to coloured threads. Sew in Sleeves. Fold hem to wrong side at ridge and slip-stitch in position. Press seams.

Patchwork

See Basic Instructions (page 164), allowing approximately 3 balls navy (Totem 244), 1(1, 1, 2, 2) ball/s each red (Totem 1221) and blue (8MW 2332), and 1 ball each green (Totem 1391), yellow (Totem 2453) and hot pink (8MW 2334).

DIRECTIONS

Foll Basic Jumper Patt (page 165), using navy for ribbed bands and noting foll changes. For Back, work st st area in blocks of 23 (24, 26, 27, 28) sts hot pink, 23 (25, 25, 27, 29) sts navy and 23 (24, 26, 27, 28) sts green for first 34 (36, 36, 38, 40) rows; 23 (24, 26, 27, 28) sts navy, 23 (25, 25, 27, 29) sts yellow and 23 (24, 26, 27, 28) sts navy for next 34 (36, 36, 38, 40) rows; then 23 (24, 26, 27, 28) sts blue, 23 (25, 25, 27, 29) sts navy and 23 (24, 26, 27, 28) sts red for rem. Note that when changing colour in the middle of a row, twist the colour to be used (on wrong side) underneath and to the right of the colour just used to avoid holes in work. For Front, work as for Back but reverse positions of hot pink and green, and blue and red. For Left Sleeve, work st st in blue. For Right Sleeve, work st st in red.

Presents

See Basic Instructions (page 164), allowing approximately 4 (5, 5, 6, 6) balls white (Totem 51) and 1 ball each blue (Totem 1435), pale pink (8MW 2325), teal (8MW 2331), and hot pink (8MW 2334). One crochet hook for ties. If desired, you will also need diamantes for trimming.

DIRECTIONS

Foll Basic Jumper Patt (page 165), noting foll changes. Use white for main part of jumper, working st st areas from Presents Graphs (pages 168 to 169) using winding yarn method (see page 191). Using hook and colour to match ribbon on each parcel, make a length of chain for ties. Thread ties through jumper at places marked on Graphs and tie in bows where indicated. Sew securely in position through centre of bow. If desired, trim with diamantes (be sure to attach them securely).

Clown

See Basic Instructions (page 164), allowing approximately 3 balls yellow (8MW 2010), 2 (2, 2, 3, 3) balls hot pink (8MW 2334), and 1 ball each teal (8MW 2331), blue (8MW 2336) and white (8MW 51). Three purchased pompoms.

DIRECTIONS

Foll Basic Tunic Patt (page 165), noting foll changes. For Back and Front, use teal for hem and first 2 rows of st st above ridge, then change to yellow and work a further 10 (14, 18, 22, 26) rows st st before beg to work larger areas from Clown Graph (page 170), using winding yarn method (see page 191), then use yellow st st for rem. For Sleeves, use hot pink for ribbed bands, then work st st area from Clown Graph for Sleeves (page 169). Use teal for Neckband. Using knitting-stitch, embroider spots on suit. Embroider facial features on Front only. Make loops of blue yarn for hair and attach to each side of head on Front, and all across head on Back. Sew purchased pompoms on Front of suit, as photographed.

Cool!

See Basic Instructions (page 164), allowing approximately 2 balls each red (8MW 2338), yellow (8MW 2010) and white (8MW 51), and 1 ball each green (8MW 2329), blue (8MW 2332) and black (8MW 52).

DIRECTIONS

Foll Basic Jumper Patt (page 165), noting foll changes. For Back and Front, use green for ribbed bands, then foll Cool Graph (page 171) for st st area. Use winding yarn method (see page 191) for background and 'bubbles', but we suggest embroidering words afterwards in knitting-stitch (see page 191). For Left Sleeve, use yellow for ribbed band, foll Left Sleeve Graph (page 170) until complete, then use blue to complete Sleeve. For Right Sleeve, use red for ribbed band, foll Right Sleeve Graph (page 174) until complete, then use green to complete Sleeve. Use blue for Neckband. Use black to embroider words and outline 'bubbles' in stem-stitch.

Nautical Stripes

See Basic Instructions (page 164), allowing approximately 4 (4, 4, 5, 5) balls navy (Totem 244) and 1 (1, 2, 2, 2) ball/s cream (Totem 100). You will also need one purchased motif, if desired.

DIRECTIONS

Foll Basic Tunic Patt (page 165), noting foll changes. For Back and Front, use navy for hem, then work in stripes of 22 rows navy and 8 rows cream throughout. For Sleeves, cast on and work 2 rows in cream at edge of ribbed band, then work rem of Sleeve in same stripes as Back and Front. For Neckband, work cast-on and first 7 rows in navy, then work last 2 rows of Neckband and cast-off in cream. Stitch motif to Front, if desired.

PRESENTS GRAPH FOR BACK AND FRONT

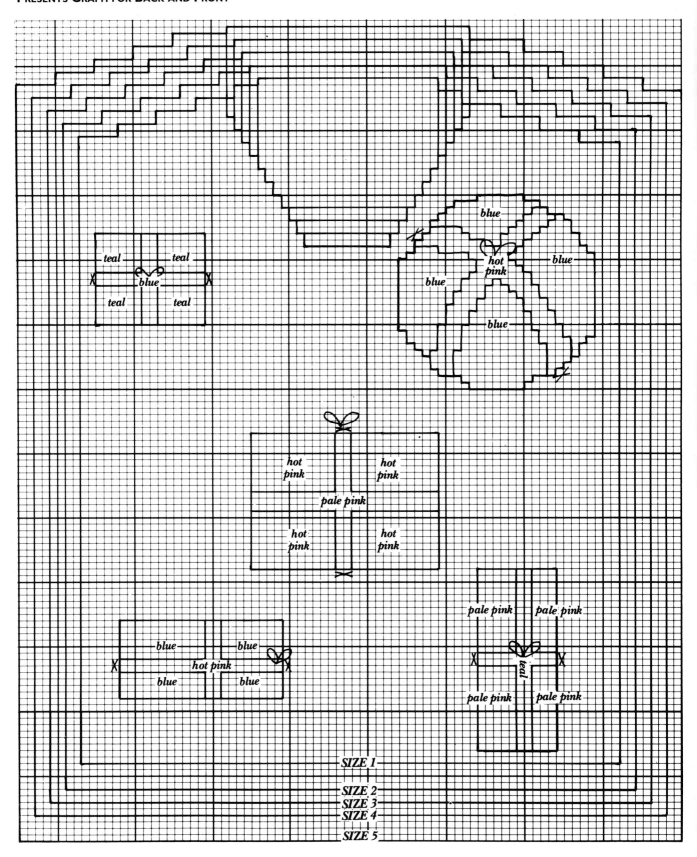

Heavy lines represent changes in colour.

Thread ties at points marked by crosses and tie at bows. Work background in white. ISQ = IST

PRESENTS GRAPH FOR SLEEVES

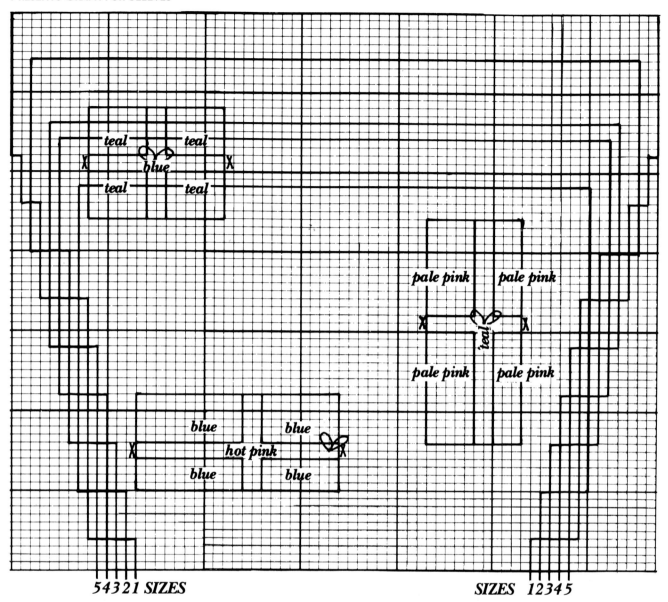

54321 SIZES   **SIZES 12345**

Heavy lines represent changes in colour.
Thread ties at points marked by crosses and tie at bows.
Work background in white. Only work complete parcels.

CLOWN GRAPH FOR SLEEVES

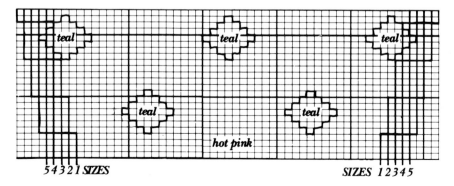

54321 SIZES   **SIZES 12345**

Heavy lines represent changes in colour.
These 24 rows form patt, noting to work extra sts at side edges in hot pink st st.

CLOWN GRAPH FOR BACK AND FRONT

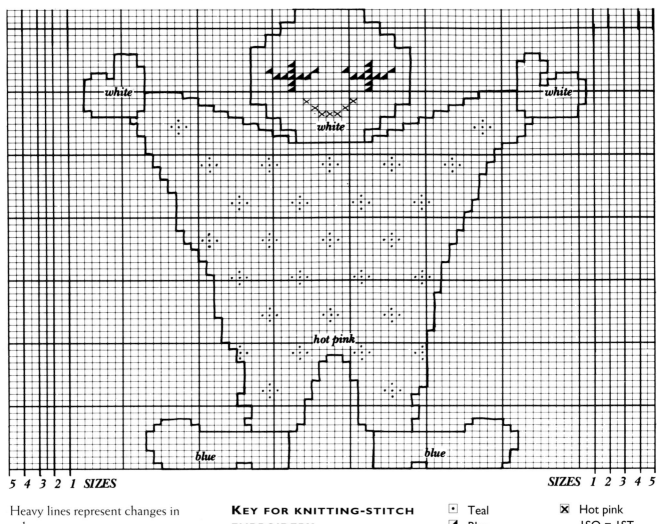

5 4 3 2 1 SIZES   SIZES 1 2 3 4 5

Heavy lines represent changes in colour.

KEY FOR KNITTING-STITCH EMBROIDERY

- • Teal
- ◢ Blue
- ☒ Hot pink

1SQ = 1ST

COOL! GRAPH FOR LEFT SLEEVE

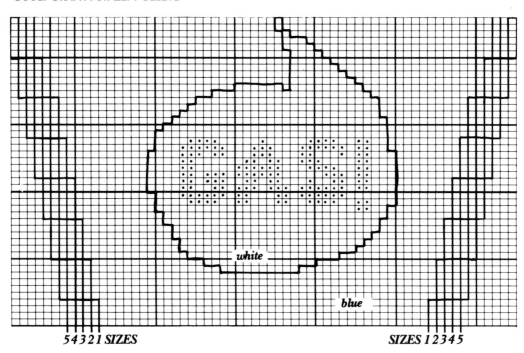

Heavy lines represent changes in colour.

KEY FOR KNITTING-STITCH EMBROIDERY

- • Black

1SQ = 1ST

5 4 3 2 1 SIZES   SIZES 1 2 3 4 5

COOL! GRAPH FOR BACK AND FRONT

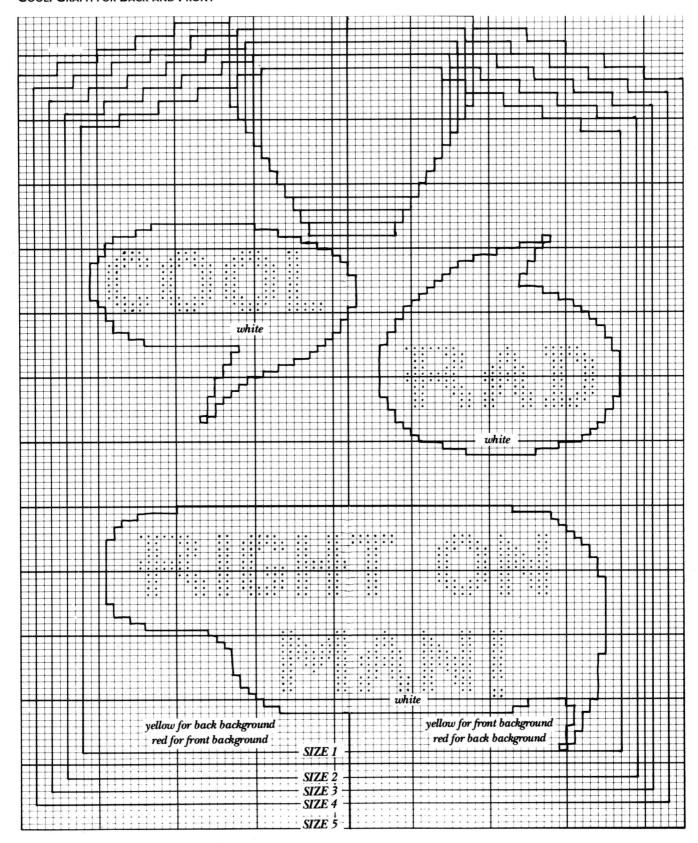

Heavy lines represent changes in colour.

KEY FOR KNITTING-STITCH EMBROIDERY

⊡ Black

1SQ = 1ST

Tumbling Teddies

See Basic Instructions (page 164), allowing approximately 5 (5, 6, 6, 7) balls white (Totem 51) and 1 ball each yellow (Totem 2453), hot pink (8MW 2334), blue (8MW 2332) and jade (8MW 2328). You will also need a scrap of black for features.

DIRECTIONS

Foll Basic Jumper Patt (page 165), noting foll changes. Use yellow for lower bands, hot pink for Sleeve bands and jade for Neckband. Work all st st areas in white. We suggest you embroider teddies to Front, but if you prefer, you could use the winding yarn method (see page 191) and knit them in from Teddies Graph (page 175) as you knit the Front. After working rib for Front, work 4 (8, 10, 12, 16) rows white st st, work from Graph, then complete Front in white st st.

Argyle

See Basic Instructions (page 164), allowing approximately 3 (3, 3, 4, 4) balls red (Totem 1221) and 3 balls navy (Totem 244).

DIRECTIONS

Foll Basic Jumper Patt (page 165), using red for ribbed bands, then working st st areas from Argyle Graph (page 174), using winding-yarn method (see page 191).

Thomas the Tank Engine

See Basic Instructions (page 164), allowing approximately 3 (4, 4, 5, 6) balls green (8MW 2329) and 1 ball each blue (8MW 2332), yellow (8MW 2010), red (8MW 2338), black (8MW 52) and white (8MW 51).

DIRECTIONS

Foll Basic Jumper Patt (page 165), noting foll changes. For Back, use blue for ribbed band and green for st st. For Front, use blue for ribbed band and green for first 2 (6, 8, 10, 14) rows of st st. Work rows 1 to 75 incl from Thomas Graph (page 176) using winding yarn method for larger areas and knitting-stitch embroidery for intricate areas (see page 191), then complete Front using green or, if preferred, knit all in green and embroider in knitting-stitch from Graph afterwards. For Sleeves, use yellow for ribbed bands and Green for st st. Use red for Neckband. Use stem-stitch and back-stitch in black, red and yellow to embroider outlines and details on train, as photographed.

Circus

See Basic Instructions (page 164), allowing approximately 4 (5, 5, 6, 6) balls navy (Totem 244) and 1 ball each red (Totem 33), yellow (Totem 2453), blue (8MW 2332) and hot pink (8MW 2334).

DIRECTIONS

Foll Basic Jumper Patt (page 165), noting foll changes. For Back and Front, use navy for ribbed band, then work st st areas from Circus Graph, on page 177, using winding-yarn method for larger areas and knitting-stitch embroidery for intricate areas (see page 191) or, if preferred, work all in navy and embroider in knitting-stitch from Graph afterwards. Use stem-stitch and navy to embroider outlines and features. For Sleeves, use yellow for ribbed band on Right Sleeve and blue for ribbed band on Left Sleeve, then work st st areas in navy, embroidering star shapes from Graph afterwards at random, in colours as desired. Use red for Neckband.

Bananas in Pyjamas

See Basic Instructions (page 164), allowing approximately 4 (4, 4, 5, 5) balls red (Totem 33), and 1 ball each blue (8MW 2332), yellow (8MW 2010), green (8MW 2329) and white (8MW 51), and a small amount of black.

DIRECTIONS

Foll Basic Jumper Patt (page 165), noting foll changes. For Back, use blue for ribbed band and red for st st. For Front, use blue for ribbed band, red for first 2 (6, 8, 10, 14) rows st st, work from Bananas in Pyjamas Graph (page 180), then complete Front in red st st. We suggest that you use the winding-yarn method for the areas outlined with heavy lines on Graph, then use knitting-stitch embroidery for the more intricate areas marked by symbols (see page 191). For Sleeves, use yellow for ribbed bands and red for st st. Use green for Neckband. Use black to work stem-stitch details and French knots for buttons and eyes. Use white stem-stitch for bikini straps.

Cool! Graph for Right Sleeve

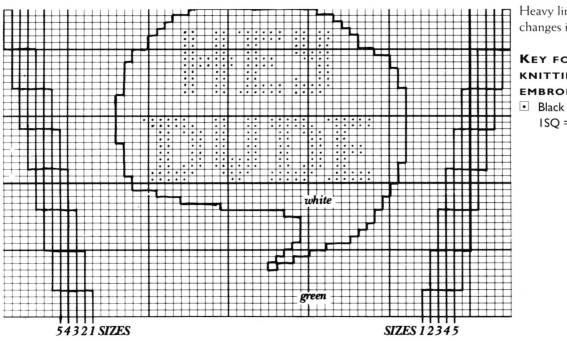

Heavy lines represent changes in colour.

KEY FOR KNITTING-STITCH EMBROIDERY

⊡ Black
1SQ = 1ST

white

green

5 4 3 2 1 SIZES

SIZES 1 2 3 4 5

Argyle Graph

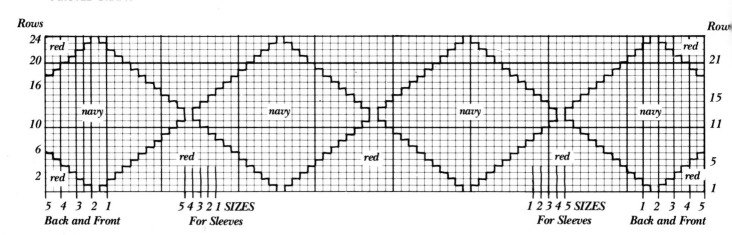

Heavy lines represent changes in colour. Rows 1 to 24 incl form patt.

TUMBLING TEDDIES GRAPH

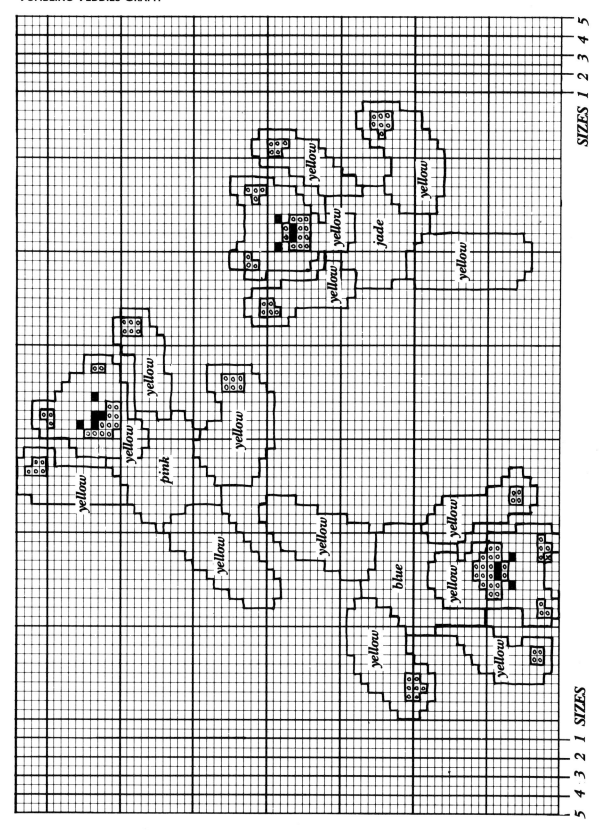

Heavy lines represent changes in colour. Work background in white.

KEY FOR KNITTING-STITCH EMBROIDERY

- ⊡ White
- ⊠ Yellow
- ■ Black
- 1SQ = 1ST

THOMAS THE TANK ENGINE GRAPH

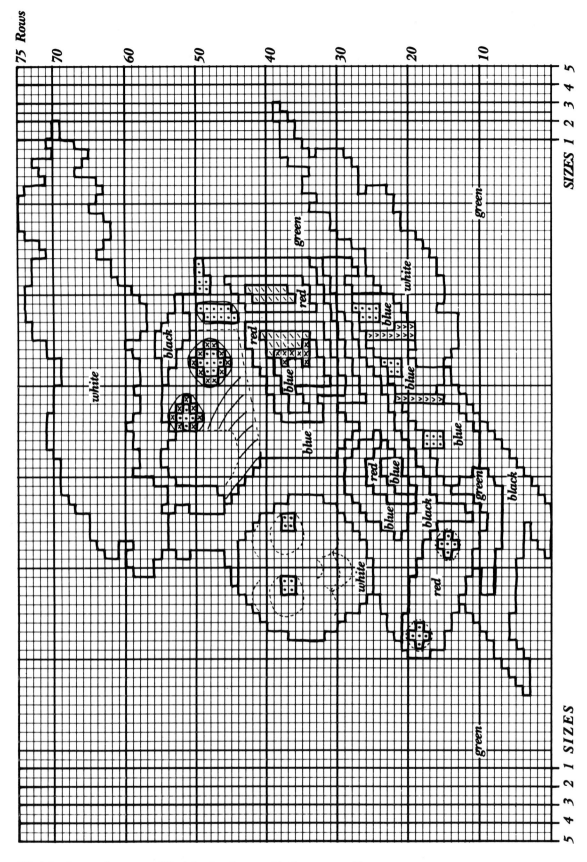

Work background in green. Work broken lines in black stem-stitch or back-stitch. Work diagonal lines on top of train in red back-stitch. Work lines around windows in yellow back-stitch. Heavy lines represent changes in colour.

KEY FOR KNITTING-STITCH EMBROIDERY

• Black	☑ Green	ISQ = IST
☑ Blue	☒ Yellow	

CIRCUS GRAPH

red

yellow

blue

blue

pink

blue

red *red*

yellow

pink

yellow

SIZE 1
SIZE 2
SIZE 3
SIZE 4
SIZE 5

Heavy lines represent changes in colour. Work background in navy. Work broken lines in navy stem-stitch

KEY FOR KNITTING-STITCH EMBROIDERY

⊠ Blue	◪ Navy	⊡ Yellow
◼ Hot Pink	Ⓨ Red	1SQ = 1ST

Angora Bunny

See Basic Instructions (page 164), allowing approximately 5 (5, 5, 6, 6) balls vanilla (Totem 1996), and small amounts each mauve (Totem 1992) and white (for a fluffy rabbit, we used Patons Chantal 9634). You will also need rose pink, green and grey stranded cottons.

DIRECTIONS

Foll Basic Jumper Patt (page 165), noting foll changes. Use vanilla for Back, Sleeves and Neckband. For Front, use vanilla for ribbed band and first 11 (15, 17, 19, 23) rows of st st, then work rows 1 to 55 incl from Angora Bunny Graph (page 181), noting to purl 1st row, using winding yarn method for rabbit and mauve background only (see page 191), then complete Front using vanilla. Cross-stitch flowers from Graph to Front, then embroider flowers all over Back and Sleeves, foll Graph for placement. Cross-stitch rose pink border around rabbit. Embroider features, using rose pink cross-stitch for ear and nose. Using grey stranded cotton, work satin-stitch for eye and stem-stitch for whiskers and detail on ear and leg. Embroider rose pink grub roses and green lazy daisy leaves in garland round neck (see Embroidery Stitch Guide, page 55).

Daisies

See Basic Instructions (page 164), allowing approximately 4 (4, 5, 5, 5) balls pale pink (8MW 2325) and small amounts white (Totem 51), dusty pink (Totem 2495), mauve (8MW 2324), green (8MW 2322) and yellow (8MW 2010).

DIRECTIONS

Foll Basic Jumper Patt (page 165), noting foll changes. Use pale pink for Back, Sleeves and Neckband. For Front, we suggest that you use the winding yarn method for areas outlined with heavy lines on Daisies Graph (page 182), then use knitting-stitch embroidery for more intricate areas marked by symbols (see page 191). For Front, use pale pink for ribbed bands and first 2 (6, 8, 10, 14) rows st st, then work from Graph and complete Front in pale pink st st.

Pastel Stripes

See Basic Instructions (page 164), allowing approximately 4 (4, 5, 5, 5) balls cream (Totem 100) and 1 ball each sand (Totem 1999) and sage (Totem 2626).

DIRECTIONS

Foll Basic Jumper Patt (page 165), using cream for ribbed bands, then working st st in stripes of (2 rows cream, 6 rows sand, 2 rows cream, 2 rows sage, 2 rows cream, 2 rows sage) 2 (2, 2, 3, 3) times, then rem in cream.

Baby Hippo

See Basic Instructions (page 164), allowing approximately 2 (2, 2, 3, 3) balls navy (Totem 244) and 3 (4, 4, 5, 5) balls cream (Totem 100).

DIRECTIONS

Foll Basic Jumper Patt (page 165), noting foll changes. For Back and Front, use navy for ribbed band. For st st area, work (4 rows navy, 2 rows cream) 1 (1, 2, 2, 3) time/s, 8 rows navy, 2 rows cream, 4 rows navy, then rem in cream. Embroider Baby Hippo Graph (page 183) to Front, noting to embroider eye and leg detail in navy stem-stitch. For Sleeves, use navy for ribbed band. For st st area work (4 rows navy, 2 rows cream) 3 (4, 4, 5, 5) times, then rem in cream. For Neckband, knit up sts and work 2 rows navy, 5 rows cream, then 2 rows and cast-off in navy.

Cross-Stitch Flowers

See Basic Instructions (page 164), allowing approximately 4 (4, 5, 5, 5) balls white (Totem 51) and 1 (1, 1, 2, 2) ball/s pink (8MW 2325). You will also need green, pale pink and rose pink stranded cottons for embroidery.

DIRECTIONS

Foll Basic Jumper Patt (page 165), noting to use white for ribbed bands, then work st st areas in stripes of 14 rows white and 4 rows pink throughout. Using stranded cottons and cross-stitch, embroider flowers from Cross-stitch Flowers Graph (on page 183) to centre of one white stripe on Front, as photographed (see page 191 for basic cross-stitch instructions).

BANANAS IN PYJAMAS GRAPH

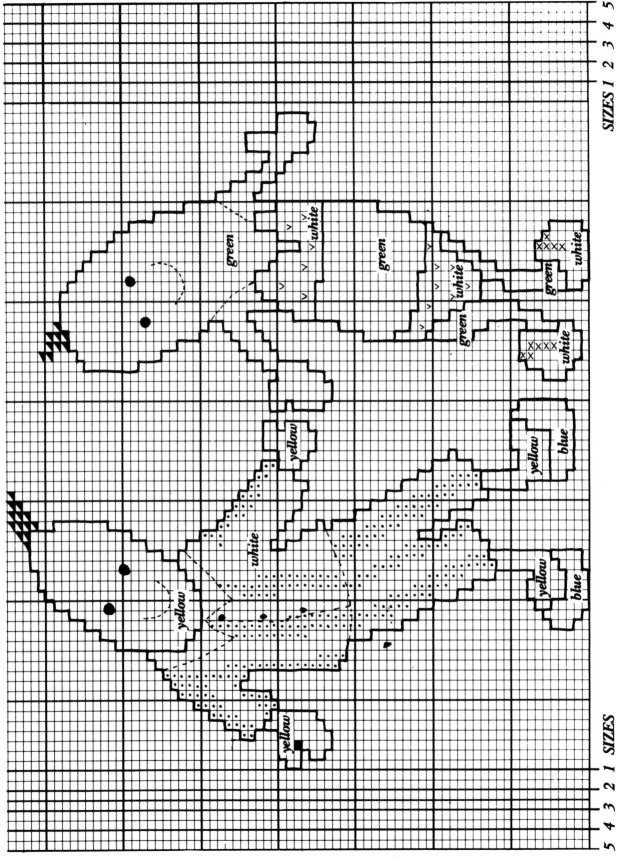

Heavy lines represent changes in colour. Work broken lines in black stem-stitch (except bikini straps which are worked in white stem-stitch). Work eyes and buttons in black French knots. Work background in red.

KEY FOR KNITTING-STITCH EMBROIDERY

• Blue	☑ Yellow	◤ Black
☒ Green	■ Red	ISQ = IST

ANGORA BUNNY GRAPH

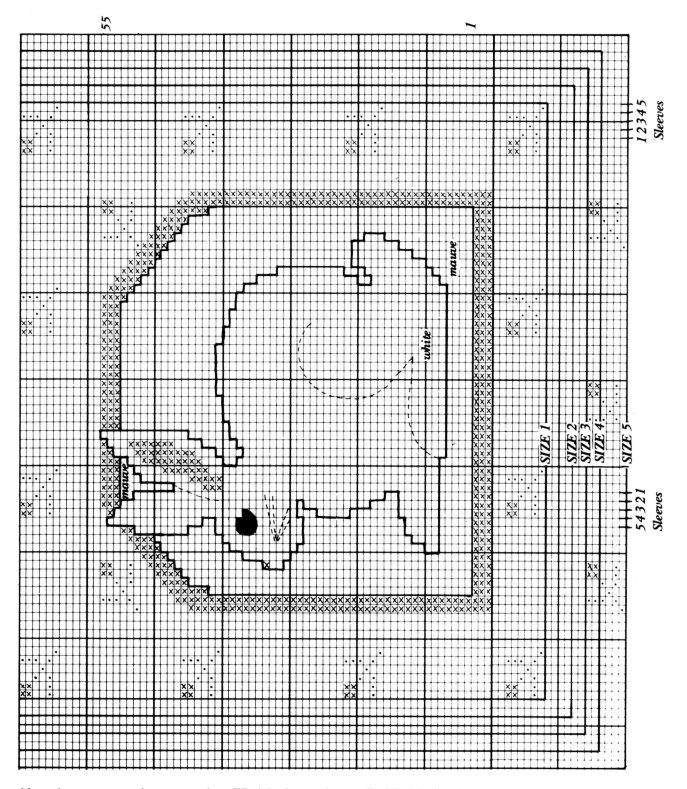

Heavy lines represent changes in colour. Work background in vanilla. Work broken lines in grey stem-stitch.

KEY FOR CROSS-STITCH

ISQ = IST   • Green   ☒ Rose pink

DAISIES GRAPH

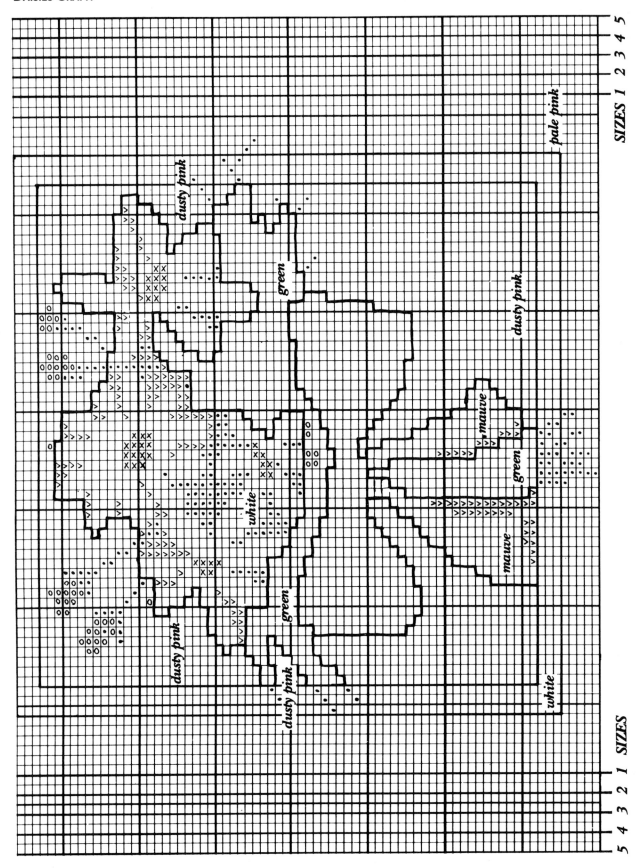

Heavy lines represent changes in colour.

KEY FOR KNITTING-STITCH EMBROIDERY

• Green	⊙ White	ISQ = IST
⋁ Dusty pink	✗ Yellow	

BABY HIPPO GRAPH

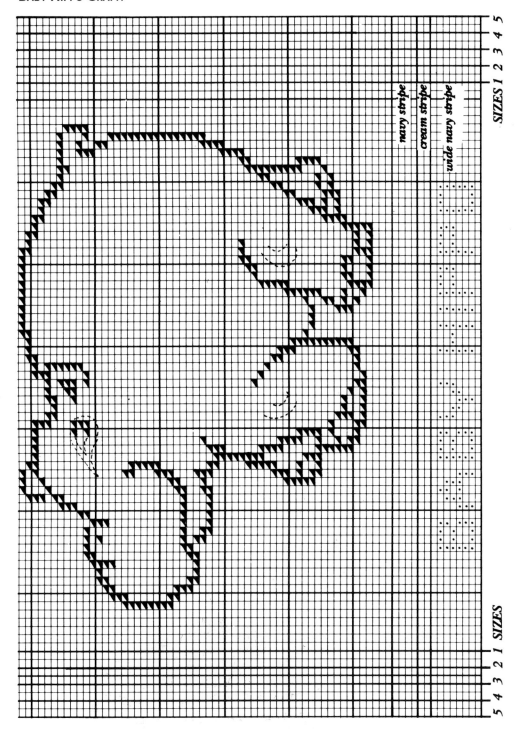

navy stripe

cream stripe

wide navy stripe

SIZES 1 2 3 4 5

SIZES 1 2 3 4 5

Work broken lines in navy stem-stitch.

KEY FOR KNITTING-STITCH EMBROIDERY

◤ Navy

◉ Cream

1SQ = 1ST

CROSS-STITCH FLOWERS GRAPH

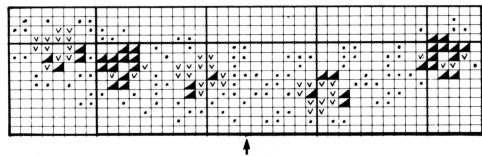

↑
Centre stitch

KEY FOR CROSS-STITCH

◉ Green

☑ Pale pink

◤ Rose pink

1SQ = 1ST

Sailing Boats

See Basic Instructions (page 164), allowing approximately 4 (5, 5, 6, 6) balls blue (8MW 2332), 1 (1, 1, 2, 2) ball/s pale blue ((8MW 321) and small amounts of navy (8MW 2342), red (8MW 2338), yellow (8MW 2010), green (8MW 2328), and white (8MW 51).

DIRECTIONS

Foll Basic Jumper Patt (page 165), noting foll changes. Use blue for Back and Sleeves. For Front, use blue for ribbed band and first 2 (6, 8, 10, 14) rows of st st, then work rows 1 to 60 incl from Sailing Boats Graph (page 186), using winding yarn method for larger areas and knitting-stitch embroidery for intricate areas (see page 191), noting change of background colour at row 47 for sky (or if preferred, work all in background colour and embroider in knitting-stitch afterwards). Complete Front in pale blue. Use pale blue for Neckband.

Bright Stripes

See Basic Instructions (page 164), allowing approximately 3 balls black (Totem 52) and 1 ball each red (Totem 33), green (Totem 1391), yellow (Totem 2453) and blue (Totem 1435).

DIRECTIONS

Foll Basic Jumper Patt (page 165), using black for ribbed bands, then working st st areas in stripes throughout of 4 rows black, 6 rows red, 4 rows black, 4 rows green, 4 rows black, 2 rows yellow, 8 rows blue, 2 rows yellow.

Scarecrow

See Basic Instructions (page 164), allowing approximately 4 (5, 5, 6, 6) balls yellow (Totem 2453) and small amounts of red (Totem 33), blue (Totem 1435), white (Totem 51), green (Totem 1391) and brown (8MW 220). You will also need black stranded cotton.

DIRECTIONS

Foll Basic Jumper Patt (page 165), noting foll changes. Use yellow throughout (Scarecrow is worked on Front only). For Front, we suggest working large red area from Scarecrow Graph (page 187) using winding yarn method, then embroidering other areas in knitting-stitch afterwards (see page 191). After working rib for Front, work 3 (7, 9, 11, 15) rows yellow st st, work from Graph (noting to purl the first row at base of pole), then complete Front in yellow st st. Embroider grass in green stem-stitch, mouth in red stem-stitch, coat detail in black straight-stitch, and eyes and buttons in black French knots. Make loops of blue for hair over blue base area.

Doodles

See Basic Instructions (page 164), allowing approximately 5 (5, 6, 6, 7) balls black (8MW 52) and small amounts of red (8MW 2338), blue (8MW 2332) and yellow (8MW 2010).

DIRECTIONS

Foll Basic Jumper Patt (page 165), using black throughout, then embroider detail from Doodles Graphs (pages 188 to 189). See page 191 for information on knitting-stitch embroidery.

Tip-Truck

See Basic Instructions (page 164), allowing approximately 4 (5, 5, 6, 6) balls blue (Totem 1435) and 1 ball each black (Totem 52) and yellow (Totem 2453).

DIRECTIONS

Foll Basic Jumper Patt (page 165), noting foll changes. For all pieces, cast on and work 2 rows in black, 2 rows in yellow, then work rem (except for Front) in blue. For Front, we suggest working larger areas from Tip-Truck Graph (page 190) using winding yarn method, then embroidering any intricate areas in knitting-stitch afterwards (see page 191). After working rib for Front, work 18 (22, 24, 26, 30) rows in blue st st, work from Graph, then complete Front in blue st st. For Neckband, knit up sts and work first 5 rows in blue, 2 rows in yellow, then 2 rows and cast-off in black.

SAILING BOATS GRAPH

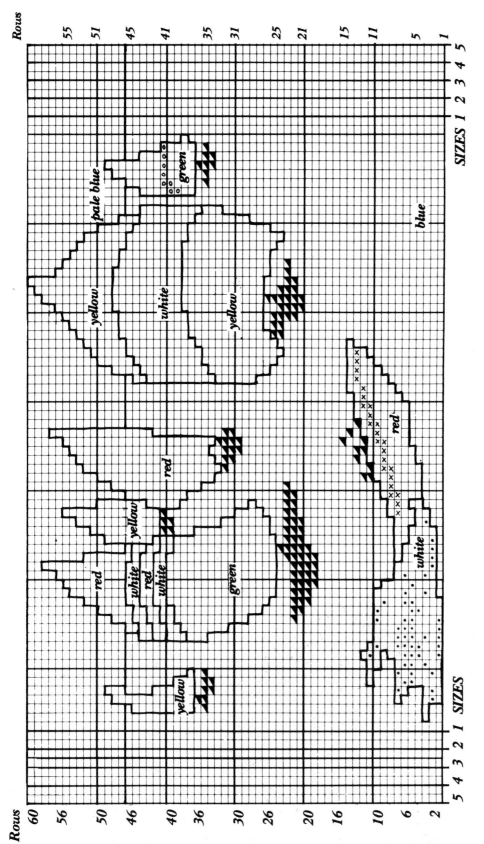

Heavy lines represent changes in colour. Change background colour to Pale blue at Row 47.

KEY FOR KNITTING-STITCH EMBROIDERY

- ⊡ Blue
- ◢ Navy
- ☒ Green
- ⊙ White

1SQ = 1ST

SCARECROW GRAPH

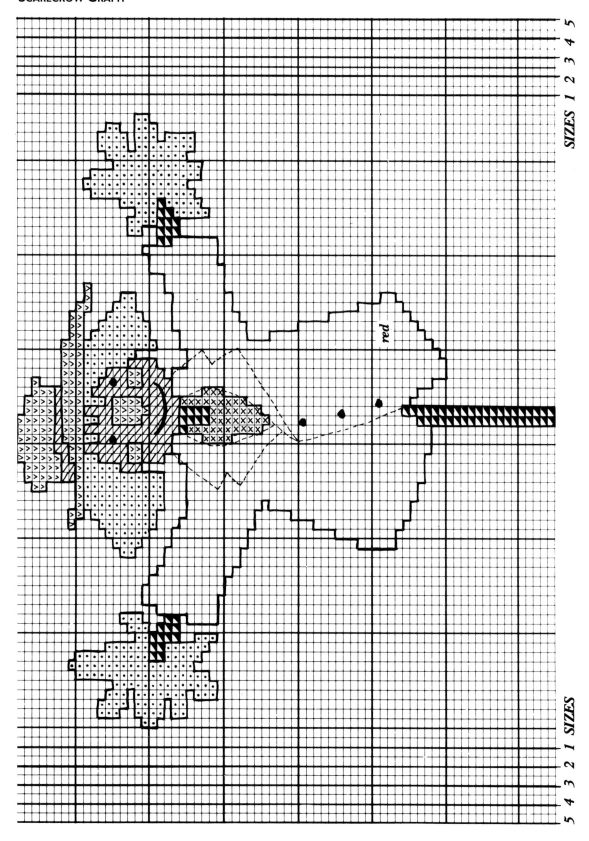

Heavy lines represent changes in colour. Work background in yellow. Work broken lines in black straight-stitch. Work buttons and eyes in large black French knots.

KEY FOR KNITTING-STITCH EMBROIDERY

1SQ = 1ST	◢ Brown	⊻ Red
▪ Blue	⊠ Green	⧄ White

DOODLES GRAPH FOR SLEEVE

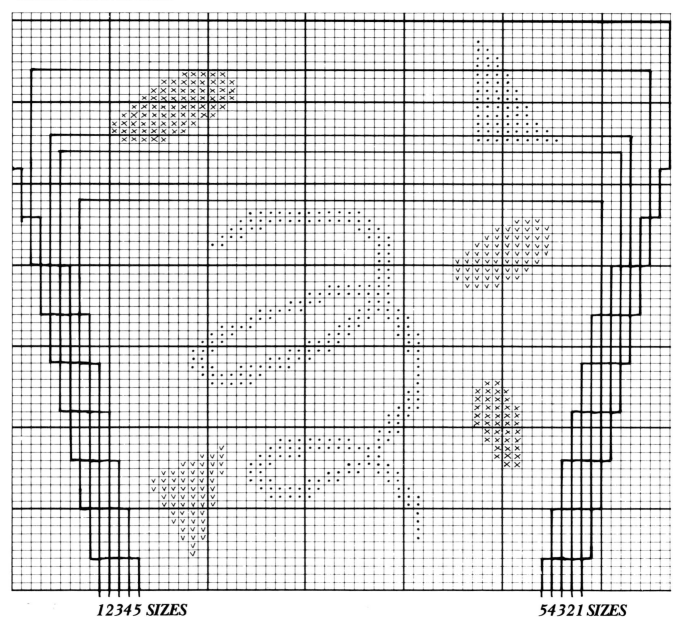

12345 SIZES   *54321 SIZES*

KEY FOR KNITTING-STITCH EMBROIDERY

ISQ = IST   ☒ Red

⊡ Yellow   ⓥ Blue

DOODLES GRAPH FOR BACK AND FRONT

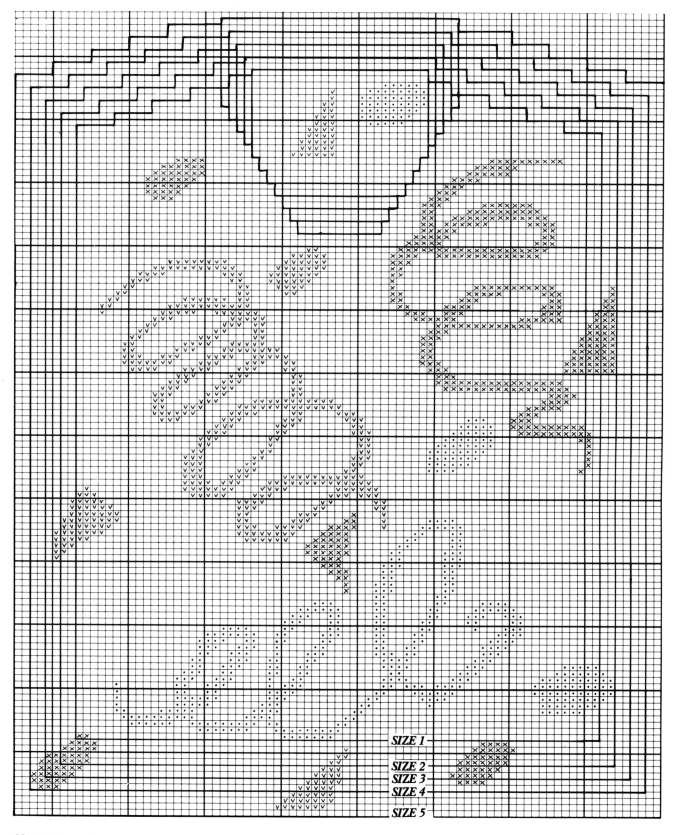

SIZE 1
SIZE 2
SIZE 3
SIZE 4
SIZE 5

KEY FOR KNITTING-STITCH EMBROIDERY

ISQ = IST   ☒ Red
▪ Yellow   ☑ Blue

TIP-TRUCK GRAPH

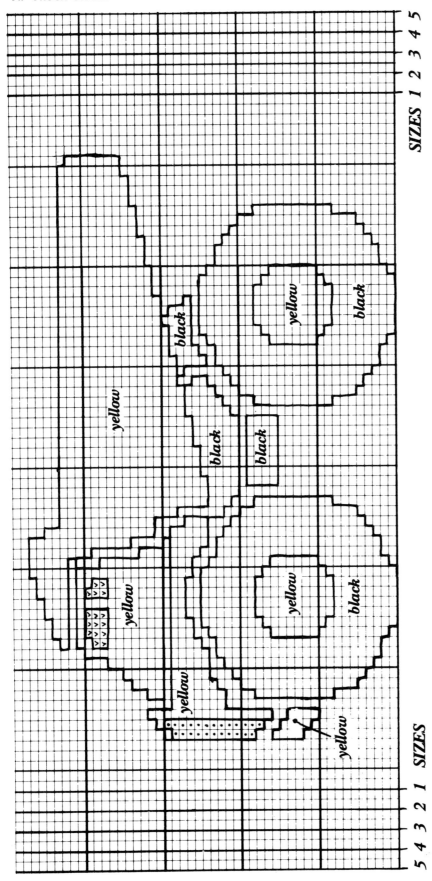

Heavy lines represent changes in colour. Work background in blue.

KEY FOR KNITTING-STITCH EMBROIDERY

- ⊡ Black
- ⊽ Blue

ISQ = IST

PICTURE KNITTING USING THE WINDING YARN METHOD

This is a simple method of knitting-in motifs. It must not be interchanged with Fair Isle. When changing colours in middle of row, twist colour to be used (on wrong side) underneath and to right of colour just used. As you begin each colour, give a gentle tug to even up loose stitches.

It is necessary to use a separate quantity of yarn for each section of colour. To minimise tangles, wind small amounts of yarn onto yarn bobbins. Unwind only enough yarn to knit required stitches, keeping bobbin close to work.

You may find it helpful to colour-in each section of your graph before beginning.

When working from graphs, knit all sts on right-side rows, reading graphs from right to left, and purl all sts on wrong-side rows, reading graphs from left to right.

KNITTING-STITCH EMBROIDERY

Interest can be added to garments with knitting-stitch embroidery — this is very easy to do, especially if you do embroidery before you sew up garment. Knitting-stitch is worked over each knitted stitch with a contrasting colour (see Embroidery Stitch Guide on page 55). It is necessary to use yarn of same thickness as knitted garment. Be careful not to pull stitch too tightly and it will cover existing stitch completely.

A completed stitch looks like a 'V'. Each square on graph represents one stitch. It is a good idea, before beginning, to colour-in graph in colours to be used.

Begin at lower edge of graph, on righthand side.

Using a tapestry or knitter's needle, bring needle from back through centre of stitch below the one to be covered.

*Take needle from right to left under both strands of stitch above the one to be covered.

Bring needle back to start of stitch, take needle behind 2 strands in row below and across into centre of next stitch. You have worked one knitting stitch.

Repeat from *, following graph for required number of stitches. To finish, bring needle back to start of stitch and through to back of work.

To begin second row, bring needle from back to centre of stitch below the one to be covered. Working from left to right, pick up both strands of stitch in row above the one to be covered.

Take needle back to beginning of stitch, pick up 2 strands which brings needle across into centre of next stitch. When working stitch above one worked in previous row your needle will come up in centre of this worked stitch. Repeat this, following graph for number of stitches to be worked.

CROSS-STITCH EMBROIDERY ON KNITTED FABRIC

A new dimension can be added to garments with cross-stitch embroidery — this is very easy to do, especially if you do embroidery before you sew up garment. It is advisable to use a finer yarn than that in which garment was knitted (see Embroidery Stitch Guide on page 55).

Each square on your graph represents one stitch. It is a good idea before beginning to colour graph in colours to be used.

Begin on lefthand side.

1. Using a tapestry needle or knitter's needle, bring needle from back through space to left of stitch to be covered.

2. *Take needle to back through space to right of stitch above the one being covered.

3. Bring needle from back through space to left of next stitch. Repeat from * following graph for required number of stitches (don't pull yarn too tightly or work will pucker). If you find it difficult to work stitches loosely enough, you may prefer to work 2 and 3 as separate operations).

Begin second half of row on righthand side of graph and work back the other way to complete crosses.

To stop yarn from twisting and tangling as you work, drop needle at back after every few stitches and let it hang freely until yarn unwinds.

CARNIVAL COLLECTION

Colour a little one's world with these brilliant knits. Both rug and jumper feature a happy clown motif that's sure to brighten any tiny tot's day.

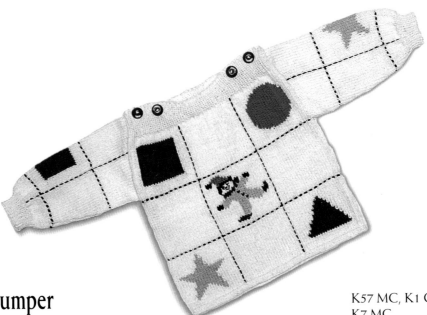

Carnival Jumper

MEASUREMENTS

To fit underarm: 50cm. Garment measures: 57cm. Length: 32cm. Sleeve fits: 19cm.

MATERIALS

Patons Bluebell 5-ply (50g):
- Main Colour (MC): 4 balls
- 1st Contrast (C1): 1 ball
- 2nd Contrast (C2): small quantity for embroidery
- 3rd Contrast (C3): 1 ball
- 4th Contrast (C4): 1 ball
- 5th Contrast (C5): 1 ball
- One pair each 3.00mm (No 11) and 3.75mm (No 9) knitting needles
- Tapestry needle for embroidery
- Four buttons

TENSION

See Knitting Notes on page 158.
26 sts and 35 rows to 10 cm over st st, using 3.75mm needles.

BACK

Using MC and 3mm needles, cast on 77 sts.
Knit 3 rows garter st (first row is wrong side).
Change to 3.75mm needles.
1ST ROW K26, tie a coloured thread around loop which lies before next st, K25, tie a coloured thread around loop which lies before next st, K26.
Work 3 rows st st, beg with a purl row.
NOTE: When changing colours in the middle of a row, twist colour to be used (on wrong side) underneath and to the right of colour just used, making sure both yarns are worked firmly at joins. Use a separate ball of yarn for each section of colour; wind yarn into smaller balls where necessary for easier usage.
PLACE GRAPH D (page 197). 5TH ROW

K57 MC, K1 C1, K11 MC, K1 C1, K7 MC.
6TH ROW P7 MC, P2 C1, P9 MC, P2 C1, P57 MC.
PLACE GRAPH E. 7TH ROW K5 MC, K17 C3, K35 MC, (K3 C1, K7 MC) twice.
Cont working from row 8 of Graphs, as placed in last 3 rows, until row 32 has been completed.
Tie a coloured thread at each end of last row to mark position of embroidery.
Work a further 32 rows st st, tying a coloured thread around centre st in first row.
Tie a coloured thread at each end of last row to mark position of embroidery and beg of armholes.
Work a further 5 rows in st st.
PLACE GRAPH A. 6TH ROW P61 MC, P5 C5, P11 MC.
PLACE GRAPH C. 7TH ROW K9 MC, K9 C5, K37 MC, K17 C4, K5 MC.
Cont working from row 8 of Graphs,

Baby will be warm and enjoy hours of fun wearing a clown motif jumper knitted in Patons Bluebell 5-ply.

as placed in last 2 rows, until row
32 has been completed.
Use MC only for rem.
NEXT ROW K2, *P1, K1; rep from * to
last st, K1.
NEXT ROW K1, *P1, K1; rep from * to
end.**
Rep last 2 rows 6 times more.
NEXT ROW Rib 22, cast off 33 sts
loosely in rib, rib 22.
Work a further 5 rows rib on last
22 sts for underlap.
Cast off loosely in rib.
With wrong side facing, join yarn to
rem 22 sts and work to correspond
with other underlap.

FRONT

Work as for Back to**.
Shape neck. When turning, bring
yarn to front of work, sl next st on
righthand needle, ybk, sl st back on
lefthand needle, then turn and
proceed as instructed, to avoid holes
in work.
1ST ROW Rib 30, turn.
2ND AND ALT ROWS Rib to end.
3RD ROW Rib 26, turn.
5TH ROW Rib 22, turn.
7TH ROW Rib across all sts to end.
Rep rows 1 to 7 incl once.
NEXT ROW (Rib 8, yfwd, K2tog)
twice, rib 38, yfwd, K2tog, rib
8, yfwd, K2tog, rib 7...4 buttonholes.
Work a further 3 rows rib.
Cast off loosely in rib.

LEFT SLEEVE

Using MC and 3mm needles, cast on
37 sts.
Work 11 rows rib as before.
12TH ROW Rib 4, *inc in next st, rib
1; rep from * to last 5 sts, rib 5...51 sts.
Change to 3.75mm needles.
1ST ROW K13, tie a coloured thread
around loop which lies before next st,
K25, tie a coloured thread around
loop which lies before next st, K13.
Work 9 rows st st, beg with a purl row
and inc one st at each end of 4th
row...53 sts.
Tie a coloured thread at each end of
last row to mark position of
embroidery.***
Work a further 4 rows st st, inc one st
at each end of first row...55 sts.
PLACE GRAPH D. NEXT ROW K21 MC,
K1 C1, K11 MC, K1 C1, K21 MC.

Keeping patt correct from 6th row of
Graph D until motif is complete, then
working rem in MC st st only, inc one
st at each end of foll 6th rows from
previous inc until there are 63 sts,
then work a further 7 rows.
Tie a coloured thread at each end of
last row to mark position of
embroidery.
Cont straight in MC st st until work
measures 18 cm from beg, ending with
a purl row.
Cast off 5 sts loosely at beg of next
10 rows.
Cast off rem 13 sts.

RIGHT SLEEVE

Work as for Left Sleeve to***.
Work a further 6 rows st st, inc one st
at each end of first row...55 sts.
PLACE GRAPH C. NEXT ROW Using
MC, inc in first st, K18 MC, K17 C4,
K18 MC, using MC, inc in last st...
57 sts.
Keeping patt correct from 8th row of
Graph C until complete, then working
rem in MC only, inc one st at each
end of foll 6th rows until there are
63 sts, then work a further 7 rows.
Tie a coloured thread at each end of
last row to mark position of
embroidery.
Cont straight in MC st st until work
measures 18cm from beg, ending with
a purl row.
Cast off 5 sts loosely at beg of next
10 rows.
Cast off rem 13 sts.

TO MAKE UP

Using knitting-stitch, embroider
clown motif from Graph F in centre of
Front and Back, as photographed,
using thread tied around centre st as a
guide for positioning. Embroider
features as photographed. Using C2,
embroider horizontal and vertical lines
of running-stitch on all pieces where
indicated by coloured threads (do not
remove coloured threads for
armholes). With a slightly damp cloth
and warm iron, press lightly. Lap
Front shoulders over Back for 6 rows
and oversew tog at armhole edge.
Using back-stitch, join Sleeve seams
and side seams to coloured threads.
Sew in Sleeves. Sew on buttons. Press
seams.

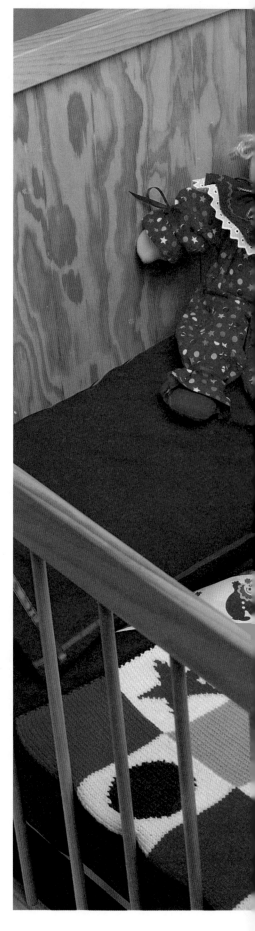

This warm snuggly rug in bright primary colours will be an instant hit with any baby or toddler.

Carnival Cot Cover

MEASUREMENTS
Width: 67cm. Length: 100cm.

MATERIALS
Patons Totem 8-ply (50g):
- Main Colour (MC): 4 balls
- 1st Contrast (C1): 1 ball
- 2nd Contrast (C2): 2 balls
- 3rd Contrast (C3): 1 ball
- 4th Contrast (C4): 2 balls
- 5th Contrast (C5): 1 ball
- 6th Contrast (C6): 2 balls
- One pair 4mm (No 8) knitting needles
- Tapestry needle for embroidery
- One 3.50mm (No 9) crochet hook for Edging

TENSION
See Knitting Notes on page 158 and Crochet Notes on page 201.
22.5 sts and 30 rows to 10cm over st st, using 4mm needles.

STRIP I
NOTE: When changing colours in the middle of a row, twist the colour to be used (on wrong side) underneath and to the right of the colour just used, making sure both yarns are worked firmly at joins. Use a separate ball of yarn for each section of colour; wind yarn into smaller balls where necessary.

Using MC, cast on 27 sts.
Using MC and C1, work rows 1 to 32 incl from Graph A on page 197.
Using C2, work 32 rows st st.
Using MC and C3, work rows 1 to 32 incl from Graph B.
Using C1, work 32 rows st st.
Using MC and C4, work rows 1 to 32 incl from Graph A.
Using C5, work 32 rows st st.
Using MC and C4, work rows 1 to 32 incl from Graph C.
Using C2, work 32 rows st st.
Using MC and C5, work rows 1 to 32 incl from Graph A.
Cast off loosely.

STRIP 2
Using C6, cast on 27 sts.
Work 32 rows st st.

Using MC, work 32 rows st st, tying a coloured thread around centre st in first row.
Using C4, work 32 rows st st.
Using MC and C6, work rows 1 to 32 incl from Graph D.
Using C3, work 32 rows st st.
Using MC and C2, work rows 1 to 32 incl from Graph E.
Using C6, work 32 rows st st.
Using MC, work 32 rows st st, tying a coloured thread around centre st in first row.
Using C4, work 32 rows st st.
Cast off loosely.

STRIP 3

Using MC, cast on 27 sts.
Using MC and C4, work rows 1 to 32 incl from Graph D.
Using C5, work 32 rows st st.
Using MC and C1, work rows 1 to 32 incl from Graph C.
Using C2, work 32 rows st st.
Using MC, work 32 rows st st, tying a coloured thread around centre st in first row.
Using C1, work 32 rows st st.
Using MC and C2, work rows 1 to 32 incl from Graph D.
Using C5, work 32 rows st st.
Using MC and C1, work rows 1 to 32 incl from Graph B.
Cast off loosely.

STRIP 4

Using C3, cast on 27 sts.
Work 32 rows st st.

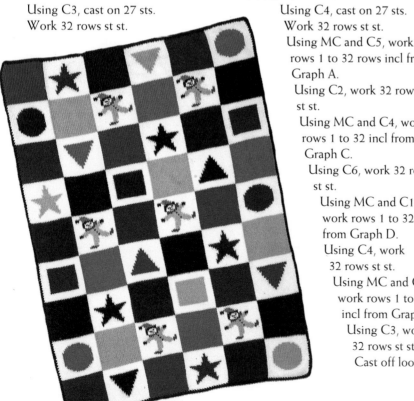

Using MC, work 32 rows st st, tying a coloured thread around centre st in first row.
Using C6, work 32 rows st st.
Using MC and C3, work rows 1 to 32 incl from Graph E.
Using C4, work 32 rows st st.
Using MC and C6, work rows 1 to 32 incl from Graph C.
Using C3, work 32 rows st st.
Using MC, work 32 rows st st, tying a coloured thread around centre st in first row.
Using C6, work 32 rows st st.
Cast off loosely.

STRIP 5

Using MC, cast on 27 sts.
Using MC and C2, work rows 1 to 32 incl from Graph B.
Using C1, work 32 rows st st.
Using MC and C2, work rows 1 to 32 incl from Graph D.
Using C5, work 32 rows st st.
Using MC, work 32 rows st st, tying a coloured thread around centre st in first row.
Using C2, work 32 rows st st.
Using MC and C5, work rows 1 to 32 incl from Graph B.
Using C1, work 32 rows st st.
Using MC and C4, work rows 1 to 32 incl from Graph D.
Cast off loosely.

STRIP 6

Using C4, cast on 27 sts.
Work 32 rows st st.
Using MC and C5, work rows 1 to 32 rows incl from Graph A.
Using C2, work 32 rows of st st.
Using MC and C4, work rows 1 to 32 incl from Graph C.
Using C6, work 32 rows st st.
Using MC and C1, work rows 1 to 32 incl from Graph D.
Using C4, work 32 rows st st.
Using MC and C6, work rows 1 to 32 incl from Graph A.
Using C3, work 32 rows st st.
Cast off loosely.

TO MAKE UP

Using knitting-stitch, embroider clown motif from Graph F on all MC squares, using thread tied around centre st as a guide for positioning. Embroider features as photographed. With a slightly damp cloth and warm iron, press lightly. Using back-stitch, join Strips tog as shown in diagram. With right side facing, using hook and C2, work 2 rounds double crochet around outside edges of Cover, taking care not to stretch work and inc at corners to keep work flat. Fasten off. Press seams and Edging.

KEY FOR KNITTING-STITCH EMBROIDERY

- ⊡ C1
- ◩ C2
- ◪ C3
- ◼ C4
- ⊠ C5
- ☐ MC background stitches

1SQ = 1ST

Knit all sts on right-side (odd-numbered) rows, reading Graphs from right to left, and purl all sts on wrong-side (even-numbered) rows, reading Graphs from left to right. Heavy lines represent areas to be worked in contrast colours as instructed in pattern. All background areas are worked in MC.

DIAGRAM FOR JOINING STRIPS FOR COT COVER

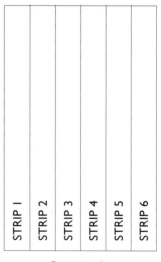

STRIP 1 | STRIP 2 | STRIP 3 | STRIP 4 | STRIP 5 | STRIP 6

Cast-on edge

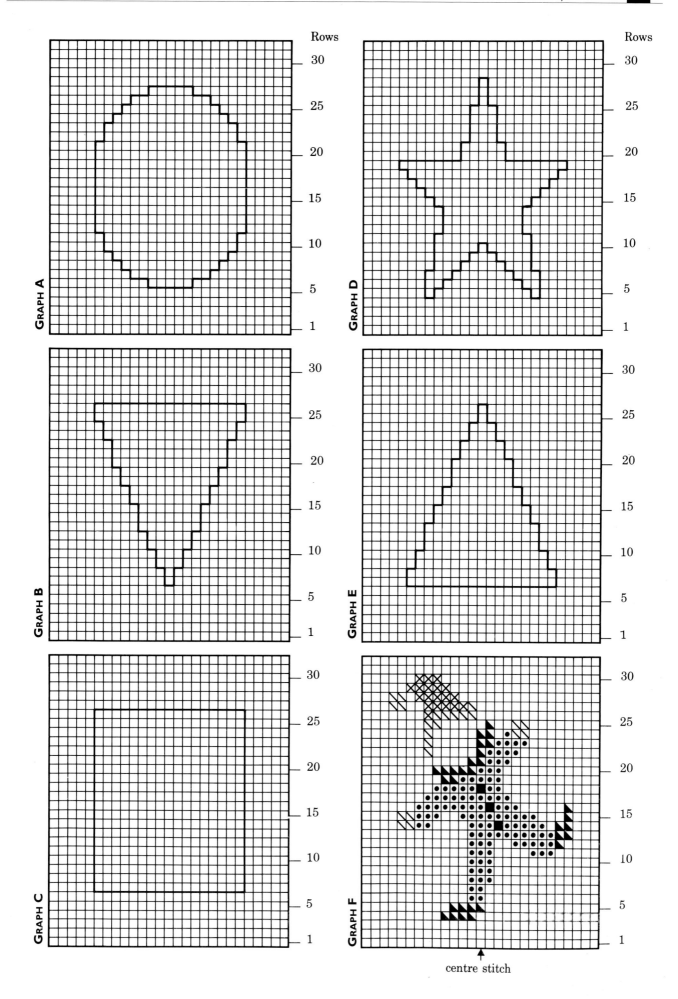

Rows

GRAPH A

GRAPH B

GRAPH C

GRAPH D

GRAPH E

GRAPH F

centre stitch

Crochet and Tatting

The origins of crochet are obscure, but for thousands of years crochet has been worked in the Middle East. During the Renaissance crochet patterns were developed to imitate the beautiful Guipure and Richelieu laces. In the 1800s these beautiful patterns were developed further by nuns and crochet workers in Ireland.

Though a shuttle is used instead of a hook, the nature of tatting gives this craft a close affiliation with crochet. Tatting is composed of knots and picots from which various types of designs are produced. Tatting, like crochet, has obscure origins, though references have been made to tatting in the history of many countries.

Crochet and tatting are gaining popularity today, as people long for the beautiful edgings on clothing and household items of yesteryear.

NERÉE HARTOG

A HIGHLAND FLING

The thrifty Scots certainly knew what they were doing when they invented tartan. Its deceptively simple patterning is so versatile, never dates and is bright enough to cheer up the bleakest winter weather. Two bright rugs designed by Kath Baker in authentic Scottish tartans will be essentials for travelling on cool days, or as ground covers at picnics or at the weekend football game.

MacLeod Hunting Tartan Rug

MEASUREMENTS
Finished rug is approximately 134.5cm square.

MATERIALS
8-ply acrylic yarn (100g):
- 4 balls blue; 3 balls black; 3 balls green; 1 ball yellow; 1 ball red
- One each 4mm (No 8) and 5.50mm (No 5) crochet hook
- Knitter's needle

RUG
Using 4mm hook and black yarn, make 254 chain.
1ST ROW Miss 5ch, 1tr into next chain, *1ch, miss 1ch, 1tr in next ch;

rep from * to end...125 spaces.
2ND ROW Using green yarn, 4ch, *1tr in next tr, 1ch; rep from * to end, 1tr in 2nd turning ch.
Rep 2nd row, working 5 more rows green, *4 rows black, 8 rows blue, 1 row black, 1 row yellow, 1 row black, 8 rows blue, 4 rows black, 6 rows green, 1 row black, 1 row red, 1 row black; rep from * twice, omitting last 2 rows...125 rows.

WEAVING CHAINS
Using 4mm hook and blue yarn, make a 152cm length of chain, leaving 8cm yarn at each end for darning in. Fasten off. The chain should be long enough to weave through spaces without being too tight.
Using blue yarn, make 47 more chains the same...48 blue chains.
Make 36 lengths of chain each from

green and black yarn.
Make 3 lengths of chain in yellow and 2 lengths of chain in red.
Beg at last row of sps, weave a black chain vertically through this row.
Continue weaving *6 rows green, 4 rows black, 8 rows blue, 1 row black, 1 row yellow, 1 row black, 8 rows blue, 4 rows black, 6 rows green, 1 row black, 1 row red, 1 row black; rep from * twice omitting last red and black rows...all spaces filled.
Darn all ends and trim neatly.

EDGING
Using 5.5mm hook and red yarn, work 2 rows of dc evenly around rug, working extra dc in each corner.
Fasten off.

MacGregor Tartan Rug

MEASUREMENTS

Finished rug is approximately 132cm square.

MATERIALS

8-ply acrylic yarn (100g):
- 5 balls red; 5 balls green; 1 ball black; 1 ball white
- One each 4mm (No 8) and 5.50mm (No 5) crochet hook
- Knitter's needle

RUG

NOTE: 3ch at beg of row stands for 1tr.

Using 4mm hook and red yarn, make 250 chain.

1ST ROW Miss 5ch, 1tr in next ch *1ch, miss 1 ch, 1tr in next ch; rep from * to end...123 spaces.

2ND ROW 4ch *1tr in next tr, 1ch; rep from * to end, 1tr in 2nd turning ch.

Rep 2nd row, working 10 more rows red, *6 rows green, 2 rows red, 3 rows green, 1 row black, 1 row white, 1 row black, 3 rows green, 2 rows red, 6 rows green, 12 rows red; rep from * twice...123 rows.

WEAVING CHAINS

Using 4mm hook and red, make a 147cm length of chain, leaving 8cm yarn at each end for darning in. Fasten off. The chain should be long enough to weave through spaces without being too tight.

Using red, make 59 more lengths of chain the same...60 red chains. Using green, make 54 lengths of chain.

Using black, make 6 lengths of chain. Using white, make 3 lengths of chain. Beg at last row of sps, weave a red chain vertically through this row and next 11 rows of spaces. Continue weaving *6 rows green, 2 rows red, 3 rows green, 1 row black, 1 row white, 1 row black, 3 rows green, 2 rows red, 6 rows green, 12 rows red; rep from * twice...all spaces filled.

Darn all ends and trim neatly.

EDGING

Using 5.5mm hook and green yarn, work 2 rows of dc evenly around rug, working extra dc in each corner. Fasten off.

CROCHET NOTES

CROCHET ABBREVIATIONS

Bl: block = 3tr;
ch: chain;
cl: cluster;
crab st: work as for dc, working from left to right instead of from right to left;
dc: double crochet;
dec: decrease (insert hook into first st, draw through and leave on hook, insert hook into next st, draw yarn through, yoh and draw through all 3 lps);
dtr: double treble;
htr: half treble;
lp/s: loop/s;
rep: repeat;
rnd/s: round/s;
sl st: slip-stitch;
sp: space;
st/s: stitch/es;
tr: treble;
yoh: yarn over hook.

The MacGregor tartan (below) and the MacLeod tartan (opposite) are made by first crocheting a mesh through which chains of colour are then woven.

OLD-FASHIONED FAVOURITES

R emember the days before plastic wrap, when no bride's 'glory box' was considered complete without a set of beaded crochet covers for the tops of jugs and bowls? Well, here they are again, practical and pretty as ever, and decorated with perfect miniature teapots, cups and saucers — a lovely touch of whimsy for your breakfast table or tea-tray.

Each of the doilies is slightly different. The tall jug is topped with a classic filet cover; the next two, with their quaint decoration, are worked in a pretty lace pattern, and the front doily is a fluted design with an interesting border detail. Crochet instructions begin opposite.

Filet Jug Cover or Doily

MEASUREMENTS
Approximately 23cm diameter.

MATERIALS
- No 30 crochet cotton: 1 ball
- 0.75mm crochet hook
- 8 glass beads (for jug cover only)

COVER
Make 8 ch, join with sl st to form ring.
NOTE: 3 ch at beg of rnd stands for 1tr.
1ST RND 3 ch, 15tr in ring, sl st in 3rd ch at beg.
2ND RND 3 ch, 1tr in same place as sl st, 1tr in next tr, *2ch, 2tr in next tr, 1tr in next tr; rep from *6 times, 2ch, sl st in 3rd ch at beg.
3RD RND 3 ch, 1tr in same place as sl st, 1tr in next tr, 2tr in next tr; *2ch, 2tr in next tr, 1tr in next tr, 2tr in next tr; rep from *6 times, 2ch, sl st in 3rd ch at beg.
4TH RND 3ch, 1tr in same place as sl st, 1tr in each of next 3tr, 2tr in next tr, *2ch, 2tr in next tr, 1tr in each of next 3tr, 2tr in next tr; rep from *6 times, 2ch, sl st in 3rd ch at beg.
5TH RND 3ch, 1tr in same place as sl st, 1tr in each of next 5tr, 2tr in next tr, *2ch, 2tr in next tr, 1tr in each of next 5tr, 2tr in next tr; rep from *6 times, 2ch, sl st in 3rd ch at beg.
Cont in this way working an extra tr in each rep until 10th rnd has been completed...19tr in each rep.
11TH RND 3ch, *1tr in each of next 3tr. (2ch, miss 1tr, 1tr in next tr) 6 times, 1tr in each of next 3tr, 2ch, 1tr in next tr; rep from * around, omitting 1tr in last rep, sl st in 3rd ch at beg.
12TH RND 3ch, *1tr in each of next 3tr, 2ch, (1tr in next tr, 1tr in each of next 2ch) twice, 1tr in next tr, (2ch, 1tr in next tr) 3 times, (2ch, miss 1tr, 1tr in next tr) twice, 2ch, 1tr in next tr; rep from * around, omitting 1tr in last rep, sl st in 3rd ch at beg.
13TH RND 3ch, *1tr in each of next 3tr, 1tr in each of next 2ch, 1tr in next tr, (2ch, miss 1tr, 1tr in next tr) twice, (2ch, 1tr in next tr) 6 times; rep from * around, omitting 1tr in last rep, sl st in 3rd ch at beg.
14TH RND 5 ch, *miss 2tr, 1tr in next tr, 2ch, miss 2tr, 1tr in next tr, (1tr in each of next 2ch, 1tr in next tr) 3 times, (2ch, 1tr in next tr) 4 times, 1tr in each of next 2ch, 1tr in next tr, 2ch; rep from * around, omitting 1tr and 2ch in last rep, sl st in 3rd ch at beg.
15TH RND 5ch, *1tr in next 2ch-sp, 2ch, 1tr in next tr, 1tr in each of next 2ch, 1tr in each of next 10tr, 1tr in each of next 2ch, 1tr in next tr (2ch, 1tr in next tr) twice, 2ch, 1tr in next 2ch-sp, 2ch, 1tr in each of next 4tr, 2ch; rep from * around, omitting 1tr and 2ch in last rep, sl st in 3rd ch at beg.

16TH RND 5ch, *1tr in next tr, 2ch, 1tr in each of next 7tr, (2ch, miss 2tr, 1tr in next tr) twice, 1tr in each of next 3tr, (2ch, 1tr in next tr) 4 times, 2ch, miss 2tr, 1tr in next tr, 2ch; rep from * around, omitting 1tr and 2ch in last rep, sl st in 3rd ch at beg.

17TH RND 5ch, *1tr in next tr, 2ch, 1tr in each of next 7tr, 2ch, 1tr in next tr, 1tr in each of next 2ch, 1tr in each of next 4tr, (2ch, 1tr in next tr) 5 times, 2ch; rep from * around, omitting 1tr and 2ch in last rep, sl st in 3rd ch at beg.

18TH RND 5ch, *1tr in next tr, 2ch, 1tr in next tr, 2ch, miss 2tr, 1tr in each of next 4tr, 1tr in each of next 2ch, 1tr in each of next 4tr, 2ch, miss 2tr, 1tr in next tr, (2ch, 1tr in next tr) 5 times, 2ch; rep from * around, omitting 1tr and 2ch in last rep, sl st in 3rd ch at beg. Complete each star point by working in rows.

1ST ROW 5ch, 1tr in next tr, (2ch, 1tr in next tr) twice, (2ch, miss 2ch, 1tr in next tr) 3 times, (2ch, 1tr in next tr) 5 times, turn...11 sps.

2ND ROW Sl st in each of 2ch and 1tr, 5ch, 1tr in next tr, (2ch, 1tr in next tr) 8 times, turn...9sps.

3RD ROW Sl st in each of 2ch and 1tr, 5ch, 1tr in next tr, (2ch, 1tr in next tr) 6 times, turn...7sps.

4TH ROW Sl st in each of 2ch and 1tr, 5ch, 1tr in next tr, (2ch, 1tr in next tr) 4 times, turn...5 sps.

5TH ROW Sl st in each of 2ch and 1tr, 5ch, 1tr in next tr, (2ch, 1tr in next tr) twice, turn...3 sps.

6TH ROW Sl st in each of 2ch and 1tr, 5ch, 1tr in next tr...1 sp.
Fasten off.
Miss 2ch on 18th rnd, join thread to next tr and work rows 1 to 6 incl for next point.
Cont in this way until all 8 points have been worked, noting for jug cover, to thread beads onto cotton before commencing last point and push along until needed for edging. Do not fasten yarn off after completing last point.

EDGING

1ch, 1dc in same place as ch, *5ch, (sl st in 3rd ch from hook = picot), 2ch, 1dc in corner of next row; rep from * around, picking up a bead instead of working a picot at each point.
Fasten off and weave all ends securely into work.

Lace Cover with Teapot and Blue Beads

Lace Cover with Teapot and Blue Beads

MEASUREMENTS
Approximately 15cm diameter.

MATERIALS
- No 40 crochet cotton: 1 ball
- 0.6mm crochet hook
- 23 glass beads
- 5cm fine wire
- Small amount polyester filling
- Petal Porcelain or craft glue

COVER

Thread 18 beads onto cotton and push along until needed in 13th rnd.
Make 10ch, join with sl st to form ring.
NOTE: 3ch at beg of rnd stands for 1tr.

1ST RND 3ch, 1tr in ring, (3ch, 2tr in ring) 7 times, 3ch, sl st in 3rd ch at beg.

2ND RND 3ch, 1tr in next tr, *5ch, 1tr in each of next 2tr; rep from * 6 times, 5ch, sl st in 3rd ch at beg.

3RD RND 3ch, 1tr in next tr, *3tr, 2ch, 3tr in 5ch-sp, 1tr in each of next 2tr; rep from * 6 times, 3tr, 2ch, 3tr in 5ch-sp, sl st in 3rd ch at beg.

4TH RND 3ch, 1tr in each of next 2tr, *2tr, 5ch, 2tr, in 2ch-sp, miss 2tr, 1tr in each of next 4tr; rep from * around, ending last rep with 1tr instead of 4tr, sl st in 3rd ch at beg.

5TH RND 3ch, 1tr in each of next 2tr, *3ch, 6dtr in 5ch-sp, 3ch, miss 2tr, 1tr in each of next 4tr; rep from * around, ending last rep with 1tr instead of 4tr, sl st in 3rd ch at beg.

6TH RND 3ch, 1tr in each of next 2tr, *4ch, (1tr in next dtr, 2ch) 5 times, 1tr in next dtr, 4ch, 1tr in each of next 4tr; rep from * around, ending last rep with 1tr instead of 4tr, sl st in 3rd ch at beg.

7TH RND 3ch, 1tr in each of next 2tr, *5ch, miss 4ch-sp, 1dc in next 2ch-sp, (3ch, 1dc in next 2ch-sp) 4 times, 5ch, miss next 4ch-sp, 1tr in each of next 4tr; rep from * around, ending last rep with 1tr instead of 4tr, sl st in 3rd ch at beg.

8TH RND 3 ch, 1tr in each of next 2tr, *6ch, 1dc in next 3ch-lp, (3ch, 1dc in next 3ch-lp), 3 times, 6ch, 1tr in each of next 4tr; rep from * around, ending last rep with 1tr instead of 4tr, sl st in 3rd ch at beg.

9TH RND 3ch, 1tr in each of next 2tr, *2tr in next 6ch-sp, 6ch, 1dc in next 3ch-lp, (3ch, 1dc in next 3ch-lp) twice, 6ch, 2tr in next 6ch-sp, 1tr in each of next 4tr; rep from * around, ending last rep with 1tr instead of 4tr, sl st in 3rd ch at beg.

10TH RND Sl st in each of next 3tr, 3ch, 1tr in next tr, *2tr in next 6ch-sp, 6ch, 1dc in next 3ch-lp, 3ch, 1dc in next 3ch-lp, 6ch, 2tr in next 6ch-sp, 1tr in each of next 2tr, 4ch, miss 4tr, 1tr in each of next 2tr; rep from * around, omitting last 2tr from last rep, sl st in 3rd ch at beg.

11TH RND Sl st in each of next 2tr, 3ch, 1tr in next tr, *2tr in next 6ch-sp, 6ch, 1dc in next 3ch-lp, 6ch, 2tr in next 6ch-sp, 1tr in each of next 2tr, 4ch, 1tr in next 4ch-sp, 4ch, miss 2tr, 1tr in each of next 2tr ; rep from * around, omitting last 2tr from last rep, sl st in 3rd ch at beg.

12TH RND 3ch, 1tr in next tr, *6ch, 1dc in next 6ch-sp, 6ch, 1dc in next 6ch-sp, 6ch, miss 2tr, 1tr in each of next 2tr, 2tr in next 4ch-sp, 4ch, 2tr in next 4ch-sp, 1tr in each of next 2tr; rep from * around, omitting last 2tr from last rep, sl st in 3rd ch at beg.

13TH RND Sl st in each of next 1tr and 3ch, *6ch, pick up bead, 6ch, miss 6ch-sp, 1dc in next 6ch-sp, 4ch, miss 2tr, 1tr in each of next 2tr, 2tr in next 4ch-sp, pick up bead, 2tr in same sp, 1tr in each of next 2tr, 4ch, 1dc in next 6ch-sp; rep from * around, omitting last dc from last rep, sl st in first ch at beg.

Fasten off and weave end securely into last rnd.

TEAPOT

Join thread to right side of centre of cover.

1ST RND 1ch, 15dc in ring, working between tr of 1st rnd of cover, sl st in first ch at beg.

2ND RND 1ch, 1dc in each dc around, sl st in first ch at beg.

3RD RND 2ch, 1htr in same place, 2htr in each dc around, sl st in 2nd ch at beg.

4TH RND 2ch, 1htr in each htr around, sl st in 2nd ch at beg. Rep 4th rnd twice more.

7TH RND 2ch, 1htr in each of next 2htr, *miss 1htr, 1htr in each of next 3htr; rep from * around, sl st in 2nd ch at beg.

8TH RND 2ch, 1htr in next htr, *miss 1htr, 1htr in each of next 2htr; rep from * around, sl st in 2nd ch at beg.

9TH RND 2ch, *miss 1htr, 1htr in next

htr; rep from * around, sl st in 2nd ch at beg. Fasten off.

LID

Leaving a 10cm end, make 2ch, join with sl st to form a ring.

1ST RND 2ch, 8htr in ring, sl st in 2nd ch at beg, using a sl st, fasten edge of lid to one side of opening of teapot. Work 12ch for handle and fasten to side of pot with sl st, work 15dc over ch.

Fasten off. Attach a bead to centre of lid, using starting thread.

Finish off all ends securely.

SPOUT

Following illustration, fold wire in half leaving a small loop at centre and twist wire under loop. Thread 4 beads on wire, insert ends of wire in pot opposite handle then separate wires inside pot, turning ends over. Bend wire in a curve.

TO FINISH

Fill pot with polyester filling and coat pot with craft glue or Petal Porcelain to stiffen, and allow to dry to desired shape.

The cup and saucer and tiny teapot, complete with opening lid, are crocheted to the finished doilies and stiffened lightly to keep their shape.

Lace Cover with Cup and Saucer

MEASUREMENTS

Approximately 15cm diameter.

MATERIALS

- No 40 crochet cotton: 1 ball
- One 0.6mm and one 0.75mm crochet hook
- 18 glass beads
- Petal Porcelain or craft glue
- Plastic thimble

COVER

Work as for Lace Cover With Teapot, see opposite, until 12th rnd has been completed.

13TH RND Sl st in each of next 1tr and 3ch, 1ch to stand for 1dc, *5ch, miss 2ch in next 6ch-sp, 2tr in next ch, 2ch, 2tr in next ch, 5ch, 1dc in next 6ch-sp, 5ch, miss 2tr, 1tr in each of next 2tr, 4tr in next 4ch-sp, 1tr in each of next 2tr, 5ch, 1dc in next 6ch-sp; rep from * around, omitting last dc from last rep, sl st in first ch at beg.

14TH RND 1ch, *6ch, 1htr in 2ch-sp, 3ch, pick up bead, 1htr in same sp, 6ch, 1dc in next dc, 7ch, miss 2tr, 1tr in each of next 4tr, 7ch, 1dc in next dc; rep from * around, omitting last dc from last rep, sl st in first ch at beg. Fasten off and weave end securely into last rnd.

Fluted Cover with Teapot

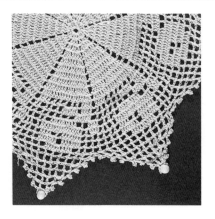

MEASUREMENTS
Approximately 15cm diameter.

MATERIALS
- No 40 crochet cotton: 1 ball
- 0.6mm crochet hook
- 21 glass beads
- 5cm fine wire
- Small amount polyester filling
- Petal Porcelain or craft glue

COVER
Thread 16 beads onto cotton and push along until needed in 14th rnd.

Make 10ch, join with sl st to form ring.

1ST RND 2ch, 15htr in ring, sl st in 2nd ch at beg.

NOTE: 3ch at beg of rnd stands for 1tr.

2ND RND 3ch, 1tr in same place as sl st, 2tr in each htr around, sl st in 3rd ch at beg...32tr.

3RD RND 3ch, keeping last lp of each st on hook, work 1tr in each of next 3tr, yoh and draw through all lps on hook, *5ch, keeping last lp of each st on hook, work 1tr in each of next 4tr, yoh and draw through all lps on hook; rep from * 6 times, 5ch, sl st in cl at beg...8cl.

4TH RND 2ch, 6htr in each 5ch-sp around, working only 5htr in last 5ch-sp, sl st in 2nd ch at beg.

5TH RND 3ch, 1tr, 2ch, 2tr in same place as sl st, *5ch, miss 6htr, 2tr, 2ch, 2tr in sp between htr over cl in 3rd rnd; rep from * 6 times, 5ch, sl st in 3rd ch at beg.

6TH RND Sl st in next tr and in 2ch-sp, 3ch, 1tr, 2ch, 2tr in same 2ch-sp, *5ch, 1dc in 5ch-sp, 5ch, 2tr, 2ch, 2tr in 2ch-sp; rep from * 6 times, 5ch, 1dc in 5ch-sp, 5ch, sl st in 3rd ch at beg.

7TH RND Sl st in next tr and in 2ch-sp, 3ch, 1tr, 2ch, 2tr in same 2ch-sp, *(5ch, 1dc in 5ch-sp) twice, 5ch, 2tr 2ch, 2tr in 2ch-sp; rep from * around, ending with 5ch, sl st in 3rd ch at beg.

8TH RND Sl st in next tr and in 2ch-sp, 3ch, 1tr, 2ch, 2tr in same 2ch-sp, *5ch, 1dc in next 5ch-sp, 5ch, 2tr, 2ch, 2tr in centre ch of next 5ch-sp, 5ch, 1dc in next 5ch-sp, 5ch, 2tr, 2ch, 2tr in 2ch-sp; rep from * around, ending with 5ch, sl st in 3rd ch at beg.

9TH RND As 7th rnd.

10TH RND Sl st in next tr and in 2ch-sp, 1dc in same 2ch-sp, *(5ch, 1dc in next 5ch-sp) 3 times, 5ch, 1dc in next 2ch-sp; rep from * around, ending with 5ch, sl st in 1st dc at beg.

11TH RND Sl st in each of next 3ch, 1dc in 5ch-sp, *5ch, 1dc in next 5ch-sp; rep from * around, ending with 5ch, sl st in 1st dc at beg.

12TH RND 3ch, 4tr in 5ch-sp, 5tr in each 5ch-sp around, sl st in 3rd ch at beg.

13TH RND 4ch, *miss 1tr, 1tr in next tr, 1ch; rep from * around, sl st in 3rd ch at beg.

14TH RND 6ch, 1tr in 4tr ch from hook, (2tr in next ch) twice, *miss 1tr of 13th rnd, 1tr in next tr, 3ch, pick up bead, 5tr around stem of last tr worked; rep from * around, picking up bead on every 5th rep only, sl st in 4th ch at beg.

Fasten off and weave end securely into last rnd.

TEAPOT
Work as for Lace Cover with Teapot, on page 204.

CUP
Using a 0.75mm hook, join thread to foundation ch of cover.

1ST RND 2ch, *1dc between tr of 1st rnd of cover, 1ch; rep from * around, sl st in first ch at beg.

2ND RND 2ch, 1htr in next ch, *1htr in next dc, 1htr in next ch; rep from * around, sl st in 2nd ch at beg...16htr.

3RD RND 2ch, *1dc in each of next 2htr, 1ch; rep from * around, ending 1dc in last dc, sl st in 1st ch at beg.

4TH RND 2ch, *1htr in next ch, 1dc in each of next 2dc; rep from * around, ending with 1htr in last dc, sl st in 2nd ch at beg...24htr.

5TH RND 1ch, 1dc in each htr around, sl st in 1st ch at beg.

HANDLE
Work 5ch and sl st to side of cup. Fasten off.

SAUCER
Using a 0.75mm hook, pass cotton through base of tr of 1st rnd of cover and fasten securely to form a foundation ring on right side between cup and cover.

1ST RND 3ch, 2tr in foundation ring between tr of 1st rnd of cover, 1ch, *3tr in foundation ring between tr of 1st rnd of cover, 1ch; rep from * around, sl st in 3rd ch at beg...24tr.

2ND RND 2ch, 1htr in each of next 2tr, *2htr in 1ch-sp, 1htr in each of next 3tr; rep from * around, sl st in 2nd ch at beg...40tr.

3RD RND S 1ch, 1dc in next htr, 2ch, *1dc in each of next 2htr, 2ch; rep from * around, sl st in ch at beg. Fasten off.

TO FINISH
Weave in all ends securely. Coat cup and saucer with craft glue or Petal Porcelain to stiffen and allow to dry using a plastic thimble to hold desired shape.

PRESENT FROM THE PAST

Those quaintly posed and precious sepia photos of Grandma as a baby often featured exquisite little clothes that perhaps *her* grandmother had made. This pretty crocheted dress and bootees are just the sort of heirloom outfit that today's doting Granny might have the time to make for a very special new grand-daughter.

Crochet Dress and Bootees

MEASUREMENTS
To fit baby 3 (6) months. Height: 34 (38) cm. Sleeve length: 4cm (both sides).

MATERIALS
Panda Lyscot (100g):
- 2 balls (both sizes)
- 2mm crochet hook
- Four small buttons
- Ribbon

TENSION
See Crochet Notes on page 201.
33 sts and 17 rows to 10cm over treble fabric, using 2mm hook.

Crocheted in easy care Panda Lyscot, the dress and bootees will fit a baby from three to six months old. The circular yoke is in plain treble, the sleeves and skirt feature a lacy pattern with a delicate picot edge.

SPECIAL ABBREVIATIONS
Half cluster: yoh, draw up a lp in next tr or half cluster, yoh and draw through all 3 lps on hook;

cluster: yoh and draw up a lp in same tr or cluster just used, yoh, draw up a lp in next tr or cluster, yoh and draw through all 5 lps on hook;

crab st: work as for dc, but work from left to right instead of right to left, so that sts are worked backwards;

picot: 3ch, sl st into first of these 3ch.

DRESS

YOKE (BEGIN AT NECKLINE)
With 2mm hook, make 74 (88) ch.
1ST ROW (wrong side). Miss 3 ch, 1tr in each of next 2 (3) ch, *2tr in next ch, 1tr in each of next 4 (5) ch, rep from * to last 4ch, 2tr in next ch, 1tr in each of next 3ch...86 (100) tr, counting 3ch as 1tr.
2ND ROW (1dc, 1ch) in first tr, 1tr in each of next 3tr, *2tr in next tr, 1tr in each of next 5 (6) tr, rep from * to last 4 (5) sts, 2tr in next tr, 1tr in each of next 2 (3) tr, 1tr in top of turning ch...100 (114) tr, counting (1dc, 1ch) as 1tr.
3RD ROW (1dc, 1ch) in first tr, 1tr in each of next 3 (4) tr, *2tr in next tr, 1tr in each of next 6 (7) tr, rep from * to last 5 sts, 2tr in next tr, 1tr in each of next 3tr, 1tr in top of turning ch...114 (128) tr, counting (1dc, 1ch) as 1tr.
4TH ROW (1dc, 1ch) in first tr, 1tr in each of next 4tr, *2tr in next tr, 1tr in each of next 7 (8) tr, rep from * to last 5 (6) sts, 2tr in next tr, 1tr in each of next 3 (4) tr, 1tr in top of turning ch...128 (142) tr, counting (1dc, 1ch) as 1tr.
5TH ROW (1dc, 1ch) in first tr, 1tr in each of next 4 (5) tr, *2tr in next tr, 1tr in each of next 8 (9) tr, rep from * to last 6 sts, 2tr in next tr, 1tr in each of next 4tr, 1tr in top of turning ch...142 (156) tr, counting (1dc, 1ch) as 1tr.
6TH ROW (1dc, 1ch) in first tr, 1tr in each of next 5tr, *2tr in next tr, 1tr in each of next 9 (10) tr, rep from * to last 6 (7) sts, 2tr in next tr, 1tr in each of next 4 (5) tr, 1tr in top of turning ch...156 (170) tr, counting (1dc, 1ch) as 1tr.
7TH ROW (1dc, 1ch) in first tr, 1tr in each tr to end, 1tr in top of turning ch.
Work a further 7 (9) rows tr, inc 14 sts (as before) in next and alt rows 4 (5) times in all...212 (240) sts. Fasten off.

SKIRT (BACK/FRONT ALIKE)
Begin at top. Using 2mm hook, make 65 (74) ch loosely.
1ST ROW Miss first ch, 1dc in each ch to end...64 (73) dc.
2ND ROW 1ch, 1dc in first dc, *miss 1dc, 5tr in next dc, 1dc in next dc, rep from * to end.
3RD ROW (3ch, 2tr) in first dc, *miss 2tr, 1dc in next tr, 1ch, miss next (2tr and 1dc), 'Half cluster' in next tr, 2ch, ('Cluster', 2ch) 4 times, 'Half cluster' in same tr just used, 1ch, miss next (1dc and 2tr), 1dc in next tr, miss next 2tr, 5tr in next dc, rep from * to end, ending last rep with 3tr in last dc instead of 5.
4TH ROW 1ch, 1dc in first tr, *miss next (2tr, 1dc and 1ch), 'Half cluster' in top of next half cluster of previous

row, 2ch ('Cluster', 2ch) 5 times, 'Half cluster' in same half cluster just used, miss next (1ch, 1dc and 2tr), 1dc in next tr, rep from * to end, working last dc in top of turning ch.

5TH ROW 1ch, 1dc in first dc, *2dc in next 2ch sp, (1dc in top of cluster, 2dc in next 2ch sp) 5 times, 1dc in next dc, rep from * to end.

6TH ROW 1ch, 1dc in first dc, *miss 2dc, 5tr in next dc, mibss 2dc, 1dc in next dc, rep from * to end.

Rows 3 to 6 incl form patt. Tie marker at each end of last row to mark end of armholes. **

Cont in patt until work measures 24 (27) cm from markers, ending with a 5th row of patt, do not turn, 1ch, 'Crab st' to end. Fasten off.

SLEEVES (BEGIN AT TOP)

Using 2mm hook, make 47 (56) ch. Work as for Skirt to **. Work a further 4 rows patt.

NEXT ROW (3ch, 1tr) in first dc, * miss 2tr, 1dc in next tr, miss 2tr, 2tr in next dc, rep from * to end.

NEXT ROW 1 ch, 1dc in each tr and dc to end, 1dc in top of turning ch...47 (56) dc.

NEXT ROW 1ch, 1dc in each dc to end. Rep last row 3 more times.

NEXT ROW 1ch, 1dc in each of first 2dc, *'Picot', 1dc in each of next 3dc, rep from * to end. Fasten off.

TO MAKE UP

Join side seams of skirt to markers. Join beg and end of last row of Yoke tog. Placing this join to centre back, and centre of Yoke to centre front, sew Yoke to Skirt, easing in fullness on Skirt and leaving 14 (15) cm free each side for tops of sleeves. Join Sleeve seams to markers, then sew Sleeves in position.

With right side facing, work 71 (86) dc evenly around neck. Work 1 row dc.

NEXT ROW. 1 ch, 1dc in each of first 2dc, *'Picot', 1dc in each of next 3dc, rep from * to end. Fasten off.

With right side facing, work 2 rows dc evenly around back opening, working four 3ch buttonloops evenly along right side of back opening in first row. Sew on buttons. Thread ribbon around yoke.

BOOTEES

Before beg, wind off approximately 3m of yarn for each bootee and reserve for instep.

Beg at sole. Using 2mm hook, make 20 (24) ch.

1ST ROUND Miss 3ch, 4tr in next ch, 1tr in each of next 1 (2) ch, 1htr in each of next 2ch, 1dc in each of next 3 (4) ch, 1htr in each of next 2ch, 1tr in each of next 3 (4) ch, 1dtr in each of next 4 (5) ch, 11dtr in last ch, working along other side of foundation ch (excluding ch just used), work 1dtr in each of next 4 (5) ch, 1tr in each of next 3 (4) ch, 1htr in each of next 2ch, 1dc in each of next 3 (4) ch, 1htr in each of next 2ch, 1tr in each of next 1 (2) ch, 5tr in next ch, sl st in 3rd ch at beg.

2ND ROUND 3ch, 2tr in next tr, 1tr in next tr, 2tr in next tr, 1tr in each of next 17 (21) sts, (2tr in next dtr, 1tr in next dtr) 4 times, 2tr in next dtr, 1tr in each of next 17 (21) st, (2tr in next tr, 1tr in next tr) twice, sl st in 3rd ch at beg...60 (68) tr, counting 3ch as 1tr.

3RD ROUND 3ch, 1tr in back lp of each tr to end, sl st in 3rd ch at beg. 4th round. 3ch, 1tr in each tr to end, sl st in 3rd ch at beg. Rep last round 1 (2) time/s.

Draw lp on hook up to a height of approx 3cm to prevent unravelling, then remove hook from lp.

Shape instep. With right side facing and using reserved yarn, miss first 23 (26) tr (counting 3ch as 1tr), join yarn with a sl st in next tr, miss 1tr, 1tr in each of next 8 (10) tr, miss 2tr, sl st across next 2tr, turn.

NEXT ROW Miss 2 sl sts, 1tr in each of next 8 (10) tr, miss 2tr, sl st across 2tr, turn.

Rep last row 2 (3) times.

NEXT ROW Miss 2 sl sts, 1tr in each of next 8 (10) tr, miss 1tr, sl st in next tr. Fasten off.

Return to main work and complete top (noting not to work into tr's where sl sts were worked for instep) thus:

1ST ROUND 3ch, 1tr in each of next 3 (5) tr, 2tr in next tr, (1tr in each of next 3 (7) tr, 2tr in next tr) 8 (4) times, 1tr in each of next 3 (5) tr, sl st in 3rd ch at beg...49tr.

2ND ROUND 4ch, miss 1tr, 1tr in next tr, *1ch, miss 1tr, 1tr in next tr, rep from * to end, sl st in 3rd ch at beg.

3rd round. 1ch, 1dc in same place as sl st, 1dc in each ch sp and tr to end, turn...49dc.

NEXT ROW 1ch, 1dc in first dc, *miss 1dc, 5tr in next dc, miss 1dc, 1dc in next dc, rep from * to end, turn.

Work 7 rows (not rounds) patt as for Skirt of Dress, beg with a 3rd row of patt. Do not turn at end of last row, 1ch, 'Crab st' to end. Fasten off.

TO MAKE UP

Join back seam of Bootees. Thread length of ribbon through row of holes at ankle and tie in a bow at front.

The delicate look of lace can be added to a handkerchief using fine cotton, as here. A more robust trim can be made using the same pattern for towel trims.

A TOUCH OF LACE

Although we live in the age of the ubiquitous tissue, a fine linen handkerchief with delicately crocheted edging is still a gift to be treasured. Rosemary Borland has worked these two pretty edgings for you to add to purchased handkerchiefs, or wherever a little lace would add a special touch.

*Crocheted
Fan Edging*

Crocheted Fan Edging

MEASUREMENTS

Edging is approximately 13mm deep.

MATERIALS

DMC No 40 Crochet Cotton:
- 1 ball
- 1.00mm crochet hook
- 27cm purchased or handmade fine linen handkerchief
- Embroidery needle and thread

FAN EDGING

Join thread to one corner of handkerchief.

1ST RND *(6ch, miss about 7mm, 1dc in edge of handkerchief) to end of first side, work 6ch, 1dc into same place as last dc; rep from * along each of rem 3 sides; sl st to join.

2ND RND Sl st to centre of first sp, *3ch, (1tr, 1ch, 1tr, 1ch, 1tr) into next sp, 3ch, 1dc into next sp; rep from * all round, working 5tr divided by 1ch, into each corner sp; sl st to join.

3RD RND Sl st to first tr of previous rnd, 5ch, 1tr in sl st, *2ch, 1tr in 2nd tr, 2ch, (1tr, 2ch, 1tr) in 3rd tr, (1tr, 2ch, 1tr) in first tr of next block of 3tr; rep from * to end of first side, work (1tr, 2ch, 1tr, 2ch) into each tr of corner. Cont thus to end; sl st to join.

4TH RND *2dc into each of first 2 sps of 2ch, 4ch, 2dc in each of next 2 sps, 1dc into sp between last 2ch-sp and next 2ch-sp; rep from * to end of first side. In corner, work: (2dc in each of first 2 sps) twice, 4ch, 2dc in each of next 2 sps, 1dc into sp between last 2ch-sp and next 2ch-sp. Cont thus to end; sl st to join.
Fasten off.
If desired, embroider motif on one corner of handkerchief (see Embroidery motif, below), using lazy daisy and stem-stitch.

Embroidered handkerchief motif.

Crocheted Lattice Edging

MEASUREMENTS

Edging is approximately 13mm deep.

MATERIALS

DMC No 40 Crochet Cotton:
- 1 ball
- 1.00mm crochet hook
- 25cm purchased or handmade fine linen handkerchief
- Embroidery needle and thread

LATTICE EDGING

1ST RND Work 141dc along each side of handkerchief and 3dc into each corner; sl st to join.

2ND RND *6ch, miss 3dc, sl st to next dc; rep from * to last dc of first side of handkerchief, (6ch, miss 1dc, sl st to next dc) twice.
Work rem sides in same way; sl st to join.

3RD RND Sl st to centre of first sp, 3ch, 1tr in same sp, *3ch, 2tr in next sp, rep from * to end of first side, 3ch, (2tr, 3ch, 2tr) in next sp, 3ch, (2tr, 3ch, 2tr) in next sp; rep from * for each rem side, finishing with 3ch; sl st to join.

4TH RND Sl st to centre of first sp, *6ch, 1dc in next sp; rep from * to end of rnd; sl st to join.

5TH RND Sl st to centre of first sp, 2ch, (1tr, 1dc) in same sp, *3ch, (1dc, 1tr, 1dc) in next sp; rep from * to end of rnd, 4ch; sl st to join.
Fasten off.
If desired, embroider motif on one corner of handkerchief (see Embroidery motif, above), using lazy daisy and stem-stitch.

*Crocheted
Lattice Edging*

THE GENTLE ART OF TATTING

So simple, once the fingers feel confident, the age-old art of knotting lace, or tatting, can be a joy to work. The French and Dutch call this 'frivolité', while the English and Italian names relate the work to gossip. Both suggest the light-hearted ease with which lace-makers of the past approached their work. If you've not tried it before, here's a guide to how easy it is to make beautiful borders. Jenny Oliver's step-by-step guide and pretty designs will have you tatting in no time. Unlike crochet, the edgings are worked separately and are sewn on once completed.

Step-By-Step Tatting

Once you've mastered making the knots, then tatting is easy! For beginners, it's easier to use two threads in two different colours so that the formation of the knots can be clearly seen. Once you are confident that you've got the technique correct, you can work with the one thread. The most basic knot is called double stitch.

MAKING THE KNOTS

Step 1. Wind one of the two colours (here, pink) onto the shuttle. Wind a small ball of the other colour (here, blue). The blue is the work thread; the pink is the shuttle thread.

Take ends of work thread and shuttle thread between thumb and forefinger of left hand. Wind thread from ball a couple of times around little finger of left hand, so that it forms a large loop around hand. Take shuttle between thumb and forefinger of right hand, so that shuttle thread is on righthand outside edge. With little finger of right hand, hold shuttle thread away from shuttle at right angles and guide shuttle under work thread between forefinger and middle finger of left hand.

Step 2. Push shuttle under both shuttle thread and work thread.

Step 3. Then pull shuttle back between shuttle thread and work thread. Release thread from right little finger. Steps 2 and 3 should be a smooth movement.

Step 4. Relax middle finger of left hand then carefully and slowly pull shuttle thread taut, so that work thread 'springs' around into the first loop of a knot.

Step 5. In this picture, work thread has now sprung around. This is the slightly tricky bit. Look carefully at

Face washer and guest towel have generous matching borders of white cotton, while the pretty floral table napkins are trimmed in écru. These elegant patterns can be used wherever else a touch of lace is called for.

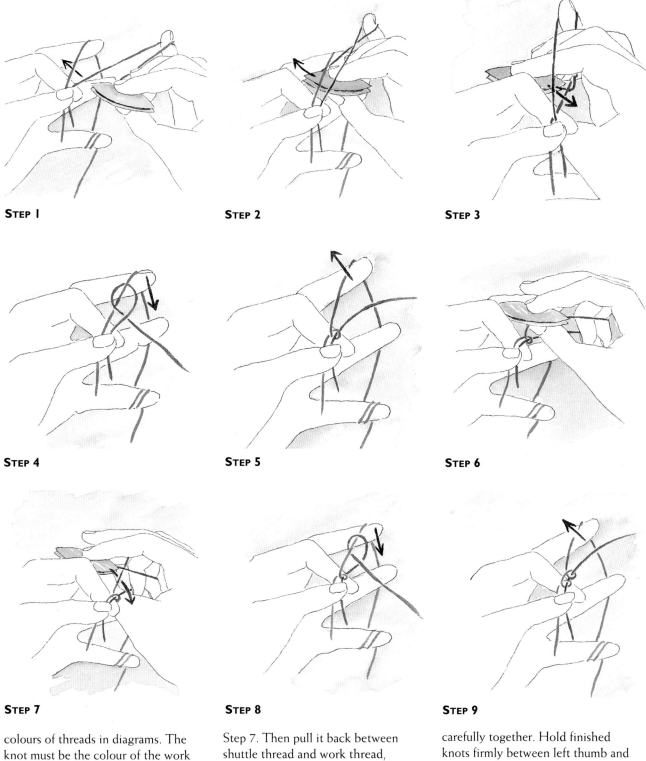

STEP 1

STEP 2

STEP 3

STEP 4

STEP 5

STEP 6

STEP 7

STEP 8

STEP 9

colours of threads in diagrams. The knot must be the colour of the work thread and it must be able to be pulled to and fro along shuttle thread. Check this. If it's not right, begin again! Now hold loop firmly between thumb and forefinger of left hand so that it can't jump back around.

Step 6. Reverse process for second half of knot. Hold shuttle thread towards palm with right little finger and push shuttle over both shuttle thread and work thread.

Step 7. Then pull it back between shuttle thread and work thread, releasing shuttle thread from right little finger. Steps 6 and 7 should be a smooth movement.

Step 8. Relax middle finger of left hand and carefully and slowly pull shuttle thread taut, so that work thread springs around into a second knot and shuttle thread loops to right.

Step 9. The first double stitch is made. Continue in this manner from Step 1 again, pushing knots thus formed

carefully together. Hold finished knots firmly between left thumb and forefinger. Keep checking colour of knots and make sure they can be pushed along shuttle thread (and not vice versa).

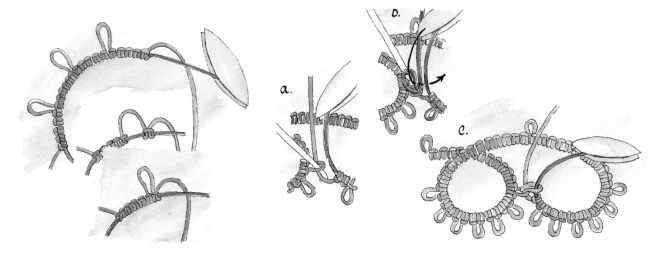

STEP 10

STEP 11

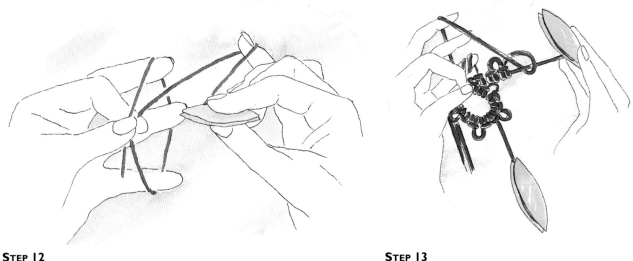

STEP 12

STEP 13

TO MAKE PICOTS

Step 10. Instead of moving first half of a double stitch up against previous knot, position it about 4mm away. Work second half of stitch, then push complete knot up, so that a loop is formed.

JOINING

Step 11. Insert crochet hook through picot loop and pull work thread upwards. Thread shuttle through loop thus formed and pull taut. Continue with double stitches.

TATTING WITH ONE COLOUR

Step 12. Once you have mastered the technique using two colours, you can dispense with second ball of thread and just use one shuttle. Take thread between thumb and forefinger of left hand, loop it around fingers and

catch it again between thumb and forefinger. Now make knots, as above.

TO FORM A RING

Step 13. When given number of stitches are complete, draw up thread

holding securely between thumb and forefinger. Draw shuttle thread tight so that first and last stitches meet, forming a ring.

Tatted Edge for Table Napkin

MATERIALS
• One tatting shuttle
• One ball No 20 crochet cotton

SPECIAL ABBREVIATIONS
See under Hand Towel, on page 215.
NOTE: 'One picot' (p) means the

thread that remains between two double stitches. This thread forms a loop when double stitches are pushed up against one another (see Step 10 above).

METHOD
Before beginning, carefully read Step-By-Step Instructions on pages 212 to 214.
1ST RING 4ds, p, 4ds, p, 2ds, p, 2ds, p, 4ds, p, 4ds, close ring, rw.
CHAIN *4ds, p, 4ds, rw.

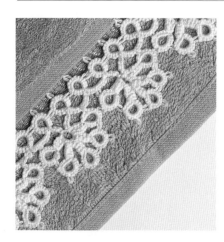

Tatted Edge for Hand Towel

MATERIALS
• One tatting shuttle
• One ball 4-ply cotton

SPECIAL ABBREVIATIONS
R (s): ring(s); sr: small ring; lr: large ring; ds: double stitch; p: picot; smp: small picot; lp: long or large picot; sep: separated; cl: close; rw: reverse work; sp: space; ch(s): chain(s); tog: together.
NOTE: 'One picot' (p) means the thread that remains between two double stitches. This thread forms a loop when double stitches are pushed up against one another (see opposite).

METHOD
Before beginning, carefully read Step-By-Step Instructions, on pages 212 to 214.
1ST RING 4ds, p, 4ds, p, 4ds, p, 4ds, close ring, rw.
CHAIN 4ds, p, 4ds, rw.

2ND RING 4ds, join to p of previous ring, 4ds, p, 4ds, p, 4ds, close ring.
REVERSE CHAIN 4ds, 1lp, 4ds, rw.
FLOWER, 1ST RING 4ds, join to p of first chain, 4ds, p, 4ds, p, 4ds, close ring, rw.
CHAIN 4ds, join to lp, 4ds.
2ND RING *4ds, join to last p of previous ring, 4ds, p, 4ds, p, 4ds, close ring, rw.
CHAIN **4ds, join to lp, 4ds*. Repeat from * to * three times. Do not reverse work at end of last chain.
3RD RING 4ds, join to last p of 2nd ring, 4ds, p, 4ds, p, 4ds, close ring, rw.
CHAIN 4ds, join to last p of last ring of flower, 4ds, rw.
4TH RING 4ds, join to last p of previous ring, 4ds, p, 4ds, p, 4ds, close ring, rw.
CHAIN 4ds, p, 4ds.
5TH RING 4ds, join to last p of previous ring, 4ds, p, 4ds, p, 4ds, close ring.
CHAIN 4ds, lp, 4ds, rw.
6TH RING 4ds, join to p in second last ch, 4ds, join to p of last ring, 4ds, p, 4ds, close ring.
Repeat from ** until edging measures required length for sewing to hand towel.

Tatted Edge for Face Washer

MEASUREMENTS
Finished edge measures 32cm square, or as desired.

MATERIALS
• One tatting shuttle
• One ball 4-ply cotton

SPECIAL ABBREVIATIONS
See under Tatted Edge for Hand Towel.
NOTE: 'One picot' (p) means the thread that remains between two double stitches. This thread forms a loop when double stitches are pushed up against one another (see page 214).

METHOD
Before beginning, carefully read Step-By-Step Instructions, on pages 212 to 214.
1ST RING 4ds, p, 4ds, p, 4ds, p, 4ds, close ring, rw.
CHAIN 4ds, p, 4ds, rw.
2ND RING 4ds, join to last p on previous ring, 4ds, p, 4ds, p, 4ds, close ring.
REVERSE CHAIN 4ds, lp, 4ds, rw.
FLOWER, 1ST RING 4ds, join to p on first chain, 4ds, p, 4ds, p, 4ds, close ring, rw.
CHAIN *4ds, join to lp, 4ds.
2ND RING 4ds, join to last p of previous ring, 4ds, p, 4ds, p, 4ds, close ring *, rw.
Repeat from * to * three times, rw.
CHAIN 4ds, join to lp, 4ds, do not turn work.
3RD RING 4ds, join to p on second ring from start, 4ds, p, 4ds, p, 4ds, close ring.
CHAIN 4ds, join to last p of last ring of flower, 4ds, rw.
4TH RING *4ds, join to p of previous ring, 4ds, p, 4ds, p, 4ds, close ring, rw.* Repeat from * to * seven times.
NOTE: For smaller or larger washers, lengthen or shorten here.
Repeat from beginning until length required. Join ring to first ring, making sure lace is not twisted.
LAST RING 4ds, join to last p of previous ring, 4ds, p, 4ds, join to p of 1st ring, 4ds, close ring, rw.
CHAIN 4ds, p, 4ds, join to start, tie off.

2ND RING 4ds, join to p on previous ring, 4ds, p, 2ds, p, 2ds, p, 4ds, p, 4ds, close ring.*
Repeat from * to * until desired length to corner, ending on a ring.
NEXT RING 4ds, join to p of previous ring, 4ds, p, 2ds, p, 2ds, p, 4ds, p, 4ds, close ring.
CHAIN 4ds, join to p of last chain, 4ds, rw.
LAST RING 4ds, join to last p on previous ring, 4ds, p, 2ds, p, 2ds, p, 4ds, p, 4ds, close ring, tie and cut.

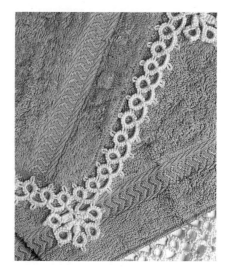

Paper Crafts

Traditional crafts which originated in the Orient, particularly handmade paper, evolved into more than a method of preserving information. Paper was used in wonderful works of art, with the imaginative additions of paints — fans, screens, kites, origami and paper cutting.

The Egyptians' papyrus are well known. In Europe in the 17th century the Venetians developed 'Lacce Povera', followed by the English embracing 'Japanning', a centuries-old approximation of early Oriental lacquerware. These were the precursors of eighteenth century French Découpage. The nineteenth century Victorians promoted whimsical paper scraps used to decorate books and screens and this was extended by the Germans into their beautiful postcard industry.

Papier Mâché, the European method of pulping or laminating newspaper into furniture, decorative objects, bowls and plates, is then painted or découpaged to produce highly individualistic pieces of art.

Working with paper is enjoying a great resurgence of popularity. Increased leisure time allows creative people to experiment with a diversity of paper crafts with modern technology providing improved materials.

NERIDA SINGLETON

PAPER, PASTE AND POLISH

A gentle art from a bygone era — découpage — adds old-world appeal to the plainest of objects. This enthralling art, which began in the 18th century, has become a passion for Nerida Singleton. In these pages, Nerida demonstrates the basic techniques and shows how to make a delightful brooch, following simple step-by-step instructions. The same technique can be applied to bracelets, wooden boxes or any old favourite piece which needs reviving.

HISTORICAL NOTE

Découpage was devised in the 18th century by clever but fraudulent craftsmen. They used it to fake the Japanese furniture that was enjoying a vogue in Europe at that time. The furniture was noted for its intricate painted designs, which were painstakingly applied and lacquered. The Venetian fakers found a way to speed up this laborious and time-consuming procedure. Rather than painting designs on individual pieces, they etched and printed multiple copies of the same design, which were then hand-painted by apprentices. These coloured prints were glued to screens, wall panels and furniture, then many coats of varnish were applied and the articles were sanded and polished.

Somewhere along the line, these merchants of Venice were sprung, and their technique was unmasked. However, by this time, the technique itself was celebrated and was known throughout the polite society of Victorian England as japanning.

Découpage is enjoying a contemporary renaissance, largely due to the work of an American, Hiram Manning, whose interest in the art led to teaching others the technique and finally to the formation of an influential body called the Découpage Guild of America.

Purists still hand-colour black-and-white prints of roses, cupids, garlands, and the like, and apply these to a hand-painted background, but what we present here is a more attainable technique of découpage, using images cut from art books and magazines.

Previous page: Découpage projects can be as small as a pretty wooden brooch or as ambitious as one of Nerida's intricately finished hatboxes. The technique is always the same, and patience is a vital ingredient!

Step-by-Step Découpage

MATERIALS

- Object to be covered (for example, hatbox, handbag, brooch)
- Good quality pictures from magazines (non-porous paper)
- Sealer (Atelier or Liquitex Gloss Medium and Varnish)
- Brush for sealer
- 600 and 1200 wet and dry sandpaper
- Long bladed scissors
- Sharp curved cuticle scissors
- Clag glue
- Aquadhere
- Wallpaper roller (optional)
- Sponge
- Oil-based pencils
- Good quality, soft bristle brush
- Varnish (Walpamur or Estapol)
- Scotchbrite or 000 steel wool (very fine, available from hardware stores)
- Beeswax
- Muslin, to polish

PREPARING PICTURES

Before cutting your pictures, seal both sides with Liquitex Gloss Medium and Varnish or equivalent. If using a colour photocopy of an image, it is sometimes necessary to paint a sparing amount of sealer over the picture three times, brushing it in different directions.

Preparing Pictures

Preparing Objects

PREPARING OBJECTS

Lightly sand and seal object to be covered, to prevent glue leaking into its surface. If glue does leak, picture will not adhere to object and stress from many coats of varnish will cause air bubbles to appear.

CUTTING

Remove excess paper around image to allow easy manoeuvring of cuticle scissors. With curved point of scissors facing outwards, feed picture into scissors, moving picture through scissors to achieve a smooth finish. This also gives a crisp edge, and a white rim will appear around picture.

GLUING

Mix together a paste of three parts Clag to one part Aquadhere on a saucer, then apply it, small blobs at a time, to the object you are covering (not to back of picture, as this will make picture soggy, stretched and unmanageable). When pasting images onto a wooden object, be generous

with glue; dab a little on top of picture, and rub it with fingertips to spread it evenly, ensuring there are no hard lumps or bare spots where air bubbles could eventuate.

GLUING (CONTINUED)

Next, excess glue has to be removed from behind picture. This can be done with a wallpaper roller, or by pressing it from under image with a thumb, then sponging over image. Put a dab of glue on top of picture, as this helps prevent it from tearing. It also avoids the danger of overworking the colour, which can cause picture to fade.

Starting from centre, use roller or your thumb, and radiating out to edges, press image firmly in place. Be sure you don't remove all glue, or there will be no adhesion. Wipe over picture gently with a damp sponge and remove glue from surface of picture. If this is not done, brown smudges will appear after varnishing. If glue persists, add a little vinegar to water and sponge it off.

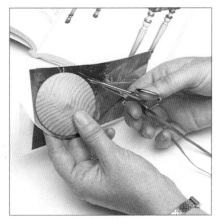

Cutting

Gluing

Gluing Continued

Varnishing

When picture is completely dry, touch up any white spots with oil-based colour pencils, then smudge edge of pencil line, so it is not obvious.

Seal entire object again before varnishing. This is your insurance against 'a bleed'.

If covering a large object, continue to glue images, overlapping them until whole surface is covered.

VARNISHING

Using a good brush (Raphael No 24) apply a light film of varnish, brushing in one direction. (Brushing back and forth promotes air bubbles.) Change direction of your brush strokes with each new application.

Varnish needs 24 hours to dry completely, so apply only one coat per day. Never varnish if it is raining or the humidity is high, as varnish will not dry properly.

If wrinkles appear on varnished surface, object should be left for

Sanding

Waxing

several days to ensure it is totally dry before revarnishing. Apply 20 coats before beginning sanding process.

SANDING

The aim of découpage is to achieve a silky surface similar to French polishing, so once 20 coats of varnish have been applied, object is lightly sanded using No 600 wet and dry sandpaper and a few drops of water for a better finish.

Apply seven more coats of varnish, sanding with No 600 after each coat.

Apply another three coats of varnish (making 30 coats in all). After each, sand with No 1200 wet and dry sandpaper which is finer.

WAXING

Use Scotchbrite or No 000 steel wool to remove all traces of gloss. No highlights should remain, as these will be obvious under waxed surface. When surface is silky smooth and uniformly dull, wipe clean, allow to dry and apply beeswax in very small sections. Rub with muslin to achieve a

silk sheen (Goddards Cabinetmaker's Polish with Beeswax is also good).

Because of the many coats of varnish needed, surface will take six months to cure (that is, harden completely) and it should be treated with respect for this period. Do not allow object to be subjected to sunlight, and wax it periodically during this time.

TIP FOR RECTIFYING AIR BUBBLES

This can be treated by cutting into the picture with a scalpel blade and pushing the glue behind it to ensure it sticks, and then removing excess glue. However, it is far better to prevent bubbles by sealing the object before you begin gluing and varnishing.

Nerida Singleton displays the diversity and beauty of découpage with a selection of her exquisitely crafted boxes.

SECOND TIME AROUND

Beautiful paper to make from scrap

Discover the ancient and satisfying craft of papermaking. Using simple traditional hand methods, and all your scrap paper and envelopes, you'll be surprised at the wonderful results you can achieve. Professional papermaker, Gretchen Forrest, who made all the beautiful paper on these pages, takes you step-by-step through the process, but be warned — it becomes completely addictive.

Soaking

Blending

Step-by-Step Papermaking

MATERIALS

- Mould and deckle (see Note)
- 30–40 sheets white, scrap paper, such as office or computer paper (not newspaper)
- Two large plastic buckets, or similar containers
- Kitchen blender
- Sieve
- Large rectangular plastic vat, such as baby's bath, larger than mould and deckle
- Couching pad (see opposite)
- 12–15 couching cloths (rectangular pieces of closely-woven cotton fabric, cut a little larger all round than mould)
- Two 10–20mm-thick pressing boards, cut from waterproof wood, such as marine ply, a little larger all round than couching cloths
- Two or four G-cramps (depending on size)

Combining

- Two rectangles of old blanket or towel, cut to fit pressing boards
NOTE: A mould is a wooden frame covered with mesh, used to strain the paper pulp. A deckle is a frame without mesh, used to define the edges of the paper. Moulds and deckles can be purchased from specialist craft stores in a variety of sizes.

SOAKING

Tear paper into small pieces, about the size of a postage stamp, and soak in a container of water overnight. The length of soaking time will depend on thickness of paper, and process can be speeded up by using warm water. The end result should be a pulpy mass that is easily blended.

BLENDING

Take a handful of paper pieces and place in blender with about three cups of water — proportions should be ½ cup of pulp to 3 cups water. Blend this mixture until it is finely pulped. To

Previous page: Wonderful texture can be added to handmade paper with a variety of items readily to hand. Experiment with flowers, of course, but don't forget tea leaves, cinnamon, cotton thread and fern fronds, for interesting and varied results.

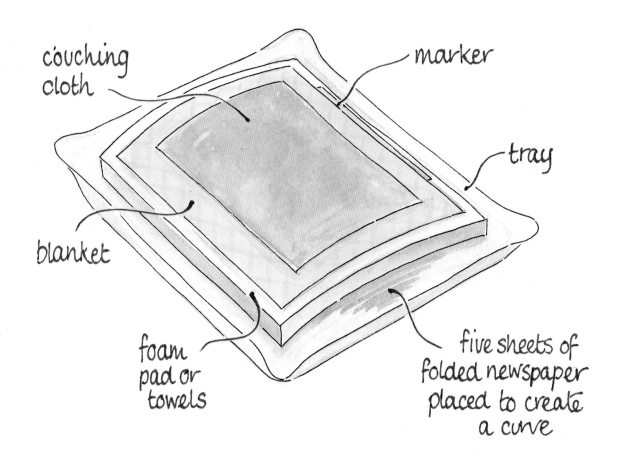

couching
cloth

marker

tray

blanket

foam
pad or
towels

five sheets of
folded newspaper
placed to create
a curve

HOW TO MAKE A COUCHING PAD

This pad is used when laying paper onto cloths, ready for pressing.

MATERIALS

- Large waterproof tray, with lipped edges
- Five sheets of newspaper
- A piece of thick (5cm) plastic foam, or an old blanket or folded towels — this should be a few centimetres bigger all round than your mould
- A strip of fabric, the same length as your mould and about 10cm wide, for a couching marker (this strip should have a very straight edge and a sharp corner)
- Piece of blanket, a little wider all round than your couching cloths

METHOD

Take five sheets of newspaper and fold each along its spine. Fold first piece lengthways into a strip about 5cm wide, wet it and lay it down middle of tray. Fold second sheet into a strip a few centimetres wider, wet it, and put it on top of the first. Proceed in this manner, making each strip a little wider, until all five sheets have been used to form a mound down middle of tray.

Saturate foam and place this over newspapers to form a convex curve.

On top of foam, place marker strip, so that it lines up with left edge of foam.

Now cover foam with a wet piece of woollen blanket, allowing a narrow strip of marker to show.

Just before you begin couching, pour water onto couching pad until it is saturated, then position the first of your couching cloths, smoothed wrinkle-free, onto blanket.

Paper Transfer

Transfer Complete

Paper Layering

test if you have blended mixture enough, put two or three teaspoonfuls into a glass of water, stir and hold up to the light. It should be cloudy with minute particles of paper. If you can see any large pieces, you need to blend next batch for longer.

As each batch is blended, strain it through a sieve over a bucket or other container. Let water drain away unaided — if you squeeze it with your hands it makes the pulp lumpy.

If you are not proceeding with your papermaking immediately, pulp can be placed in a covered container and stored in fridge with a few drops of disinfectant, until needed.

If you want to add small flowers as decoration to your paper, they need to be prepared at this stage. Use tiny whole flowers, such as forget-me-nots, or shred petals from larger flowers, such as cornflowers and geraniums.

COMBINING

Three-quarters fill vat with clean water and place it on a table next to your couching pad (see instructions for making couching pad, on page 223). On the other side of vat, place pulp and shredded flowers. Put a few handfuls of pulp into vat with a handful of flowers and agitate vigorously. You can't feel if there is enough pulp in the water — you need to take a 'pull' and look at the pulp on

the mould. The more pulp in bath, the thicker the paper will be. It is better to err on the thick side at first, as this is easier to couch, but with a little practice, you will be able to tell whether the pulp on your mould is too thick or too thin. If you can see the mesh through the wet paper, it is probably too thin. If, when you take deckle off, the sheet has a thick edge, then paper will probably be too thick.

Before beginning, place a wet couching cloth onto couching pad, making sure that it is completely smooth.

To 'pull' a sheet of paper, place mould wire-side up and put deckle on top of it. Hold the two together with your thumbs on deckle, in the centre of each side. Now dip mould and deckle through mixture in vat. This dip can be done towards you or away from you, or by plunging mould straight down to bottom and straight up again. Keep pressure of water against wire throughout dip. Don't slow up, but move mould in one even movement through water to bottom of bath, and straight up out of water in a horizontal position. Keep mould and deckle firmly together while water drains. When water has drained away, a sheet of paper is left on mould. Now carefully remove deckle.

Pressing

Securing Boards

PAPER TRANSFER

You now have to transfer wet sheet of paper on mould to cloth on couching pad.

Stand mould on its edge on marker side of couching pad, lining mould up with marker. Gently tilt mould towards couching cloth at a 45 degree angle and in one smooth movement, press bottom corner of mould into pad and 'roll' mould across pad, releasing sheet of paper onto couching cloth and avoiding bubbles.

PAPER LAYERING

Lay another smooth, wet couching cloth carefully on top of this piece of paper, and proceed with another pull, lining up each sheet of paper directly with one beneath it, using marker as a guide. Repeat this process until 8–10 sheets are ready for pressing, adding a little more pulp to water every two or three pulls, or when paper starts to look too thin.

If you damage paper at any time, you can return it to vat. If it is on mould, simply turn mould over and return pulp to vat by 'kissing it off', that is, touching it onto surface of water, where it will fall off. If paper on couching cloth is damaged, simply rinse couching cloth in vat.

PRESSING

The paper now needs to be pressed to remove excess water and to strengthen it. Lay one rectangle of blanket on a pressing board (blanket is better than

Different Effects

towel, as the latter can leave an impression on paper when it is pressed). Place pile of couching cloths and paper on this blanket and cover with second piece of blanket.

SECURING BOARDS

Place remaining pressing board on top and use G-cramps to hold boards tightly together. Tilt to allow water to run away, then leave for about an hour. Tighten G-cramps again and leave for another 20 minutes or so.

Remove pressed paper from press and carefully separate cloths. Hang each cloth (with its paper) to dry, away from direct hot sunlight and out of wind.

Before removing paper from its

cloth, make sure that both are thoroughly dry. Carefully peel cloth from paper — if cloth is stretched a little, paper should release easily.

DIFFERENT EFFECTS

Various different effects can be achieved by adding different things to pulp in vat, such as tea leaves, turmeric, torn postage stamps, paper table napkins and threads, to name but a few. You can also place whole ferns and leaves onto a piece of paper and either completely or partially cover them with another thin pull, giving the effect of embossing.

Once you've mastered the basic technique, you'll be hooked!

GOOD NEWS!

Recycle your morning paper into fabulous designer tableware

Chances are, the last time you had anything to do with papier mâché, you stuck little pieces of soggy paper all over a balloon (and yourself) to produce an outlandish puppet head, that was loudly admired when you took it home. But papier mâché, that great mainstay of schoolroom craft, has far greater possibilities — and, considering how little it costs to make and how easy it is to do, it's time to look again at this ancient art.

We had a wonderful time creating these colourful bowls and plates, inspired by imported peasant-style ceramics found in shops and magazines.

On the following pages, you can see, step-by-step, how simple it is to produce spectacular results from very humble beginnings.

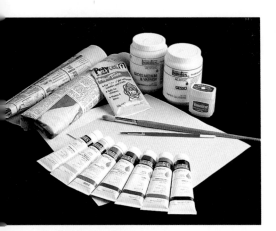

Papier Mâché Bowls and Plates

MATERIALS
- Newspapers (including coloured stock, such as the TV guide)
- A mould (such as a plate or bowl)
- Petroleum jelly
- Wallpaper paste
- Stanley knife
- Acrylic gesso (from artists' supplies)
- Paintbrushes
- Fine and very fine sandpaper
- Selley's Rapidfilla (optional)
- Acrylic paints
- Acrylic varnish

Papier mâché bowls are colourful, cheap and durable. They shouldn't be immersed in water, but are terrific for fruit or dry food. Just wipe the surface to clean.

METHOD

Make up wallpaper paste according to instructions on packet and leave for 30 minutes. In the meantime, tear (do not cut) newspapers (including coloured stock) into strips about 3cm wide and 10 to 20cm long, depending on size of finished vessel.

Rub a generous layer of petroleum jelly onto surface of your chosen mould. We used plates and bowls and also a spherical glass lampshade, which proved to be an excellent mould. You can also blow up a balloon and use it by inverting knotted end into a bowl, while covering rounded end with papier mâché.

APPLYING PAPER

Place wallpaper paste in an open bowl and dip strips of newspaper into it, removing excess paste by drawing strips between your fingers. Apply strips of paper to mould, overlapping edges a little and varying direction in which they are applied. Try not to allow excess paste or air bubbles to remain under strips — squeeze them out as you work.

You can apply several layers at the one time, using alternate layers of plain or coloured newsprint each time you begin a new layer, so that you can keep track of layers. However, we found that the most satisfactory results were achieved if each layer or two was allowed to dry before next was added. This means that the process is a rather drawn-out affair, but the finished product seemed much sturdier and less prone to air pockets.

The total number of layers you apply is up to you, but eight is about the minimum. Our large bowl has sixteen layers and is very strong. If you are making a large plate, you will need to weight the work with something as it dries, since flat shapes are very prone to warp.

Applying Paper

When you have applied and dried about six layers, you can remove the papier mâché object from the mould, prizing it from edges with a blunt knife. It should come easily away from mould. If it does not, leave it to dry for another 24 hours.

NEAT FINISH

You will find when mould is removed, that edges may be a little uneven or ragged. Trim ragged pieces with a stanley knife, then apply another layer of small pieces around edge, lapping them from outside to inside to give a firm, neat finish.

MAKING A BASE

The base for the small round bowl was made from a circle of cardboard, placed on bottom of bowl and held in place, initially, with a couple of pieces of sticky tape. Small pieces of paper were then stuck over and around this cardboard ring, to cover it and sticky tape completely with papier mâché.

After all layers have been applied, vessel should be allowed to dry thoroughly — perhaps for three or four days, depending on weather. We found that attempting to hurry this process in the oven tended to cause distortion in shape.

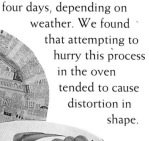

Neat Finish

Making a Base

APPLYING GESSO

When vessel is dry, apply a coat of gesso and allow to dry. Gesso will fill slight imperfections and give a smooth white surface on which to paint. You will probably need to apply about four coats of gesso, lightly sanding vessel in between each coat.

Now comes our shocking admission which will horrify papier mâché purists. We wanted our bowls to look like expensive Italian ceramics, so we filled the dents with Selley's Rapidfilla, then sanded it back for a lovely smooth finish. If you work carefully with your newspaper and strips, you will probably not have to resort to this, or you may like the slightly uneven look of papier mâché, but if not, there is help at hand.

Once you are satisfied with the finish of your work, you can apply the design and paint it. We haven't given designs to trace, because the idea is to make your design look as freehand as possible, not slavishly copied. The intricacy of Limoges or Wedgwood is not called for here. Look for

Applying Gesso

Painting

inspiration in magazine advertisements, or go to a department store and check their collections of peasant-style china. You'll notice that the designs are usually quite rough and unsymmetrical — this is what gives them their charm. So don't be afraid to try your own design. All your mistakes will be covered over by the final layer of paint anyway.

PAINTING

When you're happy with the design, paint it carefully with acrylic paints, keeping colour vibrant by not diluting it too much with water. Allow first coat to dry completely before applying second.

When paint is completely dry, vessel can be varnished and allowed to dry in a dust-free area. If applying two coats of varnish, for extra strength and durability, make sure you allow first coat to dry thoroughly before applying second.

Now sit back and allow your work to be loudly admired! You can get the glue off everything tomorrow.

WRAP SESSION

For our gift packages, we've used two patterned wallpapers from Laura Ashley — Palmetto and Albert, two plain sheets purchased from Woolworths and a scrap of foil we had lying about collecting dust. If you have masses of presents to wrap, wallpaper could offer a cost-conscious alternative to gift wrap. It comes in 10m rolls, is strong, easy to work, and, for price, compares well with papers you purchase by the sheet.

You've made the perfect gift —
here are ways to enhance its presentation

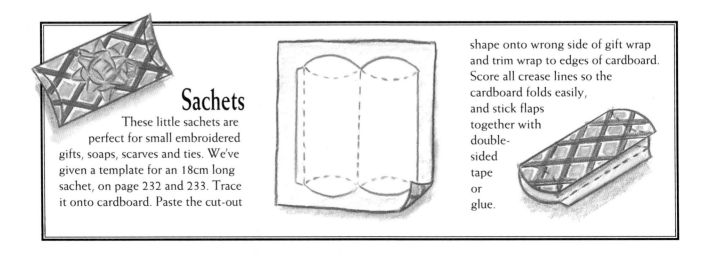

Sachets

These little sachets are perfect for small embroidered gifts, soaps, scarves and ties. We've given a template for an 18cm long sachet, on page 232 and 233. Trace it onto cardboard. Paste the cut-out shape onto wrong side of gift wrap and trim wrap to edges of cardboard. Score all crease lines so the cardboard folds easily, and stick flaps together with double-sided tape or glue.

Carrier Bags

Get carried away with these carrier bags which can be made to accommodate anything awkward. The only restriction on their size is the size of the gift wrap sheet. You'll need something to use as a mould — a bundle of books is ideal. Cut gift wrap wide enough to fit mould, with an allowance at top and bottom. Fold over top allowance and wrap paper around mould so that edges meet at centre back.

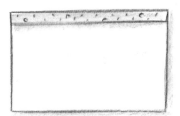

Glue edges together. Fold in bottom just as you would wrap a normal parcel and glue or seal with double-sided sticky tape. Slip mould out, punch holes at top, and, for a professional-looking finish, fold in sides of bag. Add handles knotted on inside.

Recycled Milk Cartons

Wide cylinders and milk cartons make great recycled containers for bottles or home-made goodies. Simply cut cylinders to size and cover with paper. Use the metal or plastic ends for bases only, and tie attractive bows, or rosettes around the neck of bottles at the top. Present homemade biscuits or sweets à la carton.

Cut the top off a well-washed milk or juice carton so that you get a V-shape on opposite sides, and a point on the other two. Cover with gift wrap, allowing about a 1cm overlap at top. This is clipped at the apex, turned in and glued. Punch holes in both points to take a ribbon tie.

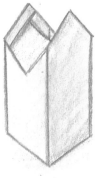

Beautiful Boxes

Beautiful little boxes are just right for gifts of homemade beauty preparations, jewellery or pot-pourri sachets. Cut out a cross-shaped piece as shown, which will give you four sides and a base. It's important that sides and base are true squares. The lid is cut about 5mm larger than the base, with sides about 2cm deep. Paste both shapes onto wrong side of gift wrap

and trim paper to leave a 1cm turning around all edges.

Clip paper at inner four corners, and fold in and glue turning on left of each side of box. Score along centre square

edges so that it is easy to turn up sides. Bend sides up, glue patterned side of unfolded gift wrap turnings on each side, and stick these inside box to their adjacent sides.

Finally, fold in overlapping paper around top. The lid is finished in the same way. Templates for box and lid appear on page 232 to 235.

A   PATTERN PIECES FOR WRAPPINGS AND BOXES

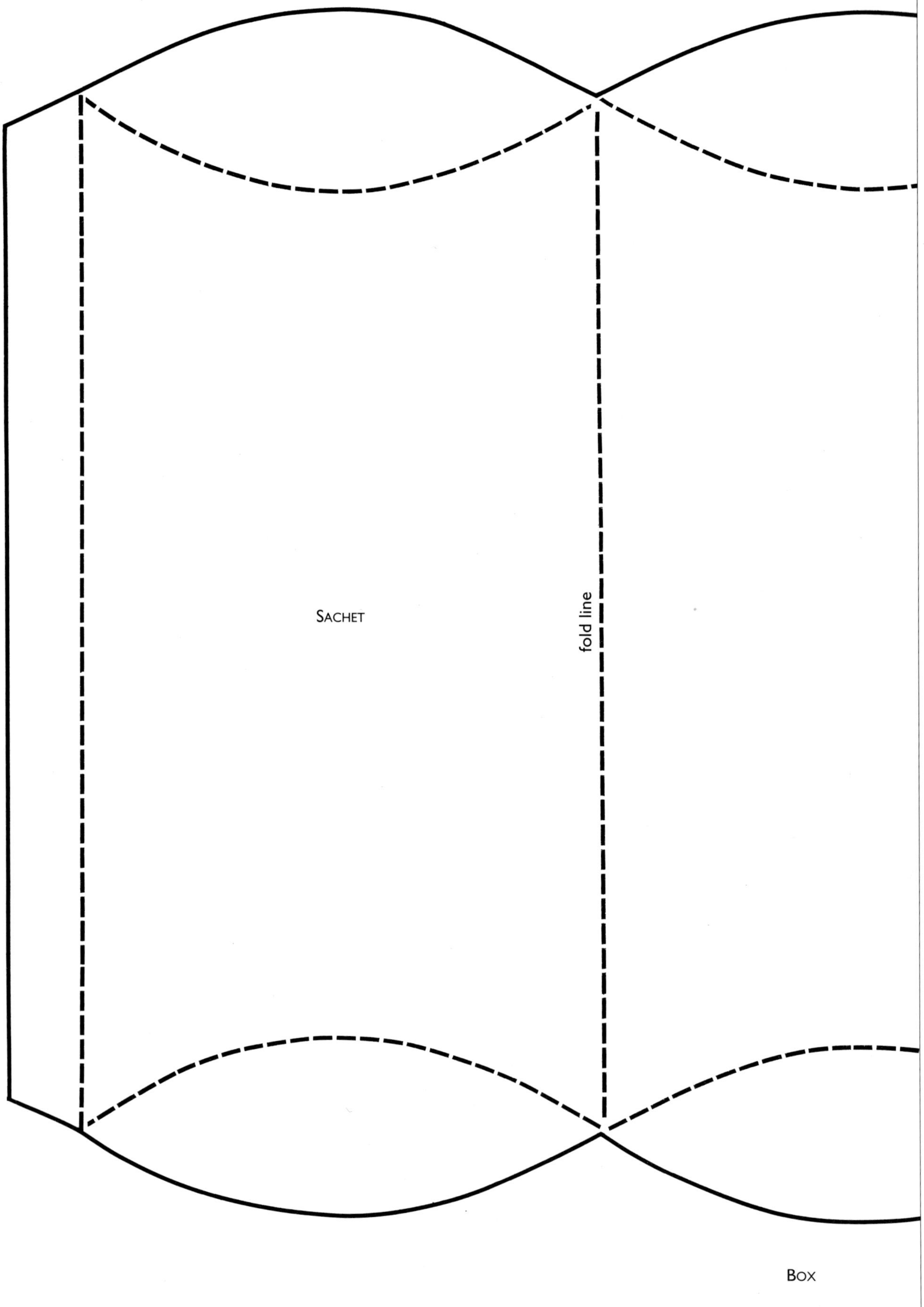

A JOINS B

SACHET

fold line

BOX

A JOINS C

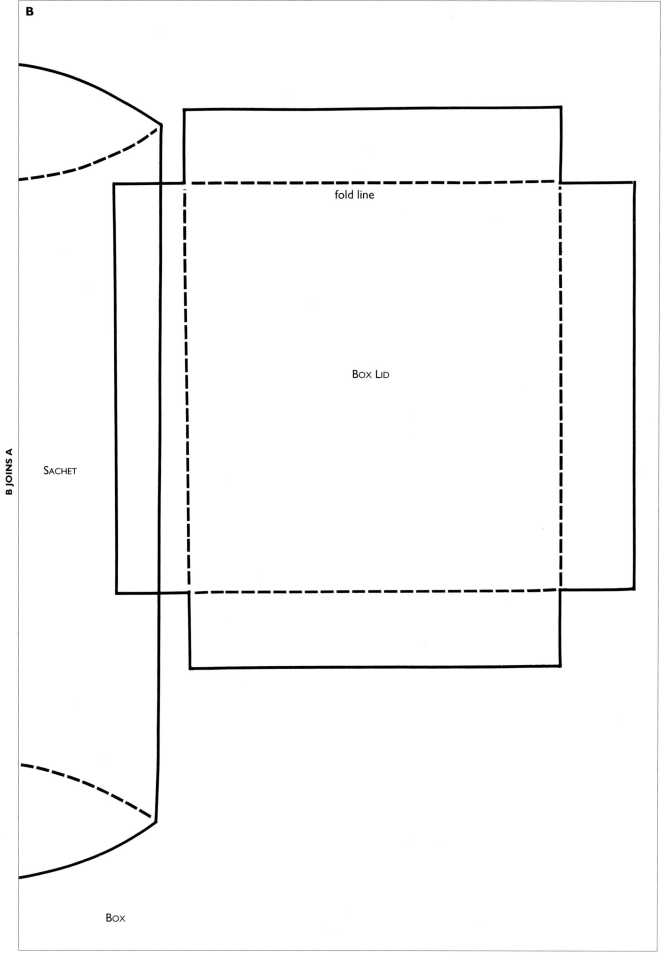

B

fold line

Box Lid

Sachet

Box

C

Box

fold line

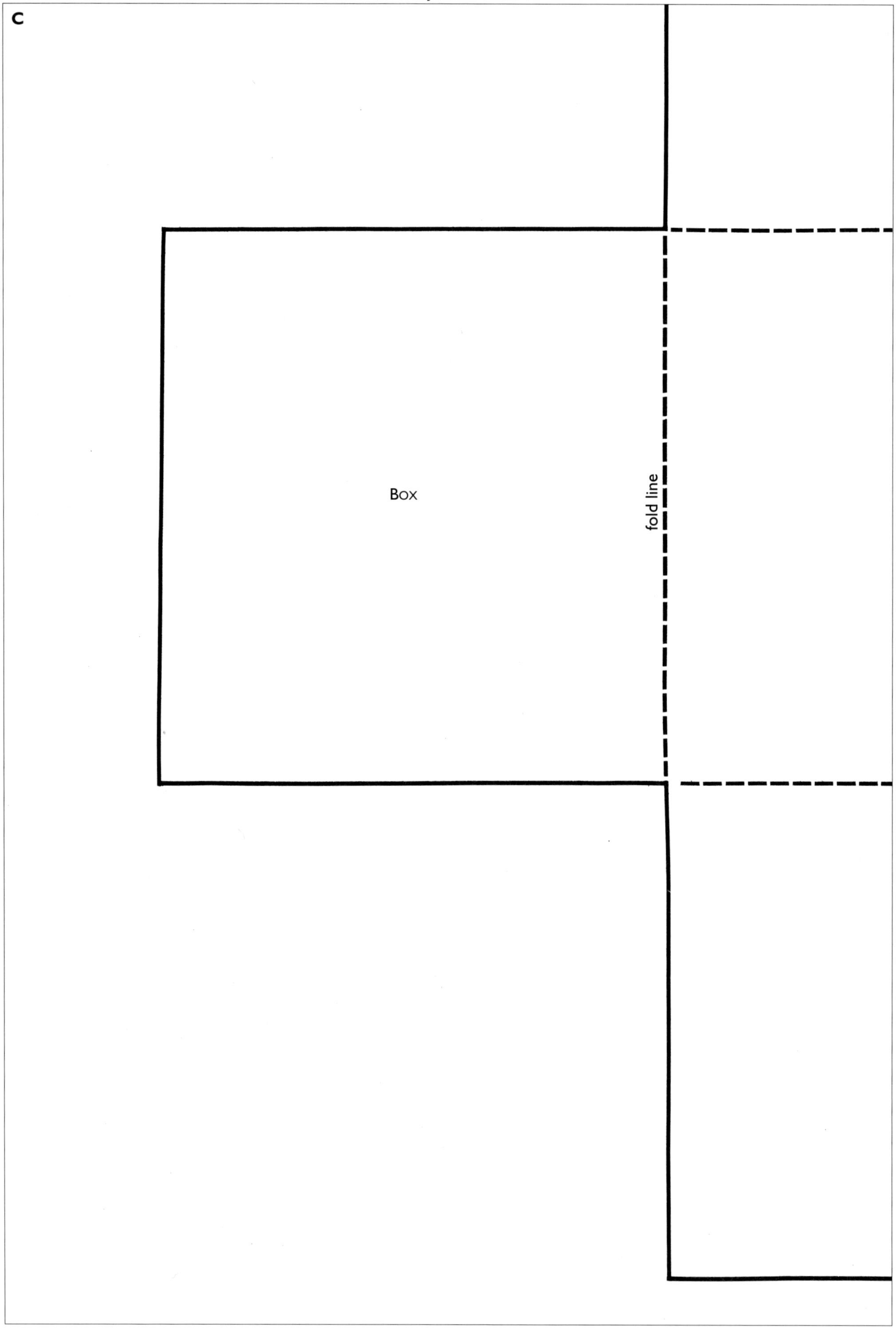

C JOINS D

C

D JOINS B

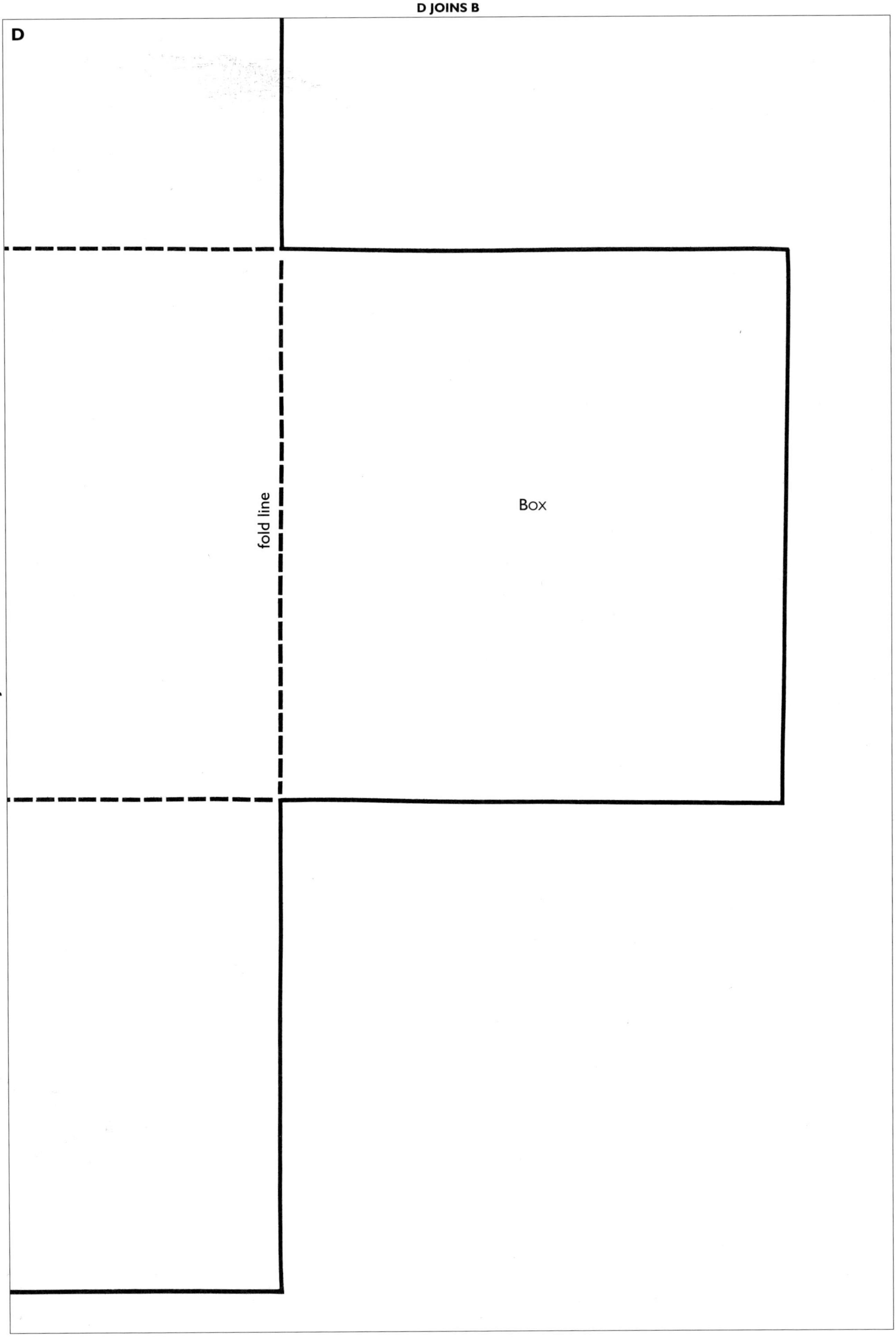

D

D JOINS C

fold line

Box

D JOINS B

D

Folk Art,

Stencilling & Marbling

Folk Art, Stencilling and Marbling have captured the creative instinct we all possess. Beginning with the early home makers who wished to decorate their simple furniture pieces with paint and colour, these techniques have been passed on over the centuries to the people of the modern world to learn and enjoy. Folk Art patterns were created by unskilled artists who drew their ideas and patterns from their basic way of life. Traditional Folk Art is meant to show a simplistic style with no need for the realistic look of a trained artist.

It is with gratitude to the people who began these traditions so many years ago that the artist of today can create beautiful pieces for future generations to admire.

Janet Klepatzki

SCENES FROM A COUNTRY CHILDHOOD

Folk art made easy!

Out beyond the suburbs, you'll still find the small selections with their weatherboard houses and barns among the gumtrees. Here, chooks roam free and scratch a living from the dusty soil, and there's always a load of washing flapping and a rusty windmill creaking in the breeze. Or so it seems ...

Country Childhood Canisters

MATERIALS
- Rust free tins of various shapes and sizes, with lids (we used Milo, International Roast, Twinings tea and a biscuit tin)
- Vinegar

Previous page: These canisters designed by Lorell McIntyre, depict simple, comforting scenes that are just as enjoyable to paint. So, if you've longed to try this wonderful craft, here's the very project.

- Fine grade wet and dry sandpaper or 0000 steel wool
- Lint-free tack cloth
- Rust inhibitor in spray or brush-on form
- FolkArt Acrylic Basecoat: Porcelain White
- Sponge brush
- Chalk or graphite transfer paper
- Tracing paper
- Scotch Magic Tape
- Stylus
- FolkArt Extender
- FolkArt Acrylic Colors: Vanilla Cream (VC), Barnwood (BW), Dapple Gray (DG), Green Olive (GO), Coffee Bean (CB), Earthenware (E), Rusty Nail (RN), Indigo (I), Wrought Iron (WI), Licorice (L)
- Brushes: FolkArt No 6 flat; No 2 round; No 00 script liner; ¼ inch deerfoot brush
- Palette
- Paper towels or soft cloth
- Kneadable rubber or eraser
- FolkArt Clearcote Acrylic Sealer

PREPARATION
Wash tins in warm soapy water to remove any traces of food, paying particular attention to any tiny crevices. Rinse in a solution of 1:1 water and vinegar to eliminate grease, then dry by shaking off excess water and placing tins in a warm oven, which will dry seam lines without leaving lint.

Scuff surface of tins lightly with very fine wet and dry sandpaper or 0000 steel wool. This will allow paint to adhere to slick surface of tin. Wipe with a tack cloth.

Apply rust inhibitor. Follow manufacturer's instructions and allow 24 hours for surface to dry.

After wiping again with a tack cloth, use sponge brush to apply 2–3 even coats of FolkArt Basecoat in Porcelain White. DO NOT paint inside of tins if you intend to store food in them.

ADJUSTING THE DESIGN
It will be necessary to photocopy design and decide on how you need to adjust it to suit your particular tins. The design has been drawn in four sections, so that you can alter spacing of these to suit the width of your tins. Design can also be enlarged or reduced on a photocopier. You can also re-arrange the picture blocks or repeat them in a number of different combinations and so create your own country scenes.

TRANSFERING THE DESIGN
Trace or photocopy design onto tracing paper.

Chalk back of tracing paper and position it onto tins, securing with Magic Tape. If using graphite paper, slip this between tracing and tin after positioning design. Use a stylus to draw lightly over tracing, using a ruler to help with straight lines.

Cottage and Farmhouse Tins

NOTE: See page 242 for an explanation of Folk Art terms.

Apply a float of WI to top and bottom edges of tin, close to seam line.

LEAVES

Double-load flat brush in GO and WI and paint S-strokes in the leaf shape, keeping WI on under side. Outline in WI using 00 Script Liner. 'Pull' stems by loading script liner in WI, then tipping in CB. The brown will be predominant at beginning of the stem, but as brush moves up towards leaf tip, WI will become dominant colour. The little gumnuts are painted as 'sit-down' strokes (see under Double-loading, page 242) with the round brush loaded in CB and tipped in GO.
NOTE: Do not paint blossoms at this stage.

HILLS

The background hills are a float of E. The foreground hills are a float of GO.

SKY

Float I underneath gum leaves and above hills. The clouds are added in VC as finger print dabs. Touch your finger to the extender, then the paint, picking up very little of each. Blot off excess on palette, then pat lightly onto sky area.

GUM BLOSSOMS

Using liner brush loaded in RN, pull thin straight lines of varying lengths, in a fan shape, from each gumnut. Add tiny dots of RN just beyond ends of lines to give a light, airy look.

BASING-IN BUILDINGS AND ANIMALS

Base-in walls of two houses, right side of barn and barn loft doors, with BW Also paint in circle of windmill and top of water tank.

Paint cow bails, left side of barn, front door of farm house and water tank with DG.

Use RN to base-in cottage roof, tractor and socks on clothesline. For finer areas, use a round brush.

Farmhouse roof is EA. With round brush, paint EA on towel on clothesline, tank stand, cow's udders and faces.

Use WI on liner brush for fences around cow bails and in front of barn. Also paint wires of farmhouse fence.

Use liner in DG to paint railings of cottage fence, while palings and posts of farmhouse fence are VC.

Load round brush in CB to paint trees, clothesline poles and washing basket. Side-load flat brush in CB for vegie patch. Pick up a little RN with CB and float in furrows of earth around tractor. Begin at back and come forwards.

Cows, sheep and hens can be painted with round brush in VC. Don't forget to include milk cans outside cow bails, shirt on clothesline, sacks in front of barn and inner circle on windmill.

All people are wearing I clothes and L hats.

Tractor wheels, tyre swing and patches on cows are L, using a round brush.

FLOATS AND SHADING

Side-load flat brush in DG and add shadows to houses and barns by floating down left side of buildings and under eaves.

Also float DG close to houses to indicate verandahs, and to add shadows to barn doorways. Float DG down left sides of tree trunks.

Float L on left sides as well as under eaves of cow bails, barn and water tank.

With round brush, add a crescent of L to left of tractor wheels and tyre swing.

Shade left side and centre line of cottage roof, with CB. Shade tractor near large wheel.

Float RN along left edge and centre of farmhouse roof.

Float E below cow bails fences, under barn and windmill.

Float GO below other fences and in front of the two houses.

DETAIL AND LINER WORK

Load liner in RN to add roof to cow bails.

Load liner in DG to paint roof gap, chimneys and verandah posts on farmhouse.

Mix some L into the DG on liner to paint in barn roof.

Thin I with a little water to make a wash. Use round brush to lightly colour windows.

Paint front door and shutters of cottage with VC on round brush. Then add details around window sills and verandah posts with VC on liner.

Foliage is stippled in with deerfoot brush. Pick up GO on one side of brush and WI on the other. 'Pounce' up and down on palette to remove almost all paint. Then lightly dab areas around branches, keeping WI on underside and GO to the tree top. Practise first, to get a light airy touch.

Load round brush in GO with a little WI mixed in, to dab vegetation along verandah in front of cottage. Pick up tiny dots of RN to make little flowers amongst this foliage.

Add a larger dot of RN to centre of tractor wheels.

Use liner loaded in mix of GO and WI to paint fine lines of grass along fences and in front of farmhouse verandah. Vegetables in the vegie patch are painted in a similar way.

Thin L with water and/or extender and outline all buildings, animals, people, trees, tractor, water tank and windmill.

Remove any traces of graphite design with kneadable rubber then seal tins with Clearcote Acrylic Sealer.

Photocopy these designs, enlarging or reducing them to the size you need, then vary the arrangements to create a variety of country scenes.

Farm Animal Tin

HEN AND ROOSTER

Head and neck are based-in with E.

Body has a double-load of VC and CB. Make sure that darker colour is towards wings. Upper back is again a double-load of CB and RN, keeping RN to top of back and CB towards wing. Allow RN to blend into CB. Rooster's tail has streaks of WI and RN. Chickens are VC.

SHEEP

Sheep are based-in with BW, with faces, legs and ears of VC. Float DG around head of righthand sheep. Mix DG with L. Load liner and paint spirals on left sheep's back. Spirals on right sheep are VC.

COWS

Base-in cows in VC. Patches are L. Udders and horns are E. Float DG around calf's head and chest, and under cow's neck, ear, front and hind leg.

Grass is a float of GO with small tufts defined with liner in mix of GO and WI.

Flowers are dots of RN with a swirl of VC.

Float I above animals and along top of tin.

Design on lid is made up of gum leaf motif, painted in same way as previously.

Finish tins as for Cottage and Farmhouse Tins.

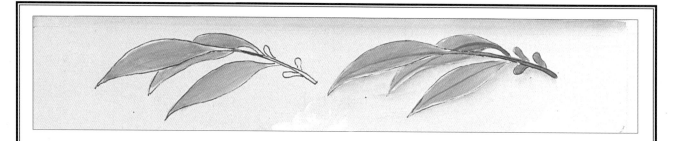

PAINTING TECHNIQUES

BASE PAINT

Most of the work in this country scene is 'based-in' with smooth, even strokes. This can be done more easily using FolkArt Extender. Moisten flat brush in water, blot it on a cloth, then pick up some extender. Blend brush back and forwards to work extender into fibres. It is better to use too little extender rather than too much. Load brush by picking up some colour and then working it into fibres in the way just described. It is important to have brush fully loaded, but over-loading will produce thick ridges of paint. Blend by stroking brush on your palette and work by building up several light even coats of paint rather than one thick coat.

FLOATING AND SHADING

Floating adds shadow and dimension to based-in objects.

Load flat brush with water and/or extender. Dip one corner of brush into paint so that you pick up a triangle of colour. Stroke brush in one direction on palette so that paint gradually blends from coloured edge to fade away across brush to clear extender on the other side. If colour flows right across brush, rinse and begin again. Blend each time you pick up more colour. When painting your project, place side of brush with deepest colour against area you want to be darkest.

LINE WORK AND HIGHLIGHTS

Line work is a feature of this design as the details are outlined. To ensure good line work, thin paint with water and/or extender, to an ink-like consistency, fully load 00 Script Liner and use it up on its tip at right angles to the surface.

DOUBLE-LOADING

Double-loading of flat brush requires two colours to be carried on brush at the same time. Do this by picking up a triangle of colour on one side of brush, then picking up a triangle of a different colour on other side of brush. Blend slightly in the middle.

A round brush can also be double-loaded, but in this project it will only be necessary to tip the loaded brush in a second colour and place it down, then lift, to make 'sit-down' strokes.

Where dots are required it is important to use fresh paint.

The use of the deerfoot brush is described in painting the foliage.

HEARTS AND FLOWERS

Captivating folk art designs for beginners

It's simple, it's a pleasure to do and the results are delightful. Folk art is the perfect answer for the many of us who believe we can't draw or paint but are itching to try. These designs can be worked on wood, fabric or terracotta, as shown.

Folk Art Painting Instructions

MATERIALS
- Fine glass sandpaper
- Lint-free tack cloth
- FolkArt Acrylic Basecoat: Indigo and Bottle Green
- Sponge brush
- Tracing paper
- Stylus
- White graphite transfer paper
- FolkArt Acrylic Colors: Raspberry Sherbert (RS), Wicker White (WW), Apricot Cream (AC), Brownie (B), Bayberry (BB), Green Meadow (GM), Harvest Gold (HG), Porcelain Blue (PB), Taffy (T), Poppy Seed (PS) and Indigo (I).
- FolkArt Extender
- FolkArt Thickener (for fabric painting)
- FolkArt Textile Medium (for fabric painting)

Previous page: The wooden box, bracelet, scissors holder, thread holder, terracotta pot and fabric jam cover were designed by Janet Klepatski. All use very simple motifs that can be traced from the FolkArt pattern sheet on page 246, if you are at first unsure of your skill. There's also a worksheet opposite, which shows the steps for painting and shading each motif.

- Brushes: FolkArt No 3 round; No 6 flat; No 00 script liner
- FolkArt Waterbase Varnish
- Palette

PREPARATION
Lightly sand wooden articles and wipe with a tack cloth.

Seal wood with FolkArt Basecoat in desired colour. Apply two coats with sponge applicator, allowing each coat to dry thoroughly.

Use tracing paper to copy pattern from design sheet onto object, using white graphite paper and stylus to trace design onto dark coloured basecoat.

Paint designs onto objects, following individual instructions, below.

PAINTING TECHNIQUES

BASE PAINT
Most of the work on these pages is 'based-in' with smooth, even strokes. This can more easily be done using FolkArt Extender. Moisten flat brush in water, blot it on a cloth, then pick up some extender. Blend brush back and forwards to work extender into fibres. It is better to use too little extender rather than too much. Load brush by picking up some colour and then working it into fibres in the way just described. It is important to have brush fully loaded, but over-loading will produce thick ridges of paint. Blend by stroking brush on your palette and work by building up several light even coats of paint rather than one thick coat.

FLOATING AND SHADING
Floating adds shadow and dimension to based-in objects.

Load flat brush with water and/or extender. Dip one corner of brush into paint so that you pick up a triangle of colour. Stroke brush in one direction on palette so that paint gradually blends from coloured edge to fade away across brush to clear extender on the other side. If colour flows right across brush, rinse and begin again. Blend each time you pick up more colour. When painting your project, place side of brush with deepest colour against area you want to be darkest.

LINE WORK AND HIGHLIGHTS
Line work is a feature of this design as the details are outlined. To ensure good line work, thin paint with water and/or extender, to an ink-like consistency, fully load 00 Script Liner and use it up on its tip at right angles to the surface.

DOUBLE-LOADING
Double-loading of flat brush requires two colours to be carried on brush at the same time. Do this by picking up a triangle of colour on one side of brush, then picking up a triangle of a different colour on other side of brush. Blend slightly in the middle.

A round brush can also be double-loaded, but in this project it will only be necessary to tip the loaded brush in a second colour and place it down, then lift, to make 'sit-down' strokes.

Where dots are required it is important to use fresh paint.

Additional border designs

Brought to you with the compliments of FolkArt paints

Designs to trace brought to you with the compliments of FolkArt paints

Wooden Box

Use preparation method described on page 238.

BASECOAT Indigo.

TULIPS Base in centre area with RS. Shade and scallop edges with WW. Base in petals with AC. Two coats may be necessary. Shade with B. Highlight with WW.

LEAVES Base in with BB. Shade with B.

FLOWER GARLAND SCROLL Line in WW, using script liner. Sponge in mixture of GM, HG and WW gently over scroll line. Apply small leaves in GM, with BB shading, then dot in daisies with wooden end of paintbrush, using AC, PB, T, and centres in HG.

TULIP BORDER LEAVES In BB, shaded with GM. Tulip in RS, shaded with WW. When paint is completely dry, varnish with two coats of FolkArt Waterbase Varnish.

Scissors Holder

Use preparation method described on page 238.

BASECOAT Indigo.

DUCK Base in body in WW. Shade with PS. Outline feathers with PS. Eye in I. Beak in HG.

HEART Base in with RS. Shade with T. Dot outline of heart in T with wooden end of a paintbrush. Commas from the heart in T. Daisy is PB with a HG centre.

FLOWER (under duck) Sponge in mixture of GM, HG and WW gently under Duck. Apply small leaves with GM. Shade with BB. Daisies are dotted in with AC, PB and T, with their centres in HG.

When paint is completely dry, varnish with two coats of FolkArt Waterbase Varnish.

Thread Holder

Use preparation method described on page 238. Painting of design is the same as for Scissors Holder.

Garden Pot

Use preparation method described on page 238.

BASECOAT Bottle Green.

HEART Base in with PB. Shade in WW. Dots in WW.

DAISY RS, centre in HG.

LEAVES T.

When paint is completely dry, varnish with two coats of FolkArt Waterbase Varnish on design area only.

Bracelet

Use preparation method described on page 238. Painting is the same as for Tulip Border on wooden box.

Fabric Jam Cover

Pre-wash all fabrics before painting. Suitable materials for jam cover fabric are calico and cotton.

Apply FolkArt Thickener to areas before application of paint. This will eliminate the necessity of thick application of paint, thereby allowing fabric to remain soft and pliable.

Let Thickener dry on fabric, then apply paint details.

Pre-mix colours – Using two parts FolkArt Acrylic Color to one part of FolkArt Textile Medium, prepare paints.

LEAVES Base in with GM. Shade in BB.

DAISY Base in petals with HG, shade with T.

Centre is in BB with dots of WW and B.

Heat-set paints before washing fabric. Place fabric with painted side up on an ironing board. Place a cloth dampened with vinegar over top of painted area and a piece of waxed paper between vinegar cloth and iron. Press with a warm iron by just pressing down and lifting iron. Remove cloth and waxed paper and press wrong side of fabric.

HISTORICAL NOTE

Folk Art began in Europe before the Middle Ages, and the original painted pieces were simply decorated, reflecting the lifestyle of the period. Animals, flowers and religious scenes were favoured motifs.

Throughout the generations, folk art has evolved differently in Europe compared to the US. The US designs feature motifs from the home and use softer colours, whereas European designs feature stronger shades and many motifs from nature.

HOME SWEET HOMEWARE

Give inexpensive enamelware a pretty new look with sprays of simple folk art roses and forget-me-nots, designed by Annette Johnson. Once the paint has been fixed in an oven, it is remarkably resilient — even dishwasher-proof — so the pieces you choose to decorate can be functional as well as decorative. A set of mugs would make a delightful gift; larger pieces add a lovely, old-fashioned cottage look to a bathroom or dresser.

Folk Art Enamel Bowls

MATERIALS

- Enamelware of your choice (from camping or disposal stores)
- Vinegar
- Non-waxy graphite paper (or a carbothello pencil, or chalk and tracing paper)
- Scotch brand Magic Tape
- Stylus
- Liquitex Glossies Acrylic paints in blue, green, white, black, yellow and red
- No 4 and No 6 flat brushes
- No 2 round brush
- Liner brush

METHOD

NOTE: Although non-toxic, Glossies should not be used on actual food contact areas. Paint on the outside only of food containers.

Wash enamel in a 1:1 solution of warm water and vinegar and dry thoroughly.

Transfer patterns, below and on page 251, to graphite paper, or trace pattern onto tracing paper and apply chalk or carbothello pencil to wrong side of tracing paper. Tape pattern in place and transfer onto enamelware, using a stylus. The placing of patterns will depend on the size of your container. You may need to enlarge or reduce pattern, or shift placement of ribbon to accommodate the curve of a bowl or plate.

Mix black, yellow and white to make a dull grey-green and paint leaves with a No 2 round brush, tipped with white.

Mix blue with a touch of black and white to give a dusty blue colour and paint ribbons with a No 2 round brush, side-loaded with white.

To paint the roses, first study step-by-step illustrations on page 250. Mix red and green to make a dark burgundy and, using a No 6 flat brush, block in whole rose shape of pink rose (Step 1). Mix red, yellow and a touch of green (to mute orange colour) and block in peach rose. Let dry thoroughly before doing overstrokes. All petals are stroked in with a No 4 flat brush, using blocking-in colour on one side of brush and white on other side; that is, for pink rose, load one side of brush with burgundy mix and other side with white; for peach rose, load one side with dark peach mix and other side with white. Blend well before painting in petals.

Start at outer edge of block and work towards centre, keeping darker side of brush towards centre (Steps 2, 3, 4, 5 and 6).

For forget-me-nots, mix blue, black and white and apply with a No 2 round brush, side-loaded with white. Paint five dot petals. Centres are a mix of yellow, with a touch of red and a side-load of white.

Tendrils are painted in same colour as leaves, using a liner brush.

If you need more than one coat of paint for good coverage, let first coat dry thoroughly before overpainting.

Paint will be permanent without baking, but for a harder finish that is also dishwasher-proof, pre-heat oven to 160 degrees Celsius and bake for 30–40 minutes in a well-ventilated area. (If painting on glass, place glass into cold oven and bring up to 160 degrees C.)

Brushes can be washed in soap and water.

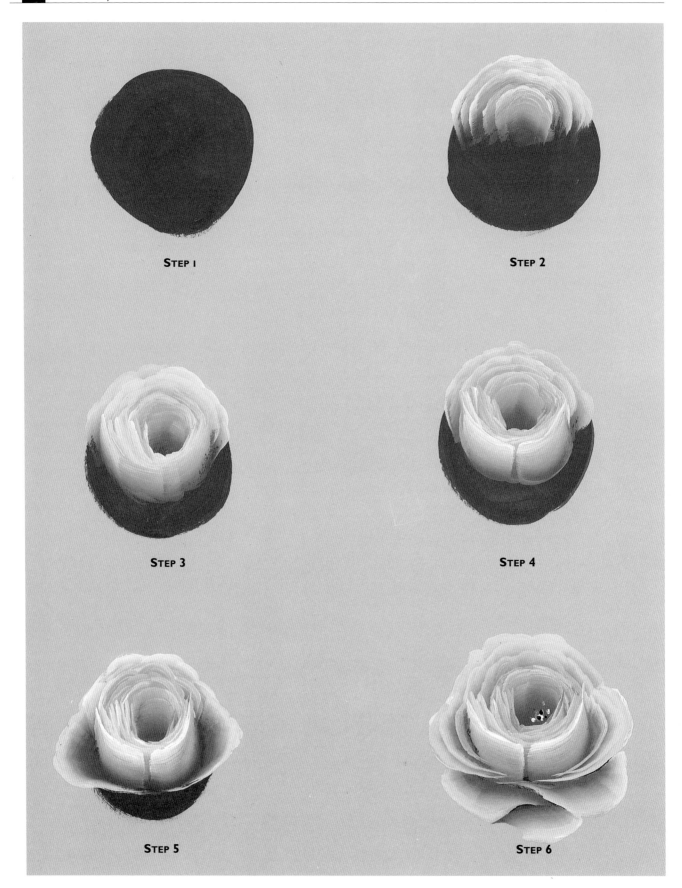

STEP 1

STEP 2

STEP 3

STEP 4

STEP 5

STEP 6

Step-by-step illustrations to paint roses in conjuntion with instructions on page 249.

SOMETHING TO CROW ABOUT

Maybe one of these days, you'll get the space for your big vegie garden and a chook-run, but in the meantime, why not add a whimsical barnyard touch to your favourite chair with this magnificent stencilled rooster? Using homespun as a base, designer Annette Allen shows how to cut and stencil the rooster and checked border, then make it up into a country style cushion. At least a cushion won't wake you at dawn ...

Stencilled Cushion

MEASUREMENTS

Finished cushion is 45cm square.

MATERIALS

60cm x 30cm Mylar (acetate) for stencils
- Fine permanent marker pen
- Sharp craft knife
- Craft cutting mat (optional)
- Repositional adhesive spray (such as Stick it Again)
- 0.5m x 115cm cotton fabric (homespun is ideal)

- Permaset fabric paints in Venetian Red, Navy, Mid Green, Mid Red, Black, available through artists' supply stores, or use any fabric paint
- Three stencil brushes
- Paper towels
- 50cm square wadding
- 2m x No 2 piping cord
- 2m x 2.5cm wide colour co-ordinating bias binding (or purchase ready-made piping)
- 35cm zip, to match fabric colour
- Cushion insert, 45cm square

STENCILLING

Trace rooster, heart and chequerboard stencil designs on page 254 onto Mylar, using a fine permanent marker pen. Note that there are three overlays to the rooster design, each represented by a different colour. You need to trace the complete rooster three times (as a positional guide), then cut out different sections on each of the three stencils.

We've only given a section of the border pattern, which you need to repeat to make a border, 29cm x 6cm.

Cut out designs, using a sharp craft knife. This is easier if you use a craft cutting mat. It is sometimes difficult to cut out a square, as used in the borders, without getting edges uneven. If in difficulty, neaten with masking tape.

Cut fabric in half, giving two rectangles each 50cm x 57.5cm. Trim one piece into a 50cm square.

Fold square piece of fabric lightly into quarters to indicate centre point, then unfold.

Place rooster body stencil in centre of fabric, using repositional adhesive spray on back of stencil to hold it firmly in place.

Mix Venetian Red and Navy (70/30) and load stencil brush with paint. Work paint into bristles, and take off excess paint at the same time, by using a circular movement onto paper towels. Aim to have a very dry brush. Again using circular movements, apply paint to stencil, keeping to the edge of design so that centre of body remains colour-free. Carefully remove stencil.

Now lay tail and feathers stencil on fabric, using traced outline to position it accurately over rooster body.

Mix Mid Green and Navy (50/50). With a new stencil brush, apply paint in the same way as before. This time, make sure application of paint is heavy enough to hide edge of body that is directly underneath feathers. Rather than overloading your brush with too much paint, however, which could seep under stencil, make several applications with a very dry brush to get desired depth of colour.

Remove stencil, then lay comb stencil on design. Mix Mid Red and Venetian Red (70/30) and apply paint

*King of the roost, an elegant
stencilled cockerel takes pride of
place on a country-style cushion.*

as before. Remove stencil and return
to first stencil to paint in eye, using
Black.

Centre border stencil on each side,
approximately 3cm in from raw edge,
so that inside corner squares are
almost touching at their diagonal
points. Mark position on each side
before stencilling. Mix Venetian Red
and Navy (70/30) and apply paint as
before. Remove stencil.

Position heart stencil in centre of
square created in each corner. Mix
Navy and Black (70/30) and stencil as
before.

Press completed design with an
iron to set colour.

TO MAKE UP CUSHION

Pin and baste stencilled top to wadding and, using
a large stitch on sewing machine, quilt around
outside edges of chequerboard bands and define
square around hearts. Quilt around hearts
themselves. Make another row of quilting stitches
around whole design. The rooster could also be
quilted, if desired.

Fold bias binding over piping cord and sew to
cushion top with a large machine-stitch, easing it
around corners to avoid pulling. Use last row of
quilted stitches as a guide.

To accommodate zip, which is fitted across
centre back, cut remaining piece of fabric in half
crosswise and over-sew cut edges to neaten. Stitch
centre seam 7.5cm in at each end, leaving 35cm
opening for zip. Pin zip in place and stitch, using
a zipper foot.

Leaving zip partly open, and with right sides
together, attach back and stencilled top together.
Using a zipper foot and with piping stitching line
as a guide, sew close to piping cord. Oversew
edges, snip corners and turn inside out. Add
cushion insert.

Wash strictly according to instructions given
by manufacturer on fabric paint.

THE EGG AND DYE

Marbling is the creation of patterns of paint on the surface of liquid, and the transfer of these patterns to an object. The most intricate designs can be achieved with a minimum of skill and applied to all sorts of surfaces. As a quick, easy Easter idea, Diana Cross shows how to marble eggs for an eye-catching display, or to give away — if you can bear to part with them.

STEP 1

STEP 2

Marbled Eggs

MATERIALS
- Large bowl or plastic container
- Marble Magic (see Note)
- Hen or goose eggs
- Metal skewer
- Spray-on mould remover
- Household cream cleanser
- Scourer
- Wooden satay skewers
- Elastic bands
- Polystyrene box or block, for drying
- Alum (available from the chemist)
- Acrylic paints in clear and metallic colours (see Note)
- Long-toothed comb (optional)
- Rubber gloves
- White gift tags (optional)
- Paper towel
- Newspaper
- Quick-drying varnish
- Paintbrush
- Gold crowns (from bead suppliers)
- Craft glue

NOTE: We used a product called Marble Magic. If this is not available, use powdered carrageen, instead, which is available from craft shops or by mail order from Batik Oetoro, Sydney, ph (02) 398 6201. The paint used was an acrylic model paint called Tamiya, available from hobby/model shops.

STEP 1
First, prepare marbling solution. Measure quantity of warm water needed to three-quarters fill large

Previous page: Glowing with colour — and a dash of varnish — marbled eggs are fun, easy and creatively satisfying to make.

bowl or plastic container. Sprinkle evenly over the surface one level lid full of Marble Magic per one litre of water. (If using carrageen powder, mix one dessertspoon of carrageen with a little cold water, then, using an blender or egg beaters, beat into a thick paste. Add 1.4 litres hot water and beat for about 5 minutes, until solution becomes like egg white in consistency.)

Leave your solution to stand overnight. Next day, stir gently. You should have a clear, thick solution with a slippery feel. Extra solution can be prepared ahead and kept in an air-tight container, to be added as marbling and cleaning lowers solution level.

STEP 2
Meanwhile, prepare eggs. They must be at room temperature before you attempt to blow out the contents. Make a small hole in pointed end of egg with a metal skewer, and a slightly larger hole in opposite end. Insert skewer to break up yolk, then blow into small hole, forcing egg contents out through larger hole into a small bowl.

When eggshell is empty, carefully suck water up into shell, shake to clean inside thoroughly, then blow it out again. Continue doing this until expelled water is clear.

Outside of egg must also be cleaned, especially if using the larger goose eggs, which have a rather waxy coating. Spray egg with mould remover to remove any marks left by hatchery. Rinse, then scrub gently with a scourer pad and cream cleanser. Rinse. Handle with care once eggs are clean, as oils in your hands can affect marbling.

STEP 5

STEP 3
Break wooden skewers into lengths about 5cm longer than length of eggs. Wind an elastic band tightly around a stick, about 2cm in from one end, leaving just enough stick to grip while dipping and painting eggs. Slip an egg onto skewer, resting on elastic band. Insert skewer into polystyrene as far as elastic band, and leave egg to dry after cleaning.

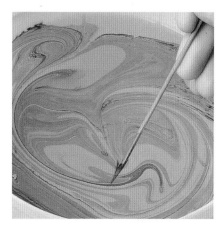

STEP 6

STEP 7

STEP 8

STEP 9

STEP 4

Mix 30g of alum to 1 litre of water in a glass jar. Paint eggs with two coats of alum mixture, leaving to dry about 5–10 minutes between coats. Alum acts as a mordant, encouraging colour to adhere to surface of egg. Insert skewered egg into foam to dry, as previously.

STEP 5

Break more skewers in half, to make individual stirrers for each colour. Stir paint and then, using mixing skewer, drop a few drops of your chosen colours onto surface of prepared marbling solution. Ideally, each spot should float on surface and slowly spread to form a circle.

STEP 6

Using pointed end of a clean skewer, the circles of colour can now be pushed, pulled or swirled, dragged into stripes, or left as dots. An intricate scalloped effect can be achieved by gently dragging a long-toothed comb through colours. Do not hurry, and don't overwork paint — sometimes the simplest pattern is the most effective.

STEP 7

When you are satisfied with design, hold skewered egg at either end and, wearing rubber gloves, lower egg steadily and horizontally into solution until it is completely immersed. Egg will collect colour as it passes through floating design.

STEP 8

Lift out vertically and quickly so egg will not be marbled twice. If colours begin to run, immediately place egg under gently running tap water for a few seconds and colour running will cease. If desired, after each egg is marbled, you can marble a matching card by lowering it onto surface of solution. Place each marbled egg in foam block to dry.

STEP 10

STEP 11

STEP 9

To clean solution between each dipping, lay a piece of paper towel on surface to soak up any remaining colour.

STEP 10

Then skim surface until it is clean, using strips of newspaper.

STEP 11

Paint dried eggs with varnish to give colours depth and gloss, as well as greater durability to finished egg. Use at least two coats, following manufacturer's instructions, applying brush in one direction only. When dry, cover holes at either end of egg by gluing on gold crowns.

General Crafts

I have often said that there is a craft for everyone — no matter what level of skill or confidence people may claim to have — even levels that seem non-existent. The clever editors at *Handmade* magazine have always placed a creative emphasis on easy, stylish and unusual crafts that seem to stimulate people into thinking "I can do that" — and they do!

Over the years, readers have been shown the most amazing variety of crafts and home decorating ideas — and some of the best of these follow for you to try. You'll find that these crafts may give you new techniques and introduce you to unfamiliar materials — and you know what fun it can be making that sort of crafty discovery.

Your mind will be spinning with the possibilities of adaptation — for I'm sure that, once learned, these crafts will re-appear shaped to your own individual interpretations. Now, isn't that what craft is all about?

TONIA TODMAN

GRANNY SMITHS

These must be the original Granny Smiths! If you look closely at the faces of this trio of old ladies, designed by Georgina Bitcon, you'll see that they're fashioned from dried apples. When filled with pot-pourri, lavender, or even dried herbs, they will hang in your kitchen indefinitely, their wonderful expressions changing as they become more wizened.

Granny Smiths

MEASUREMENTS
Finished doll is about 19cm high, excluding hanging loop.

MATERIALS
- One apple (we used a Granny Smith)
- Sharp knife
- Pencil or chopstick
- Small amount thin cardboard (from an empty packet will do)
- Craft glue
- Four ordinary white pipe-cleaners
- 34cm x 20cm piece fabric, for dress
- Approximately 1/3 cup lavender, pot-pourri or mixed dried herbs
- Sewing thread and needle
- 17cm square contrasting fabric, for shawl
- Very small amount stuffing
- Old pantihose or stockings
- 0.2m narrow ribbon, for hanging
- Hair material, such as wool, cotton wool, steel wool or synthetic craft hair (from craft shops)
- Small twigs and a little wool (for besom), or two satay sticks, two small wooden beads and small amount of wool (for knitting), or small purchased basket and apple green and brown modelling compound (for basket of apples)

METHOD
Peel apple and, with a sharp knife, carve a rudimentary face on one side. There is no need for fine detail, as the face will develop as the apple dries and wrinkles. Cut two eye sockets, a single slit above each socket to make brows protrude and two or three tiny slits at corners of eyes. Cut away a little apple on either side of centre of face, to create a nose, and make a single slit for mouth. Cut away a little apple below mouth to define chin. Push a pencil or chopstick into core from bottom, stand apple in a bottle or jar to support it and leave on a sunny window sill to dry. If weather is cold or wet, dry apples in a very slow oven with door slightly ajar.

When apple is dry and wizened (this usually takes a couple of weeks), remove it from pencil. Cut a rectangle of thin cardboard approximately 11cm x 7cm and roll into a cylinder about the width of a pencil. Smear end of cylinder with craft glue and insert into core of apple. This will provide a 'neck' on which to attach arms and clothes. Allow to dry.

Take two pipe-cleaners and overlap them enough so that when twisted together they form a length of about 21cm. Repeat this process with the other two pipe-cleaners. Now twist the two double sets together, leaving a gap at centre, for inserting neck, and curving ends into circles, to form basis for hands. Finished length is approximately 19cm.

Smear a little glue around neck, immediately below head, and insert neck into gap in centre of pipe-cleaners. Move pipe-cleaners up neck till they are directly below head, then twist 'arms' in opposite directions until neck is held tightly in place (see diagram below).

Fold rectangle of fabric in half crosswise and cut along fold line. With right sides facing, and allowing 5mm seams, stitch two pieces together, leaving a 6cm neck opening in centre of one 20cm side and 4cm armhole openings at top of each 17cm side. Turn right side out and press, pressing raw edges of openings to inside along seam line.

Fill bag thus created with about ⅓ cup lavender, pot-pourri or dried mixed herbs. Use a funnel to fill the bags if necessary. It is important not to fill bag too full — a small amount in bottom of 'skirt' is all that is required to provide scent and a little shaping to body.

With a needle and thread, run a gathering thread around neck and armhole edges of dress but do not pull up. Bending pipe-cleaners as necessary, insert neck and arms into dress, pulling hand ends out through armholes. Pull up gathering thread tightly around neck edge and secure.

Take a small piece of stuffing, about the size of the tip of your little finger, and wind around pipe-cleaner hand. Cut a double piece of pantihose, stretch it over stuffing and bind in place with cotton around 'wrist'. Trim away excess pantihose close to binding. Press hand to flatten slightly and define 'fingers' with a few stitches, if desired.

Pull up gathering threads around sleeve edge, covering binding, and secure.

Fold ribbon in half lengthwise and attach cut ends to back of dress, just below head.

Pull a few threads away from each edge of shawl square to give a frayed effect, fold shawl in half diagonally, then wrap around doll, covering ends of ribbon hanger, and secure in place with a stitch at centre front.

Tease out wool or synthetic curls and glue to head, as desired.

To make a besom, simply bind a bunch of small twigs around a longer, thicker one and secure with wool.

To make miniature knitting, trim satay sticks to 7cm from point and attach a small wooden bead to each end with glue (whittling ends to fit hole of bead, if necessary). When glue is dry, cast on about 15 stitches and knit, as normal, until desired length. Roll leftover wool into a little ball and secure end with a drop of glue so it can't unravel.

To make a basket of apples, roll small balls of apple green modelling compound, press top end with a skewer and insert tiny brown stalks, as well as a little leaf or two, if desired. Dry in oven, according to manufacturer's instructions and use to fill miniature basket (which can be purchased from a craft shop).

Although apple head may go on drying and become even more wrinkled after doll is finished, these dolls will last indefinitely. They are traditionally hung in kitchens.

Small details give individuality to each of your dolls. These grannies have knitting on tiny satay stick needles, a basket of modelled apples and a traditional besom, made from twigs, to keep them busy. Dressed as witches, the dolls also make marvellous decorations for Halloween.

OLD-FASHIONED FUN AND GAMES

From the days when the nursery was a small child's kingdom, when *Coles Funny Picture Book* made Bad children Good, and old Scrooge was finally softened by the spirit of Christmas, these beautiful Victorian-inspired toys will delight new generations of kids — and not-so-small kids — all over again.

Designed by Maria Ragan, jack-in-the-box, weight-lifting muscle man, pop-up harlequin, rocking bunny and adorable crocheted lamb will more than repay the little bit of extra effort required to make them. Jack and the harlequin both have original Victorian faces. For these, a reproduction Victorian scrap or face cut from découpage paper is glued to a wooden bead for an instant antique look.

Rocking Bunny

MATERIALS

- 20cm square 4mm plywood
- 8cm x 25cm x 20mm pinewood
- Coping saw
- Fine sandpaper
- Dark tan shoe polish
- Neutral shoe polish
- Non-toxic, water-based paints
- Paintbrush
- Black pencil
- Rit liquid dye, Fuchsia 12
- Small cut-out of flowers, or other decorative image (from magazine)
- Craft glue
- Matt spray varnish

PATTERN PIECES

All pattern pieces, printed below, are actual size. Trace Rabbit Body and Rabbit Base.

METHOD

Trace Rabbit Body pattern onto plywood. If making more than one, do not forget to reverse pattern so that some face other way. With coping saw, cut out one Rabbit Body. From pinewood, trace and cut out one Rabbit Base. Smooth edges with sandpaper.

Paint bunny front white and let it dry thoroughly. Rub dark tan shoe polish into wood on both sides. On white side only, rub in neutral shoe polish to give an antique stained look.

Paint flowers and eyes as shown. With black pencil, outline back leg.

With a rag, apply liquid dye to base and let it dry thoroughly. Rub in dark tan shoe polish. Attach bunny to base with craft glue, and decorate base with cut-out images.

Spray all over with matt varnish. NOTE: If making bunny for a baby, be sure to use non-toxic paint and varnish. We used FolkArt paint from Myart. They also make a non-toxic antiquing medium and a water-based varnish. Do not use shoe polish.

Weight-lifter

MATERIALS

- 40cm x 30cm x 4mm plywood
- Coping saw
- Fine sandpaper
- Water-based paints
- Paintbrush
- Neutral shoe polish
- Drill
- 8 small nails (about 1.5cm long)
- Pliers
- 1.5m strong thread
- Craft glue
- Small wooden bead
- Matt spray varnish

PATTERN PIECES

All pattern pieces, printed opposite, are actual size. Trace Body, Head, Arm A, Arm B, Thigh and Leg.

METHOD

Trace pattern pieces onto plywood. Do not forget to reverse pattern for one Arm A and one Leg so that finished figure is symmetrical. Using a coping saw, cut out one Body, one Head, two Arm A's, two Arm B's, two Thighs and two Legs. Smooth rough edges with sandpaper.

Paint weight-lifter with colours as shown. For skin, mix one part yellow ochre, half a part of white and one drop each of lemon yellow and vermilion.

For an antique finish, apply neutral shoe polish, colour by colour, and rub in until it shines. (Do not rub over two colours because they may smudge.)

Drill holes in body parts as indicated. Join parts with nails which have had their points removed. With pliers, bend nails so parts are joined securely but still allow free movement.

Assemble thread at the back of figure, as shown. Glue head to body, covering thread holes in neck. Knot a wooden bead on bottom of thread. Finally, spray finished weight-lifter with a matt varnish.

RABBIT BODY

RABBIT BASE

WEIGHT-LIFTER PATTERN PIECES

POP-UP HARLEQUIN PATTERN PIECES

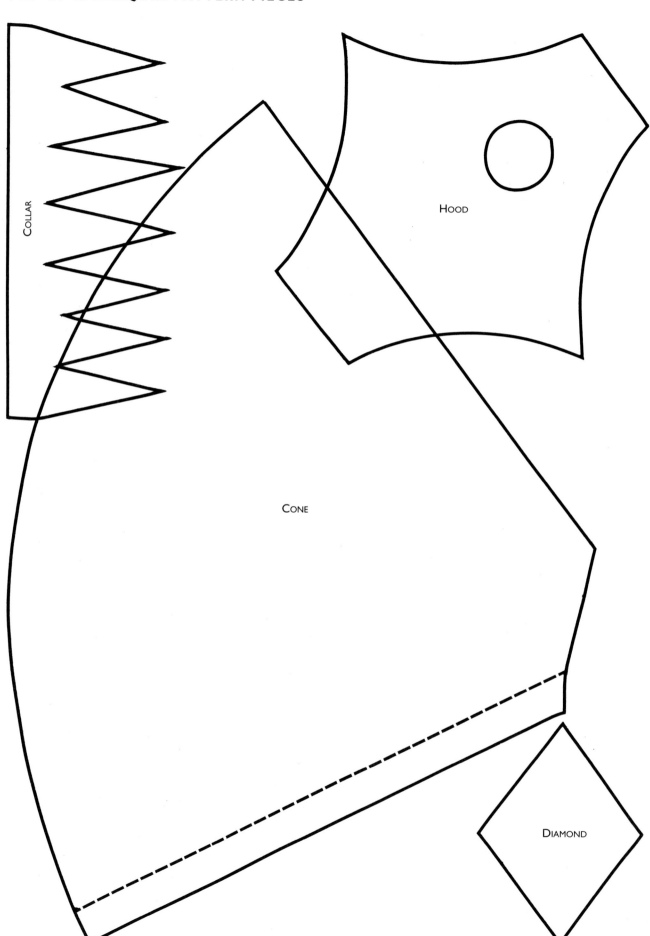

Collar

Hood

Cone

Diamond

Pop-up Harlequin

MATERIALS
- 10cm square each of grey, sky blue, bright red and rose pink felt
- 15 cm square each of peppermint green, violet and dusty pink felt
- Paper doll's face, 3.5cm diameter
- 3cm-diameter wooden bead
- Craft glue
- Clear nail polish or varnish
- 9 small gold beads
- One pipe-cleaner
- 40cm x 5mm-diameter dowel (it should fit hole in bead)
- Sheet of thin construction cardboard
- 25cm x 25mm-wide strip lightweight fabric
- 30cm x 10mm-wide green ribbon

PATTERN PIECES
All pattern templates, printed opposite, are actual size. Trace Hood, Collar, Diamond and Cone.

CUTTING
From peppermint green felt, cut one Hood; from dusty pink felt, cut one Collar; using colour guides opposite, cut Diamonds from remaining felt. From cardboard sheet, cut one Cone.

METHOD
With right sides together, and using the two colour guides, blanket-stitch felt patches together for both Top and Cone. Fold and blanket-stitch side seams together. Turn right way out.

Cut out doll's face and stick carefully to wooden bead using craft glue, working creases to edge as much as possible. Varnish with three or four coats of clear nail polish or varnish, letting each coat dry thoroughly before applying next.

Glue Hood around doll's face and blanket-stitch Hood together around outer edges. Decorate both ends with a gold bead. Place a small piece of pipe-cleaner into each point of Hood, to help keep its shape.

Push dowel into wooden bead and secure with a drop of glue. Gather lower edge of Hood around dowel and secure firmly. Run a gathering thread around neck edge of Top and secure firmly around dowel.

Decorate ends of Collar with gold beads. Slip into place around neck, gather up and secure firmly.

Glue sides of cardboard Cone together. Glue 25mm-wide fabric strip to inside lower edge of harlequin's Top, leaving half width of fabric extending. Slip dowel through cone, and glue extending edge of fabric to inside top edge of Cone.

Position felt Cone over cardboard one and glue in place. Glue dark green ribbon over join. Wind rest of ribbon around bottom part of Cone and secure with glue.

COLOUR GUIDES FOR DIAMONDS

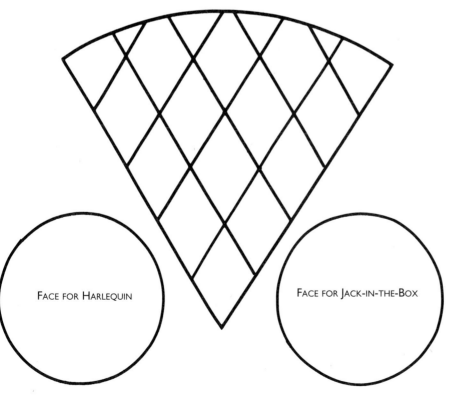

FACE FOR HARLEQUIN

FACE FOR JACK-IN-THE-BOX

Jack-in-the-Box

MATERIALS

- 14cm square wooden box with lid (made-to-order from Timber Turn, ph (08) 277 5056)
- FolkArt acrylic colour paints: Rose Shimmer; Antique Gold; Persimmon; Evergreen; Taffy; Turquoise; Frosted Berry
- No 4 flat and No 1 paintbrushes
- Craft glue
- Matt spray varnish
- Brass catch (from hardware shops)
- Small amount polyester filling
- Paper doll's face, 3.5cm diameter
- 47mm-diameter

wooden bead
- Clear nail polish or varnish
- 9cm length of dowel (diameter must fit hole in bead)
- 30cm x 40cm light-weight fawn fabric
- 10cm x 40cm calico
- 50cm x 20cm lightweight mid-blue fabric
- Scraps of navy blue, grey and green fabric
- Small piece white construction cardboard
- Horse and palm tree motifs, cut from wrapping paper (you could choose any motifs that you like)
- One pipe-cleaner
- Three small gold bells
  - Five 11mm-diameter, self-cover buttons
  - 22.5cm x 3.5cm-diameter spring (made-to-order for about $60 from Worthwhile

Springs, ph (02) 519 4415)
- 7cm x 5cm-diameter rigid plastic, or thick cardboard, tube
- Selley's Kwik Grip glue
- 3.5cm-diameter piece of cork

PATTERN PIECES

All pattern pieces, opposite and on page 270, are actual size. Trace Sun Face, Sun Rays, Hat Side, Hat Top, Hand and Collar.

CUTTING

- From fawn fabric, cut four rectangles 20cm x 12cm for Sleeves, one rectangle 20cm square for Hood and one 8cm square for Hood Facing.
- From calico, cut four Hands and two Sun Faces.
- From mid-blue fabric, cut two 20cm x 25cm rectangles for Dress.
- From grey scrap, cut two Collars.
- From navy blue scrap, cut four Hat Sides and one strip, 2.5cm x 20cm, for dress trim.
- From green scrap, cut two Hat Tops.

From construction cardboard, cut two Sun Rays, cutting one with straight edges and the other with wavy edges, as shown.

From wrapping paper, cut out motifs and a 2cm border for inside lid.

METHOD

Paint outside of box and lid with Persimmon; paint inside of lid and inside edges with Rose Shimmer. Glue cut-out border to inside of lid. Using photograph as a guide, decorate outer panels of box and attach cut-out motifs with craft glue.

Spray entire box with matt varnish. When thoroughly dry, attach brass catch to outside of box for closing.

To construct Sun, cut a small opening along diameter of one of the calico circles, then, with right sides facing, oversew them together around circumference. Turn right side out and press. Insert small piece of polyester filling and embroider features in running-stitch, using ordinary sewing cotton, following diagram. Using craft glue, stick finished face to wavy-edged Sun Ray and oversew edges of face through both fabric and cardboard, if desired. Paint this part of sun with

JACK-IN-THE-BOX PATTERN PIECES

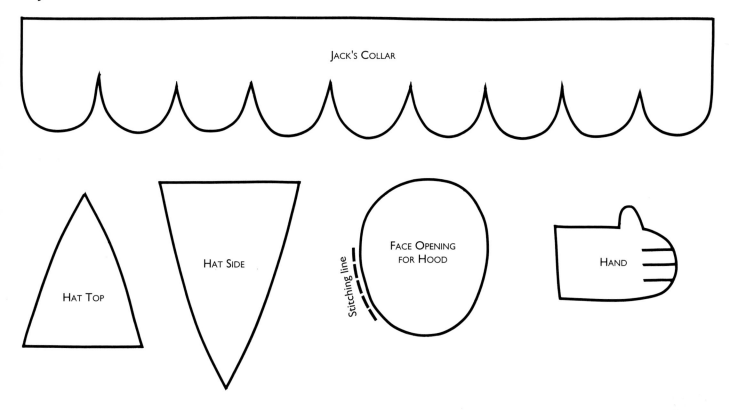

Antique Gold. Paint straight-edged Sun Ray with Taffy. Allow both parts to dry thoroughly. Glue Sun Face portion to straight-edged Sun Ray, positioning lower rays to appear between upper rays. Glue whole sun onto box lid.

Cut out doll's face and glue carefully to wooden bead with craft glue, keeping it as wrinkle-free as possible. Let it dry and then varnish with 34 coats of nail polish or varnish, letting each coat dry thoroughly before applying next. Push dowel through bead and fix with glue.

Using diagram, trace face opening for Hood onto centre of wrong side of Hood. Position Hood Facing underneath Hood (on right side) so that it extends beyond tracing line on all sides. Stitch both pieces together along stitching line. Carefully slash and cut out face opening close to stitching, clipping to curve so that it will lie flat. Turn facing to wrong side and press.

With right sides together, oversew side seams on blue Hat Sides and green Hat Top. Turn right side out. Before sewing them onto Hood, insert a piece of pipe-cleaner in each to

enable hat to be bent into position. Hand-sew Hat Sides and Top to Hood, about 2cm from face opening. Stitch small bells to each point of hat.

Wrap Hood around bead as shown in diagram. Blanket-stitch along folds to hold in place. Stick Hood around face using craft glue. Gather lower part of Hood around dowel and secure firmly. Trim excess fabric.

Press under 5mm on long edges of navy dress trim and neatly hand-sew down centre front of one piece of Dress. Decorate with self-covered buttons, painted as shown in photograph and positioned as shown on diagram.

Using a pencil, lightly rule Sleeve pieces into 1.5cm squares. Creating a chequerboard effect, paint alternate squares on one Sleeve in Antique Gold and on the other in Rose Shimmer. Allow to dry.

With wrong sides together, join Sleeve sections to Dress sections. Stitch front to back at side seams, underarm seam and top sleeve seam. Turn right side out.

To make Hands, oversew edges of two Hand pieces together, with right sides facing. Turn right side out and

fill with polyester filling. Define fingers with running-stitch, as indicated on pattern.

Turn in raw edge on cuff edge of Sleeves, and run a gathering thread around edge. Place Hands into Sleeves and draw up gathers to fit. Secure gathers and catch Hands to Sleeves in one or two places. On wrong side, run a gathering thread along upper Sleeve seams and draw up slightly to lift Hands into position.

With right sides facing, over-sew Collar sections together. Trim seam, clip curves, turn right side out and press. Run a gathering thread around neck edge.

Using Selley's Kwik Grip, glue spring onto base of box. Place plastic or cardboard tube over spring and glue to base with Kwik Grip. (This will stop spring from lolling sideways when box is opened.)

To join head to spring, push dowel through cork from top and push cork into spring.

Glue bottom of Dress around insides of box. Gather neck edge of Dress, pull up tightly and secure around neck. Place Collar around neck, draw up gathers and secure.

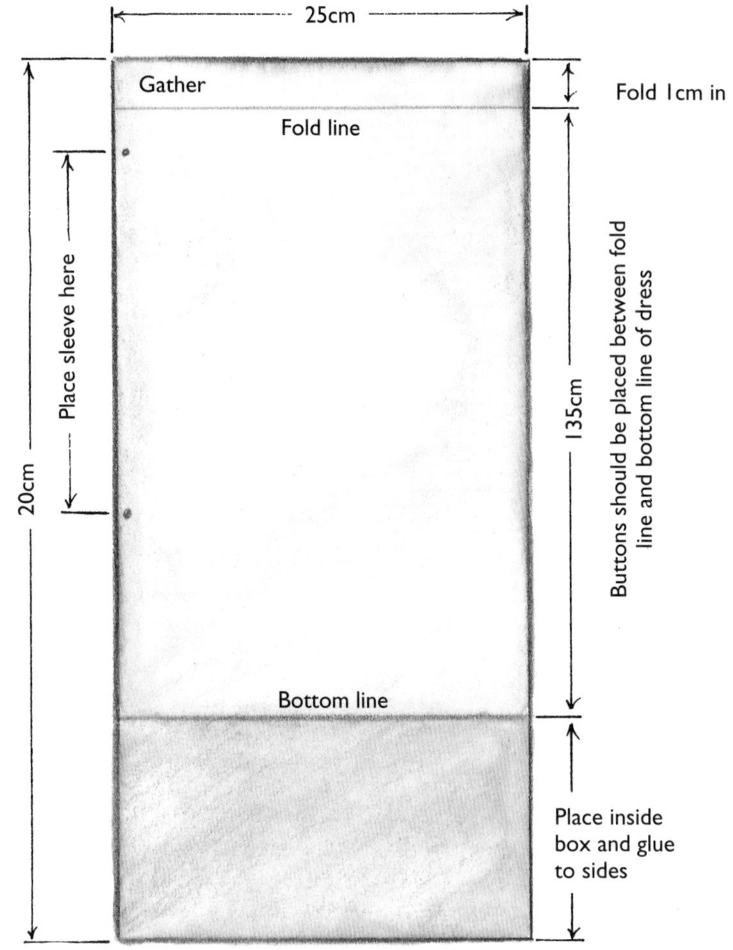

25cm

Gather

Fold line

Fold 1cm in

Place sleeve here

20cm

135cm

Buttons should be placed between fold line and bottom line of dress

Bottom line

Place inside box and glue to sides

DIAGRAM FOR JACK'S BODY

SUN FACE

CUT-OUT MOTIFS FOR BOX LID

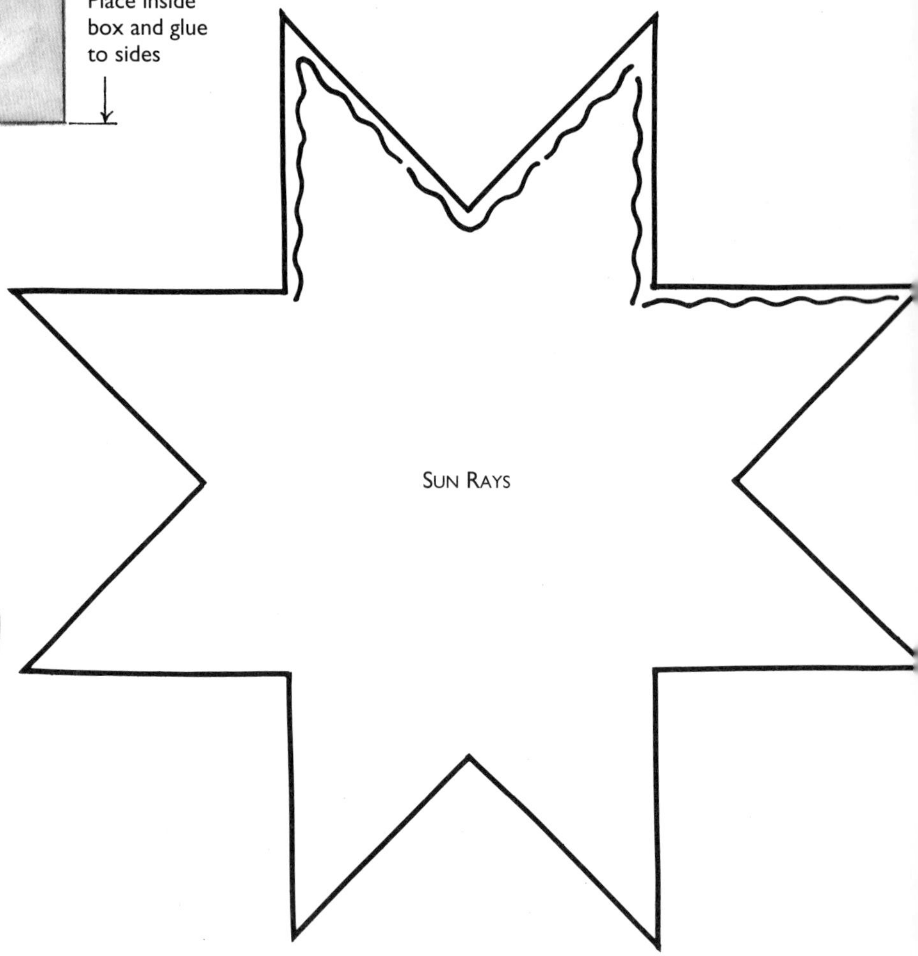

SUN RAYS

Antique Pull-along Lamb

MATERIALS

LAMB

- 200g white 8-ply bouclé cotton/acrylic
- 3mm (No 10–11) crochet hook
- Two 25cm squares black felt
- 1.5m x 10mm-wide green ribbon
- Scraps of fabric (for flowers)
- 60cm x 6cm lace fabric (for flowers)
- 11 pearl beads
- Craft glue
- Tapestry and sewing needles
- Polyester fibre filling
- 32cm x 15mm-diameter dowel (for leg support)

CART

- 39cm x 20cm x 15mm pinewood
- Four 15mm x 8cm-diameter circles of wood
- Eight 35mm brass screws
- Rit liquid dye, Fuchsia 12
- Dark tan shoe polish
- Cotton or silk cord

PATTERN PIECES

All pattern pieces are printed on page 273. Trace Lamb Ear and Lamb Head.

CUTTING

- From felt, cut two Lamb Heads, two Lamb Ears, and four 10cm x 7cm rectangles for Legs.
- From fabric scraps, cut four 20cm x 6cm pieces for Flowers.
- Cut lace into three 20cm lengths.
- From pinewood, cut one Cart Base, to specified size.
- From dowel, cut four 8cm lengths.

CROCHET LAMB

Pieces are worked in dc fabric with inc and dec as shown in diagrams on page 272.

TENSION

See Crochet Notes on page 201.

20dc and 20 rows to 9cm over dc fabric.

SIDE

Begin with back Leg. Make 11 ch.
1ST ROW 1dc in 2nd ch from hook, 1dc in each ch to end...10dc. Continue in dc fabric, foll diagram 1, to 14th row. Fasten off and break off yarn.

Beg front Leg. Make 11 ch and work 1st row as for back Leg. Cont in dc fabric, foll Diagram 1, to 14th row. **15TH ROW** Foll diagram, dc across front Leg, 9ch, dc across back Leg.

Work rows 16 to 41, foll Diagram 1.

Divide for back and head. 42nd row. Foll diagram 1, work Back only. Fasten off and break off yarn.

Join yarn to 41st row and work Head, foll diagram.

Fasten off.

Following Diagram 2, complete second side.

UNDERSIDE GUSSET

Work as for first Side to end of 29th row, foll Diagram 3.
30TH ROW Beg working back Leg, as

shaded on diagram. Fasten off and break yarn.

Join yarn where indicated on 29th row and complete front Leg from 30th row on Diagram 3.

EARS (MAKE 2)

Make 11 ch.
1ST ROW Miss 1 ch, 1dc in each ch...10dc. Cont in dc fabric, foll Diagram 4.

TAIL (MAKE 2)

Make 5 ch.
1ST ROW Miss 1 ch, 1 dc in each ch...4dc. Cont in dc fabric, foll Diagram 5.

TO MAKE UP

Using tapestry needle and matching yarn, join Underside Gusset to both Sides, then join Sides at front and along back, leaving a small opening in back, and bottom of Legs and face side of Head open.

Using blanket-stitch, join Head pieces, with wrong sides together, around outside edges. With right sides together, stitch Head to body.

Fold Leg pieces in half cross-wise and stitch short sides together. Stitch a felt leg to bottom of each Leg.

Turn lamb to right side and fill with polyester fibre. Stitch back opening closed.

Join Tail pieces together, leaving an opening as indicated on graph. Turn to right side and slip-stitch to body.

Insert one piece of 8cm dowel into each Leg for support.

Stitch black felt Ear pieces to crocheted ear pieces around outside edges, leaving open on bottom edge, as indicated on graph. Turn to right side and stitch Ears to Head.

Fold each Flower piece in half, with right sides together, and stitch along short sides. Turn to right side.

Fold in half again and gather raw edges. Stitch a pearl bead inside each Flower. Dab craft glue on raw edges to stop fraying.

Cut 110cm length of green ribbon, then cut remaining ribbon into six equal pieces. Fold each of these and attach ribbon between flowers. Tie ribbon necklace around lamb's neck in a bow.

ANTIQUE PULL-ALONG LAMB CROCHET CHARTS

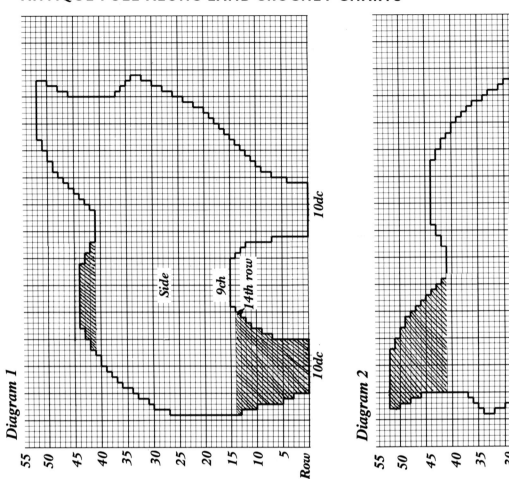

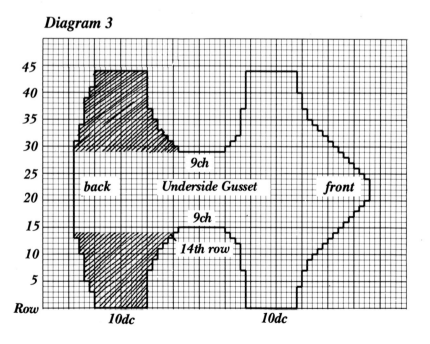

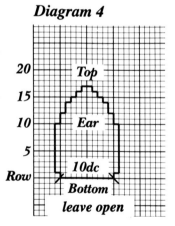

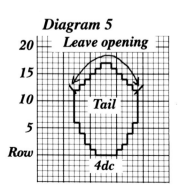

ANTIQUE PULL-ALONG LAMB BLACK FELT PIECES

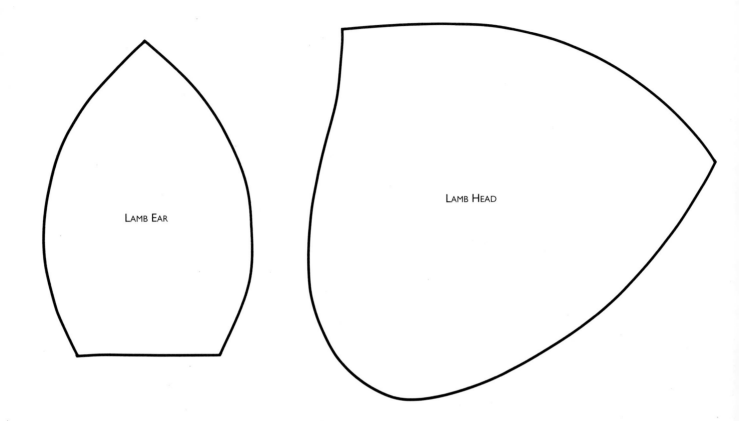

LAMB EAR

LAMB HEAD

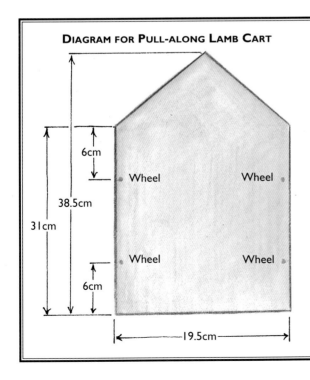

DIAGRAM FOR **PULL-ALONG LAMB CART**

6cm

38.5cm

31cm

Wheel   Wheel

6cm

Wheel   Wheel

19.5cm

Pull-along Lamb's Cart

Using an old rag, rub dye straight from bottle onto all wooden parts. Allow to dry thoroughly.

Apply dark tan shoe polish and rub to give a shine. Join wheels to Base with brass screws, in positions indicated on pattern piece.

Drill holes for screws through Base into dowel support in each Leg.

Screw lamb to base. Glue felt parts of each Leg to base.

Make hole for pull-along cord. Knot one end of cord and pass remaining end through hole, tying another knot to prevent fraying.

Kitchen Garden Pot-pourri

WILDFLOWER POT-POURRIS

~

Capture the essence of the Australian bush with fragrant pot-pourris. Author Denise Greig gives tempting recipes, using readily available bush or garden flowers.

Kitchen Garden Pot-pourri

Many culinary herbs blend beautifully with dried native plant materials. The powerful scent of rosemary harmonises especially well with that of eucalyptus in this aromatic pot-pourri. The rosemary oil may be omitted.

- 2 cups dried strongly aromatic eucalypt foliage
- 1 cup dried rosemary
- 1 cup dried bay leaves
- 1 cup dried agonis flowers and foliage
- ½ cup dried basil leaves
- ½ cup coriander seeds, lightly crushed
- ½ cup each dried orange and lemon peel
- 4 cinnamon sticks, broken into large pieces
- 10 star anise pods
- 1 cup oakmoss
- 1 cup yellow or orange flowers for colour (optional)
- A few drops rosemary oil (optional)

Blend all the foliage and petals together in a bowl and lightly crush with your hands. In a separate container, mix coriander seeds, citrus peel, cinnamon sticks, star anise and oakmoss. Add rosemary oil and mix thoroughly. Combine spice mixture with leaves and mix well. This pot-pourri can be used immediately, or stored in a sealed container for two weeks, stirring occasionally. Transfer to open bowls.

Bush Pot-pourri

Bush Pot-pourri

This extremely handsome pot-pourri contains lots of woody fruits and gumnuts that give it texture and invite handling. Experiment with your choice of foliage. Some mint bushes and boronias have very little scent, while others have a strong incense-like aroma.

- 4 cups dried gumnuts, small cones and other woody capsules
- 2 cups dried eucalypt leaves
- 1 cup dried mint bush or boronia foliage
- 1 cup dried lemon peel (coarsely ground)
- 1 cup aromatic timber shavings, if available
- 6 cinnamon sticks broken into chunks
- 1 cup oakmoss
- A few drops sandalwood or cedarwood oil
- A few drops huon pine oil
- Tufts of lichen and shredded bark, for decoration

Mix together woody fruits, eucalypt, mint bush or boronia leaves, lemon peel, timber shavings and cinnamon sticks in a large bowl. In a separate small bowl, place the oakmoss and add the oils a drop at a time, working them well into the oakmoss with your fingers. Combine and blend thoroughly. Place in a container with a tight lid and allow to mature for a month, stirring often. To use, place in an open bowl and top with lichen and pieces of bark.

Citrus Pot-pourri

Citrus Pot-pourri

Lemon-scented leaves are found in several groups of Australian plants and form a strongly perfumed basis for this crisp, fresh mix.

- 2 cups dried lemon-scented tea-tree leaves
- 2 cups other lemon-scented foliage such as Eucalyptus citriodora, Backhousia citriodora or Boronia citriodora.
- 2 cups culinary herbs such as lemon thyme, lemon verbena or young bergamot leaves
- ½ cup each dried lemon and orange peel, coarsely ground
- 1 cup oakmoss
- A few drops bergamot oil
- Some bright yellow flowers, such as paper daisies, wattle sprigs and pressed native buttercups, for decoration

Combine foliage, herbs and peel in a large bowl. In a separate bowl, place the oakmoss and add the oil, a drop at a time. Work the oil well into the oakmoss with your fingers. Combine and blend thoroughly. Store in airtight container for four weeks to mature. Place the mixture in open bowls and decorate with dried yellow wildflowers.

Wildflower Garden Pot-pourri

A spicy pot-pourri that has the tang of the bush. Lots of red and white flowers evoke the feeling of summer. This decorative pot-pourri could be packed into glass jars and decorated with Christmas ribbon for gift giving.

- 2 cups dried red flowers such as eucalyptus blossoms, bottlebrush, kangaroo paws and flame tree
- 1 cup dried white flowers, such as melaleuca, sago flower, angophora, everlastings or ixodia
- 1 cup dried lemon-scented tea-tree leaves and flowers
- 1 cup of any strongly-scented dried eucalyptus leaves
- 1 cup aromatic foliage from your native garden
- 1 cup small woody capsules
- 1 cup oakmoss
- A few drops boronia oil
- 1 or 2 drops tea-tree oil

NOTE: Reserve a few of the best dried flowers and use some pressed flannel flowers for decoration.

Mix all the dried flowers and foliage in a large mixing bowl. In a separate bowl, mix oakmoss and woody capsules. Add boronia and tea-tree oils carefully to oakmoss and mix thoroughly with your hands. Add this mixture to flowers and foliage and blend thoroughly. Store in airtight containers for about a month, to mature. Transfer to open bowls or containers and decorate with reserved flowers and flannel flowers.

Wildflower Garden Pot-pourri

TIPS FOR PREPARATION

- Pick unblemished flowers and foliage on a day when humidity is low, and dry them in an airy spot away from direct sunlight (a hallway, garage or attic is ideal).
- Lay each flower out separately on paper, flat baskets or screens. Air must be able to circulate around the flowers. Small bunches of leaves can be loosely tied together and hung to dry. When leaves become crackly dry, strip them from their stalks.
- Even flowers without scent can be dried and used for colour, bulk and decoration. Try to include a blend of colours and textures, with a combination of petals, foliage, buds and fruiting capsules.
- Woody fruiting capsules, such as gumnuts and casuarina cones, can be collected and then hung in plastic mesh onion bags. Toss regularly to allow air to circulate. Dispersed seeds and fluff will fall through the mesh, leaving clean, dry capsules, after about a month.
- For those in a hurry, a microwave oven can be used to quickly dry small quantities of flowers and leaves. As the timing of microwave ovens differs slightly, you will need to experiment a little. Spread ingredients on absorbent paper. Start with a low heat and check after two or three minutes. Re-bake, always in short bursts, as necessary.
- Store all dried ingredients in labelled airtight containers until you have sufficient for a pot-pourri.
- A fixative, such as gum benzoin, orris root powder or oakmoss (available through craft shops or nurseries), preserves the scent of a pot-pourri. Oakmoss is especially good in a native plant pot-pourri, as it does not cloud the mixture, but adds its own dainty grey foliage to the mix.

AUTUMN STORY

Dried Flower Flair

*Hydrangea heads will dry once picked, and will lose their colour, though they maintain their shape.
Designer Helen Norton provides a charming solution. The thoroughly dry hydrangea heads have been
lightly spray-painted a soft turquoise (not all over — just enough to give a semblance of fading colour),
and then embellished with sprigs of statice, baby's tears, feverfew, bunches of berberis berries and tiny bows.*

The fine flush of flowering that lights up spring and summer gardens from early September, starts
giving notice to quit as Autumn approaches. In the gardens of those lucky enough to be able to
grow them, roses burst forth in a final showing, fighting for attention (as if they needed to fight)
before the season finishes. Autumn is also the season when those most agreeable of summer flowers,
hydrangeas, begin drying themselves on the bush and in the process, toning down their colours to
lovely muted greens and pinks. It's the time to arm yourself with secateurs, to snip and to store up
colour for the cooler months. Here are three pretty ideas for using your stored bounty.

Lavender and Rose Ball

MATERIALS

- 10cm diameter polystyrene ball
- 85cm x 2cm-wide ribbon
- Craft glue
- Approximately 45 dried red roses
- Dried lavender stalks
- Knitting needle

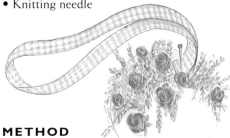

METHOD

Fold ribbon in half and glue ends to ball. Hold in place with pins until glue has dried. Cut off roses to leave about 2.5cm of stem and shorten lavender stalks to match. Densely cover entire surface of polystyrene ball with holes made with knitting needle. Insert lavender and rose stalks to completely cover surface of ball.

As the perfume of dried flowers diminishes with time, freshen up this floral pomander with drops of lavender or rose oil.

Above: A scented ball of dried rose and lavender heads is both decorative and useful when hung among precious linens.

Hydrangea Wreath

MATERIALS

- Polystyrene wreath base
- Hydrangea heads and dried leaves
- Florist wire

Below: Enjoy the muted colours of autumn hydrangeas by displaying them in a garland. The deeper colours seen here come from a really cold climate garden and these colours still endure for several months.

METHOD

The ideal time to pick hydrangeas for drying is once they have turned their heads to muted autumn tonings. Pick heads with about 10cm of stem and wind stalks with florist wire. Attach small bundles of blooms to polystyrene base with wire and fill in any holes with dried leaves.

FABULOUS FAKES

With glittering metallic brush-on powders and lots of wonderful faux gems and exotic findings, modelling clay jewellery has really come of age. Leave the family jewels in the vault and make up some fakes, the more extravagant and baroque the better!

'Antique Gold' Drop-Earrings

STEP 1
Roll three different-sized balls from modelling clay, and make holes through centre with a skewer, taking care not to put balls out of shape. Decorate beads as follows:

STEP 2
Roll a very thin sausage and wind it around bead in two directions, anchoring it at top and bottom holes by pressing with skewer.

STEP 3
With a very sharp knife, cut tiny indentations in the thin sausage, around middle of bead, in order to lay another cable in it.

STEP 4
Twist two fine modelling clay 'threads' together, to form a fine cable. Do this as evenly as possible.

STEP 5
Wrap each cable around the bead, in gaps that you cut in Step 3.

STEP 6
Paint bead with metallic powder — we used Fimo Antique Gold — and bake according to instructions.

STEP 7
Cut an oval shape from rolled modelling clay, and press a black 'stone' in centre. Cut a very narrow flat strip of modelling clay for a bezel, and surround stone with this.

STEP 8
Make a cable, as in Step 4, and press around edge of oval. Roll tiny balls and press these between bezel and cable. Don't forget to make a hole in one end with a skewer. Gild and bake. Varnish when cool.

Copy old jewellery you see in antique shops, and create your own heirloom.

Press a simple twist around large fake pearls for a super-quick pair of earrings.

Give modelling clay beads a filigree look with added decoration. The basic technique is described on page 283.

Diamantes and mirrors are pressed into modelling clay bases for wonderful sparkle.

Make your fakes big and bold. This one was inspired by a 19th century mourning brooch in an old family photograph.

A fake turquoise is surrounded by 'silver' leaves and flowers.

Jewellery findings are available for both clip-on earrings and pierced ears. Often, the findings can inspire the finished design.

These 'silver' earrings would also look terrific in 'antique gold'.

Modelling clay hearts are decorated with tiny balls and strips, then gilded with metallic powder.

With modelling clay and a little imagination, you can make a limitless range of fabulous jewellery. When Handmade had a try, we got metallic powder on everything, but also managed to produce some pieces that prove you don't have to be a professional to produce great results. Have a go! You can copy ours, if you're feeling uninspired, but it's more fun to design your own.

Decorated Heart Earrings and Pendant

STEP 1

Knead modelling clay well, roll out to about 2mm thick, then, using a very sharp knife, cut out a heart shape. We used a metallic sheen clay, but any dark colour will do.

STEP 2

Make a hole with a skewer at centre top. Roll a very thin sausage of clay, and place onto heart shape. Press markings into it with a blunt edge.

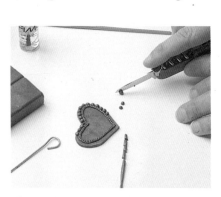

STEP 3

Cut even-sized pieces from a roll of modelling clay and shape into tiny balls. Cut each ball in half, and use to decorate edge of heart. Try not to squash balls out of shape as you place them on base.

STEP 4

Finish decorating, using the photograph as a guide, and make top parts of earrings to match. Brush metallic powder carefully over back and front surfaces of hearts and earring tops. We used Fimo Gold Bronze powder. Place on aluminium foil and bake in oven, according to instructions. Varnish when cool.

The golden hearts can be worn as earrings, or threaded on leather thongs for pendants. Smaller linked hearts could also be used for a necklace. Although it looks heavy and metallic, modelling clay is very light to wear.

TEXTURE AND DECORATION

STEP 1

Pressing lace or tulle into rolled modelling clay gives an interesting texture, which is then highlighted with metallic powder. Scrunched paper can also be used to impress a textured pattern onto clay. Experiment — it's fun!

STEP 2

Real leaves can be pressed firmly into modelling clay, the finely-veined outline carefully cut out and then gilded with metallic powder, or decorated with chain.

STEP 3

'Stones' and chain are added to modelling clay bases before baking. Glass stones and metal chains will survive their time in the oven, but you should take care with plastic — you may have to stick them on after. Add leaves, and any other decoration that you wish, and paint carefully with metallic powder — a little goes a very long way! Place clay on a baking tray lined with aluminium foil, and bake in a pre-heated oven at 130 degrees C, for 20 minutes. When cool, piece should be coated with varnish, to stop metallic powder rubbing off. Any loose stones or leaves can be fixed in place with a drop of super adhesive. Findings should be glued to pieces after varnishing.

MARBLING

STEP 1

It is easy to obtain a marbled effect by combining two colours. Place two equal rolled lengths of modelling clay together.

STEP 2

Now twist them around one another to obtain a coil.

STEP 3

Squash this coil in your hands, roll into a sausage again, and twist round itself to obtain another coil. You will see that it has started to give a marbled effect.

STEP 4

Roll coil into a ball again, and then roll out flat, and cut to desired shape.

PERFECT PASSEMENTERIE

Passementerie is the French word for a very specialised craft — the making of tassels and trimmings. Used extensively from the 17th to the early 19th century, elaborate trimmings were used to add colour and richness to upholstery and furnishings. Today, passementerie is in demand again, but because of the handwork involved, even the smallest tassel can be alarmingly expensive. Don't despair — they may look complex, but expert Effie Mitrofanis shows how, having mastered a basic tassel, you can produce splendidly luxurious trimmings at a fraction of their retail cost.

Basic tassel

Basic Tassel

MATERIALS
• Small amount heavy cardboard
• Yarn of desired thickness (see Note)
• Large-eyed tapestry needle
NOTE: Almost any yarn can be used to make a tassel. For our tassels, Effie used DMC Coton Perle No 5 (Art 116). As a guide to quantities, a 4cm-long tassel, wound 50 times around with Coton Perle No 5, requires approximately 5m. It is advisable to keep a notebook handy when making tassels to record measurements and yarn amounts.

STEP I

METHOD
Cut a piece of cardboard, approximately 30cm long x desired length of finished tassel, to make a template. The width of card in our photograph is 3.5cm. Now, wind yarn around one end of template until desired thickness is achieved (about 50 times, if using Coton Perle No 5), starting and finishing yarn at bottom of card. This forms body of tassel.

Next, take yarn, without cutting it, about 2.5cm further along card and start winding another tassel. Continue in this manner until card is full. This is

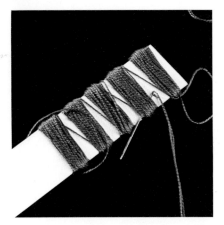

STEP 2

STEP 3

a quick method of producing lots of same-sized tassels (Step 1).

While yarn is still on card, cut a separate length of yarn about 45cm long (one length for each tassel, if mass producing), thread it through a needle so that it becomes double, and thread it under wound yarn at top of tassel, tying ends in a firm granny or double knot. This is called the holding cord (Step 2).

Remove each tied tassel from card (snipping joining threads between). Cut another length of yarn, about 30cm long (one for each tassel) and wrap tassel a short distance below holding cord to form neck (Step 3). To keep them secure, loose ends are tied off, then threaded with a needle behind neck and left to blend with bottom of tassel, which is called the skirt.

Cut loops at bottom of tassel, to form skirt. Trim if necessary.

Multiple or Family Tassel

This tassel is made with a total of 32 basic tassels — 16 x 3.5cm tassels and 16 x 4.5cm tassels, attached to a plastic ring suspended between two wrapped balls and held by a twisted cord.

STEP 2

STEP 1

MATERIALS

- Heavy cardboard for templates
- DMC Coton Perle No 5 (Art. 116) in following colours and amounts: 2 balls each of blue (930), red (816), gold (977) and green (991), and one ball of écru
- One reel DMC Fil or Clair
- Large-eyed tapestry needle
- One 3.5–4cm polystyrene ball
- Metal skewer, or other sharp tool, such as pointed scissors

Multiple or family tassel

- One large wooden macramé bead, slightly smaller than polystyrene ball
- One 3.5cm plastic curtain ring

METHOD

Winding yarn 50 times around template, make 16 basic tassels, each 4.5cm long: four each of blue, red, gold and green.

In the same manner, make another 16 basic tassels, each 3.5cm long: four each of red, gold, green and écru.

With a metal skewer, make a large hole through middle of polystyrene ball and wrap or satin-stitch it with a double thread of blue Coton Perle No 5 (Step 1). Knot ends when finished and work them round into centre hole, so they can't be seen.

Using double threads of metallic gold yarn in needle, wrap or satin-stitch

STEP 3

STEP 4

decorative lines on top of blue yarn.

Wrap wooden bead with blue yarn, as for polystyrene ball, omitting metallic gold.

Now, attach the 16 x 3.5cm tassels to curtain ring, alternating colours, one after the other, until all are attached (note that in our photograph,

STEP 5

we've attached a blue tassel, which should be a green one)(Step 2). Attach each tassel with a chain stitch then anchor thread in bar of holding cord with two buttonhole stitches. Bury ends of holding cord by threading them through into skirt and trimming off ends to match skirt (Step 3).

Lift these 16 smaller tassels out of the way into centre of ring and then attach the 16 x 4.5cm tassels, alternating between each of the shorter tassels, forming a top row of 3.5cm tassels and a bottom row of 4.5cm tassels (Step 4).

Make a twisted cord, approximately 50cm long, using 4–6 lengths of blue

STEP 6

yarn (see Making a Twisted Cord on page 288). Thread ends into a large-eyed needle and knot other end. If needle eye is too narrow to thread, simply stitch cord to eye of needle, using an ordinary needle and thread.

(Step 5) Take needle firstly through polystyrene ball, then through ring of tassels, and lastly through wooden bead, to hold it in place.

(Step 6) Stitch other end back into cord to form a loop above polystyrene ball.

(Step 7 — we've used contrast thread, to make it easier to see). Snip off original knot, then knot the now double cord and use a needle to move knot into hole of ball in order to conceal stitching.

Hang completed tassel from loop formed by cord.

STEP 7

Ring of tassels

STEP 1

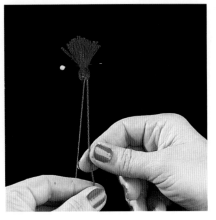

STEP 2

Ring of Tassels

A wooden ring, covered with detached buttonhole stitch, holds three groups of six tassels. The twisted cords of each group have first been held together with an overhand knot, then the cords have been plaited together and stitched to the ring.

MATERIALS

• Heavy cardboard for templates
• One ball DMC Coton Perle No 5 (Art 116) in each of following colours: red (816), green (991) and gold (977)
• Large-eyed tapestry needle
• One 7.5cm wooden curtain ring

METHOD

Cover wooden curtain ring, using detached buttonhole stitch and double lengths of green yarn (Step 1).

Make 18 tassels, each 4.5cm long,

six of each of the three colours. Use two 60cm lengths of yarn to tie tassel and form holding cord.

Make a twisted cord out of holding cord by separating each cord into two threads. Pin tassel to your ironing board, or a heavy cushion, and twist each length of yarn separately in the same direction, that is, both either to the right or to the left (Step 2). Tie a knot at end. Unpin tassel from ironing board and, while holding knotted end, let tassel drop, allowing cord to twist. Repeat for all 18 tassels.

Combine each group of colour together and tie a simple overhand knot in holding cords, approximately 6cm above heads. Bring three groups of cords together and plait them. Stitch plait to covered ring and trim ends at back.

Add a fat twisted cord, made by using 14 lengths of yarn (see Making a Twisted Cord below). Tassel is now ready to hang.

Making a Twisted Cord

Any kind of yarn is suitable for inclusion in twisted cords. Experiment with each yarn to see the effects and thickness created. If a twisted cord is too thin, multiply number of threads before twisting. A different type of cord is created

by re-twisting together two previously twisted cords.
1. Take a length of yarn, approximately eight times desired finished length.
2. Double it by hooking it over a door knob or door key.

3. Twist doubled cord between thumb and index finger, until it is tightly coiled.
4. Find halfway point, carefully double cord, then let it twist together in small sections, to prevent knotting.

Hooded Cushion Tassels

Tassels with detached buttonhole stitch heads decorate a cushion edged with a twisted cord.

MATERIALS

• Heavy cardboard for templates
• One ball each DMC Coton Perle No 5 (Art 116) in following colours: red (816), gold (977) and écru
• One reel DMC Fil or Clair
• Large-eyed needle
• Tapestry needle

METHOD

Make three basic tassels with twisted holding cords, as described for Ring of Tassels. Make a 10cm red tassel, an 8cm gold one, and a 6cm écru one. Wrap each tassel 100 times, blending metallic gold yarn with last 60 wraps of each tassel.

To form 'hood', proceed as follows. Thread a tapestry needle with yarn, about 1–1.5m long. Bring needle up through skirt, to just above neck. With head of tassel held towards you, make about ten detached buttonhole stitches, evenly spaced around the neck (Step 1). When you reach the first stitch, stitch into it, and keep on stitching into previous row, spiralling up to holding cord (Step 2 and Diagram A). As head curves, tighten stitches rather than decreasing number. Finish off remaining thread by running it around top row like a draw-string, then pulling up thread and taking it down into skirt.

Twist holding cord, as described for Ring of Tassels.

To trim cushion, make a twisted cord with five lengths of yarn (see opposite, Making a Twisted Cord).

STEP 1

STEP 2

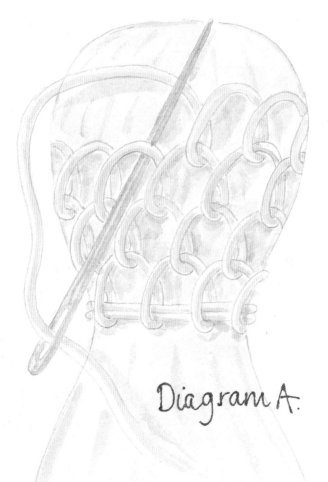

Diagram A.

Hooded cushion tassel

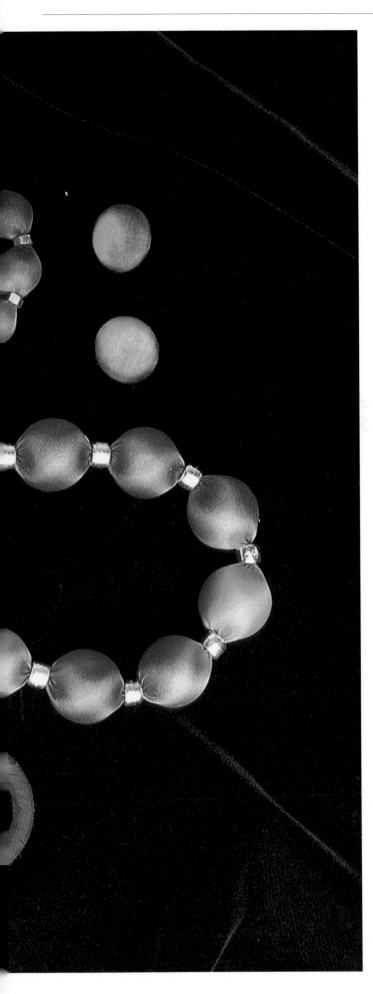

BEAUTIFUL BEADS

Ever wanted to have a go at silk painting? Here's a manageable and inexpensive project to begin with. Designer Jo Beard, who makes and sells a range of breathtaking hand-dyed silk items, has come up with an unusual string of beads to make. Cocooned in their close-fitting tube of silk, the plain wooden beads are transformed into brilliantly coloured baubles, each one slightly different from the rest. Once you've mastered the basic technique, make a scarf to match, or earrings.

Silk Beads

MATERIALS
- 70cm x 20cm piece of silk fabric (this will be sufficient for one large bead necklace)
- Two wooden blocks, approximately 20cm long (see Step 1)
- Masking tape or sticky tape
- Silk dyes (available from art supply and craft stores)
- No 11 paintbrushes, one for each colour
- Aluminium foil
- Steamer or pressure cooker
- Firm cardboard or plastic strip, for making template
- Rotary cutter
- Needle and thread
- 12–14 large wooden beads (approximately 15mm diameter)
- 15–18 gold or silver spacer beads
- Four small wooden beads (two 10mm diameter and two 5mm diameter, approximately)
- Two flat gold or silver rings
- Two gold or silver cord caps
- Strong craft glue
- Gold or silver bolt ring and tag

Wooden beads are threaded inside a tube of hand-painted silk for a necklace that's as individual as it is beautiful.

METHOD

Cut a piece of silk, 67cm x 20cm, or to desired length. (When making necklaces or scarves, always cut silk a little longer than necessary so it can be trimmed later.) Apply sticky tape or masking tape to upper edges of wooden blocks, to give a smooth pinning surface, then stretch silk between wooden blocks, pinning ends of fabric to the upper edges of the blocks (Step 1).

Mix dyes with water, following manufacturer's instructions. Before painting silk, decide which colour is to be dominant, then apply colours accordingly, remembering that dyes spread rapidly. If choosing a light colour to be dominant, apply large areas of this colour and only a few touches of the dark dye. Apply dyes to silk in stripes, beginning with lightest colour and working through to darkest colour, using a different brush for each colour (Steps 2, 3, 4). Do not overload brush with dye.

Allow dyes to soak into fabric for a few minutes, then wrap silk in aluminium foil. Roll up and boil in a steamer or pressure cooker for one hour. Remove from heat and foil, and allow silk to dry.

Make a template for large bead necklace, using cardboard or plastic sheet. Cut template 17cm wide x length desired.

Lay silk flat on cutting board and cut along template lines using a rotary cutter (Step 5). Shape ends of silk into points. With right sides together, fold fabric in half and stitch along length to form a tube, allowing 1cm for seam. Trim seam and turn right side out.

Make a few small stitches in one end of fabric tube, using needle and thread and leave attached. Push one large bead inside tube. Next, thread a small metal spacer bead onto fabric, using needle to thread fabric through its centre (Steps 6, 7).

Repeat this step until one half of necklace is complete. Repeat for other side until necklace is almost desired length. Taper ends of necklace by pushing a 10mm bead and then a 5mm bead into each end of fabric tube, using spacer beads to separate them. Thread a flat spacer ring onto each end of necklace.

Trim off excess fabric and glue a cord cap onto each end. Attach a bolt ring to one end and a tag to other end to form necklace closure (Step 8). NOTE: Silk scarves can be made by following this dyeing technique. You will need a large frame for painting scarves. Cut fabric to desired size allowing 1cm for hems.

STEP 1

STEP 2

STEP 3

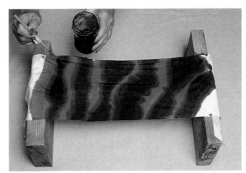

STEP 4

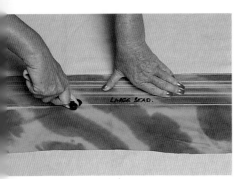

STEP 5

STEP 6

STEP 7

STEP 8

FRIENDSHIP FUN

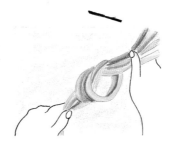

STEP 1

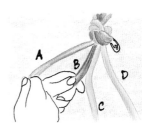

STEP 2

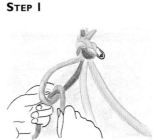

STEP 3

STEP 4

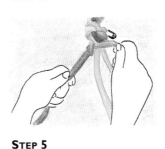

STEP 5

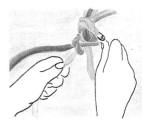

STEP 6

STEP 7

STEP 8

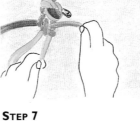

STEP 9

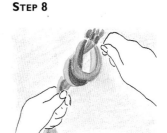

STEP 10

Colourful cotton friendship bracelets are a hit everywhere. You can match them to whatever you're wearing, or swap them with friends. *Best of Handmade* shows you how it's done. Follow the simple step-by-step diagrams for a slim-line bracelet, and double, or treble, the quantities of thread used to make a thicker bangle.

Friendship Bracelets

MATERIALS
- 3–4 skeins DMC Coton Perle No 3 (Art 115) in different colours (this is enough for several bracelets)
- Adhesive tape or a safety pin

METHOD
To make a basic friendship bracelet, you can either use three colours and repeat one colour in the band, or, as we have done, use four different colours.

1. Cut one-metre strands of each colour and tie an overhand knot about 10cm from strand ends.
2. Pin to firm surface. Reach under strand A with your left hand and hold strand B.
3. Wrap A under B. Pull A through loop with your right hand.
4. Tighten knot by holding strand B taut and pulling A up.
5. Make a second knot with strand A over B. Pull up taut.
6. Drop strand B and pick up C. Make two knots with A over C.
7. Drop strand C and pick up D. Make two knots with A over D.
8. Begin second row. Make 2 knots with strand B over C.
9. To complete row, make 2 knots with B over D, then B over A.
10. Work until bracelet is 15cm long. Tie strands with a knot and trim ends to 10cm.

FRENCH CLASS

Remember French knitting —
that circular knitting done on
looms made with nails and cotton
reels? Wooden cotton reels may no
longer be readily available, but we
experimented and found that some
of the modern cotton reels
work just as well!

*Right: French knitting makes
colourful trims for your
favourite clothes. We
appliquéd a paint tube
to our model's
sweatshirt — and
made the knitting
squeeze from the tube
like paint! It's just one
idea for your French
knitting. Experiment
with your own
designs.*

*Below: Pull down
gently on tail of yarn
below reel as work
progresses.*

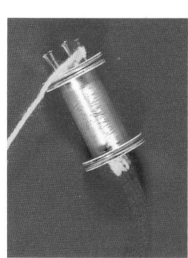

French Knitting Step-by-Step

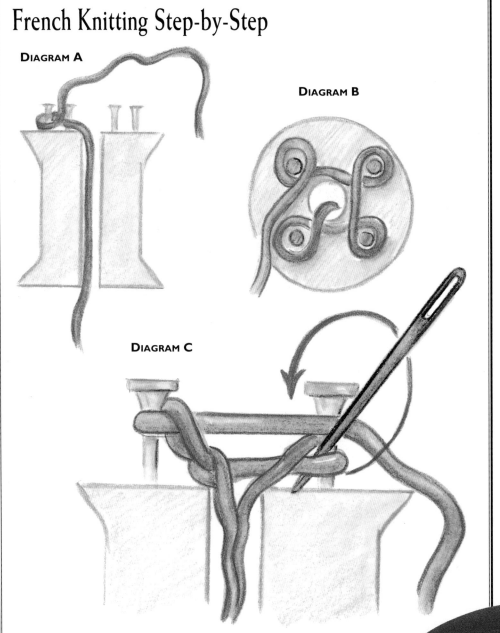

DIAGRAM A

DIAGRAM B

DIAGRAM C

Small nails hammered into Coats metallic-looking cotton reels make ideal 'looms'. Droop the end of your wool down centre of reel (Diagram A), then wrap the ball of wool around each of the four nails, following Diagram B.

Now wrap wool around outside of nails. With a large tapestry needle or a fine crochet hook, pick up the loop already on the nail and pull it up and over the wrapped wool, to make a new stitch (Diagram C).

Keep repeating this process until you have a rope of wool the desired length. Pull down gently on tail of yarn below reel as work progresses.

Cast off the stitches, one by one over each other, then knot the last one.

Add twists of colour to your winter socks, or trim a hat, as shown on the right.

DESIGNER PROFILES

Annette Allen

SOMETHING TO CROW ABOUT

pages 252 – 254

Annette Allen mastered the art of stencilling in England and, since coming to Australia, has developed her art into a thriving business. As well as selling stencilling materials, Annette also designs and markets her own stencils and gives workshops to beginners and specialists alike, sometimes in her own home or in shops, and occasionally 'going bush' to teach people in the country. Her gorgeous cushions and boxes are also sold in various retail outlets around Melbourne.

Contact: Creative Stencilling 21 Champion St, Brighton, Victoria 3186. Telephone (03) 592 8630.

Kath Baker

HIGHLAND FLING

pages 200 – 201

Kath Baker is fascinated by the beauty of Scottish tartans and has adapted 180 different patterns to magnificent crochet rugs, which she has collected together in a recent book and published herself, *Tartan Crochet*.

Kath has spent many hours researching tartans and says that the patterns are very easy to do providing the instructions are followed carefully.

Contact: PO Box 136, Beaconsfield, Victoria, 3807.

Georgina Bitcon

FABULOUS FAKES

pages 280 – 283

GRANNY SMITHS

pages 260 – 261

Georgina Bitcon joined *Handmade* as Assistant Editor in 1990 and ever since has rued the fact that she hasn't enough time to make anything featured. She does, however, design and make the most delightful and unusual originals that prove irresistible and become featured. Each demonstrates, in its individuality, an eye delighted by detail.

Before joining *Handmade* Georgina studied then worked at Sydney University, first gaining her MA then tutoring in the English Department before becoming Assistant Director of Continuing Education. The step from Dickens to dollies is one she has made with great grace and, to the entertainment of her colleagues, with great wit.

Rosemary Borland

A TOUCH OF LACE

pages 210 – 211

Rosemary Borland is representative of many Australian women — someone who can turn her hand to anything. From building a chook house to cooking a great meal from leftovers, from knitting a garment each winter for a growing number of grand-children to making patchwork quilts of mouth-watering colour mixes. Roe follows in the self-sufficient traditions of colonial women and later settlers

who, with warmth and ingenuity, made their houses homes. It is small wonder *Handmade* turns to her whenever a spot of help is needed.

Alison Bushell

THREE LITTLE MAIDS

pages 58 – 65

Alison Bushell has had a passion for making cloth dolls for as long as she can remember. As a child she amused herself by making clothes for her dolls and toy animals and constructed dolls out of anything useful she could find. While her own children were growing up she began to design cloth doll patterns for magazines and made storybook characters for collectors. A school teacher for many years, she now owns a craft shop and continues to design and make dolls.

Contact: (069) 77 1346 after hours.

Diana Cross

THE EGG AND DYE

pages 255– 257

Diana Cross has been actively involved in all the different aspects of craft in Australia and New Zealand. In 1975 she established her own craft business, Strawberry Patches Handcrafts and Gifts, importing craft raw materials and designing specialised craft kits.

Since 1987 Diana has concentrated on writing for craft magazines and her own books. Contributions as a freelance writer have appeared in *Handmade, Australian Women's Weekly, Craft and Home* and *Craft and Decorating.*

Diana's most recent books are *More Crafts Throughout the Year*, *Craft from Recycled Material* and *Quilted Clothing and Accessories*.

Contact: 10 Bilkurra Avenue, Bilgola Plateau, New South Wales, 2107. Telephone (02) 973 1655.

Cassie Donnellan

PERFECT POSIES

pages 52 – 53

Needlecraft has been an important part of Cassie's life since her school days in Kuala Lumpur, Malaysia. Now, as a graduate in fashion technology and commercial needlecraft, Cassie has been able to integrate the two disciplines in her work. She is strongly influenced by the beauty of nature and has a love of country craft.

Cassie's work has been published in various craft magazines and over the past few years she has introduced many of her students to the charm of creative embroidery. Now with a young son, she enjoys teaching from home and working on commissioned projects.

Contact: 94 Vivian Street, Inverell, New South Wales, 2360.

Dianne Finnegan

PERFECTLY PATCHED

Pages 144 – 153

Dianne learnt quilting when she lived in Canada 13 years ago. Since returning to Australia she has been president of The Quilters' Guild. Besides writing and exhibiting, Dianne gives classes, workshops and lectures. Her two publications *Piece by Piece* and *The Quilters Kaleidoscope* were published by Simon and Schuster in 1990 and 1992. She has been named International Quilting Teacher of the Year for 1993/4 and awarded the Jewel Pearce Patterson Scholarship for Quilting Teachers, to be taken in Houston, Texas.

Contact: PO Box 1108, Lane Cove, New South Wales, 2066. Telephone/facsimile (02) 427 1724.

Gretchen Forrest

SECOND TIME AROUND

pages 221 – 225

Gretchen Forrest was born and educated in Western Australia. In 1978 she learned to make handmade paper from plant fibres and recycled papers. Almost immediately she began teaching the craft to others as well as experimenting with and exploring all aspects of the craft.

In 1987 her book *Papermaking My Way* was produced in a limited edition of 55 copies. Printed on 21 of Gretchen's own papers using a hand-operated press, the book was hand-stitched and bound. It is now a collector's item. Also in 1987, her papers appeared with those of 50 other papermakers from 17 countries in *A Book of Strange Papers* published in Switzerland.

Gretchen has been a member of the International Association of Papermakers and Paper Artists since its inception in 1987 and is the President of the Papermakers' Guild of Western Australia. She continues to make paper in her Mouse and Butterfly Studio in Bicton, Perth.

Contact: Mouse and Butterfly Studio, 75 Beach Street, Bicton, Western Australia, 6157. Telephone (09) 339 2732.

Vivienne Garforth (Chinnery)

A STITCH IN TIME

pages 16 – 19

A CALENDAR OF WILDFLOWERS

pages 20 – 23

Vivienne is a self-taught embroiderer with a great love of craft and embroidery. Finding that there was a lack of Australian designs for cross-stitch, she wrote her first book *Australian Cross-Stitch Designs* which was published in 1989. Since then she has written several others: *Colonial Embroidery*, *Australian Themes in Cross-stitch*, *Découpage with Scrapbook Pictures*,

Our Heritage in Cross-stitch and Embroidery. Vivienne has had articles published in *Handmade* and *Australian Women's Weekly*, *New Idea* and *Needlecraft*.

Denise Greig

WILDFLOWER POT-POURRIS

pages 274 – 277

Denise is a writer on and a photographer of Australian and exotic plants covering natural history, gardening, pot-pourri, plant craft and flower arrangements. She is a regular exhibitor at the annual Australian Craft Show selling home grown and prepared pot-pourri, art works and books, including *Pot-Pourri & Perfumery* and *Catalogue of Australian Native Plants*.

Contact: 27 Cascade Street, Paddington, New South Wales, 2021. Telephone (02) 361 4894.

Janet Klepatzki

HEARTS AND FLOWERS

pages 243 – 247

Janet Klepatzki is an experienced artist painting traditional and decorative work over many years. From her studio, Janet conducts classes in traditional folk art and all the techniques for decorative flat brush work.

The experience she gained from working with American and European artists, plus her own unique style of decorative painting, provides the beginner and experienced painter with the opportunity to gain the full enjoyment of creating and painting.

Janet's recent publication *Traditional Folk Art*, published by Simon and Schuster, was received with success and she has just returned from Germany, Holland and Switzerland where she studied new techniques which she will use for future classes and publications.

Contact: Boronia Cottage, 53 Broughton Street, Camden, New South Wales, 2570. Telephone (046) 55 2420.

Effie Mitrofanis

PERFECT PASSEMENTERIE

pages 284 – 289

Effie Mitrofanis is an experienced teacher with an Associate Diploma of Fine Art. She has taught embroidery workshops for many years throughout Australia and New Zealand.

Effie is the author of *Tassels and Trimmings* and *Creative Canvas Embroidery* published by Simon and Schuster.

She is a member of the Embroiderers' Guild of the United Kingdom, the Embroiderers' Guild of NSW and the Creative Embroiderers' Association.

Contact: (02) 661 4495.

Jenny Oliver

THE GENTLE ART OF TATTING

pages 212-215

For the past two years Jenny Oliver has been teaching ceramics to an Aboriginal class at Casino TAFE. She finds this a very rewarding and full-time job.

Tatting is one of the crafts she enjoys as a hobby because of the sense of achievement she obtains from creating new designs.

Contact: (066) 29 3327, after hours.

Marianne Porteners

NATURE NOTES I

pages 24 – 29

NATURE NOTES II

pages 30 – 35

VICTORIAN SPLENDOUR

pages 36 – 39

As an eight-year-old schoolgirl in her native Holland, Marianne Porteners was given her first piece of cross-stitch to do. She still remembers it vividly. 'It was roses — two shades of red and two of green. And I couldn't stop doing it. It seemed magic that the graph should turn into those beautiful flowers. I was hooked.'

For Marianne, this was the beginning of a lifetime's devotion to handiwork of all kinds — embroidery, patchwork, tapestry, knitting and crochet, among many others.

Since coming to Australia in 1958, she has taught handicraft both to children and adults, studied colour and design, contributed regularly to craft magazines, written a number of books, and raised a family of daughters all interested in craft.

She is fascinated by the Australian bush. 'Although my heritage is European, all my influences are now Australian,' she said when interviewed by *Handmade*. 'I love to bushwalk with my husband, who is very interested in photography. I think that when you come to a landscape as a foreigner, you look at it with new eyes. Maybe if you're used to something, you don't see so much. For me, it is a constant source of inspiration.'

She is also inspired by historic buildings, and her enthusiasm for The Strand Arcade has resulted in a beautiful cross-stitch design of The Strand's magnificent floor tiles.

Maria Ragan

IN AND OUT THE WINDOW

pages 86 – 93

ANIMATED ANIMALS

pages 94 – 105

SEND IN THE CLOWNS

pages 106 – 113

BUSH BABIES

pages 114 – 127

STACKING UP THE ODDS

pages 154 – 155

OLD FASHIONED FUN AND GAMES

pages 262 – 273

Toymaker and craftsperson extraordinaire, Maria Ragan's visits to the *Handmade* office are always exciting events. From Maria's tiny studio come marvellous felt toys and mobiles, music boxes, knitted animals, beautifully finished decorating items and fantasies from modelling clay.

Maria, who migrated from her native Czechoslovakia in 1980, has been interested in every kind of craft from early childhood. This interest was fostered by her mother, herself the daughter of a professional artist. Although Maria received no real formal training, beyond a period studying painting, which she modestly says she was no good at, she clearly has a gift in her exquisite colour sense and eye for detail. 'I love strong, bright colours,' she said, when interviewed by *Handmade*, 'especially for children. I think coming to Australia has influenced my colour choices — the colours in the landscape are so much more intense than Europe. The light is so bright!'

As a young mother with two small daughters, and speaking almost no English, Maria occupied herself with making toys and clothes for her girls. When they started school, she gradually became known among their friends for her homemade birthday presents and party favours, and her work was in constant demand for the school fête craft stall. Maria was happy to oblige.

Now her daughters are in high school, Maria still maintains her links with the local primary school, teaching craft at the after-school care centre, and assessing Girl Guides for their craft badges.

Nerida Singleton

PAPER, PASTE AND POLISH

pages 218 – 220

Turning tired trinket boxes, plain wooden bracelets and old hatboxes from the pedestrian into treasured possessions is Nerida Singleton's speciality. Nerida, a mother of seven, from Brisbane, has dedicated herself to découpage for the past eight years and has experimented with covering jewellery, hatboxes, handbags and many other surfaces with hundreds of lovely images.

What began as a hobby has become a demanding business, and Nerida regularly has numerous orders to complete at any one time. There is no limit to the objects which can be decorated with découpage, and Nerida's work ranges from decorating small items, such as old cigarette boxes, clocks, violin cases and knife handles, to large wooden screens.

As well as her own découpage work, Nerida conducts classes designed to introduce students to the basic techniques of découpage. She is the author of *Découpage An Illustrated Guide*, published by the Milner Craft Series, has designed sheets of découpage paper, and is working on the first of a series of découpage calendars.

Betty Smith

OF MICE AND MARRIAGE

pages 74 — 85

Betty Smith trained at a leading milliner's establishment and later started her own business. She has worked for the *Australian Women's Weekly* for the past 13 years, and also, more recently, contributed to *Handmade* and the *AWW Home Library Series*, where her expert sewing and craft skills are in great demand. She collects old sewing equipment, buckles and buttons, and is actively involved with helping the Smith Family.

Contact: (02) 949 5257.

Alison Snepp

PINS AND NEEDLES

pages 40 — 41

Alison Snepp has been embroidering and sewing since she was a small child. She taught embroidery and marbling around Australia and New Zealand for ten years. She has written several books: *The Australia and New Zealand Book of Cross-Stitch and Counted Thread Embroidery*, *Babies Names and Embroidery* and *Jenny Kee Needlepoint*.

Tonia Todman

WELCOME HOME

pages 135 — 143

Tonia Todman is Australia's best known craft and decorating television personality. She has been presenting regular craft and decorating sessions on Channel 10 for many years via the shows *Good Morning Australia* and *Healthy, Wealthy and Wise*.

After ten years with Vogue Patterns in various educational and craft positions, she went on to become craft editor for *Family Circle*, teach Textile and Design to High School students, enter into partnership in Australia's largest cushion manufacturer, edit several craft and homemaker magazines, and more recently was in-house author and craft editor for J.B. Fairfax Press for three years. She has written six craft books over the last year and a half which form the start of

the *Tonia Todman Collection* published by Sally Milner, has written regular decorating features for *Handmade*, and recently became craft editor for the retail chains of David Jones and Lincraft on home decorating and craft.

Tonia is married to Tony, has two teenage sons and lists her interests as her family, home and pets, her career, good food and company, and sleep!

Catherine Woram

BABES IN THE WOOD

pages 43 — 48

Catherine Woram studied fashion and journalism at St Martins School of Art in London where she completed her BA Hons Degree in 1987. Since that time she has worked as a freelance fashion writer, stylist and designer for a number of magazines including *Handmade* magazine for whom she works as European Fashion Adviser. She completed a Masters Degree by thesis at London's Royal College of Art in 1991 where her chosen subject was the history of the British Fashion industry since 1930. Her books include *Wedding Dress Style* (Apple Press UK, New Burlington Press, Australia), 1993 and *Contemporary Fashion* (St James Press) 1994, to which she contributed a series of critical essays on international fashion designers.

PHOTOGRAPHER AND STYLIST CREDITS

Needlework

HONEYEATERS AND BANKSIA
Photography by André Martin and Catherine Muscat

A STITCH IN TIME
Photography by Scott Cameron

CALENDAR OF WILDFLOWERS
Photography by Joseph Filshie

NATURE NOTES I
Photography by Jaime Plaza

NATURE NOTES II
Photography by Joseph Filshie

VICTORIAN SPLENDOUR
Photography by Scott Cameron

PINS AND NEEDLES
Photography by André Martin
Styling by Fiona Connolly

BABES IN THE WOOD
Photography by Alfalfa
Styling by Catherine Woram

PERFECT POSIES
Photography by Tim Cole

Soft Toys

THREE LITTLE MAIDS
Photography by André Martin

BEAR ESSENTIALS
Photography by Joseph Filshie

OF MICE AND MARRIAGE
Photography by André Martin

IN AND OUT THE WINDOW
Photography by Justine Kerrigan and Tim Cole

ANIMATED ANIMALS
Photography by Ashley Mackevicius and Justine Kerrigan

SEND IN THE CLOWNS
Photography by Scott Cameron

BUSH BABIES
Photography by André Martin

Patchwork and Appliqué and Quilting

QUILT QUICK STEP
Photography by André Martin and Catherine Muscat

WELCOME HOME
Photography by Andrew Elton

PERFECTLY PATCHED
Photography by Steven Lowe

STACKING UP THE ODDS
Photography by André Martin

Kids Knits

SMALL BEGINNINGS
Photography by Scott Cameron

TOTS TOP 20
Photography by Scott Cameron and Catherine Muscat

CARNIVAL COLLECTION
Photography by Georgia Moxham
Styling by Louise McGeachie

Crochet and Tatting

HIGHLAND FLING
Photography by Joseph Filshie

OLD FASHIONED FAVOURITES
Photography by Joseph Filshie and Tim Cole

PRESENT FROM THE PAST
Photography by Joseph Filshie

A TOUCH OF LACE
Photography by André Martin

THE GENTLE ART OF TATTING
Photography by Joseph Filshie

Paper Crafts

PAPER, PASTE AND POLISH
Photography by Glenn Weiss

SECOND TIME AROUND
Photography by André Martin and Justine Kerrigan

GOOD NEWS
Photography by André Martin

WRAP SESSION
Photography by Catherine Muscat

Folk Art Painting, Stencilling and Marbling

SCENES FROM A COUNTRY CHILDHOOD
Photography by André Martin

HEARTS AND FLOWERS
Photography by Catherine Muscat

HOME SWEET HOMEWARE
Photography by André Martin

SOMETHING TO CROW ABOUT
Photography by André Martin

THE EGG AND DYE
Photography by Justine Kerrigan

General Crafts

GRANNY SMITHS
Photography by André Martin

OLD FASHIONED FUN AND GAMES
Photography by Joseph Filshie
Illustrations by Enrico Giametta

WILDFLOWER POT POURRI
Photography by Catherine Muscat

AUTUMN STORY
Photography by Andrew Elton
Styling by Louise Owens

FABULOUS FAKES
Photography by Catherine Muscat

PERFECT PASSEMENTERIE
Photography by André Martin

BEAUTIFUL BEADS
Photography by Catherine Muscat
and Tim Cole

FRIENDSHIP FUN
Photography by Scott Cameron

FRENCH CLASS
Photography by Georgia Moxham

FRONT COVER
Photography by Andrew Elton
Styling by Louise Owens
Chair and sewing companion from
Cane and Cottage, Lindfield, NSW.
Poppies from Lisa Milasas, Gymea,
NSW.
Lengths of fabric from Wardlaw,
Pyrmont NSW.

SUPPLIERS AND STOCKISTS

Appletons crewel yarns are available from specialist needlework stores nationally or by mail order through Anne's Glory Box, 60-62 Beaumont Street, Hamilton, NSW 2303. Telephone (049) 61 6016.

Cleckheaton yarns are available nationally. In case of difficulty, contact Cleckheaton Head Office, 314 Albert Street, Brunswick, VIC 3056. Telephone (03) 380 3888.

DMC stranded cottons are available from department, sewing and craft stores nationally. In case of difficulty contact the head office at 51-55 Carrington Road, Marrickville, NSW 2204. Telephone (02) 599 3088.

Fimo is available nationally from craft stores and toy shops. In case of difficulty, contact the distributors, Assembly Crafts, Unit 3, 28 Martha Street, Granville, NSW 2142. Telephone (02) 637 0677.

FolkArt products are available at department and craft stores nationally. In case of difficulty, contact DMC/Myart, 51-55 Carrington Road, Marrickville, NSW 2204. Telephone (02) 559 3088.

Liquitex paints and sealers are available through craft stores nationally. In case of difficulty, contact Binney & Smith, 611 Blackburn Road, North Clayton, VIC 3168. Telephone (03) 560 5633.

Myart products are available at department and craft stores nationally. In case of difficulty, contact the head office of DMC.

Panda Yarns are available nationally. In case of difficulty, contact Panda Cleckheaton Head Office, 314 Albert Street, Brunswick, VIC 3056. Telephone (03) 380 3888.

Patons yarns are available nationally. In case of difficulty, contact the Coats Patons office in your state (check the Yellow Pages for details).

Permaset fabric paints are available through artist supply shops nationally and through selected craft stores.

Ray Toby fabrics are available through selected department, sewing and craft stores nationally. In case of difficulty contact the head office at 134 Cambridge Street, Collingwood, VIC 3066. Telephone (03) 416 3966.

DISCLAIMER
The publisher has made every effort to ensure that all contact details were correct at the time this book went to print.

INDEX